MEDIEVAL THEORY OF AUTHORSHIP

Second edition

MEDIEVAL THEORY OF AUTHORSHIP

Scholastic literary attitudes in the later Middle Ages

Second edition

A. J. MINNIS

Scolar Press

First published in 1984
This second edition published 1988 by
SCOLAR PRESS
Gower Publishing Company Limited
Gower House, Croft Road
Aldershot GU11 3HR

British Library Cataloguing in Publication Data
    Medieval theory of authorship.—2nd ed.
    1. Literature—Philosophy
    I. Title
    801   PN45
    ISBN 0–85967–641–2

Printed and bound in Great Britain by
Billing and Sons Limited, Worcester.

Contents

Preface   *vii*

Abbreviations   *xx*

Notes on style   *xxvi*

Introduction: the significance of
the medieval theory of authorship   1

1 Academic prologues to *auctores*   9

2 Prologues to scriptural *auctores*   40

3 Authorial roles in the 'literal sense'   73

4 Literary forms in the 'literal sense'   118

5 Literary theory and literary practice   160

Epilogue: The familiar authors   211

Notes   218

Bibliography   282

Index of Latin terms   312

General index   317

FOR MY FATHER

AND

TO THE MEMORY OF MY MOTHER

Preface

The second edition of this book incorporates some minor alterations, corrections and additions of material. Moreover, I have updated the notes and the bibliography to take account of several important books which were not in print when the first edition went to press, most notably Judson B. Allen's *The Ethical Poetic of the Later Middle Ages* (Toronto, 1982) and Glending Olson's *Literature as Recreation in the Later Middle Ages* (Ithaca and London, 1982). Writing in 1980 (the year in which the first edition was actually completed) I complained that 'The study of late medieval literary theory is still in its infancy' (see p. 3 below). There has been considerable growth since then, thanks in large measure to the two books just mentioned, but the subject has still a long way to go before it reaches full maturity.

My main objective in writing was to demonstrate the considerable importance of scholasticism for the development of literary theory, a phenomenon which earlier writers had either ignored (leaping from twelfth-century 'humanistic' literary theory to that produced in the early Renaissance) or belittled and misunderstood. In particular, scholastic Scriptural exegesis was a central force in the re-shaping of literary values in the later Middle Ages. The central event, from my point of view, was the emergence (in Bible commentaries) of the view that the human author possessed a high status and respected didactic/stylistic strategies of his very own—in short, *auctoritas* moved from the divine realm to the human.

The ramifications of this event were many and varied, and so I limited myself, for the most part, to two areas of inquiry. The first was, the main implications thereof for Scriptural exegesis from the time of the *Summa theologiae* associated with Alexander of Hales until the time of Nicholas of Lyre and the 'classicizing friars' (as they were dubbed by the late Beryl Smalley). The second chosen area was the influence of a few aspects of scholastic literary theory on vernacular writers of the later Middle Ages, with special reference to two major English authors, Chaucer and Gower. The fact that my final chapter focuses on those two writers should not be taken as a tacit statement that scholastic literary theory is more important for the study of literature in Middle English than for that in any other vernacular—for this is certainly not the case. Italy and Spain yield far more obvious data than England does. Moreover, medieval Latin literature and scholastic culture influenced all the emergent vernacular literatures of the later Middle Ages, and so to pick on one may give a false impression. But one must start somewhere, and I chose to begin with Middle English literature, even though I recognized then (and my subsequent research has overwhelmingly confirmed) that the richest vein to mine was the outstanding literary theory and criticism of Dante, Petrarch and Boccaccio, so innovative and yet so traditional in many ways. Anyone interested in that area of enquiry can now turn to the texts and annotation in the relevant sections of A. J. Minnis and A. B. Scott (eds.), *Medieval Literary Theory and Criticism c. 1100–c. 1375: The Commentary Tradition* (Oxford, 1987). When, in literary discourse, *auctoritas* moved from the divine realm to the human, and (as an intriguing concomitant) in some measure from the past to the present, certain 'moderns' found in it a means not only of describing recent literary enterprises (including their own) but also of elevating them. This *translatio auctoritatis*, to coin a phrase on the model of the term *translatio imperii*, was one of the most significant movements in the history of vernacular literature. And nowhere was the sense of change felt more keenly than in late-medieval Italy.

Since it is the implications of scholastic literary theory for vernacular literature which seem to have been the main source of interest to readers of the first edition of this book, it seems appropriate, in this the Preface to the second edition, to offer a few comments on the kinds of relationship which may be posited between that theory and the literary practice of some of the *moderni*. Here we are approaching, of course, the ultimate question: to what extent should twentieth-century critics take medieval literary theory and criticism into account in the contemporary appreciation of medieval literature? It is hoped that the following categories and examples will serve as pointers for further investigation, despite the summary form in which they must necessarily be presented here.

Commentary as source. In many cases, medieval commentaries on classical and Scriptural *auctores* were the direct sources of certain statements, attitudes, images, etc., as found in the works of major vernacular writers. Late-medieval vernacular versions of the Bible, in part or whole, clearly reveal the influence of Latin Scriptural exegesis; very often a gloss would provide a translator with details not found in the text itself, or determine his preference for a particular word, phrase or idiom, in rendering a certain passage. For instance, Peter Lombard's commentary on the Psalter is reflected by Richard Rolle's Middle English psalm versions, while the *Glossa ordinaria* on the Psalter and especially Nicholas of Lyre's superb exposition thereof lie behind the Lollard Psalter in its 'second version' (as Harry Hargreaves has demonstrated). The influence of Latin commentaries on secular authorities was just as pervasive. The anonymous author of the Old French *Les faits des Romains* used a glossed copy of Lucan's *Pharsalia*; the French translation of Ovid's *Ars amatoria* which recently has been edited by Bruno Roy was influenced by, and is accompanied by, glosses, which are rendered in the vernacular to provide a running commentary on the text. Jean de Meun consulted William of Conches's popular commentary on the *De consolatione philosophiae* when writing the Boethian passages in *Le Roman de la Rose* and subsequently in making his complete French translation of the *Consolatio*. Nicholas Trevet's commentary on Boethius was especially popular among English writers: its influence is writ large in Chaucer's *Boece* and it has also been detected in Boethian passages in such works as *Troilus and Criseyde* and *The Monk's Tale*. Trevet on Boethius was used also by John Walton in making his all-verse English Boethius (completed 1410), and by Robert Henryson, grammar master at Dunfermline in the early fifteenth century, who found in Trevet's exposition of the story of Orpheus in the underworld the inspiration, and much of the information, for his Middle Scots poem *Orpheus and Eurydice*. Glosses on, and medieval adaptations of, Aesop suggested to Henryson touches which appear in both the *narrationes* and the *moralizationes* in his *Moral Fables of Aesop*. Then again, clear evidence of the influence of glosses on Ovid's *Heroides* may be found in certain stories included in

Chaucer's *Legend of Good Women* and John Gower's *Confessio amantis*. The class of commentary known to Chaucer has even been identified (by M. C. Edwards).

This list of examples could be extended indefinitely, but enough has been said, we trust, to make the point that it is quite crucial for modern scholars to be aware of the manuscript contexts of the Latin sources of vernacular literature. One might go so far as to say that it is the original text *together with* its accompanying commentary (often, it must be remembered, written around the actual text in the manuscript margins) that should be regarded as the source. At any rate, it is obvious that some effort should be made to divest oneself of assumptions engendered by the reading of texts in modern editions, apart from their medieval apparatus of glosses (the 'Loeb Classics' syndrome). How can one possibly begin to ascertain what a major writer like Dante or Chaucer is doing to his source-text unless one is aware of how that text had been expounded and elaborated in medieval scholarship of a kind readily available to (and often demonstrably consulted by) the writer concerned?

Academic prologue as literary model. It is obvious that in many cases writers modelled their own prefaces on one or other of the types of prologue which they had encountered during their grammar-school education (wherein standard prologue headings provided the basis of the introductory lecture on each and every 'set text') and in subsequent readings of commentaries in manuscripts.

Some of the vernacular prologues of this type are, as one would expect, either straight translations or faithful adaptations of their Latin equivalents, as is the case with the following Middle English examples: the prologue to the translation, attributed to John Trevisa, of Giles of Rome's *De regimine principum*, the English version of the standard 'Paris Bible' prologue to the Apocalypse, the prologue to Rolle's English Psalter (see pp. 190–91 below), and the *accessus* in an English commentary on the first book of the *Consolatio philosophiae* as translated by Chaucer (preserved in Oxford, Bodleian Library, MS Auct. F.3.5), which owes its basic form to the 'type C' prologue as described in our first chapter. Others are far more original in purpose and application, good examples being the prologue to the Old French *Livre du Chevalier de la Tour*, the Latin prose preface (in some measure modelled on twelfth-century type *accessus* to Ovid) to Juan Ruiz' *Libro de buen amor*, the introductions to such reference-books as Vincent of Beauvais's *Speculum maius* and Pierre Bersuire's *Reductorium morale*, all the prologues used by John Gower in his Latin poem *Vox clamantis* (on which see pp. 168–77 below), the Messenger's introductory speech in the English morality play *Everyman* (cf. p. 272 n. 14), and many of William Caxton's prologues and epilogues, including his preface to Malory's *Morte Darthur* (cf. pp. 206, 279 n. 117). For the various and varied works introduced by 'Aristotelian prologues' see pp. 161–2. Sometimes the prolegomena may be of a more complicated type, a good example being afforded by the beginning of Gower's *Confessio amantis*, on which see pp. 177–81.

There is, then, plenty of evidence to suggest that major writers of the later Middle Ages found in academic prologues idioms which they regarded as being sophisticated enough (and of course distinguished enough) to provide a basis for the description and justification of their own writings—although it must be recognized, of course, that often they made quite unusual use of traditional materials. Knowledge of the traditions of the academic prologue is, therefore, quite indispensable in our own attempts to comprehend and assess those same descriptions and justifications.

'Modern' commentary and 'self-commentary'. Thus far we have been considering how certain medieval writers responded to the elements of medieval commentary, i.e. the particular glosses and the general prologues. But the influence of the commentary tradition did not stop there, since it was often drawn upon by those who wished to provide vernacular texts with an apparatus which at once described certain aspects of those texts and tacitly claimed a degree of prestige for them (because that apparatus was of the type which conventionally had accompanied the works of the revered *auctores*). A good case in point is the mise-en-page of the most popular of all the vernacular translations of the *Consolatio* of Boethius, the 'Anonymous Verse-Prose Version' or 'Revised Mixed Version' as it is variously called (which has been studied intensively, and is being edited, by Glynnis Cropp). In some manuscripts the text is divided into short sections, each of which is followed by a section of French commentary, often marked 'glose' (the information coming, it would seem, from some version of the William of Conches commentary on Boethius). Here features of layout which had been developed in generations of scholastic manuscripts are being

used in presenting a translation of an *auctor* to an audience of wealthy layfolk.

Of even greater significance for the history of literary theory and criticism are the changes of attitude revealed by the treatment of vernacular works which, while in many instances still heavily dependent on Latin models, were beginning to demand attention of a kind which hitherto had been afforded only to established Latin authorities. Academic commentary became a precedent and source for 'new' commentary and even 'self-commentary': certain *moderni* set about the business of producing commentaries on 'new' works, works written by their medieval contemporaries and indeed by themselves.

Some of these appropriations of method and matter were more daring than others. Certain moral and didactic vernacular works received, quite naturally, moral and didactic glossing, the latter serving to enhance the prestige of the former with little sense of disjunction existing between text and gloss. A good example of this is provided by what is, to the best of my knowledge, the most heavily glossed original work written in Middle English: two copies of the mid-fifteenth-century *Court of Sapience* contain an extensive and erudite apparatus of Latin glosses, probably provided by the writer himself. The *Echecs amoureux*, by contrast, was something of a risqué poem, yet the person responsible for the French commentary on it—probably the first commentary to be written on any original poem in Medieval French—is hardly self-conscious about his hermeneutic activity, since he limits his justification to the claim that he is bringing out the profit and delight offered by the text under scrutiny. In *La Vita nuova* Dante applied to his own poetry certain scholastic techniques of textual exposition (most notably a type of *divisio textus* which grinds exceedingly fine) with apparent ease and freshness, without drawing attention to the pedagogic contexts which were their normal environment.

The glosses (in Italian) which Boccaccio appended to his *Teseida* are, however, a very different case, and a special one. This Italian epic was studiously equipped with apparatus of a kind which accompanied its Latin models in manuscript (e.g. the *scholia* on the *Thebaid*, the *Aeneid* and that highly popular Medieval Latin facsimile of a classical epic, Walter of Châtillon's *Alexandreis*), an apparatus calculated to dispose the discerning reader in favour of the poem and underline for his benefit the superlative literary criteria in accordance with which it had to be judged and esteemed. Here, techniques of exposition traditionally used in interpreting 'ancient' authorities are being used to indicate and announce the literary authority of a 'modern' work. No criticism is value-free (to cite a commonplace of contemporary literary theory), the truth of which is borne out by the glossing of the 'modern' commentators and 'self-commentators' of the later Middle Ages, who sought to aggrandize vernacular literature by applying to it a value-bestowing type of criticism.

The most articulate of all the self-commentators was certainly Dante. *Il Convivio* constitutes at once a commentary on three of his own *canzoni* and on the methods of commentary themselves. Dante gives a fascinating explanation of the reasons why he decided to write an Italian, rather than a Latin, commentary on Italian texts, and his famous explanation of the two types of allegorical exposition, the 'allegory of the poets' and the 'allegory of the theologians', is found at the beginning of his exposition of the first poem, *Voi che'ntendendo*. Literally, this *canzone* is supposed to record the conflict in Dante's mind between the memory of the lost Beatrice and a gentle lady—usually identified as the 'lady of the window' of *La Vita nuova*—whose pity sought to console him. Allegorically, this new love is Lady Philosophy (here Dante is, as he himself admits, influenced by the female personification created by Boethius); no rival to Beatrice, but rather a means towards her now-glorified self. Twelfth-century Bible commentators had used allegorical interpretation to establish the *auctoritas* of holy Scripture (as is explained in Chapter 2 below): here Dante, with a similar purpose and result, is applying the very same method to *Voi che'ntendendo*. Once again, appropriation of hermeneutic idioms and techniques may be identified as a strategy for the *translatio* of literary *auctoritatis* from Latin into the vernacular.

Medieval literary theory as interpretive aid. It has already been suggested that, with regard to textual details, knowledge of how a writer's source-text was understood by medieval scholars can be of considerable importance in our own attempt to grasp the significance of what he wrote. On many occasions it is possible to go much further than this, and claim that knowledge of how a given source was integrally interpreted and evaluated in medieval scholarship (or 'medievalized', as some would call it) can provide vital clues to the plans and purposes of some of the writers who drew on that source.

For example, the last book of the *De amore* (1184–6) of Andreas Capellanus, in which the addressee Walter is advised to refrain from the love of women, has been described by P. G. Walsh, the work's most recent editor, as an utter volte-face which has no real precedent in Ovid: 'The chasm between Andreas' first two books and the third is thus much more profound than is that between Ovid's *Ars* and his *Remedia*, in both of which the mock-didactic tone is uniform throughout'. However, as the *accessus* to Ovid make perfectly clear, medieval readers were taught to consider the *Remedia* as a genuine retraction, an attempt to make amends for the *Ars* which (so the story goes in the *vitae Ovidii*) had misled many men and women into reprehensible amours. Those same medieval readers, it may be inferred, would have regarded Andreas's transition as more essentially Ovidian, and hence more conventional and precedented, than his modern editor would allow. I endorse Walsh's remark that Andreas is proclaiming himself 'the medieval *magister amoris*, a twelfth-century Ovid', but would wish to add that the Ovid whom Andreas was imitating was the twelfth-century Ovid, i.e. Ovid as interpreted in that century.

Knowledge of the way in which Ovid was commonly interpreted is of considerable value in our approach to another work which owes much to that *auctor*, namely John Gower's *Confessio amantis*. How can a work which professes to treat of human love admit consideration of such political matters as the qualities required in a good ruler and the current sorry plight of the 'three estates' in medieval society? Gower's basic rationale becomes clearer when it is remembered that, in medieval literary criticism, Ovid's love-poetry was described as 'pertaining to ethics' (*ethice subponitur*). As one branch of practical philosophy as defined by Aristotle, ethics is related to politics, which is another branch of the same subject (cf. pp. 177–90). In sum, the *Confessio amantis* seems to operate through an assimilation of materials which, although they may appear heterogeneous to the modern reader, would have been regarded as quite compatible by the medieval reader who had learned his Ovid in grammar school.

These two cases may be regarded as manifestations of the late-medieval attitude to *intentio auctoris*, the intention of the author, in this case Ovid—by which was understood not any highly personal preoccupations but rather the author's pedagogic purpose, whether explicit or implicit; what was meant in ultimate terms. Medieval commentators were more interested in Truth than in the personal and subjective areas wherein we individualistic moderns are accustomed to seek the true intention of an author. Should we, then, moralize medieval texts in this manner, on the ground that, as an authentically medieval interpretive method, it must reveal the intended meaning of those texts? Our answer must surely be in the negative. We can treat a medieval work in the way in which medieval commentators treated their authorities *only* if the work in question clearly demands such treatment. Otherwise we are simply perpetuating the medieval interpretive system in an unthinking and highly reductive kind of way, with little regard for that rich diversity of style and sense which is such a marked feature of medieval textuality.

Since this point is of the first importance, we must dwell on it for a moment. The last major attempt to relate medieval hermeneutics (particularly Scriptural exegesis) to vernacular literature, led by D. W. Robertson, produced an interpretive determinism, and there seems to be little scholarly advantage in replacing one kind of interpretive determinism with another, by making pan-allegorization give way to pan-moralization. And that is why I have reservations about one aspect of the late Judson Allen's stimulating book *The Ethical Poetic of the Later Middle Ages*. 'For the Middle Ages', Professor Allen wrote, 'meanings tended to be multiple but not at all random or unpredictable; they existed in an array of possibilities'. Once this 'normative array' is defined—and we are assured that relatively few levels of meaning are possible—the critic is supposed to possess the definitive interpretive programme for revelation of the meaning of complex medieval poems. In a far more controversial book, which Allen wrote in collaboration with T. A. Moritz, these principles are pursued relentlessly in an interpretation of Chaucer's *Canterbury Tales* based on what medieval commentators had to say about the *Metamorphoses*; in particular, the practice of classifying Ovid's stories according to whether they were natural, moral, magical or spiritual is deemed to provide the system with which Chaucer's stories must also be classified. In this regard it is necessary, I feel, to enter some caveats.

To claim or imply that late-medieval moral interpretation should become a critical 'skeleton key', able to open any literary lock, is going too far. The truth seems to be far more complex and pluralistic, and therefore less reducible to rule or 'normative array'. What in the hands of medieval commentators was an evaluative method became in the hands of certain practising poets a possible literary strategy. By 'possible strategy' is meant a certain well-defined literary procedure which medieval poets could use but did not feel obliged to use. Sometimes that strategy is dominant, as for example in the attempts by John of Garland (*Morale scolarium*) and John Gower (*Vox clamantis*) to produce satire according to the medieval understanding of the genre, which involved the commendation of virtue and the castigation of vice. Sometimes the strategy is one among several, perhaps the best example being Juan Ruiz' *Libro de buen amor*, in which critical commonplaces relating to the ethical function of love-stories (derived, most likely, from *accessus* to Ovid's *Ars amatoria* and *Remedia amoris*) are interspersed with anecdotes of a lascivious and naturalistic kind; here the impeccably pious is juxtaposed with the energetically profane. Ruiz, it would seem, is providing instant commentary on his own text; the 'good men' in the audience (to echo Chaucer's Nun's Priest) can take the morality if they want to. But only if they want to.

The problem becomes even more acute when we consider late-medieval self-commentary. In *Il Convivio* Dante provides us with a learned philosophical and in part allegorical interpretation of a text (*Voi che'ntendendo*) which seems originally to have been written as a poem of human love. In the Latin glosses on his *Confessio amantis*, Gower provides us with the basis of an exclusively moral interpretation of his lover's confession. Neither writer seems to have envisaged his commentary as revealing the determinate meaning of his text, but rather one possible meaning thereof. The fact that the moral understanding is the one which any wise man would adopt does much to recommend it but does not enshrine it as the one and only 'real' understanding. A single text can have different kinds of meaning, depending on the kind of reader, or the kind of reading in which the reader is engaged at a given time. Conversely, in the hands of different writers a single story can take on different significations (as is obvious from medieval manipulations of *exempla*, for instance), and some writers imposed more semantic restrictions than others. This is, to be sure, at variance with the spirit of certain forms of modern 'New Criticism', wherein interpretation of a text is envisaged as being rather like many people climbing a single mountain, confident that, on its sun-kissed summit, they will all meet, shake hands and reconcile their differences, discussing (often wryly, for some took wrong turnings) the relative merits of the several routes to the top, but now united in the conviction that they share the secret of F6 (or wherever). But medieval textuality seems to offer a veritable range of mountains which are very different in shape and size, and hence demand different strategies: a method which ensures success with one may spell disaster with another. Any one of these mountains, moreover, may have several peaks, of varying or equal importance as the case may be—and certain climbers will turn out to be blind to some of them. Indeed—and here our metaphor breaks down completely—one often perceives a medieval reader/author making his own mountain in the very act of climbing.

Sometimes medieval poets thought and wrote like medieval commentators, and sometimes they did not; on occasion they assumed what the *Epistle to Can Grande della Scala* called the 'office of the commentator' (*lectoris officio*) but elsewhere quite different stances were adopted. Certainly, the ethical justification and moral interpretation of poetry were of crucial importance in the later Middle Ages, and every major poet took them seriously (a claim which quite definitely cannot be made for the 'allegory of the theologians'). But *how* they informed poetic purpose and plan was a matter for the individual poet. In short, much medieval textual meaning was pluralistic in nature. And such pluralism of meaning makes interpretive determinism impossible.

Medieval literary theory and criticism, of which medieval theory of authorship forms just one part, should not, therefore, be reduced to a rigid interpretive programme which brooks no exceptions to its rules. That attitude cannot be justified either diachronically or synchronically: it is indefensible in historical terms and also in terms of the complexities presented by so many of the most interesting texts. There is no skeleton key. What is offered are bunches of specific keys which fit specific locks: to refuse to use them would be surely perverse. Of course, literature is not firmly controlled by the literary theory contemporaneous with it (to think otherwise is, in my view, to be very naive about the nature of literary theory), yet, particularly in the case of writers whose works were demonstrably influenced thereby, such theory can assist us in identifying the criteria in accordance with which those works should be judged. Thus, theory becomes part of the process of contextualization which is necessary for the meaning of a text to be grasped. There is little credit to be gained in assessing texts with reference to an alien system of value, in punishing them

> under a foreign code of conscience.
> The words of a dead man
> Are modified in the guts of the living.
>   (W. H. Auden, 'In Memory of W. B. Yeats')

Cultural change is one thing: cultural imperialism is something else. One can only hope that greater awareness of medieval literary theory and criticism will help us to go back to the texts and their contexts with the desire to listen and learn, not to shout down and dominate.

It is a great pleasure to acknowledge those scholars who have helped me to pursue my research. My greatest debt, personal as much as academic, is to Mr M. B. Parkes. To Malcolm I owe (among other things) hours of stimulating and companionable discussion, precise reading of every draft of first my thesis and then my book, and constant encouragement. Those who know the late Beryl Smalley's work well will recognise her as the 'primary efficient cause' of the present book. Indeed, she managed—a feat unprecedented in my scholastic prologues—to combine that office with the role of instrumental cause, in so far as she provided invaluable information and advice, and carefully perused my material in an earlier form.

Generous advice and information on specific matters was provided by the following scholars: the late R. W. Hunt, Richard H. Rouse, the late Judson B. Allen, James J. Murphy, Éamonn Ó Carragáin, Nigel Palmer, Pamela R. Robinson, Pamela de Wit, the late J. A. W. Bennett, John Burrow, Paul Miller, the late Elizabeth Salter and the late William A. Pantin. I am very grateful to Dr Brian Scott for his considerable and meticulous help with passages of medieval Latin, and to Dr Alan Press and Miss Evelyn Mullally for discussion of some passages of Old French. To Dr Scott and Miss Robinson I owe careful proof-reading.

I was particularly fortunate, during my time at The Queen's University of Belfast, in being able to draw on the resources of a unique department, the Department of Scholastic Philosophy. Professor Theodore Crowley helped me to attain that familiarity with medieval philosophy and theology which was the main basis of my research, and his successor, Professor James McEvoy, answered a host of technical queries which arose in the course of my work.

Generous research grants from The Queen's University of Belfast made much of my research possible. An award from the British Academy enabled me to study in Paris libraries during the Summer of 1978.

Some of the material included in this book has appeared, in different forms and in different contexts, in the following periodicals: *Beiträge zur Geschichte der deutschen Sprache und Literatur*, *Medium Ævum*, *Mediaeval Studies*, and *New Literary History*.

Photographs are reproduced here by kind permission of the Trustees of the British Library and the Curators of the Bodleian Library, Oxford. For permission to print brief extracts from manuscripts I am indebted to the following: the Conservateur en chef of the Bibliothèque Nationale, Paris, the British Library Board, the Curators of the Bodleian Library, Oxford, the President and Fellows of Trinity College, Oxford, the President and Fellows of Corpus Christi College, Oxford, the Warden and Fellows of New College, Oxford, the Master and Fellows of Balliol College, Oxford, the Warden and Fellows of Merton College, Oxford, the Syndics of the University Library, Cambridge, the Master and Fellows of Corpus Christi College, Cambridge, the Master and Fellows of Christ's College, Cambridge.

Finally, some very personal acknowledgements. My wife Florence spent many hours discussing ideas, reading and improving drafts, compiling the index, and in general hastening the progress of this book. I have dedicated my work to my parents in grateful recognition of their constant understanding and support. It is impossible to describe my debt to my mother, who died in 1972, for the intellectual companionship which I enjoyed with her since I was old enough to think.

Bristol, Winter 1986   *A. J. M.*

Abbreviations

The following abbreviations have been used
in the Notes and Bibliography.

Accessus ad auctores, etc. ed. Huygens
Accessus ad auctores; Bernard d'Utrecht; Conrad d'Hirsau, édition critique
entièrement revue et augmentée, by R. B. C. Huygens (Leiden, 1970)

Ad Herennium
(Pseudo-) Cicero: Rhetorica ad Herennium, ed. with an English trans. by
H. Caplan (Cambridge, Mass. and London, 1954)

AFH
Archivum Franciscanum historicum

AFP
Archivum Fratrum Praedicatorum

AHDLMA
Archives d'histoire doctrinale et littéraire du moyen âge

Alberti opera, ed. Borgnet
S. Alberti Magni opera omnia, ed. A. Borgnet (Paris, 1890–9)

Allen, *Ethical Poetic*
Judson B. Allen, *The Ethical Poetic of the Later Middle Ages* (Toronto,
1982)

Aquinatis opera
S. Thomae Aquinatis opera omnia (Parma, 1852–72)

Biblia glossata
Biblia sacra cum Glossa ordinaria et Postilla Nicolai Lyrani (Antwerp, 1634). References are to numbered columns.

BLR
Bodleian Library Record

Bonaventurae opera
S. Bonaventurae opera omnia (Quaracchi, 1882–1902)

Bull. du Cange
Archivum latinitatis medii aevi, Bulletin du Cange

Camb. Hist. Jour.
Cambridge Historical Journal

CCCM
Corpus christianorum, continuatio medievalis

CCSL
Corpus christianorum, series latina

Chenu, *Toward understanding St Thomas*
M.-D. Chenu, *Toward understanding St Thomas*, trans. A.-M. Landry and D. Hughes (Chicago, 1964)

Cicero, *De inventione, etc.*
Cicero: De inventione, etc. ed. with an English trans. by H. M. Hubbell (Cambridge, Mass. and London, 1949)

CIMAGL
Cahiers de l'Institut du Moyen-Age Grec et Latin, Université de Copenhague

CP
Classical Philology

CSEL
Corpus scriptorum ecclesiasticorum latinorum

Curtius, *European Literature*
E. R. Curtius, *European Literature and the Latin Middle Ages*, trans. W. R. Trask (London, 1953)

Dom. Stud.
Dominican Studies

EETS (ES)
Early English Text Society, Extra Series

EETS (OS)
Early English Text Society, Original Series

Fran. Stud.
Franciscan Studies

HSCP
Harvard Studies in Classical Philology

Hugonis postilla
Hugonis Cardinalis postilla seu expositiones in Veteris et Novi Testamentum
(Paris, 1530–45). References are to numbered folios.

Hunt, 'Introductions to the *Artes*'
R. W. Hunt, 'The Introductions to the *Artes* in the Twelfth Century',
Studia medievalia in honorem R. M. Martin, O.P. (Bruges, 1948), pp.
85–112

JEGP
Journal of English and Germanic Philology

JEH
Journal of Ecclesiastical History

JWCI
Journal of the Warburg and Courtauld Institutes

Kristeller, *CTC*
*Catalogus translationum et commentariorum: Medieval and Renaissance Latin
Translations and Commentaries*, ed. P. O. Kristeller *et al.* (Washington,
1960–   )

Lottin, *Psychologie et morale*
O. Lottin, *Psychologie et morale aux XIIe et XIIIe siècles* (Louvain and
Gembloux, 1942–60)

de Lubac, *Exégèse médiévale*
H. de Lubac, *Exégèse médiévale* (Paris, 1959–64)

MARS
Medieval and Renaissance Studies

Med. et hum.
Medievalia et humanistica

Med. Stud.
Mediaeval Studies

Miller, 'John Gower, Satiric Poet'
Paul Miller, 'John Gower, Satiric Poet', in *Gower's Confessio amantis: Responses and Reassessments*, ed. A. J. Minnis (Cambridge, 1983), pp. 79–105

Minnis, 'Moral Gower'
A. J. Minnis, '"Moral Gower" and Medieval Literary Theory', in *Gower's Confessio amantis: Responses and Reassessments*, ed. A. J. Minnis (Cambridge, 1983), pp. 50–78

MP
Modern Philology

New Schol.
The New Scholasticism

PBB
Beiträge zur Geschichte der deutschen Sprache und Literatur

PL
Patrologia latina, ed. J.-P. Migne (Paris, 1844–64). References are to numbered columns.

PMLA
Publications of the Modern Language Association of America

RAM
Revue d'ascétique et mystique

Rev. bén.
Revue bénédictine

Rev. bib.
Revue biblique

Rev. thom.
Revue thomiste

RFN
Rivista di filosofia neo-scolastica

RHE
Revue d'histoire ecclésiastique

RSPT
Revue des sciences philosophiques et théologiques

RTAM
Recherches de théologie ancienne et médiévale

Sandkühler, *Die frühen Dantekommentare*
B. Sandkühler, *Die frühen Dantekommentare und ihr Verhältnis zur mittelal-terlichen Kommentartradition*, Münchner Romanistiche Arbeiten, xix (Munich, 1967)

Smalley, *English Friars and Antiquity*
B. Smalley, *English Friars and Antiquity in the Early Fourteenth Century* (Oxford, 1960)

Smalley, 'Sapiential Books I'
B. Smalley, 'Some Thirteenth-Century Commentaries on the Sapiential Books', *Dom. Stud.*, ii (1949), 318–55

Smalley, 'Sapiential Books II'
B. Smalley, 'Some Thirteenth-Century Commentaries on the Sapiential Books, contd.', ibid., iii (1950), 41–77

Smalley, 'Sapiential Books III'
B. Smalley, 'Some Thirteenth-Century Commentaries on the Sapiential Books, concl.', ibid., iii (1950), 236–74

Smalley, 'Sapiential Books IV'
B. Smalley, 'Some Commentaries on the Sapiential Books of the Late
Thirteenth and Early Fourteenth Centuries', *AHDLMA*, xviii (1950),
103–28

Smalley, *Study of the Bible*
B. Smalley, *The Study of the Bible in the Middle Ages* (Oxford, 1952)

SP
Studies in Philology

Spicq, *Esquisse*
P. C. Spicq, *Esquisse d'une histoire de l'exégèse latine au moyen âge*, Bibliothèque thomiste, xxvi (Paris, 1944)

Stegmüller, *Bibl.*
F. Stegmüller, *Repertorium biblicum medii aevi* (Madrid, 1949–61). References are to numbered items.

Stegmüller, *Bibl. suppl.*
F. Stegmüller, *Repertorium biblicum, vols. viii–ix: supplementum* (Madrid,
1976–7). Numbered items.

Stegmüller, *Sent.*
F. Stegmüller, *Repertorium commentariorum in sententias Petri Lombardi*
(Wurzburg, 1947). Numbered items.

TAPA
Transactions of the American Philological Society

TRHS
Transactions of the Royal Historical Society

Notes on Style

Quotations of prose, with the exception of passages of Middle English prose, have been translated from the original language in which they were written. In those cases where the source was an unpublished manuscript, the original has been provided in a note. Verse has always been printed as verse, in its original language, with an English translation immediately following in the text.

Although the text of the *Glossa ordinaria* published in J.-P. Migne's *Patrologia latina* is the most easily accessible, because of its general inaccuracy I have preferred usually to cite the text in the early printed edition of the *Biblia sacra cum Glossa ordinaria* which was available to me, the Antwerp edition of 1634.

Introduction:
The Significance of
the Medieval Theory of Authorship

IN RECENT YEARS, in discussions of late-medieval literature, it has become fashionable to employ a number of critical terms which derive their meaning from modern, not medieval, literary theory.[1] This practice can to some extent be interpreted as a tacit admission of defeat. There are many major aspects of medieval texts which cannot be discussed adequately in the terminology and framework of those sources of medieval rhetoric and poetic which have to date enjoyed full scholarly attention. For example, the arts of preaching are very specialised, while the arts of poetry offer practical instruction in the use of tropes, figures and other poetic devices. Neither type of source has much to say about the usual preoccupations of literary theory, namely 'the principles of literature, its categories, criteria, and the like'.[2] Faced with such apparent limitations, naturally the scholar is inclined to adopt concepts from modern literary theory, concepts which have no historical validity as far as medieval literature is concerned. Is it not better to search again, in a different range of medieval writings, for a conceptual equipment which is at once historically valid and theoretically illuminating?[3]

I suggest that such a range of writings is provided by the glosses and commentaries on the authoritative Latin writers, or *auctores*, studied in the schools and universities of the later Middle Ages (by which I mean the period extending roughly from 1100 to 1400). In particular, the prologues to these commentaries are valuable repositories of medieval theory of authorship, i.e. the literary theory centered on the concepts of *auctor* and *auctoritas*.

A medieval lecture-course on an *auctor* usually began with an introductory discourse in which the text would be considered as a whole, and an outline provided of those literary and doctrinal principles and criteria supposed to be appropriate to it. When the series of lectures was written down by pupils, or prepared for publication by the teacher himself, the opening lecture became the prologue to the commentary on the text. Thanks to the extensive research on the educational contexts of this textual explication carried out by such scholars as H. Marrou and P. Riché (for the late classical and early medieval periods) and P. Glorieux and M.-D. Chenu (for the later medieval period) I am able to concentrate on the way in which its terminology was developed by successive generations of medieval teachers into a precise and comprehensive 'critical idiom'. Thereby the academic prologue became an important vehicle for the advancement of literary theory relating to *auctores* and *auctoritas*.

It is possible to speak of 'theory' of authorship rather than 'theories' because of the high degree of consistency with which medieval scholars treated the subject and employed its characteristic vocabulary. This is hardly surprising in an age which was obsessed with classification, valuing the universal over the particular and the typical over the individual. Yet medieval theory of authorship was not homogeneous in the sense of being uncomplicated and narrowly monolithic: there was a rich abundance of kinds, degrees, properties and aspects of authorship to describe and relate to not one but several systems of classification. Neither was the theory static: it is best defined in terms of basic literary assumptions, approaches and methods of analysis which altered, sometimes considerably, over the centuries and were applied to many types of writing for many different purposes.

This book is not offered as a comprehensive 'history' of medieval theory of authorship. To attempt such a book would be premature in the present state of our knowledge. My aim has been to illuminate one area of the subject which has largely been ignored, namely the contribution made by several generations of schoolmen who, in the main, were connected with the schools and universities of late-medieval France and England. The Italian contribution is so singular and complex that it merits a study all of its own, and therefore I have confined myself to a brief mention of Petrarch and Boccaccio. Neither has an attempt been made to assess the extent to which the theory of authorship discussed below meets the demands of modern literary critics and theorists. Full historical description of the literary theory produced in the later Middle Ages naturally precedes the comparative analysis of medieval and modern literary theory.

The study of late medieval literary theory is still in its infancy. It is most unfortunate that research on it has been hindered by what I regard as an anachronistic and highly misleading notion, namely the distinction between twelfth-century 'humanism' and thirteenth-century 'scholasticism'. According to a common exposé, by the end of the twelfth century grammar had lost the battle of the seven liberal arts and Dame Logic held the field.[4] Rhetoric and poetic gave way to logic and dialectic; humanism retreated before scholasticism. Orléans, where the songs of the muses had been guarded zealously, became a law school. The pagan *Fasti* (by Ovid) was replaced by a blatantly Christian one, the *Ecclesiale* of Alexander of Villa Dei;[5] the study of grammar—and therefore of 'literature'—was generally impoverished. In such unfavourable conditions, literary theory died or at least went underground.

This view is untenable, as the evidence presented below will attest. It is impossible to square with, for example, the sophisticated literary analyses of texts—particularly Scriptural texts—produced by commentators of the thirteenth and fourteenth centuries. At a time when the study of grammar had moved a long way from explication of classical *auctores* to speculative analysis of the theoretical structures of language, theologians and Bible-scholars were elaborating a comprehensive and flexible interpretative model for the diverse literary styles and structures supposed to be present in sacred Scripture, and for the diverse roles or functions—both literary and moral—believed to be performed by the human *auctores* of the Bible.

Some recent writers have countered the facile distinction between twelfth-century humanism and thirteenth-century scholasticism with the suggestion that, in many major respects, thirteenth-century scholasticism was a natural growth out of twelfth-century scholasticism. Hence, Sir Richard Southern can speak of 'a process of accumulation and increasingly refined analysis of the deposit of the past' from the twelfth century into the thirteenth century.[6] The scholastic literary theory formulated in the thirteenth and fourteenth centuries is quite clearly a product of this process of accumulation and refinement. In the twelfth century, certain scholars—notably Peter Abelard and

Gilbert of Poitiers—had in their Bible-commentaries applied the conventions and categories of secular literary theory to sacred literature. Later scholars built on this by, for example, producing an intricate framework for discussion of each and every 'form of literary treatment' (*forma tractandi*) found in Scripture.

Another consequence of the emphasis on accumulation and refinement is that the so-called 'School of Chartres' is not afforded undue prominence on the twelfth-century intellectual landscape. The typical rather than the supposedly unique qualities of this 'school' are emphasised in my chapter on 'Academic Prologues to *Auctores*'. Hence, the standard techniques of Latin literary scholarship current in the twelfth century can emerge clearly, as can, in subsequent chapters, the ways in which these techniques were developed, adapted, and altered in later centuries.

Chapters 2–4 are chronological, tracing the development of this scholarship from the twelfth century to the fourteenth century, with special reference to commentaries on the Bible. As the authoritative text *par excellence*, the 'Book of Life' and the book of books, the Bible was for medieval scholars the most difficult text to describe accurately and adequately. Medieval theologians were eminently aware of both the comparisons and the contrasts which could be made between the Bible and secular texts. On the one hand, they stressed the unique status of the Bible; on the other, they believed that the budding exegete had to be trained in the liberal arts before he could begin to understand the infinitely more complex 'sacred page'. Consequently, in theologians' prologues academic literary theory is at its most elaborate and sophisticated.

The literary analysis in academic prologues was conducted in an orderly fashion, each and every text being discussed under a series of headings. The most popular series of headings employed in twelfth-century commentaries on *auctores* was as follows: the title of the work, the name of the author, the intention of the author, the material or subject-matter of the work, its mode of literary procedure, its order or arrangement, its usefulness, and the branch of learning to which it belonged. This system of textual explication is discussed in Chapter 2 with illustrations from commentaries on classical *auctores*, especially Ovid, and on the various books of the Bible, especially the Song of Solomon and the Psalter.

In the early thirteenth century a different series of prologue-headings came into use as a result of the new methods of thinking and techniques of study which scholars derived from Aristotle. The 'Aristotelian prologue' was based on the four major causes which, according to Aristotle, governed all activity and change in the universe. Hence, the *auctor* would be discussed as the 'efficient cause' or motivating agent of the text, his materials would be discussed as the 'material cause', his literary style and structure would be considered as twin aspects of the 'formal cause', while his ultimate end or objective in writing would be considered as the 'final cause'. In Chapters 3 and 4 this system of textual explication is illustrated with examples from major schoolmen of the thirteenth and fourteenth centuries, including Hugh of St Cher, Albert the Great, Alexander of Hales, Robert Kilwardby, Thomas Aquinas, Bonaventure, Giles of Rome, Henry of Ghent, Nicholas of Lyre, Nicholas Trevet, and Robert Holcot.

As applied in literary analysis, the 'four causes' may seem to us a contrived and highly artificial framework, but in the later Middle Ages they brought commentators considerably closer to their *auctores*. The *auctor* remained an authority, someone to be believed and imitated, but his human qualities began to receive more attention. This crucial development is writ large in the prologues to commentaries on the Bible. In twelfth-century exegesis, the primacy of allegorical interpretation had hindered the emergence of viable literary theory: God was believed to have inspired the human writers of Scripture in a way which defied literary description. Twelfth-century exegetes were interested in the *auctor* mainly as a source of authority. But in the thirteenth century, a new type of exegesis emerged, in which the focus had shifted from the divine *auctor* to the human *auctor* of Scripture. It became fashionable to emphasise the literal sense of the Bible, and the intention of the human *auctor* was believed to be expressed by the literal sense. As a result, the exegetes' interest in their texts became more literary.

Two of the most important concerns which this new interest produced are considered in detail, namely the commentators' preoccupation with authorial role and literary form. The concern with authorial role or function—sometimes termed the author's 'office' (*officium*)—is manifest by two facets of the author's individuality which the exegete sought to describe, his individual literary activity and his individual moral activity. For example, in the prologue to his commentary on

Lamentations, the Franciscan John Lathbury (whose Oxford regency must have occurred soon after 1350) pieced together a life-story of the sacred poet in which all his authorial roles are considered: Jeremiah was a prophet, writer, priest, virgin, and martyr. I have paid special attention to medieval depictions of King David in his many, and apparently contradictory, roles—*auctor* and adulterer, saint and sinner. On the other hand, the preoccupation with literary form is manifest by the two facets of a text's formal cause which the commentators were describing, namely form considered as style and form considered as structure.

The medieval theory of authorship presented in these chapters calls for a qualification of the commonly-held notion that scholasticism was not interested in art in general or poetry in particular. In fact, the influence of Aristotle, far from destroying academic literary theory, enabled it to acquire a new prestige. Such theory was not dead or even decadent, merely different, and this essential difference is the proper object of scholarly inquiry. Thirteenth-century schoolmen produced a critical vocabulary which enabled the literary features of Scriptural texts to be analysed thoroughly, and which encouraged the emergence in the fourteenth century of a more liberal attitude to classical poetry. Something of the new status which had been afforded to Scriptural poetry in particular and to the poetic and rhetorical modes employed throughout Scripture in general, seems to have 'rubbed off' on secular poetry. Scriptural *auctores* were being read literally, with close attention being paid to those poetic methods believed to be part of the literal sense; pagan poets were being read allegorically or 'moralised'—and thus the twain could meet.

Scholastic idioms of literary theory, which received their fullest development at the hands of theologians, became widely disseminated, appearing in works written both in Latin and in the European vernaculars. They influenced the attitudes which many major writers—including Petrarch, Boccaccio, Chaucer and Gower—had towards the moral and aesthetic value of their creativity, the literary roles and forms they had adopted, and the ultimate functions which they envisaged their works as performing.

This is illustrated in the final chapter, entitled 'Literary Theory and Literary Practice', which concentrates on the ways in which two practising poets of fourteenth-century England, Chaucer and Gower, exploited a few aspects of the vast corpus of literary theory indicated in the previous chapters. Then, in a short Epilogue, by way of contrast we turn to attitudes concerning authorship which are associated with the Italian Renaissance. Certain aspects of the literary theory advocated by Petrarch and Boccaccio can be regarded as imaginative extensions of ideas which had developed in scholastic literary theory. Yet along with these continuities there are new beginnings. The *auctor* is becoming the reader's respected friend.

The tacit assumption behind all these chapters is that medieval theory of authorship provides us moderns with a window on the medieval world of books. To our gaze this window may seem small and its glass unclear and distorting, but these, after all, are characteristic features of a medieval window, indications that it is genuine and historically right. Our standards must change if we are to appreciate what it has to offer. To make the same point in a different way, while we cannot re-experience the past, we can recognise the integrity of past experience and apply the resultant information in evaluating our present experience of the past. In this process of recognition and application, knowledge of late medieval literary theory must play a crucial part: it will help us to understand how major writings of the same period entered into the culture of their time, and it will provide criteria for the acceptance or rejection of those modern concepts and terms which seem to have some bearing on medieval literature.

Of course, I am not suggesting that knowledge of late medieval literary theory is the unique key to definitive understanding of late medieval literature. Literature is not rigidly determined by the literary theory contemporaneous with it. To take the case of one extraordinary writer, Chaucer often reacted against the literary theory of his day, or exploited it in a very unusual way; sometimes his narrators talk like the schoolmaster Holofernes in Shakespeare's *Love's Labour's Lost,* trotting out learned literary cliché which has little apparent relevance to the matter in hand. My point is rather that the strangeness (what some would call the 'alterity') of late medieval literary theory will to some extent free us from that 'blind modernism' which obscures our view of the past.[8] We cannot understand how Chaucer exploited or reacted against the literary theory of his day until we understand what that literary theory was; his extensive 'defamiliarization' (notably of literary convention and of genre) cannot be appreciated until we know what was normal to him and what was not[9]. How valuable would be Holofernes' reading of Shakespeare? At the very least, it would provide a register with which to measure Shakespeare's originality. More optimistically, it would focus attention on those areas of literary discourse important to him as a man of his age, and illuminate the categories and concepts which informed his thinking about literature in general and his own works in particular. If used with discretion, with what Matthew Arnold called 'tact', late medieval literary theory can serve as a stimulus and a corrective in modern speculation about authorial intention and audience expectancy in the late Middle Ages.

1

Academic Prologues to 'Auctores'

In the beginning of this book and of every other, the listeners are accustomed to ask who is the efficient cause. And it is very useful to know this, for statements of 'authentic' men are the more diligently and firmly inscribed in the mind of the hearer.[1]

The English grammarian William Wheteley (*fl.* 1309–16) is addressing his pupils in the introduction to his course of lectures on the *De disciplina scolarium*. It is very useful, he assures them, to know the name of the 'efficient cause' or writer of a book, because 'authentic' statements—statements which can be attributed to a named authority—are more worthy of diligent attention and to be committed to memory[2]. Wheteley explains that the *De disciplina scolarium* was written by Boethius, the Roman consul who died in 524. In fact, it was written between 1230 and 1240, probably at Paris[3].

This mistaken attribution of a 'modern' work to an 'ancient' and distinguished writer is symptomatic of medieval veneration of the past in general. Old books were the sources of new learning, as Chaucer remarks:

. . .out of olde feldes, as men seyth,
Cometh al this newe corn from yer to yere,
And out of olde bokes, in good feyth,
Cometh al this newe science that men lere[4].

To be old was to be good; the best writers were the more ancient. The converse often seems to have been true: if a work was good, its medieval readers were disposed to think that it was old. In order to understand such attitudes better, it will be necessary in the first place to examine the significance of the common technical term for a distinguished writer, namely, *auctor,* and then to proceed with an investigation of how the *auctores* were studied within the medieval educational system.

THE TERMS *AUCTOR* AND *AUCTORITAS*

In a literary context, the term *auctor* denoted someone who was at once a writer and an authority, someone not merely to be read but also to be respected and believed[5]. According to medieval grammarians, the term derived its meaning from four main sources: *auctor* was supposed to be related to the Latin verbs *agere* 'to act or perform', *augere* 'to grow' and *auieo* 'to tie', and to the Greek noun *autentim* 'authority'[6]. An *auctor* 'performed' the act of writing. He brought something into being, caused it to 'grow'. In the more specialised sense related to *auieo,* poets like Virgil and Lucan were *auctores* in that they had 'tied' together their verses with feet and metres[7]. To the ideas of achievement and growth was easily assimilated the idea of authenticity or 'authoritativeness'[8].

The writings of an *auctor* contained, or possessed, *auctoritas* in the abstract sense of the term, with its strong connotations of veracity and sagacity. In the specific sense, an *auctoritas* was a quotation or an extract from the work of an *auctor*[9]. Writing around 1200, Hugutio of Pisa defined an *auctoritas* as a *sententia digna imitatione,* a profound saying worthy of imitation or implementation[10]. In his *Catholicon* (finished 1286), the Dominican Giovanni de'Balbi of Genoa amplified this with the statement that an *auctoritas* is also worthy of belief: as Aristotle says, an *auctoritas* is a judgment of the wise man in his chosen discipline[11]. De'Balbi used an *auctoritas* of Plato's as an example. Plato says that the heavens are in motion; therefore, we should accept that this is indeed the case, because the man who is proficient and expert in his science must be believed[12].

The term *auctor* may profitably be regarded as an accolade bestowed upon a popular writer by those later scholars and writers who used extracts from his works as sententious statements or *auctoritates,* gave lectures on his works in the form of textual commentaries, or employed them as literary models[13]. Two criteria for the award of this accolade were tacitly applied: 'intrinsic worth' and 'authenticity'.

To have 'intrinsic worth', a literary work had to conform, in one way or another, with Christian truth; an *auctor* had to say the right things.

The Bible was the authoritative book *par excellence*. At the other end of
the scale came the fables of the poets, employed in the teaching of
grammar[14]. As fictional narrative, fable could be dismissed by its critics as lying; many medieval writers expressed their distrust of such
fabrication. According to Conrad of Hirsau (*c.* 1070–*c.* 1150), fables
have practically no spiritual significance; they are as nothing when
compared with Scripture[15]. Peter Comestor (Chancellor of Notre
Dame, Paris, between 1168 and 1178) remarked that the figments of
the poets are like the croaking of frogs[16]. The usual defence was that
fables, rightly understood, provided philosophical and ethical doctrine:
after all, Priscian had said that fable teaches and delights, and had
commended the fables of Aesop[17]. Twelfth-century grammarians rendered acceptable the licentious stories of Ovid by extensive moralisation[18]. Those thinkers influenced by Neoplatonism—notably William
of Conches (*c.* 1080–*c.* 1154) and Bernard Silvester (*fl.* 1156)—went
much further, in their elaborate mythic interpretations of pagan
fables[19].

To be 'authentic', a saying or a piece of writing had to be the
genuine production of a named *auctor*[20]. Works of unknown or uncertain authorship were regarded as 'apocryphal' and believed to possess an
auctoritas far inferior to that of works which circulated under the names
of *auctores*[21]. The standards of authenticity were applied most rigorously in the case of the books of the Bible[22]. Thus, the Dominican
Hugh of St Cher (who lectured on the Bible 1230–5) was careful in
explaining the terms on which certain apocryphal works are accepted
by the Church:

They are called apocryphal because the author is unknown. But because there
is no doubt of their truth they are accepted by the Church, for the teaching of
mores rather than for the defence of the faith. However, if neither the author
nor the truth were known, they could not be accepted, like the book on the
infancy of the Saviour and the assumption of the Blessed Virgin.[23]

It was regarded as a very drastic step to dispute an attribution and
deprive a work of its *auctor*. Much more common was the tendency to
accept improbable attributions of currently popular works to older and
respected writers. Interesting cases in point include the *De disciplina
scolarium*, discussed above, and the *Dissuasio Valerii ad Rufinum* produced by Walter Map in the late twelfth century[24]. The quality and
popularity of Map's discourse caused some of his contemporaries to
doubt that he could have written it. 'My only fault is that I am alive',

complained Map; 'I have no intention, however, of correcting this fault by my death'[25]. His title, he explained, contains the names of dead men because this gives pleasure and, more importantly, because if he had not done so the work would have been rejected. Map speculated concerning the fate of the *Dissuasio* after his death:

I know what will happen after I am gone. When I shall be decaying, then, for the first time, it shall be salted; and every defect in it will be remedied by my decease, and in the most remote future its antiquity will cause the authorship to be credited to me, because, then as now, old copper will be preferred to new gold. . . . In every century its own present has been unpopular, and each age from the beginning has preferred the past to itself. . .

In the long term, Map was right (witness the enthusiasm of recent literary critics for his works) but, in the later Middle Ages, the *Dissuasio* was attributed to the first-century Roman historian, Valerius Maximus. The 'authenticity' and *auctoritas* of the work in this attribution were defended in several medieval commentaries[26].

The thinking we are investigating seems to be circular: the work of an *auctor* was a book worth reading; a book worth reading had to be the work of an *auctor*. No 'modern' writer could decently be called an *auctor* in a period in which men saw themselves as dwarfs standing on the shoulders of giants, i.e. the 'ancients'[27]. In the treatise on the love of books which he composed in the last years of his life, Richard of Bury (Bishop of Durham 1333–45) could claim that, while the novelties of modern writers were always welcome to him, yet he always desired 'with more undoubting avidity' to explore the well-tested labours of the 'ancients'[28]. The precise reason for the ancients' excellence is unclear, according to de Bury: they may have had by nature greater mental powers, or they may have applied themselves more diligently to study. But in his opinion it is obvious that the 'moderns' are barely capable of discussing ancient discoveries, and of acquiring laboriously as pupils those things which the old masters provided[29]. Since the men of bygone days were of a more excellent degree of bodily development than the present age can produce, de Bury continued, it is plausible to suppose that they were distinguished by brighter mental faculties as well, seeing that in their works they are inimitable by posterity[30]. From all this, it would seem that the only good *auctor* was a dead one. Hence the 'fault' which Walter Map was in no hurry to correct.

THE ACADEMIC STUDY OF *AUCTORES*

Every discipline, every area of study, had its *auctores*. In grammar, there were Priscian and Donatus together with the ancient poets; in rhetoric, Cicero; in dialectic, Aristotle, Porphyry and Boethius; in arithmetic, Boethius and Martianus Capella; in astronomy, Hyginus and Ptolemy; in medicine, Galen and Constantine the African; in Canon Law, Gratian; in theology, the Bible and, subsequently, Peter Lombard's *Sentences* as well[31]. The study of authoritative texts in the classroom formed the basis of the medieval educational system.

This system had its origins in late antiquity. From the Roman grammarian *(grammaticus)* of the fifth century, the pupil learned the science of speaking with style *(scientia recte loquendi)* and heard the classical poets being explicated *(enarratio poetarum)*[32]. The first of these activities comprised explanation of the elements of language, letters, syllables and words; the second comprised explanation of the intellectual content of a text. In his *prelectio* (i.e. lecture or explanatory reading), the grammarian would describe in minute detail the verse-rhythms, difficult or rare words, grammatical and syntactical features, and figures of speech, included in a given passage. He would also elaborate on its historical, legal, geographical, mythological and scientific allusions and details. Pupils were thereby enabled to understand fully each passage of the work.

These teaching methods continued, with occasional modification, into the Middle Ages[33]. John of Salisbury's *Metalogicon* (completed 1159) provides a useful point of reference, since it refers to both past and present educational practice. After paraphrasing the account of *prelectio* which Quintilian had written in the first century, John proceeds to relate how Bernard of Chartres (†c. 1130), 'the greatest font of literary learning in Gaul in recent times', used to teach grammar[34]. In reading (i.e. lecturing on) the *auctores,* Bernard would point out what was straightforward and in accordance with the rules of composition, and also explain 'grammatical figures, rhetorical embellishment, and sophistical quibbling'. It would seem that Bernard shared some of Quintilian's principles and concerns.

Further insight into the priorities of *prelectio* is provided by a remark of one of Bernard's pupils, William of Conches, once the teacher of John of Salisbury and of the future King Henry II of England[35]. In the

prologue to his commentary on the *Timaeus,* William criticised those
commentaries and glosses on Plato which attempt to explain the *sententiae* of a work (i.e. its profound and inner meanings) without having
first carefully followed and explained 'the letter' of the text[36]. This
point of view was shared by Hugh of St Victor (writing *c.* 1127), who
advocated the following 'order of exposition' in studying the Bible: one
begins with 'the letter', working out the grammatical construction and
continuity of a passage; then, one proceeds to expound its *sensus* or
most obvious meaning; and, finally, the *sententia* or deeper meaning is
sought[37].

Analysis of both 'the letter' of authoritative texts and of the *sententiae*
found therein were, in whatever proportion, essential features of all the
teaching conducted within the medieval trivium and quadrivium. (The
trivium comprised grammar, rhetoric and dialectic, the inferior group
of the seven liberal arts; the quadrivium comprised music, arithmetic,
geometry and astronomy, the superior group). In the case of the more
specialised disciplines of law, medicine and theology, these procedures
were heavily modified to suit the special requirements of the individual
subject. But no matter what the subject, the scholar did not compete
(he did not even pretend to do so) either with his *auctores* or with the
great works which they had left. One's whole ambition was directed to
understanding the authoritative texts, 'penetrating their depths, as-
similating them and, in the fields of grammar and rhetoric, imitating
them'[38].

The explication of an *auctor* in any discipline invariably began with
an introductory lecture in which the master would say something about
the discipline in general and the purpose and contents of the chosen
text in particular. In subsequent lectures, the text would be discussed
in minute detail[39]: so thorough was this analysis that John of Salisbury
described it as a 'shaking out' of the *auctores;* they were thereby de-
spoiled of the plumes which they had borrowed from the several
branches of learning[40]. It was in the introductory lecture, and usually
only there, that the lecturer would consider the text as a whole, and
outline the doctrinal and literary principles and criteria supposed to be
appropriate to it. When the series of lectures was written down by
pupils, or prepared for publication by the master himself, the opening
lecture would serve as the prologue to the commentary on the text.

The academic prologue had different names in different disciplines.

Artistae, or students of arts subjects, called it an *accessus* (though this is essentially a feature of German manuscripts), glossators of the Roman Law called it a *materia,* while Scriptural exegetes called it an *introitus* or *ingressus*[41]. In the twelfth century, three main types of prologue were employed in introducing an *auctor.* These three types were identified and described in an article published by R. W. Hunt in 1948, a study to which the following discussion is considerably indebted[42]. Special reference will be made to the type of prologue which enjoyed the widest application and the greatest frequency of use.

THREE TYPES OF ACADEMIC PROLOGUE

Our first type of prologue (Dr Hunt's 'type B') may have originated in ancient commentaries on Virgil. Its characteristic series of headings, or paradigm, is employed in an introduction to the *Eclogues* attributed to the fourth-century grammarian, Aelius Donatus. Here the headings are divided into two groups. 'Before the work' *(ante opus)* the title, cause and intention must be investigated while, 'in the work itself' *(in ipso opere),* three things may reasonably be regarded, the number (of the constituent books or parts), order and explanation[43]. A fuller version of this type of prologue is found at the beginning of the commentary on the *Aeneid* attributed to Servius, another fourth-century grammarian. However, this elaboration probably represents the accretions of later scholarship:

In expounding authors these things are to be considered: the intention of the writer, the life of the poet, the title of the work, the quality of the poem, the number of the books, the order of the books, the explanation. This is the life of Virgil . . . The title is *Aeneis* . . . The quality of the poem is obvious, for it is heroic verse mixed with action, where the poet both speaks and introduces others speaking. Moreover, it is heroic because it is made up of divine and human characters, containing truth with fictions . . . The style is grandiloquent, which consists in high speech and in great sententious statements. For we know that there are three kinds of speaking *(genera dicendi),* the humble, the middle and the grandiloquent. The intention of Virgil is this, to imitate Homer and to praise Augustus through his ancestors . . . Concerning the number of books there is no question . . . There is no question concerning the order of the books—as is found in the case of other authors, for some say that Plautus wrote twenty-one fables, some forty, and others a hundred. The order also is manifest . . . Only the explanation remains, which will be rendered in the following exposition.[44]

Medieval scholars certainly associated this paradigm with Servius. Writing between 1076 and 1099, Bernard of Utrecht described it as an ancient schema which had fallen out of favour with the moderns, then organised his discussion of Theodulus around its seven headings, citing Servius[45]. The paradigm was applied to the *Paschale Carmen* of Sedulius because Sedulius was regarded as a Christian Virgil[46]. Even as late as the fifteenth century, when a commentator applied it to Ovid's *Metamorphoses,* he identified as his model Servius's commentary on the *Aeneid*[47].

At the head of a life of Virgil found in a ninth-century Wolfenbüttel manuscript, the usual 'type B' headings are given,

In the beginnings of books seven summaries, that is circumstances, are required: the life of the poet, the title of the work, the quality of the poem, the intention of the writer, the number of the books, the order of the books, the explanation.[48]

and then an alternative apparatus is offered, consisting of a quite different series of headings:

But John the Scot briefly wrote these summaries, saying whom, what, why, in what manner, when, where, by what means.[49]

This seems to point to a major theory of *circumstantiae* formulated by John Scotus Erigena (*c.* 810–*c.* 877), who was made head of the palace school at Laon by Charles the Bald[50]. Erigena's role in the development of prologue technique is far from clear[51]. We are on safer ground when considering the contribution made by Remigius of Auxerre (*c.* 841–*c.* 908), to whom the Wolfenbüttel life of Virgil has been attributed[52].

The main type of prologue associated with Remigius had its origin in the rhetorical circumstances *(circumstantiae)* or summaries *(periochas)*[53]. Ancient rhetoricians had taught that everything which could form the subject of a dispute or discussion was covered by a series of questions which, during successive generations of scholarship, was expanded into seven, namely, 'whom', 'what', 'why', 'in what manner', 'where', 'when' and 'whence' (or 'by what means'). When applied to the grammatical discussion of a text, these *circumstantiae* provided the basis for a comprehensive and informative prologue (cf. Dr Hunt's 'type A')[54]. A good example is furnished by Remigius's *accessus* to Martianus Capella[55]. This begins with the claim that, at the beginning of all authentic books, one must go through the seven *circumstantiae,* which are then listed in Greek together with their equivalents in Latin. The question 'who?' requires to be answered by a statement concerning the person (*persona*) responsible for the work, its *auctor*, who, in this case, is Martianus. The question 'what?' refers to the thing, the text itself, and is answered with a statement of the book-title. 'Why' did Martianus write? Because he wished to dispute concerning the seven liberal arts. The question 'in what manner?' inquires the particular mode (*modus*) or fashion in which he wrote, Remigius's answer being that, in *De nuptiis Philologiae et Mercurii* both verse and prose are used. 'Where' did Martianus write? The place (*locus*) where the book was written was Carthage. 'When' did he write? The time (*tempus*) of composition is uncertain. Finally, the question 'whence?' inquires the materials from which the book was written, namely, the marriage of Philology and Mercury, and the seven liberal arts in general.

A shortened version of this scheme, comprising the three headings *persona, locus* and *tempus,* is employed elsewhere by Remigius, for example, in his *Commentarius in artem primam Donati* and in a commentary of dubious attribution on Bede's *De arte metrica*[56]. In the *accessus* to the *Disticha Catonis* and Priscian's *Institutio de nomine, pronomine et verbo,* a fourth heading, *causa scribendi* ('why' the work was written), is added to the other three[57].

The threefold scheme had already been used by theologians. In the commentary on Ezechiel by St Gregory the Great (*c.* 540–604) and the commentary on the Apocalypse by the venerable Bede (*c.* 673–735), reference is made to the *persona, locus* and *tempus* of each Scriptural *auctor*[58]. By the time of Christian of Stavelot, the use of these headings in Scriptural exegesis seems to have been well-established: the prologue to his commentary on St Matthew's Gospel (composed shortly after 864) contains the statement that 'in the beginning of all books three things must be inquired, the time, the place, and the person'[59]. In the twelfth century, Hugh of St Victor habitually used the threefold scheme in his Bible commentaries[60]. In the thirteenth century, Hugh of St Cher made occasional use of the headings *locus* and *tempus* in prologues which derive their structure from a different series of headings[61].

But the two types of prologue described above were relatively rare in the twelfth century. The 'type B' prologue-paradigm seems to have been regarded as over-elaborate; it may have been too specialised for general use. The Servian model is not followed in the prologue to the

Aeneid commentary attributed to Bernard Silvester[62]. Hugh of St Victor's systematic use of the 'type A' prologue-paradigm is most unusual in the Scriptural exegesis of that period. However, certain items of vocabulary from both these prologue-paradigms seem to have influenced the most popular of all twelfth-century academic prologues.

The origins of this prologue (Dr Hunt's 'type C') are obscure, but it would seem that Boethius was the main channel through which it was disseminated in the Latin West[63]. In the first version of his commentary on Porphyry's *Isagoge*, Boethius listed six headings and provided their Greek equivalents: the intention of the work *(operis intentio)*, its usefulness *(utilitas)*, its order *(ordo)*, if it is indeed a genuine work of the putative author *(si eius cuius esse opus dicitur germanus propriusque liber est)*, the title of the work *(operis inscriptio)* and the part of philosophy to which it pertains *(ad quam partem philosophiae cuiuscumque libri ducatur intentio)*[64]. All these topics, Boethius claimed, must be investigated and brought forth at the beginning of every book of philosophy.

This reference to philosophical books provides a clue to Boethius's models. E. A. Quain has argued that the Greek schema cited in the *Isagoge* commentary was developed in late-antique Greek commentaries on certain works of philosophy[65]. He compares the glosses on Aristotle's *Categories* written by Ammonius of Alexandria and his disciples, Philoponus, Elias and Simplicius, which began with systematic introductions in the form of ten major questions[66]. The all-important tenth question provided a series of headings which was the basis for literary analysis of each separate work. For example, Simplicius's list is as follows: intention, usefulness, cause of the title, the order (in which the *Categories* is to be read within the Aristotelian corpus), its authenticity, and its disposition or arrangement[67]. The late-antique introductions to Porphyry, as G. L. Westerink has pointed out, were more varied; 'as time goes on, they tend to become more prolix and more schematic'[68]. In such introductions, to the six headings employed in introducing Aristotle (as noted above) was added a seventh, the branch of philosophy to which the text belongs, here said to be logic[69]. This version of the schema obviously lies behind the version used in Boethius's commentary on Porphyry. In passing, it should be noted that the Alexandrian school produced elaborate introductions to Plato also, which were organised in accordance with different principles[70]. However, this schema does not seem to have survived into the Middle Ages[71].

Whatever the origins of the 'type C' prologue may be, when it began to be popular in medieval exposition of *auctores*, its distinctive vocabulary was regarded as a 'modern' apparatus which had replaced the 'ancient' schema based on the *circumstantiae*. There are several eleventh-century statements to this effect. For example, in a reworking of Remigius of Auxerre's commentary on the *Disticha Catonis*, it is claimed that

In the exordium of every book seven things were examined beforehand by our predecessors: whom, what, where, with what aids, why, in what manner, when. . . . But in the manner used among the moderns only three things are required: the life of the poet, the title of the work and to what part of philosophy it pertains.[72]

In the late eleventh-century *Commentum in Theodulum* by Bernard of Utrecht, we are told that the 'ancients' used to apply the seven *circumstantiae* at the beginning of every book, whereas the 'moderns' investigate instead the material of the work, the intention of the writer, the part of philosophy to which the book pertains, and its utility[73]. A similar comment is found in Conrad of Hirsau's *Dialogus super auctores*, a work which seems to have been influenced by Bernard of Utrecht's commentary[74]. All these accounts seem to point to the emergence of the 'type C' prologue-paradigm as the dominant form.

In the systematisation of knowledge which is characteristic of the twelfth century, the 'type C' prologue appeared at the beginning of commentaries on textbooks of all disciplines: the arts, medicine, Roman law, canon law and theology. Its standard headings, refined by generations of scholars and to some extent modified through the influence of the other types of prologue, may be outlined as follows:

Titulus (inscriptio, nomen) libri. The title of the work.
According to Remigius of Auxerre, the title was the key to the work which followed it[75]. It could refer to the author or to some other person, or to a place, literary genre or subject[76]. The term *titulus* was supposed to be derived from *titan*, the sun: just as the sun illuminates the world, the book-title illuminates the book![77]

Discussion under this heading could involve complicated and often specious etymologies of the words that comprised the title. For example, in introducing the *Pharsalia*, Arnulf of Orléans (*fl.* 1175) gave its title as *Marci Annei Lucani Liber*. *Lucanus* is interpreted as 'lucidly singing' *(lucide canens)*; *Anneaus* is supposed to be derived from the Greek word for bees[78]. Commentators on Boethius laboriously expounded in this manner each element of the title *Anicii Mallii Severini Boetii ex magno officio viri clarissimi et illustris exconsulum ordine atque patricio liber philosophicae consolationis primus incipit*[79]. *Severinis* refers to the severity of Boethius's judgments; *Boethius* is from a Greek word which may be interpreted as 'the helper and consoler of many', and so on.

Nomen auctoris. The name of the author.
In discussion under this heading, the issue of authenticity was usually raised, the commentator either naming his author or recounting the theories concerning the author's identity. Sometimes, a short life of the author *(vita auctoris)* was provided.

Intentio auctoris (intentio scribentis). The intention of the author.
Here the commentator explained the didactic and edifying purpose of the author in producing the text in question. Sometimes, the term *finis* (i.e. 'end', 'objective') was used as an equivalent of this heading, and sometimes as an extension of it[80]. The reader of a work should regard authorial intention as the kernel, claimed Dominicus Gundissalinus (writing shortly after 1150): whoever is ignorant of the *intentio,* as it were, leaves the kernel intact and eats the poor shell[81].

Accounts of the *intentio auctoris* range from the very obvious to the very elaborate. The former may be illustrated from one of the earliest extant commentaries on Cicero's *De inventione.* Writing in the early twelfth century, Thierry of Chartres briefly stated that, in this work, Cicero had intended to treat of a single part of the art of rhetoric, namely, invention[82]. Good examples of the latter are furnished by statements concerning the purpose of the Justinian Code made by glossators of the Roman law: the different contributors to this work were supposed to have had different intentions. In the *Summa Trecensis,* which he wrote around 1150, Rogerius explained that the intention of the Roman princes was to establish laws concerning basic equity and to formulate them as precepts, while the intention of Justinian was to cull the best of this ancient material and render it in one volume[83].

In the case of the study of grammar, accounts of authorial intention were prescriptive rather than descriptive: there was rarely any attempt (at least, not until very late in the Middle Ages) to relate a person's purpose in writing to his historical context, to describe an author's personal prejudices, eccentricities and limitations. The commentators were more interested in relating the work to an abstract truth than in discovering the subjective goals and wishes of the individual author. The *intentio auctoris*—the intended meaning 'piously expounded' and rendered unimpeachable—was considered more important than the medium through which the message was expressed[84]. Texts of profane *auctores* were interpreted, and sometimes elaborately allegorised, so that they could be seen to contain nothing contrary to Christian truth. The poets had used a fictional garment or *integumentum* to clothe either truths about natural science or profound moral doctrine[85]. According to the commentators, Homer had intended to dissuade people from unlawful union which, as in the example of Paris and Helen, incurs the wrath of the gods; Ovid had intended to reprehend inchastity and to commend legal and just love; Lucan had intended to discourage his readers from engaging in civil wars[86]. On the other hand, the obviously moral statements of satirists like Horace and Persius could be taken literally[87].

In the case of sacred Scripture, no special pleading was believed to be required, because the intentions of the divinely-inspired *auctores* had been determined by the Holy Spirit.

Materia libri. The subject-matter of the work; the materials from which it had been composed.

As one might expect, some of the most sophisticated discussions of this kind are found in the Roman lawyers' *materiae* or introductions to the Justinian Code. The 'common material' of the Code consisted of those legal issues common to Justinian and the Roman princes; its 'singular and proper material' was supplied by the three ancient legal codices which Justinian had reconciled and edited[88]. A similar technique of analysis is found in the prologues to glosses on Gratian by canon lawyers[89].

Modus agendi (modus scribendi, modus tractandi). The method of didactic procedure employed in the work.

Under this heading, commentators described the stylistic and rhetorical qualities of the authoritative text, always being concerned to bring out the instructional and pedagogic value of the literary medium. For example, in an *accessus* to a 'Cornutan' commentary on Persius, the didactic efficacy of the author's 'low style' is defended with reference to an etymology of the term *satira,* whereby the literary form is supposed to be named after the goat-like satyrs[90]. The satyrs are depicted naked; similarly, satire employs a plain and unembellished style. In its use of vulgar words, it differs from tragedy, which always uses elevated language. Moreover, a satire jumps about, in the fashion of a goat, because it has neither a circumscribed theme nor a flowing rhythm. The goat is a stinking animal, and satire employs pungent and unpleasant words. By such drastic methods, the satirist made manifest his moral outrage and censured the vices of men.

The various modes of procedure used by different authors might be compared and contrasted. In William of Conches's prologue to his commentary on *De consolatione philosophiae,* it is explained that Boethius imitated the *modus scribendi* of Martianus Capella by writing in prose and verse[91]. Consolation entails both reason and delight, claimed William, and so, Boethius used two modes: in prose, he consoles by rationalisation; in metre, he interposes delight so that grief is forgotten.

Certain theologians applied secular literary theory to the stylistic analysis of sacred Scripture. In expounding the Psalter's *modus tractandi* (*c.* 1144–69) Gerhoh of Reichersberg employed the distinction between the three 'styles of writing' (*characteres scripturae*) which goes back to Servius's commentary on Virgil's *Eclogues*[92]. Gerhoh tells us that the style of a work can be called 'exegematic' when the *auctor* speaks in his own person; 'dramatic', when the *auctor* speaks 'in the persons of others'; and 'mixed', when both these styles are used. In the Pentateuch, Moses speaks in his own person; in the Song of Songs, the introduced persons speak; while, in the Apocalypse and in the *Consolatio philosophiae* of Boethius, the *auctor* speaks both in his own person and through others. The Psalter has, according to Gerhoh, a complex *modus tractandi*. Considered as a whole, it could be said to use the mixed mode, but one or other of the three *characteres* may be used in a given psalm.

Ordo libri. The order of the book.
Here the author's deployment or arrangement of his materials was discussed. Sometimes literary arrangement was discussed as a facet of the *modus tractandi;* sometimes it was allotted a separate heading. In narrative, there were believed to be two sorts of order, the natural and the artificial. According to 'Bernard Silvester', natural order follows the his-

torical sequence of events, as in the narrative of Lucan, while artificial
order begins in the middle of a narration and returns to the beginning,
as in Terence's works and Virgil's *Aeneid*[93].

Sometimes this interest in order extended to declaring the number of
chapters in a work. A book is divided in parts or chapters, said Gundissalinus, so that, when something is sought among all the things contained therein, it is the more easily found[94]. It is easier, in such a case,
to have recourse to a definite chapter than to read over the whole
volume. With the help of distinct chapters, he concluded, the memory
is much strengthened.

Of course, some works, by their very nature, were not susceptible of
chapter-division. In describing the *modus tractandi* of the *Consolatio
philosophiae,* William of Conches explained that Boethius proceeds from
one kind of proof to another, this being the basis for his organisation of
doctrine[95]. First, Boethius employs rhetorical arguments, then dialectical arguments and, finally, demonstrations.

Utilitas. Utility.

This heading introduced a consideration of the ultimate usefulness of
the work, i.e. the reason why it was part of a Christian curriculum. The
utility of the Bible was self-evident; works of lesser authority required
some justification. Hence, Arnulf of Orléans claimed that the utility of
Lucan's *Pharsalia* is very great because, through his narration of the
dreadful deaths of Pompey and Caesar, Lucan warns us not to engage in
civil wars[96]. The beast-fables of Avianus were said to be useful, in so far
as they gave delight and taught the correction of mores[97]. The more
sombre writings of the Roman satirists were useful because they harshly
reprehended vice and recommended virtue: the censures by Juvenal and
Persius of 'poets writing to no purpose' *(poetas inutiliter scribentes)* won
much approval[98]. 'Bernard Silvester' stated that some poets write because of utility, like the satirists, and some write because of delight,
like the writers of comedies, while others both instruct and please, as
do the historians[99].

Cui parti philosophiae supponitur. The branch of learning to which the
    work belonged.

In the widest sense of the term, 'philosophy' included all human
knowledge and investigation. Hence, Bernard of Utrecht defined
philosophy as the knowledge of things human and divine, joined to the

1 THE BRANCHES OF LEARNING (see pp. 23–7). London, British Library, MS Royal 15.B.III, fol. 7ᵛ. William of Conches, commentary on Boethius's *De consolatione philosophiae*.

study of living well; it comprises science, in the case of certainties, and opinion in those areas where certainty is not possible, and may be either contemplative or active[100]. Similarly, Hugh of St Victor stated that philosophy is the discipline which investigates demonstratively the causes of all things, human and divine; the theory of all pursuits, therefore, belongs to philosophy, which can be said to embrace all scientific knowledge[101]. Hugh then classified the parts of philosophy as follows:

Philosophy is divided into theoretical, practical, mechanical, and logical. These four contain all knowledge. The theoretical may also be called speculative; the practical may be called active, likewise ethical, that is, moral, from the fact that morals consist in good action; the mechanical may be called adulterate because it is concerned with the works of human labour; the logical may be called linguistic from its concern with words.[102]

The texts used in the teaching of the various disciplines had to be related to a system such as this, and given their proper status within it.

The *pars philosophiae* of the Roman law was classified as ethics, a practice which, as Kantorowicz says, 'had the advantage of reminding the budding medieval lawyer that the civil law was more than a jungle of technicalities'[103]. Much more surprising on first acquaintance is the frequent claim by *artistae* that all their *auctores* belonged to the study of ethics or practical philosophy[104]. In twelfth-century schools, the study of 'natural' or non-Christian ethics was an adjunct of the traditional studies of the trivium; its usual contexts were rhetoricians' explanations of the virtues necessary to deliberative and demonstrative oratory and grammarians' expositions of pagan literature[105]. Hence, Lucan was believed to offer us worthy models of behaviour to imitate, models exemplifying the four political virtues, which pertain to ethics[106]. Even Ovid's erotic love-poetry was supposed to have an ethical function because it exemplified the legal and chaste love which one ought to practise and the reprehensible kinds of love which one ought to avoid[107].

Of course, not everyone was in favour of such classification, as may be illustrated by the difference of opinion between Bernard of Chartres and his pupil, William of Conches, which is recorded in a twelfth-century commentary on Juvenal[108]. Having raised the issue of the part of philosophy to which Juvenal's satires belong, the anonymous commentator claims that Bernard thought this question irrelevant because poetry does not treat of philosophy. But William of Conches, he continues, made a distinction between mere writers *(actores)* and writers who are authorities *(auctores)*. The works of *actores* do not pertain to philosophy, but the works of *auctores,* although they do not teach philosophy directly, nevertheless relate to philosophy in that they provide moral instruction and, thereby, pertain to ethics. It would seem then, that to assign the *pars philosophiae* of a given text was to make a judgment concerning its *auctoritas*.

Scriptural texts presented considerable problems of classification, because of their variety and scope; moreover, one had to do justice to the general complexity and superiority of the God-given doctrine contained therein. Origen (*c.* 185–*c.* 254), as translated by Rufinus, argued that all the Greek sages had borrowed their ideas of the branches of learning from Solomon (who had acquired this information through the Holy Spirit long before their time), and that they had put them forward as their own inventions[109]. Similar theories concerning the origin of the liberal arts were held by such scholars as Jerome, Augustine and Cassiodorus[110]. According to Origen, three works traditionally attributed to King Solomon, namely, Proverbs, Ecclesiastes and the Song of Songs, taught the subjects of ethics, physics and the theoretical or contemplative science, respectively[111]. In Isidore's *Etymologiae,* it is claimed that Genesis and Ecclesiastes teach natural philosophy, which the Greeks call physics; Proverbs and other books teach moral philosophy or ethics; while the Song of Songs and the Gospels teach rational philosophy or logic, in this case to be identified with theoretical science[112]. The same basic classification is advanced in the *Glossa ordinaria* on the Song of Songs and in glosses to that same text ascribed to Anselm of Laon (†1117) and Richard of St Victor (†1173), as well as in commentaries on the Psalter attributed to Remigius, St Bruno the Carthusian (*c.* 1032–1101) and Honorius 'of Autun' (†*c.* 1156)[113].

In the prologue to the Psalter-commentary attributed to Remigius, we find this significant remark: 'Just as in mundane books so also in divine books one can inquire which part of philosophy is in view'[114]. An investigation, apparently commonplace in discussion of secular writing, is being conducted in the case of inspired Scripture, the implication being that this is something of an innovation. In reiterating the Isidorian classification, the commentator points out that one cannot speak of logic when dealing with the Bible: in its place stands theoretical science, the *pars philosophiae* of the Song of Songs and the Evangelists. Bruno the Carthusian introduced a similar threefold division with the statement that 'three things are to be considered in divine books just as in secular books'[115].

These remarks seem to indicate a conscious transition from secular to sacred which is being made with a degree of reticence. The same impression may be gained from this twelfth-century gloss on the Apocalypse:

> Just as in secular books it is asked what is the material, what is the authority, what is the intention of the author, and which part of philosophy is supposed, so also it must be asked in this prophetic writing.[116]

In order that the 'type C' prologue could be applied in Scriptural exegesis, some modification of its paradigm was necessary. Medieval theologians were very conscious of the supreme eminence of their discipline, and of the unique status of their essential textbook, the Bible. Theology was, in the words of Hugh of St Victor, the 'peak of philosophy and the perfection of truth'[117]. Hence, the heading *cui parti philosophiae supponitur* was either a challenge or an irrelevance, depending on the exegete's point of view[118]. This range of possible response may be illustrated by contrasting the notes taken by two students at Stephen Langton's lecture course on the Song of Songs (perhaps held in the third quarter of the twelfth century). One student mentions 'the aspect of philosophy or of humanity' *(pars philosophiae vel humanitatis)* to which the Scriptural text pertains; the other avoids this cumbersome heading and concentrates on Langton's discussion of the relevant 'aspect of life' *(pars vitae)*, namely, the contemplative life[119]. Most twelfth-century commentators on the Psalter ignored the heading *pars philosophiae* altogether and discussed instead the 'species of prophecy' *(pars prophetiae)* to which David's prophecies belonged[120].

This completes our illustration of the usual kinds of discussion conducted under the various headings of the most popular of all the prologue-paradigms used in the twelfth century. The felicities and limitations of prologues of this type as sources of literary theory will be discussed in our next chapter. For the moment, it must suffice to state that change came in the thirteenth century. The stock schema was supplemented; its technical idiom acquired greater precision and, in the case of prologues to Bible-commentaries, a more literary dimension. The new methods of thinking and techniques of study which thirteenth-century scholars derived from their reading of Aristotle encouraged commentators to adopt and develop a new type of prologue, based on the Aristotelian concept of 'the four causes'.

THE 'ARISTOTELIAN PROLOGUE'

Aristotle had defined the 'formal cause' of something as its substance, i.e. the essence or the pattern which 'enformed' the thing, while the 'material cause' meant its matter or substratum[121]. The 'efficient cause' consisted of motivation, the moving force which brought something from potentiality into actual being. Diametrically opposite to the efficient cause was the 'final cause', the end or objective which was aimed at and intended: Aristotle saw the function of all generation and change in terms of a hierarchy of ultimate goals and goods. To expand an illustration from the commentary on Aristotle's *Physica* by St Thomas Aquinas (written 1269–70 at Paris), the formal cause of a statue is its shape, i.e. the proportions and disposition of the constituent parts, while its material cause is the bronze from which it is made[122]. The efficient cause is the artificer or craftsman who made the statue, while the final cause is his reason for making it.

When applied to the exposition of *auctores*, this theory of causality produced a sophisticated prologue-paradigm which, hereafter, I shall refer to as the 'Aristotelian prologue'. The characteristic headings of the 'Aristotelian prologue' may be outlined as follows:

Causa efficiens
The efficient cause was the *auctor*, the person who brought the literary work into being. This heading replaced, or was used in conjunction with, *nomen auctoris*. Here the issue of authenticity was discussed which, in the case of prologues to Scriptural texts, entailed description of the causation whereby the divine *auctor* had directed the human *auctores* to write.

Causa materialis
The material cause was the substratum of the work, i.e. the literary materials which were the writer's sources. The heading replaced, or was used in conjunction with, *materia libri*.

Causa formalis

The formal cause of the work was the pattern imposed by the *auctor* on his materials. Commentators spoke of the twofold form (*duplex forma*), the *forma tractandi*, which was the writer's method of treatment or procedure (*modus agendi* or *modus procedendi*), and the *forma tractatus*, which was the arrangement or organisation of the work, the way in which the *auctor* had structured it.

Causa finalis

The final cause was the ultimate justification for the existence of a work, the end or objective (*finis*) aimed at by the writer; more specifically, the particular good which (in the opinion of the commentator) he had intended to bring about. In the context of commentary on secular *auctores*, this meant the philosophical import or moral significance of a given work[123]; in the context of Scriptural exegesis, it meant the efficacy of a work in leading the reader to salvation.

Of course, certain aspects of Aristotle's theory of causality had been known before the thirteenth century. An important *locus classicus* was provided by the brief statement in Cicero's *Topica* concerning the efficient cause and the material cause; in his commentary on this passage, Boethius had supplied a cogent summary of the four causes according to Aristotle[124]. However, while some twelfth-century commentators spoke of the *causa finalis* of a work (instead of, or in conjunction with, its *utilitas*), the complete system of the four causes was not applied[125].

The impetus for change seems to have been provided by the extensive accounts of causality contained in Aristotle's *Physica* and *Metaphysica*, works which were being admitted to the curriculum of studies in the early thirteenth century[126]. At any rate, it was during that period that the 'Aristotelian prologue' became very popular among lecturers in the arts faculty of the University of Paris[127]. Its sophisticated analytical framework soon appeared at the beginning of commentaries on the textbooks of other disciplines, including astronomy, canon law and medicine[128]. Theologians used it in introducing their commentaries on the Bible and on Peter Lombard's *Libri sententiarum*, then an established teaching-text in the faculty of theology[129]. The 'Aristotelian prologue' and, indeed, the 'type C' prologue which it never wholly superseded, continued to be employed in the study of *auctores* long into the Renaissance[130].

EXTRINSIC AND INTRINSIC PROLOGUES

All the types of academic prologue considered so far were designed to lead the listeners or readers into authoritative texts. This function was sometimes emphasised by the designation 'intrinsic': the 'intrinsic' prologue, or the 'intrinsic' component of a prologue, introduced a text. It might be preceded by an 'extrinsic' prologue or component, in which the discipline to which the text belonged was identified and described in a systematic way. Therefore, the medieval distinction between extrinsic and intrinsic analysis hinged on a difference in the object of analysis rather than differences of vocabulary or ideology: the former concerned an art or science, while the latter concerned a text. The origins and development of this distinction must now be examined.

Cicero's rhetorical theory seems to be the ultimate source of the common twelfth-century differentiation between the *ars extrinsecus* and *ars intrinsecus*. In his *Topica,* Cicero divided the topics under which arguments are included into two large groups[131]. Some are inherent in the very nature of the subject which is under discussion *(in eo ipso);* others are brought in from without *(extrinsecus).* In the first category are arguments derived from the whole, from its parts, from its meaning, and from the things which are in some way closely connected with the subject under investigation. In the second category are arguments from external circumstances, i.e. those which are removed and widely separated from the subject. In the commentary on Cicero's *De inventione* by the fourth-century rhetorician Victorinus, this approach was applied to the arts, the phrase *in eo ipso* being replaced with the term *intrinsecus*[132]. Victorinus, citing 'the precept and *sententia* of Cicero', claimed that 'every art is twofold, that is, it has a double aspect'. The extrinsic art gives us knowledge alone; the intrinsic art shows us the reasons whereby we put into practice that which knowledge gives us[133].

Thierry of Chartres (who became chancellor of Chartres in 1141) took over this distinction from Victorinus. Introducing his commentary on the *De inventione,* Thierry stated that the ancient rhetoricians, in defining and dividing an art, called the extrinsic art that which it is necessary to know in advance before commencing to practise an art, while the intrinsic art comprised the rules and precepts which we must know in order to practise the art itself[134].

Thierry also distinguished between those things it is necessary to know concerning the art *(circa artem)* and concerning the book under discussion (*circa librum*) respectively[135]. Concerning Cicero's work, two things must be considered, the intention of the author (*intentio auctoris*) and the utility of the book (*libri utilitas*): these headings are familiar to us as part of the 'type C' prologue-paradigm. Concerning the art of rhetoric, ten things must be considered: its genus (*genus*), what the art is in itself (*quid ipsa ars sit*), its material (*materia*), its office (*officium*), its end (*finis*), its parts (*partes*), its species (*species*), its instrument (*instrumentum*), its master or practitioner (*artifex*), and wherefore it is called rhetoric (*quare rhetorica vocetur*)[136]. This series of prologue-headings (Dr Hunt's 'type D') seems to have its origin in the *De inventione*; in his *De differentiis topicis* Boethius had amplified Cicero's version[137].

In the prologues to commentaries on grammatical texts, the headings *extrinsecus* and *intrinsecus* took over the functions performed by the headings *circa artem* and *circa librum* in Thierry's schema[138]. The heading *extrinsecus* introduced a discussion of the place in the scheme of human knowledge occupied by grammar, together with a summary of the defining characteristics of this art, while the heading *intrinsecus* introduced a schematic discussion of the text itself. Thus, the anonymous late twelfth century gloss on Priscian which begins *Tria sunt* proceeds as follows:

The extrinsic aspect is taught when by inquiring the nature of this same art we learn what this art is, what is its genus, material, parts, species, instrument, master, office, end, wherefore it is named, in what order it is to be taught and learned . . .

The intrinsic aspect is to be explored by considering first what is the author's intention in this work, what is its utility, what are the causes of the undertaken labour or work, what is the order, and finally what is its title.[139]

Combinations of the conventional extrinsic discussion with the 'type C' prologue-paradigm occurred from the mid twelfth century onwards, the general analysis of the relevant art or science preceding application of such characteristic intrinsic headings as *auctoris intentio, utilitas* and *modus agendi*[140]. Scholars wished to have parallel discussions of the art in general and the text in particular. As a result, the extrinsic series was sometimes modified in accordance with the usual intrinsic headings.

The most elaborate application of both series of headings occurs in the *De divisione philosophiae* of Dominicus Gundissalinus, one of the group of translators gathered together by Raymond, Archbishop of Toledo (1126–51), and still alive in 1181. In this work, a detailed analysis of the individual branches of knowledge, extrinsic headings provide the structure for discussions of the following parts of speculative philosophy: natural science, mathematics, divine science, grammar, poetics, rhetoric, logic, medicine, arithmetic, music, geometry, astrology and astronomy[141]. At the very end of the *De divisione*, Gundissalinus says that, concerning a book *(circa librum)* of any art whatsoever, seven things are to be investigated. There follows a discussion of the literary concepts of *intentio auctoris, utilitas operis, nomen auctoris, titulus operis, ordo legendi, ad quam partem philosophiae spectet* and *distinctio libri*[142].

In the thirteenth century, Aristotelian science fostered a new kind of extrinsic prologue in which the discipline was delimited and subdivided by a conceptual method of 'means' and 'ends'. The subject, mode of procedure and end of an individual art or science were discovered by defining the place it occupied within an Aristotelian hierarchy of knowledge[143]. A commentary could begin with an extrinsic investigation conducted along these lines; then the intrinsic features of the text itself would be investigated. For example, in the commentary on the recently-recovered *Nicomachean Ethics* of Aristotle which he produced around the middle of the thirteenth century, St Albert the Great first discussed the *materia, finis* and *utilitas* of moral science, then proceeded to identify the work's *titulus, materia, auctor* and *causa*[144]. Sometimes the intrinsic discussion was organised around the four causes. This practice is found in many commentaries on books of the Bible, a good example being provided by the prologue to the commentary on the Pauline Epistles written by St Thomas Aquinas between 1270 and 1272[145]. Alternatively, the four causes could provide the basic framework for a discussion of the extrinsic and intrinsic aspects of a text considered together. This is the case in two commentaries on Peter Lombard's *Libri sententiarum,* one composed by St Bonaventure between 1250 and 1252 and the other by Robert Kilwardby between 1248 and 1261[146]. By the fourteenth century, there were several possible permutations.

This completes our review of the types of academic prologue which prefaced commentaries on *auctores*. We have described the most important kind of prologue established in the twelfth century (Dr Hunt's 'type C') and its thirteenth-century successor (the 'Aristotelian prologue'). A distinction has been made between the 'extrinsic' prologue, which introduced an art or science, and the 'intrinsic' prologue, which introduced the book that taught the art or science in question. We are now in a position to begin an investigation of the theory of authorship found in prologues to commentaries on the most 'authentic' of all books, the Bible. The supreme authority of sacred Scripture must be emphasised at the outset, so that we may understand better the literary problems which it presented to its medieval readers.

THE STATUS OF HOLY SCRIPTURE

Medieval theologians were eminently aware of both the comparisons and the contrasts which could be made between the Bible and secular texts. On the one hand, they stressed the unique status of the Bible; on the other, they believed that the budding exegete had to be trained in the liberal arts before he could begin to understand the infinitely more complex 'sacred page'.

These attitudes and priorities can be traced back to the Church Fathers. H.-I. Marrou has demonstrated the influence of late-antique school practice, including the methods of grammatical training, on the Biblical exegesis of St Augustine (354–430)[147]. Yet Augustine professed a preference for substance rather than expression, for content rather than form[148]. Similarly, St Jerome insisted on the primacy of sense *(sensus)* over words *(verba)*[149]. Even Cassiodorus (*c.* 485–*c.* 580), characterised by P. Riché as 'an untitled teacher of grammar and rhetoric' in his monastery, admitted that the rules of Latin discourse are not to be followed everywhere: 'sometimes it is better to overlook the formulas of human discourse and preserve rather the measure of God's word'[150]. In the dedicatory letter to his moral commentary on Job (580–95), St Gregory the Great warned the reader not to look for 'literary nosegays', because, in interpreters of Holy Writ, 'the lightness of fruitless verbiage is carefully repressed, since the planting of a grove in God's temple is forbidden'[151]. Gregory rejected as 'unbecoming' the notion that he should 'tie down the words of the heavenly oracle to the rules of Donatus'.

The unique status of the heavenly oracle is brought out in the model of Biblical exegesis provided in Gregory's *Moralia in Job*. Traditional techniques of textual commentary have been altered to meet the special demands of divinely-inspired Scripture. Whereas the Roman *gramma-*

ticus had been interested in analysis of historical or literal sense (regarded by Gregory as explanation of all the meanings of the narrative), the exegete was obliged to concentrate on the spiritual senses. Gregory therefore offered a threefold method of exposition—

we run over some topics in historical exposition, and in some we search for allegorical meaning in our examination of types; in still others we discuss morality but through the allegorical method; and in several instances we carefully make an attempt to apply all three methods

—which was influential throughout the Middle Ages[152]. Equally popular was the fourfold method ultimately derived from John Cassian (*c.* 360–435), which was conveniently summarised in a well-known distich:

Littera gesta docet, quid credas allegoria,
Moralis quid agas, quo tendas anagogia.[153]

The literal sense provides the historical data; the allegorical, that which one should believe by faith; the tropological or moral, how one should behave; the anagogical, where one is going in terms of spiritual progress. Cassian's test-case of the word 'Jerusalem' is cogently paraphrased in the short 'treatise on the way a sermon ought to be composed' which Guibert of Nogent wrote (shortly before 1084) as a preface to his commentary on Genesis:

There are four ways of interpreting Scripture . . . The first is history, which speaks of actual events as they occurred; the second is allegory, in which one thing stands for something else; the third is tropology, or moral instruction, which treats of the ordering and arranging of one's life; and the last is ascetics, or spiritual enlightenment, through which we who are about to treat of lofty and heavenly topics are led to a higher way of life. For example, the word Jerusalem: historically, it represents a specific city; in allegory it represents holy Church; tropologically or morally, it is the soul of every faithful man who longs for the vision of eternal peace; and anagogically it refers to the life of the heavenly citizens, who already see the God of Gods, revealed in all His glory in Sion.[154]

This special type of *prelectio* had as its overriding concern the unique message of Holy Scripture[155]. Yet systematic analysis of 'the letter' was indubitably an essential part of exegesis, and, in this context, the Bible could be compared with secular works[156]. In *De doctrina christiana,* St Augustine admitted that he took great delight in the stylistic figures found in the Bible. In some cases, he explains, it is pleasanter to have knowledge communicated through figures. The Holy Spirit, 'with admirable wisdom and care for our welfare, so arranged the Holy Scriptures as by the plainer passages to satisfy our hunger, and by the more obscure to stimulate our appetite'[157]. Men of learning, Augustine continues, should know that the sacred *auctores* used all the modes of expression which grammarians call tropes, in great abundance and with great eloquence[158]. Similarly, St Jerome had believed that all kinds of figures could be found in the Bible: after all, the liberal arts had existed before the profane masters of secular letters had studied them[159]. Hence, in the prologue to his commentary on Isaiah, Jerome could claim that this work comprised the whole of physics, ethics and logic[160]. Following the lead of Jerome and Augustine, Cassiodorus managed to find some 120 rhetorical figures in the Psalter[161].

In the twelfth century, such comparing and contrasting of the Bible with other books was a regular feature of the debate concerning the true hierarchy of the branches of knowledge and the correct order in which the different arts and sciences should be studied. Hugh of St Victor believed that 'all natural arts are related to divine science in such a way that the inferior science, correctly organised in the hierarchy, leads to the superior'[162]. The declared purpose of Hugh's *Didascalicon* is to recommend proficiency in the liberal arts within a programme of study which culminated in the exposition of sacred Scripture[163]. In Conrad of Hirsau's *Dialogus super auctores*, which incorporates earlier *accessus* material on a wide range of *auctores*, the master warns his pupil that secular writings are not to be studied for their own sake, but as a necessary preparation for analysis of the more difficult texts of Holy Writ[164]. This was the intellectual milieu in which Rupert of Deutz (*c.* 1075–1129) was prepared to accept that all the artifices found in secular books were present in Scripture also: schemata, tropes, modes of verse and prose, and even fables[165]. Augustine, Jerome and Cassiodorus are echoed in Rupert's statement that Scriptural *auctores* had used these devices before their supposed inventors had even been born[166]. Here, then, is the rationale for the theologians' use of *accessus* terms of reference in their prologues.

As the 'Book of Life' and the book of books, the Bible was the most difficult book to describe with accuracy and appropriateness. To the study of the 'sacred page' a scholar would bring the procedures and techniques which he had acquired during his studies in the trivium (although it must be said that some scholars brought more of this learning to bear than others)[167]. Theologians regularly drew on the resources of secular literary theory, refining and modifying it in accordance with their special needs. When it proved inadequate, they went beyond it, thereby bringing out the uniqueness of Scripture[168]. Consequently, the study of the Bible occasioned much of the most sophisticated literary theory of the later Middle Ages.

We shall be concerned with two major aspects of the theologians' literary theory, namely, their discussions of the specific roles (both literary and moral) performed by the different *auctores* of Scripture, and of the literary forms, genres, styles and structures employed in the different books of the Bible. The changing attitudes to these issues from the twelfth through the thirteenth and fourteenth centuries can only be understood in the light of one fundamental fact about the medieval study of *auctores:* the prescribed writers, in whatever discipline, were authorities to whom the reader had to defer.

A study of the teaching of grammar in the Middle Ages led C. Thurot to the conclusion that, in explicating their texts, the glossators did not seek to understand the individual thought of each writer but rather to teach the veritable knowledge that was supposed to be contained therein. An *auctor* in grammar

could neither make a mistake, nor contradict himself, nor follow a defective plan, nor be in disagreement with another authoritative writer. They [the glossators] had recourse to extremely forced artifices of exposition to accommodate the letter of the text to what was considered to be the truth.[169]

In the teaching of theology, the obligation to defer to one's *auctores* was, of course, considerably greater, and most of all in studying the Bible. God, who had guaranteed the superlative *auctoritas* of Scripture, was the *auctor* of all created things as well as an *auctor* of words[170]. He could deploy words by inspiring human authors to write, and deploy things through his creative and providential powers. Faced with these awesome truths, theologians experienced great difficulty in assessing the relative functions of God and man in producing sacred Scripture.

The literary poles between which the medieval theologians moved may be defined by reference to St Gregory's excursus on the authorship of the Book of Job, a most striking analysis which influenced later approaches to other Scriptural *auctores*[171]. Gregory asked, who was the writer of the work in question? Was it Moses, writing about a gentile named Job? Or was it one of the prophets? Certainly, one might say that only a prophet could possibly have possessed such knowledge of the mysterious words of God as is manifest in this work. Then Gregory seems to dismiss the problem altogether, along with the human writer:

It is very superfluous to inquire who wrote the work, since by faith its author is believed to have been the Holy Spirit. He then himself wrote them, who dictated the things that should be written. He did himself write them who both was present as the inspirer in that Saint's work and by the mouth of the writer handed down to us his [i.e. Job's] acts as patterns for our imitation.[172]

The human writer of the Book of Job is then, rather disparagingly, compared to the pen with which a great man has written a letter:

If we were reading the words of some great man with his epistle in our hand, yet were to inquire by what pen they were written, doubtless it would be an absurdity, to know the author of the epistle and understand his meaning, and notwithstanding to be curious to know with what sort of pen the words were marked upon the page. When then we understand the matter, and are persuaded that the Holy Spirit was its author, in raising a question about the writer what else are we doing but making inquiry about the pen as we read the epistle?

But Gregory did not leave the matter there. He proceeded to say that, among the options concerning the human author, we may with the greater probability suppose that it was written by Job[173]. It seems reasonable to assume that the same blessed Job who bore the strife of the spiritual conflict also recorded the circumstances of his eventual victory. The author's status as a gentile is then assessed, Job being identified as a 'virtuous heathen' or 'good pagan'[174]. 'Be thou ashamed, O Zidon, for the sea has spoken' (Isaiah xxiii.4) is interpreted to mean that Christians should be shamed by the spiritual feats of those gentiles who, knowing less about God than we do, yet managed to achieve more than we have.

The impressive balance of this analysis by Gregory, in which both the divine *auctor* and the human *auctor* of Scripture are given their due, may be directly related to the principles of exegesis outlined in the dedicatory letter to the *Moralia in Job*. There Gregory explained that, while sometimes Job's words cannot be understood literally, there are times when anyone who fails to understand the text in its literal sense hides the light of truth that has been offered to him[175]. For example,

Job xxxi. 16–20 records Job's acts of generosity to the poor: if we forci-
bly twist such a passage into an allegorical sense, we make all these
deeds of mercy to be as nothing.

It is precisely this balance which was lost in much twelfth-century
exegesis, where the commentators were preoccupied with allegorical
interpretation. According to Geoffrey of Auxerre (*fl.* late twelfth century), it is not important to know who wrote the Song of Songs[176].
Perhaps the human *auctor* knew what he was prophesying but, if he did
not, the inspirer *(inspirator)* most certainly knew. What matters is the
prophecy itself, of the mystical marriage of Christ and holy Church[177].
This point of view was persistent and pervasive; we find it being reiterated by Giles of Rome (Bachelor of Theology 1276; † 1316) in the
prologue to his commentary on the Song of Songs[178]. However, by the
time of Giles, the climate of opinion had changed somewhat: he was
able to share both Gregory's metaphor (of the pen) and the balance of
the saint's analysis of authorship. It may seem superstitious, Giles says,
to inquire about the 'instrumental causes' or human writers of Scripture. On the other hand, if the writer of the Song of Songs is sought,
we may say that it was Solomon.

The Bridegroom who is the true God, that is the subject or material of sacred
doctrine, is also principally the efficient cause of this science. The instrumental
cause is not of concern to us, since causes of this type function as instruments
with respect to doctrine . . . Just as it would be superstitious, when inquiry is
made concerning the author of a certain work, to ask with what type of pen the
work was written, so after a fashion it seems superstitious that someone should
be very solicitous to seek the instrumental causes of sacred Scripture: for if it
takes its origin from truth, in that the work is from the Holy Spirit, great care
is not to be exercised in finding another author. But if, on the other hand, it
seems that care should be exercised in this, we can say that Solomon was such a
cause of this work . . .[179]

This discussion occurs within an elaborate 'Aristotelian prologue' in
which both the role of the human *auctor* and the literary form of his
work are described with care and precision.

In subsequent chapters, it will be demonstrated how different types
of academic prologue were associated with different attitudes to authorial role and literary form. As used by twelfth-century exegetes, the
'type C' prologue was mainly concerned with the *auctor* as a source of
auctoritas. The *auctoritas* of the various books of the Bible was estab-

lished through elaborate allegorical interpretation which tended to undervalue the literal sense of Scripture and the literary forms, genres, styles and structures believed to constitute part of it. But in the early thirteenth century, when emphasis came to be placed on the literal sense of the Scripture, the exegetes' interest in their texts became more literary[180]. In the 'Aristotelian prologue', the emphasis had shifted from the divine *auctor* to the human *auctor* of Scripture. As Miss Smalley puts it,

The scheme [of the four causes] had the advantage of focusing attention on the author of the book and on the reasons which impelled him to write. The book ceased to be a mosaic of mysteries and was seen as the product of a human, although divinely inspired, intelligence instead. The four causes were still an external pattern, which might be imposed on wholly unsuitable material . . . but they brought the commentator considerably closer to his authors.[181]

Because of this change of attitude, the unquestionable fact of the divine inspiration of the Bible no longer interfered with thorough examination of the literary qualities of a text. Scholars paid more attention to the instrumental causes whom God had honoured. The theory of efficient causality enabled the human *auctores* of Scripture to acquire a new dignity; the theory of formal causality provided the rationale for meticulous analysis of form both as style and as structure. Chapter 3 treats of the former theory, and Chapter 4 of the latter.

Thus far we have defined the crucial concepts of *auctor* and *auctoritas* and outlined the categories and attitudes which formed the basis of medieval theory of authorship. Summary description of the main types of academic prologue which introduced commentaries on *auctores* has been the essential preliminary to the detailed examination, carried out in the following chapters, of the literary theory conveyed by these prologues. The *auctores*, it would seem, were expected to perform certain 'offices' and to employ certain styles and structures in their writing. The most authoritative of all the authors, the inspired writers of Scripture, were credited with the most elaborate authorial roles and literary forms, and medieval expositions of these provide us with some of the most elaborate literary theory produced in the period. We shall, therefore, give the Scriptural exegetes our full attention henceforth, beginning with an assessment of the felicities and limitations of twelfth-century prologues to Bible-commentaries as vehicles for the advancement of literary theory.

2

Prologues to Scriptural 'Auctores'

THE 'TYPE C' PROLOGUE, specially adapted to meet the unique requirements of sacred Scripture, became the standard form of introduction to commentaries on the Bible. Theologians successfully exploited techniques of analysis which for generations had been employed in *accessus*. This development may be regarded as inevitable, since, in many cases, the same scholars were writing commentaries on both secular and sacred *auctores*. The outstanding example from the early Middle Ages is Remigius of Auxerre, who, apart from producing the commentaries on grammatical textbooks mentioned in the previous chapter, expounded some seven books of the Bible[1]. Among the main twelfth-century polymaths, Anselm of Laon († 1117) merits special attention. Anselm, the begetter of the *Glossa ordinaria* on the Psalter and the Pauline Epistles, was an accomplished grammarian; his glosses on Virgil, Lucan and Statius have, perhaps, been recovered[2].

It is doubtful if we will ever ascertain the identity of the scholar who first transferred the 'type C' prologue from the *artes* to theology. Indeed, in the present state of our knowledge, it is scarcely possible to determine the generation of scholars in which this transference took place. Many of the crucial texts are of dubious attribution; the differences between the suggested datings can be as large as two centuries. Moreover, in an age in which the teaching of a master was invariably elaborated and refined almost out of existence by his pupils, it is often difficult to determine just who is responsible for what.

At least it can be said that the importance of Remigius of Auxerre as a patron of several types of academic prologue was substantial[3]. His use of *accessus* in introducing commentaries on secular *auctores* has already been considered (see pp. 16–17). The headings *titulus, pars philosophiae* and *intentio* are employed in a Psalter-commentary attributed to Remigius, but this attribution has seriously been questioned[4]. In his commentary on the Pauline Epistles, the respective *causae scribendi* of the letters to the Romans and the Hebrews are discussed, but no systematic use is made of any prologue-paradigm[5]. As printed by Migne, the texts of Remigius's commentaries on the Minor Prophets, the Song of Songs and the Apocalypse are devoid of *accessus* technique[6].

The Psalter-prologue attributed to St Bruno the Carthusian, who flourished in the later eleventh century, contains a fine treatment of *intentio, titulus* and, perhaps, *modus agendi;* the notion of the *pars philosophiae* is an obvious influence, although the heading does not occur[7]. However, the authenticity of this commentary is in doubt[8]. The suggestion that Anselm of Laon was the innovator is equally attractive but equally hard to prove. Anselm cannot be credited with the interesting 'type C' prologues which are found in the early printed editions of the *Glossa ordinaria;* they seem to be later expansions of his work[9]. In a commentary on the Song of Songs ascribed to Anselm, an analysis of the reasons why and in what manner King Solomon wrote his book constitutes the basis of the prologue[10]. The technical terms *intentio, nomen libri, materia, modus agendi* and *finis* are used, and the relevant part of philosophy is assigned. Unfortunately, once again, we are dealing with a dubious attribution[11]. Extensive use is made of several 'type C' headings in the Psalter-commentary printed under the name of Haimo of Halberstat: Wilmart believed this to be by Anselm, but his theory has found few supporters[12]. We are on much safer ground when we come to the Scriptural commentaries of two of Anselm's pupils, Gilbert of Poitiers (*c.* 1080–1154) and Peter Abelard (1079–1142), and the *Expositio psalterii* which Honorius 'of Autun' wrote probably between 1115 and 1120[13]. It seems reasonable to assume that the 'type C' prologue-paradigm was coming into use in Scriptural exegesis in the first quarter of the twelfth century.

Precisely what was the function of the prologue to a commentary on a book of the Bible? It served as an introduction to, and a preparation for, the *explicatio de texte* which followed. There, the commentator attempted to get to the heart of the problems of interpretation raised by his authoritative text, summarising the methods of analysis which would be used throughout the commentary, and outlining the doctrinal issues to be considered in the course of the analysis. The prologue provided a scholar with the occasion to reiterate those received interpretations of the text which seemed most appropriate to him, and to amplify such traditional doctrine with some ideas of his own[14].

By the twelfth century, the procedures of handling received interpretations in a critical way, and of supplementing the views of the *antiqui* with more recent ones, were well established[15]. The wide use in exegesis of a modified 'type C' prologue-paradigm enabled commentators to follow both these procedures in their prologues. Much information of an introductory nature (for the most part, general comments by the Fathers on the various books of the Bible) was assimilated to, and organised around, the well-established paradigm. 'Type C' prologues were incorporated into the *Glossa ordinaria*[16]. By the middle of the twelfth century, the *Glossa ordinaria* was being employed as a teaching text; theologians were glossing the *Glossa*[17]. Each new generation of pupils was, therefore, presented with the stock prologue-headings.

Here is God's plenty. The budding theologian would make personal use of the paradigm when writing his own prologue; in the process, he drew on the prologues of his predecessors and teachers[18]. Good prologue material was appreciated, and paid the ultimate compliment of being copied and incorporated. Prologues became such common property that the same ones could be attached to different works and detached from them with what has been called a 'disconcerting facility'[19]. Sometimes, different prologues obscured the same work. There were even anthologies of prologues[20].

'TYPE C' PROLOGUES IN TWELFTH-CENTURY EXEGESIS OF THE PSALTER AND SONG OF SONGS

Two books of sacred poetry, the Psalter and the Song of Songs, furnished the commentator with a formidable nexus of problems of interpretation and, therefore, the prologues to commentaries on these texts contain intricate discussions of authorial role and literary form. The Song of Songs was supposed to be by King Solomon, a man who, according to St Augustine, had been condemned as a womaniser by Holy Scripture[21]. On the literal level, Solomon's song seemed to resemble the lascivious fables (particularly those by Ovid) studied in courses on grammar. Because they comprised the subject of a Scriptural text, the apparently erotic encounters recorded by Solomon demanded 'reverent interpretation'—and got it in abundance. The Song of Songs was read as a mystical epithalamium which celebrated the marriage of Christ and Holy Church[22], a work far superior to pagan poems of merely human love[23].

The Psalter received much more attention from medieval commentators, both because of its role in private meditation and in the liturgy, and because of the professed excellence of the prophecy it contained. In the *Glossa ordinaria* on the Psalter, we find the statement of Cassiodorus that the psalms are read in Church more often than other Scriptures because of their antiquity, spiritual content, and compendiousness: the Jews had used the psalms when worshipping in the temple, they contain more spiritual mysteries than other Biblical books, and they say briefly many things with which all the Law, prophets and evangelists agree[24].

But the authorship of the Psalter was a major problem. St Ambrose, St Augustine and Cassiodorus had thought that David, the father of Solomon, was the author of all the psalms[25]. In his *Homiliae in psalmos,* St Jerome stated two points of view: some say that David composed all the psalms which were performed by the choirmasters (Asaph, Idithun, the sons of Core, and others) whose names are found in the titles of individual psalms; others believe that these titles refer to actual authors, and that David was one psalmist among many[26]. Elsewhere, Jerome affirmed his belief in the multiple authorship of the Psalter, a view which was consistently ignored or rejected by many twelfth-century scholars[27].

Then there was the issue of the literary form of the Psalter, a work in which individual poems were brought together within a general structure. How did this grouping together of diverse items contribute to the distinctive literary quality and effect of the work as a whole? How significant was the fact that the psalms were in verse, and verse which was sung in praising God? Other books of the Bible, for example the Twelve Minor Prophets, raised similar questions of authorship and of *ordo,* but the Psalter presented an additional difficulty in so far as it consisted of hymns of divine praise. Moreover, the type of prophecy found therein was supposed to exceed in status that found in the Minor Prophets[28].

In their exegesis of the psalms, medieval commentators faced major problems of literary description, and our subsequent chapters are concerned with some of them. By comparing the prologues to the Bible-commentaries of several generations of masters, we may assess the relative functions of tradition and the individual talent in medieval discussions of authorial role and literary form.

The Psalter-prologue which, through a process of accretion, came to form part of the *Glossa ordinaria* on the Psalter, begins with details ultimately derived from St Augustine's *Enarrationes in psalmos* that constitute an explanation of the title *(titulus)* of the sacred book[29]. Augustine is reported as having said that the Jews call the Psalter 'The Book of Hymns' because a hymn is words and praise with song. Alternatively, it may be entitled 'The Book of Soliloquies', because soliloquies are said to be the result of someone having searched alone and gained knowledge only from the truth which resides within himself. Augustine's *Soliloquies* are given as an example of the genre.

The *Glossa* moves on to examine the problem of authorship. When David, ruling in prosperity, wished to glorify God, he set out to bring the Ark of the Covenant to Jerusalem (cf. II Kings vi); on which occasion, four men were appointed to perform the psalms not only with singing but also with musical instruments. These were Asaph, Idithun, and two sons of Core, namely, Eman and Ethan. Jerome is interpreted (rather freely) as having claimed that David composed all the psalms, while Asaph and the others were merely the performers who made the psalms resound in three ways, either with singing, or with musical instruments, or with both means. Various men are mentioned in the psalm-titles mainly because of the allegorical and spiritual significance of their names. This is not elaborated in the prologue, but the principle is applied in analyses of individual psalms, presumably based on the work of Anselm of Laon[30]. Augustine, Jerome and Cassiodorus are Anselm's precedents for interpreting Asaph as signifying 'assembly', Core as signifying 'Calvary', and so on[31].

To Cassiodorus, the *Glossa* is indebted for an account of the diverse types or 'modes' of prophecy found in Scripture; to Remigius of Auxerre, for number-symbolism; to St Augustine, for an explanation of the diversity and unity of the Psalter[32]. The work's *materia, intentio,* and *modus tractandi* are then described as follows:

The material is the whole Christ, groom and bride. The intention is to reform in Christ as new men those men deformed in Adam. This is the method of treatment. Sometimes he treats of Christ with regard to His head, sometimes with regard to His body, and sometimes with regard to both. With regard to the head, he speaks in three ways, either with reference to His divinity . . . or with reference to His humanity . . . or sometimes by transumption, as when he employs the voice of His members . . . Also, he speaks of the Church in three manners: sometimes with regard to perfect men, sometimes with regard to imperfect men, and sometimes with regard to evil men who are in the Church in body but not in mind, in number but not in merit, and in name but not in spirit.

Around three 'type C' headings has been organised a synopsis of material derived from Augustine's *Enarrationes in psalmos.* This deserves special attention, since it defines the range within which most twelfth-century commentators on the Psalter operated, and accounts for the limitations of their literary analyses of the psalms.

The theory that the whole of the Old Testament prefigures Christ by means of types and symbols had been developed by the Fathers, one of Augustine's main contributions being a rich elaboration of the allegory of David as a forerunner and figure of Christ. Throughout the *Enarrationes in psalmos* runs the theme of a single man, head and members, towering above the flux of centuries; Jesus Christ uniting all predestined souls within His mystical body[33]. This process of spiritual composition and discrimination proceeds despite the wicked reactions of the ungodly: the city of God is gradually disengaging itself from the city of evil. The psalms which, in their diversity of emotion and situation, embrace all life's possibilities, derive their essential unity from the whole Christ, whom we hear praying to God now as head, now as body, even as both. David-as-Christ combines within himself the functions of the groom and bride as described in the Song of Songs, interpreted as an allegory of the union of Christ with the Church or with the soul of a righteous man. This intricate interpretation of Augustine's received further elaboration at the hands of Cassiodorus; a compound of their statements formed the basis of most of the exegesis of the Psalter written by Anselm of Laon and the subsequent glossators of the *Glossa ordinaria.*

These received interpretations heavily influenced twelfth-century attitudes to David's authorial role and to the literary form of the Psalter. The Psalter speaks of the whole Christ: this is the key to the work's considerable *auctoritas* and its essential unity. Prophecies of Christ permeate the Psalter; each and every psalm has something to say about some aspect of Him, either about His godhead, His humanity, or His mystical body which is Holy Church. *Auctoritas* entails unity: the singularity of the authorship of the psalms, the unity of the diverse materials within the work, and the unity of the Psalter with the rest of the Bible.

The unity of the parts of Scripture and the harmony of the Bible were often affirmed through a metaphor derived from the Psalter. When a cithar is played, strings and wood function together to produce a unified sound by means of its diverse parts. According to Hugh of St Victor,

all of sacred Scripture is so suitably adjusted and arranged in all its parts through the wisdom of God that whatever is contained in it either resounds with the sweetness of spiritual understanding in the manner of strings; or, containing utterances of mysteries set here and there in the course of a historical narrative or in the substance of a literal context, and, as it were, connecting these up into one object, it binds them together all at once as the wood does which curves under the taut strings; and, receiving their sound into itself, it reflects it more sweetly to our ears—a sound which the string alone has not yielded, but which the wood too has formed by the shape of its body[34].

The exegetical method whereby the unity of the Bible was established was allegory. Its priorities caused considerable alteration in the denotations of the headings employed in the 'type C' prologue-paradigm. As described in the *Glossa ordinaria* and in other commentaries, the *materia* of the Psalter is not—as is usually the case with the *materia* of a secular work—the subject-matter understood literally, but rather its central allegorical referent, the whole Christ. Similarly, the heading *intentio* introduces a statement about allegorical sense rather than literal sense. This approach renders superfluous any consideration of the work's *utilitas*. In place of the artist's identification of the subdivision of philosophy relevant to the work is an identification of the subdivision of prophecy under which David's prophecy may be classified.

But the major contrast between the prologues of the artists and those of the theologians consists in differing attitudes to the historical contexts of texts. In theologians' prologues to, for example, the Psalter and the Song of Songs respectively, there is no 'Life of David' or 'Life of Solomon' to parallel the lives of Virgil, Ovid and other secular writers found in the *accessus ad auctores*[35]. When justifying the frequent use of the psalms and the Pauline Epistles in the liturgy, Remigius of Auxerre and Peter Lombard (*c.* 1100–1160) had referred briefly to David as a murderer and adulterer, and to the sins which St Paul had committed before his conversion, but they did not attempt to relate these historical facts about their authors to the issue of their authority as writers[36]. In commenting on the Psalter, exegetes sought to establish the priority of the spiritual sense (containing prophecies and prefigurations of the whole Christ) over the historical or literal sense, the consequence of which was neglect of the humanity of the psalmists. The historical context of a Biblical text, including information about the life and times of its writer, was believed to be of far less importance than the spiritual significance of the words on the page.

This is most evident in the prologue to the Psalter-commentary which Peter Lombard read in the schools shortly before his election as Bishop of Paris in 1159, a highly influential work which superseded the *Glossa ordinaria* as the standard Psalter-commentary used by students[37]. For the Lombard, David was a 'trumpet of the Holy Spirit'; his human characteristics were relatively unimportant[38]. The *auctoritas* of David is affirmed by a discussion of his kind of prophecy *(genus prophetiae),* in which it is argued that David is the prophet of whom we can say with the greatest conviction that he edited his prophecy solely under the guidance of the Holy Spirit without recourse to images of things and the veil of words[39]. Peter, delighting in allegorical speculation more than most, has elaborated on material from Cassiodorus[40]. The very identity of the human *auctores* has been put aside. The names (like Asaph and the sons of Core) which appear in the titles of the psalms are said to be there chiefly for their mystical significance:

But he [Cassiodorus] says this against some who have said that there were several writers of psalms, or authors, because in the titles are found their names, like Asaph, Heman, Ethan and Idithun. This, we have shown, was done in the work for the signification of the mysteries which is seen from the interpretations of the names.[41]

These mysterious names do not indicate the *auctores* of the psalms, but encourage the reader to think of spiritual things:

So they were not authors of the psalms, but the insertion of the names serves the purpose of the mysteries.[42]

All problems regarding the composite authorship of the Psalter are cleverly allegorised away. The Lombard seems to believe that establishment of the Psalter's *auctoritas* involves the resolution, or dissolution, of what we would regard as basic issues of literary theory. The authorship of the Psalter is problematic, and so the issue of the identity of the human *auctores* must be proved to be unimportant; any doubts concerning the work's prestige must be removed.

The Song of Songs received similar treatment. In the prologue which introduces his commentary on this work (*c.* 1130), William of St Thierry merely alluded to the historical event believed to have provided the occasion for Solomon's song, namely, the king's marriage with Pharaoh's daughter[43]. The literary form of the work, described as 'the historical drama, fable or parable', is briefly summarised:

Now the argument of the historical drama, fable or parable proposed, may be stated as follows. King Solomon took to wife the daughter of the Pharaoh of Egypt. At first he granted her certain favours of the bridal bed and of love and of the kiss. Then, after having shown her part of his riches and part of his glory, he cast her forth from their mutual union and the favour of the kiss until, by riddance of her Egyptian blackness and rejection of the customs of a barbarous nation, she might become worthy of access to the royal bed-chamber.[44]

Immediately after this, William defines the spiritual sense of the Song of Songs, thereby establishing its *auctoritas:*

But the spiritual sense is this. When the soul has been converted to God and is to be espoused to the Word of God, at first she is taught to understand the riches of prevenient grace and allowed to 'taste and see how sweet the Lord is' [Psalm xxxiii.9]; but afterwards she is sent back into the house of her conscience to be instructed, purified in the obedience of charity, perfectly cleansed of vices and richly adorned with virtues, that she may be found worthy of access to the spiritual grace of godliness and affection for virtues which is the bed-chamber of the Bridegroom.

The subsequent commentary focuses mainly on the moral sense of the work, its allegorical sense already having been expounded by St Bernard. We hear little more about the drama, fable or parable written by King Solomon, or about the king and his dark lady.

Equally striking is the implicit redefinition of the term *modus tractandi* in twelfth-century exegesis. In *De doctrina christiana,* St Augustine had provided a selective account of the ancient theory of rhetorical persuasion, quoting Cicero's recommendation that the eloquent man should speak in such a way that he teaches, pleases and persuades[45]. For Cicero, to teach is a necessity, to please, a satisfaction, and to persuade, a triumph[46]. The first of these depends on what we say; the other two depend on the manner (the *modus* or *genus*) in which we say it[47]. The manner must be suited to the material and the purpose of the speaker[48]. Augustine also outlined the three kinds of style *(genera dicendi),* the first extant formulation of which appears in the *Rhetorica ad Herennium,* a work ascribed to Cicero throughout the Middle Ages[49]. There, we are told that the grand style consists of a smooth and ornate arrangement of impressive words, the middle style consists of words of lower class, while the simple or plain style is brought right down even to the most current idiom of standard speech. Augustine's version of this theory is that the eloquent man or preacher can speak of trivial subjects in a low style in order to teach, discuss ordinary subjects in a moderate style in order to please, and treat of noble subjects in a grand style in order to persuade[50]. These styles are illustrated with examples from the Church fathers; earlier in the *De doctrina christiana,* Augustine had commended the eloquence of the Biblical prophets[51].

All this is very far from the portion of the *Glossa ordinaria* on the Psalter which may be ascribed to Anselm of Laon, even though he had probably lectured on Cicero's *De inventione* and the *Rhetorica ad Herennium,* the two authoritative texts for the teaching of rhetoric at Laon[52]. The influence of Anselm's rhetorical learning on his exegesis was minimal; he had little to say about the eloquence of the prophet David. For many of Anselm's successors, the Psalter's *modus tractandi* remained, as it were, the property of the Holy Spirit, not of the human author or authors of the Psalter.

But many exegetes did not share Anselm's reticence. The value of at least some facets of rhetorical doctrine in classifying certain literary effects found in Scripture was often recognised[53]. A good example is provided by theologians' depictions of writings which appealed to the disposition or affections *(affectus)* of the reader[54]. The notion that the orator should win the emotional support of his audience by arousing their feelings was a commonplace of ancient theory of rhetoric[55]. As applied in *accessus* to pagan poets, this notion, in some measure, functioned as a reply to the long-standing criticism that poetry inflames the passions of men and encourages vice[56]: some poems, at least, stimulate men to perform virtuous deeds, and so may be said to pertain to ethics. In the *Commentum in Theodulum* which he composed in the late eleventh century, Bernard of Utrecht gave a general account of the 'modern' concepts *materia, intentio* and *pars philosophiae* as applied in exposition of secular works, in which the affective appeal of such writings is accepted as one of the major facets of their subservience to, and support of, the sacred Scriptures:

The 'intention' is a disposition *(affectus)* of the soul concerning a matter *(materia),* or a discourse *(oratio)* which especially directs the soul in reading a book (as, in Lucan, it intends to restrain or dissuade from civil war). In accordance with that, the intention in this book [the *Eclogue* of Theodulus] seems to be to commend the truth of holy Scripture, even to condemn the literary trivia of the gentiles—not indeed that the latter should not be read, but lest, if read, they be believed or translated into action.[57]

Several exegetes recognised in this theory of affective intention a way of explaining the emotive appeal of the Psalter and the Song of Songs. Gilbert of Poiters was more interested in the persuasive force of the psalms than his master, Anselm of Laon, had been: his glosses, corrected by Anselm (before 1117), are of special interest as a development of the teaching of a master which received that master's approval[58]. Gilbert expounds the Psalter's *intentio* with reference to the notion that sacred poetry works in an affective way, that it moves the wills of men to follow the good and flee the evil. The purpose of the Psalter is not simply to teach about Christ but, by appealing to the human affections *(affectus),* to lead carnal men to praise Him.

For the prophet has in mind not only to teach those things which he propounds regarding Christ, but indeed in teaching to draw the affections of carnal men to the same end of praise.[59]

Hence, the psalms are in verse and are adorned with diverse kinds of speech *(genera loquendi).* David praised the Lord with others, in the presence of a multitude.

Whence he both wrote in metre and ornamented his work with diverse kinds of speech and, in front of the ark [of the covenant], with voice and instruments and especially with the psaltery, he sang in person with many others and in the presence of many.[60]

William of St Thierry may have disagreed with many of Gilbert's conclusions and the methods whereby he had obtained them, but his concept of the affections was basically the same as Gilbert's, though more highly developed and a more fundamental tenet of his theology[61]. In the prologue to his commentary on the Song of Songs, William appealed to the Holy Spirit to fill with love those who read Solomon's work, so that readers might understand it, and that what we read might take effect within us: 'thus we may become in some measure participants in the holy conversation of Bridegroom and Bride'[62]. This seems to be a specific application of William's belief—a belief also held by his friend St Bernard of Clairvaux—that the fear and love of God should precede all study[63]. For William 'the art of love is the art of arts' and the true master of this art is not that pagan Ovid who is so eagerly devoured in the schools, but Nature, and God who is the author of nature[64]. This is the thesis of William's *De natura et dignitate amoris,* a thorough critique of the *Ars amatoria.* Against those schools who teach the art of love according to Ovid, William would establish a school of charity or divine love[65].

However, the reader of William's commentary on the Song of Songs is constantly reminded of the common ground between these two types of 'school'. An analysis is provided of the *inscriptio, materia* and *modus agendi* of the work, in which its supreme excellence among songs is affirmed:

This book of King Solomon's, then, is entitled the Song of Songs either because, by the dignity of its sense and the pre-eminence of his material, it seems to surpass all the ancient canticles of the patriarchs or prophets, treating of the Bridegroom and Bride, Christ and the rational soul; or because it is sung with the accord of holy affections by the blessed people that knows jubilation and walks in the light of God's countenance, rather than chanted with the harmony of voices singing different notes. It treats of the love of God, either the love whereby God is loved, or the love whereby God Himself is called love. It does not matter whether we call it 'love' or 'charity' or 'dilection', except in so far as 'love' seems to indicate a certain tender affection on the part of the lover with the implication of striving or seeking; 'charity', a certain spiritual affection or the joy of possession; and 'dilection', a natural desire for an object which gives delight. But one and the same Spirit works all these things in the love of Bridegroom and Bride.[66]

The entire commentary is permeated by the conviction that the Song of Songs encourages Christians to move from a lower degree of love to a higher, from a sensitive affection for Christ to that mystical union of which it is the prelude[67].

It would seem, then, that grammarians and theologians shared a literary theory of affective intention, although they applied it in different ways and held different opinions of its purport and bearing. The links between the artists' prologues and those of theologians are many and manifold. The contrasts in priority, emphasis and content are very obvious, but certain principles of approach and techniques of literary analysis do appear to have been held in common. For example, the technique employed by several exegetes in analysing the Psalter's *intentio* was probably derived from grammarians' *accessus* to certain secular poems, as the following comparison will indicate.

The 'type C' headings provide the framework around which Gilbert of Poitiers's entire Psalter-prologue is organised. The standard opinions are expressed with great economy of statement and with a pleasing turn of phrase:

The whole Christ, head and members, is the material *(materia)* of this work, concerning which the prophet proceeds in this mode *(modus):* sometimes he speaks of the whole together, that is, Christ and the Church, and sometimes of the separate parts, that is, Christ or the Church. He speaks of Christ in three modes: sometimes concerning His divinity. . . ., sometimes concerning his proper humanity. . . , sometimes by transumption, speaking of those things which are appropriate only to the members . . . He speaks of the Church in two modes: sometimes in relation to those who are perfect; sometimes, to those who are imperfect. Moreover, sometimes he interposes, for the sake of the good, material relating to the damned. He deals with this material and in this mode with this intention *(intentio),* that those damned in Adam should be made like Christ, by whom alone their sins may be dismissed, and immortality restored; that is, just as they have borne the image of the earthly one [i.e. Adam] they may bear the image of the heavenly one [i.e. Christ]. The title of the work *(titulus libri)* is: the Book of Hymns begins. A hymn is praise of God with song . . .[68]

All this, Gilbert explains, is said about the Psalter considered as a whole. But each psalm has its special *materia, modus, finis* and *titulus*.[69] In the subsequent commentary, some or all of these headings are applied in discussion of each individual psalm. Gilbert can see the part in the whole and the whole in the part; in his glosses the commonplace belief in the unity of the Psalter is elaborated into a comprehensive view of a work in which the parts interact and ultimately harmonise

2 'THE WHOLE CHRIST IS THE MATERIAL' (see pp. 52–4, cf. p. 45). Oxford, Bodleian Library, MS Auct. D. 2. 1, fol. 147ᵛ. Gilbert of Poitiers, Commentary on the Psalter.

with each other, thereby serving the whole, while the whole accommodates a variety which is expressed through its different parts.

A similar development of Anselm's teaching is found in Peter Lombard's commentary on the Psalter.[70] Here also, the technical headings are applied both to the whole, the Psalter, and to the parts, the individual psalms.[71] Particularly interesting is the way in which the first psalm is singled out as a microcosm of the whole work.[72] Combining and amplifying statements by Jerome and Cassiodorus, the Lombard argues that Psalm i lacks a title because it functions as the beginning, preface and head of the entire Psalter. It treats of Christ who, as the beginning of all things, Himself has no beginning: this may be why it is untitled. Alternatively, the psalm may have no title because it is, as it were, the title and the prologue of the psalms which follow. The *materia* of the first psalm is identical with the *materia* of the Psalter considered as a whole; the same may be said about its *intentio*. The *modus tractandi* is described as follows:

The mode of treatment is this. The psalm is bipartite. First, it treats of the blessed man, coaxing us with blessedness. Secondly, it treats of the punishments of the unjust, alarming us by adversities . . . It treats of the blessed man in this way: in the first verse it shows him to be immune from all evil; in the second, to be full of all goodness in himself, and thereby beneficial to others, and this proceeds right up to the division of the psalm. By showing him immune from all evil it makes a comparison with the old man, namely Adam, revealing him to be full of all evil . . .

In this way, the first psalm introduces the polar opposites between which all the psalms move: from the goodness of the new man, Christ, to the evil of the old man, Adam; from the attraction of blessedness to the repugnance of whatever is contrary to it.

This sense of the interrelationships of part and whole was expressed more elaborately by another twelfth-century commentator, Pseudo-Haimo, who speaks of the *communis materia* and *communis intentio* of the Psalter in general—

The common material of the whole work is Christ, understood in three ways . . . Likewise, the common intention is that it should make us like Christ . . .

—and the diverse *materiae* and *intentiones* of individual psalms[73]. These diverse matters and intentions are subservient to the common material and common intention to which they all contribute:

Material about contrary things, that is, about impious demons, is inserted, not because it is to be the principal material, but in order that it should serve the principal material, being mixed with right things. Thus, in the first psalm he introduces the impious, so that by their torment men should be deterred from conforming with them and brought back to conforming with Christ.

Such an approach to the Psalter as a patterned collection of poems, some of which commend what is good while others describe what is evil in order that men may flee from it, is so reminiscent of *accessus* to certain secular poems that one safely may infer that twelfth-century theologians were adopting a technique of analysis which had been refined by many generations of grammarians. Within the *accessus* this technique was at its most sophisticated in introductions to Ovid's *Heroides*. The *Heroides* and the Psalter presented medieval scholars with similar problems of description: the psalms were believed to lack chronology; in much the same way, the *Heroides* was seen as a collection of verse love-letters which follow no principle of sequence.

In one of the fullest of all twelfth-century *accessus* to the *Heroides,* it is stated that Ovid's *intentio* was to write of three kinds of love: infatuation, inchastity and mad passion[74]. The first is exemplified by Phyllis, the second by Helen, the third by Canace. Moreover, Ovid intended to commend chaste love by writing of noble Greek women like Phaedra. Caesar had accused Ovid of misleading the Roman matrons with erotic poetry: in reply, he wrote the *Heroides*.

Whence he wrote a book for them, propounding by example, so that they should know in loving which things should be imitated, and which should not.

The basic notion here is that certain items within the collection work positively by describing chaste and pure love in such a way that the reader is made aware of its attractiveness, whereas inchastity is described in such a way that it appears obnoxious. The anonymous commentator speaks of the general *intentio* of the whole work and the particular *intentiones* of the different items within the collection, just like the commentators on the Psalter[75]:

Let it be known also that while in the entire book they have this and the abovementioned intentions, Ovid has over and above that two intentions in this book, one general and the other special, the general intention being to delight and to be for the general good. He has a special intention, as in individual epistles, to commend in the case of chastity or to condemn in the case of unchaste love . . . And fittingly diverse epistles have diverse intentions, because in so far as he set forth some letters to commend chastity and others to reprehend unchaste love, he intended diverse things.[76]

The epistles therefore work in a harmonious way to teach and delight[77].

The diversity of the *utilitas* or final cause of the *Heroides* is supposed to be related to the various intentions in the various epistles, some of which convey knowledge of illicit or infatuated kinds of love, while others show the benefits which accrue from chastity. Alternatively, the commentator continues, the final cause is such that, by commendation of chaste loving we should be encouraged to chaste loves; or that, by seeing the moral utility which proceeds from legal love and the misfortunes and disadvantages which arise from illicit and infatuated kinds of love, we should reject and flee from illicit and infatuated love and adhere to legal love. The work pertains to ethics *(ethice supponitur)* because it teaches us of that kind of love which is just and correct. Within a general moral framework, it would seem, some epistles function to make us reject evil love, while others function to secure our approval for good love. The general intention of the work is perfectly compatible with different intentions, materials and modes of procedure in different parts of the work; indeed, it is the very diversity of the intentions, materials and didactic methods which brings about the moral intention. One is reminded of the way in which the Psalter-commentators describe the different psalms with their diverse intentions, materials and modes as contributing to a common purpose.

Since the same twelfth-century masters lectured on both kinds of text, proceeding from the secular to the sacred, it is hardly surprising to find the same techniques of literary analysis being exploited. Both the *Heroides* and the Psalter were believed to be unified by their significance; that significance was interpreted and expounded in accordance with the available idioms of literary analysis. The significance of the Psalter consisted in its Christological level of meaning; that of the *Heroides* consisted in its contribution to a system of morality which, while non-Christian in historical terms, was not incompatible with Christian ethics. The moral significance of a work like the *Heroides* was not immediately acceptable: Ovid's *intentio* had to be piously interpreted. By contrast, the Psalter's significance was indubitable, having been guaranteed by the one true God who had inspired its human authors. Therefore, a technique of analysis which in grammarians' *accessus* formed part of the defence of a work's purpose and worth became, in the hands of theologians, a means whereby the literary features of a work which needed no apology could be adequately characterised. Sacred poetry required not justification but explanation.

Yet it cannot be assumed that all the idioms and principles of exegetical literary theory came from arts scholarship. Many different kinds of source contributed to the theologians' information and insights. Once again, we may turn to William of St Thierry for substantiation. Part of William's discussion of the *modus agendi* of the Song of Songs consists of the statement that this work is written in dramatic form and theatrical style *(modus dramatis et stylus comicus)*, as if to be acted by various characters *(personae):*

Now this song is written in the mode of a drama and in theatrical style, as if to be recited by characters and with action. Just as in the recitation of dramas various characters and various actions appear, so in this song characters and affections are seen to combine to lead to the resolution of this love-intrigue, the mystical contract of the union of God and man. The persons are four in number: the Bridegroom, His companions, the Bride, and the chorus of young maidens. The Bridegroom's companions are the angels, rejoicing with us in our good deeds and loving to serve us therein with ministrations. The maidens, in turn, are tender and new souls, who, having given their names to the instruction and profession of spiritual love, by obedient humility and attentive imitation attach themselves to the Bride, i.e. to more perfect souls. All the action of love, however, is left to the lovers themselves: while their fellow-lovers keep silence, stand still, listen and rejoice with joy at the voice of the Bridegroom and Bride, scarcely any voice is heard or any utterance introduced in this entire song, save those of the Bridegroom and Bride.[78]

This classification of the Song of Songs occurs in Bede's *De arte metrica:*

There are three types of poem. A poem is either active or imitative . . . or narrative . . . or common or mixed . . . In the dramatic or active type the characters *(personae)* are presented speaking without any intervention by the poet, as is the case with tragedies and fables . . . Among our sacred writings the Song of Songs was written in this genre. . .[79]

and a garbled version of the same is found in Bernard of Utrecht's *Commentum in Theodulum*[80]. The classification of poems on the basis of the *personae* employed therein, lacking any application to Scriptural texts, was quite commonplace throughout the Middle Ages: it goes

back to Servius's commentary on Virgil's *Eclogues* and is found in the
Etymologiae of Isidore of Seville and in twelfth-century *accessus ad
auctores*[81].

But William of St Thierry's source was not any of these. He was
drawing on the Latin translation by Rufinus of the commentary on the
Song of Songs produced by the third-century exegete Origen, a major
influence on William's commentary and, indeed, on his theology in
general. As interpreted by Rufinus, Origen had said that Solomon
wrote his song in the form of a drama:

It seems to me that this little book is an epithalamium, that is to say, a
marriage-song, which Solomon wrote in the form of a drama and sang under
the figure of the Bride, about to be wed and burning with heavenly love
towards her Bridegroom, who is the Word of God. . . . we find the Bride
speaking not to the Bridegroom only but also to the maidens; likewise the
Bridegroom's words are addressed not to the Bride alone, but also to His
friends. And that is what we meant just now, when we said that the marriage-
song was written in dramatic form. For we call a thing a drama, such as the
enaction of a story on the stage, when different characters are introduced and
the whole structure of the narrative consists in their comings and goings
among themselves. And this work contains these things one by one in their
own order, and also the whole body of it consists of mystical utterances.[82]

William's description of Solomon's *modus dramatis* reads as a reformula-
tion of this passage. In later commentaries on the Song of Songs, we
shall encounter similar descriptions, there reformulated in accordance
with the conceptual framework of the Aristotelian four causes[83].

The discussions of literary form and authorial role examined above
make clear the considerable extent to which, in twelfth-century commentaries on the Bible, God was believed to have controlled human
authors in a way which defied literary description. Literary criteria and
classifications, although not ignored altogether, were afforded a relatively unimportant place in Scriptural exegesis. Of course, there are
exceptions to this general rule, the most exceptional of all being the
exegesis of Peter Abelard (1079–1142), the great opponent of, among
others, Anselm of Laon, St Bernard and William of St Thierry.
Abelard's commentary on the Epistle of St Paul to the Romans (composed between 1135 and 1139) will be discussed at some length, as it
anticipates literary attitudes which were widely held in the thirteenth
century.

AN EXCEPTION: ABELARD ON ST PAUL

Abelard sifted all received interpretation with an unusual vigour and precision; a convenient summary of his methods is found in the preface to the *Sic et non*[84]. Here, it is argued that the obscurity and contradictions in the writings of the Fathers can be explained on many grounds, and can be examined without impugning the authors' good faith and insight. A writer may use different words to mean the same thing; indeed, different writers may use different words in discussing the same thing. Sometimes, common and vague words are employed in order that the common people may understand. Sometimes, rhetorical and poetical language is employed, which is often obscure and vague. Moreover, there are passages in which the author is speaking to exhort rather than to give information; sometimes, advice and precepts are given, which may either have general relevance or apply only to special cases. These principles reveal Abelard's interest in the historical context of authoritative statements: once this is known, a scholar can proceed to reconcile his *auctoritates* and get at the truth. Another group of principles turns on the issue of authenticity: apocryphal works are often attributed to the Saints; authors may reiterate the opinions of other men, including erroneous opinions; sometimes the Fathers themselves may err.

This acceptance of the occasional errors of the Fathers is striking. Abelard's point is that since Peter, the prince of the apostles, fell into error, it is little wonder that the Saints do not always show themselves inspired. The Fathers themselves did not believe that they, or their associates, were always right. Abelard cites the example of Augustine, who found himself mistaken in some cases and did not hesitate to compose a book of retractions[85]. Augustine warned his admirers not to look upon his writings as they would upon the Scriptures, but to accept only those things which, upon examination, they found to be true.

According to Abelard, all the patristic writings are to be read with full freedom to criticise, and with no obligation to accept anything without question[86]. By contrast, the Scriptures are of far greater authority: when anything therein strikes us as absurd, we may not say that the writer erred, but that the scribe made a blunder in copying, or we must make some similar excuse.

Such decorum is a feature of Abelard's exegesis, where many of the principles outlined above can be seen in operation. In the prologue to his commentary on St Paul's Epistle to the Romans, he attempts to reconcile those received interpretations which appear to be contradictory; in the process, he seems to get closer—in literary terms at least—to his author.

The major problem identified by Abelard is as much historical as theological: who first preached to the Romans?[87] Eusebius, Jerome and Gregory are quoted as saying that the Roman Christians were first converted by St Peter, and Haimo as being of the opinion that this was done by certain faithful Jews from Jerusalem[88]. The statements of these writers are then meticulously analysed, and the conclusion reached that, in fact, they do not disagree at all. The *Ecclesiastica historica* of Eusebius states that Peter was the first apostle—not the first doctor— to preach to the Romans. When Jerome says that the Romans accepted the faith as the result of Peter's teaching, he means, according to Abelard, that the disciples of Peter first preached in Rome. Haimo does not deny that Peter instructed the Romans, only that he was their first instructor.

The precision of this analysis of sources is impressive; it contrasts with the rather cursory resolution of the same problem found both in the *Glossa ordinaria* and in the commentary on the Pauline Epistles which Peter Lombard wrote and revised between 1148 and 1159[89].

Of a piece with Abelard's recognition that the Fathers could err (as expressed in the *Sic et non* prologue) is his acceptance that certain Scriptural *auctores* were, or once had been, great sinners. The order of words in the very first phrase of Paul's Epistle, 'Paul, a servant, called to be an Apostle . . .' provides Abelard with the opportunity to discuss Saul's rebirth as Paul, and Paul's apostolic vocation, respectively[90]. Again, one may contrast the cursory treatment by Peter Lombard[91]. Anselm of Laon, once described by Abelard as a barren tree, seems to have ignored the problem[92].

Abelard was also interested in the individual literary activity of the human *auctor* of Scripture, especially in the author's intention and the rhetorical force of his writing[93]. This emphasis on intention may be compared with Abelard's insistence, in his ethical theory, on the primacy of the motives for human actions: deeds are in themselves indifferent and are called good or evil only on account of the intention of the agent[94]. In Abelard's exegesis, the good motives of the human authors of Scripture are related directly to the appropriate literary means they employed in expressing themselves. The commentary on St Paul's Epistle begins with the statement that the intention of all divine Scripture is to teach or to move in the manner of rhetorical speech. Abelard's training in rhetoric is very much to the fore:

All sacred Scripture, in the manner of rhetorical speech, intends either to teach or to move. For it teaches when it makes known those things which are necessary to be done or avoided. But it moves when by holy admonitions it either draws back our will from evils by dissuading, or by persuading directs our will to good things: thus, forthwith we wish to implement those things which we have learned are to be implemented, or to flee contrary things.[95]

St Paul's noble motive in writing to the Romans is placed within the context of a general synopsis of the different literary techniques employed in both Testaments, in the Old as much as in the New. First of all, in the Pentateuch, the divine precepts are taught. Then, in the prophecies and histories and other Scriptures, we are exhorted to put into action what has already been given to us in the form of precepts: these writings move the affections of men to obedience of the precepts. When the prophets or holy Fathers felt that the people were not well-disposed to obey the divine laws, they applied admonitions so that, by promises or threats, the people were led to obedience. Both the reward of obedience and the punishment of transgressions are, Abelard claims, brought before our eyes by the examples provided in histories. The old cloths which were fastened around Jeremiah when he was being extracted from the pit by ropes (Jeremiah xxxviii.11) are interpreted as the examples used by the ancient Fathers, whose holy admonitions lead to the sinner being extracted from the abyss of vices.

Similarly, Abelard continues, the teaching of the New Testament is tripartite. The writings of the Four Evangelists stand as the law, which teaches the form of true justice and perfection. Then the Epistles, together with the Apocalypse, are put in place of the prophets: they encourage obedience to the law. The Acts of the Apostles and part of the evangelical narrations contain sacred histories.

From these things it follows, that since the intention of the Gospel is to teach, the Epistle and the Acts of the Apostles have this intention, that they should move us to obedience of the Gospel, or confirm us in those things which the Gospel teaches.

The Epistles are not to be regarded as superfluous: they were written for purposes of admonition instead of doctrine; they move us to action

rather than tell us what to do. Moreover, they do contain some beneficial counsels not found in the Evangelists.

From Cicero's *De inventione*, Abelard derives a distinction between
those things which are absolutely essential for the stability of a good
state (like fields, forests, etc.) and those things which contribute to the
amplification and refinement thereof (like beautiful buildings, wealth,
much dominion, etc.), thereby increasing the dignity of the state and
making it more secure[96]. The teachings of the Evangelists fall into the
category of the absolutely essential, whereas the Apostles and later
writers may be said to have added certain precepts and dispensations
with which Holy Church is adorned and increased.

Abelard then sums up the general intention *(generalis intentio)* of the
Epistles[97]. They intend to move us to obey evangelical doctrine; besides, they hand down certain things for the more secure protection of
salvation. In individual epistles, it is appropriate to inquire after special intentions, the intention of the Epistle to the Romans being the
restoration of true humility and fraternal concord amongst two groups
of Christians (converted Jews and Gentiles), each of which had engaged
in self-aggrandisement. Abelard's opinion of the individual literary
quality of St Paul's writings is manifested by the opening statement of
his commentary on the text itself. His terms of reference are from a
practical branch of rhetorical instruction, the art of letter-writing *(ars
dictaminis)*:

Paul, in the manner of those writing letters, begins with a salutation, and
exhorts them to true wellbeing. He writes this salutation, with certain things
which follow, in front, in place of a prologue, where he intends quickly to
render them (namely the recipients) docile or benevolent.[98]

The skill with which Abelard has enlisted rhetoric and *accessus* technique in the service of Scriptural exegesis is remarkable indeed. The
extent to which he was ahead of his time as a literary theorist will
emerge in subsequent chapters.

This completes our examination of the way in which literary concepts characteristic of the most important type of prologue used in the
twelfth century (in particular, those expressed by the terms *intentio
auctoris, materia* and *modus agendi* or *modus tractandi*) were exploited by
major theologians in discussions of the authorial roles and literary
forms of certain Scriptural *auctores*. Ideas taken from commentaries on
secular authors were applied, decorously modified, to the inspired au-

thors, sometimes with considerable ingenuity. I have singled out commentaries on three of the Biblical books which medieval theologians found most difficult to describe (the Psalter, the Song of Songs and the Pauline Epistles) to bring out this dexterity in the clearest manner possible. Yet, with a few notable exceptions (Abelard's exegesis being the greatest), the ventures into literary theory outlined above are severely curtailed by the commentators' preoccupation with one facet of authorship to the exclusion of others, namely *auctoritas,* a prime focus of allegorical interpretation. This preoccupation is related to the narrow range of interest in authorial intention, material and mode, which has been demonstrated by our survey.

The rest of this chapter is concerned with the fate of two other items of vocabulary from introductions to the *artes,* i.e. the terms *extrinsecus* and *intrinsecus,* in twelfth-century exegesis. In order to evaluate the extent to which the priorities of allegorical interpretation altered the scope and significance of these technical terms, we shall trace their development from their appearance in the Psalter-commentaries of a group of scholars connected with the emerging University of Paris to their widespread use in commentaries on the entire Bible produced by later Paris masters.

EXTRINSECUS AND *INTRINSECUS* IN TWELFTH-CENTURY EXEGESIS

Peter of Poitiers had studied theology under Peter Lombard; he was teaching by 1167, acceded to the chair of theology left vacant by Peter Comestor in 1169, became Chancellor of Notre-Dame in 1193, and died in 1205[99]. His *Distinctiones super Psalterium* (written shortly before 1196) is based on Peter Lombard's commentary on the Psalter[100]. In particular, a large part of the prologue to the earlier work is incorporated into the later work, being prefaced by Peter of Poitiers's own prologue. In turn, a large section of Peter of Poitiers's prologue was incorporated into the *Summa super Psalterium* of Praepositinus of Cremona, who succeeded Peter of Poitiers as Chancellor of Notre-Dame in 1206[101].

The Psalter-commentaries of Peter of Poitiers and Praepositinus are, in fact, collections of distinctions *(distinctiones)* of exegetical material related to the various psalms[102]. *Distinctiones* were widely used in the second half of the twelfth century: in them, meanings were broken down, divided into their constituent parts, so that the senses or aspects of key words were easier to grasp. Within a *distinctio,* summaries of grammatical, rhetorical and metaphorical significance could accompany concise statements of tropological, allegorical and anagogical sense, the explicatory information being taken from bestiaries and 'moral encyclopedias', as well as from Bible-glosses[103]. The *distinctio* would either be written out at length or expressed diagrammatically, with a series of arms linking the elements together. Consequently, there was a considerable gain in ease of reference, a lot of information being conveyed in a short space[104].

The prologues of Peter of Poitiers and Praepositinus are of what may be called the 'sermon-type'[105]. They begin with a text from Scripture, which is then applied to the contents of the book under discussion, just as preachers cited a text at the beginning of their sermons. Peter Comestor introduced his commentaries on the Gospels (produced between 1159 and 1178) in this way, although he was certainly not the instigator of the custom[106].

Over and over again, the writers of these sermon-type prologues turned to an Old Testament description of some aspect of the tabernacle, its trappings, decoration or furniture, to supply an initial text which could be appropriately allegorised[107]. Peter of Poitiers devoted an entire treatise to such allegories; his *Allegoriae super tabernaculum Moysi* systematically elaborates on Bede's *De tabernaculo*[108]. Exodus xxvi.36 supplies the opening quotation of Peter's *Distinctiones super Psalterium:* Moses had been commanded to make for the entrance to the tabernacle a screen or curtain consisting of four precious colours woven together.

'Make me a screen for the entrance to the tabernacle, woven together from four precious colours.' The tabernacle in which God lives in us, in which he refreshes and feasts us, is the sacred page. For just as those entering the tabernacle encountered two entrances which were distinguished by two screens, so those approaching the page of holy Scripture encounter two beginnings, namely the extrinsic and the intrinsic. And just as those screens were adorned with four precious colours, so also are these beginnings divided in four parts. For the extrinsic beginning is divided into the cause of the name, the cause of the quantity, the cause of the distinction, and the cause of the frequent use. The intrinsic beginning is divided into the title, the material, the intention and the order.[109]

The intrinsic series comprises the familiar 'type C' paradigm. The extrinsic series is an attempt to systematise material derived from Peter Lombard's Psalter-prologue[110]. The term *causa* is being used to mean something like 'case' or 'subject' and, of course, is not to be confused with the 'four causes' of the later Aristotelian prologue: the *causa nominis* refers to the familiar discussion of the name of the Psalter; the *causa quantitatis*, to the number of psalms; the *causa distinctionis*, to the divisions within the Psalter; the *causa frequentationis*, to the considerable use made of the psalms in the liturgy[111].

In using the terms *extrinsecus* and *intrinsecus* in this way, Peter of Poitiers may have been following the lead of his predecessor Peter Comestor. In a Psalter-commentary attributed to Peter Comestor, the extrinsic entrance to Solomon's temple is glossed as the entrance *to* the temple and the intrinsic entrance as the entrance *in* the temple (cf. I Kings vi), an analogy being drawn with the two entrances which Moses provided for the tabernacle[112]. This dichotomy is cited as a well-established precedent for the two 'beginnings' which holy expositors advance as being noteworthy in the beginnings of books.

The nub of Peter of Poitiers's prologue was elaborated by subsequent commentators on the Psalter, the most popular version being provided by Praepositinus (writing in the period 1196–8)[113]. The reasons for its success are not hard to find. Praepositinus delighted in exhaustive enumeration of the synonyms and antonyms of his opening *auctoritas*, and he refused to let a concept escape without providing a *distinctio* to enumerate its constituent parts. The reader who begins this prologue (which is called an *ingressus* or entry) is immediately confronted with an *egressus* or exit: 'Go out, O daughters of Zion, and behold King Solomon, with the crown with which his mother crowned him on the day of his wedding, on the day of the gladness of his heart' (Song of Songs iii. 11)[114].

Sophisticated word-play continues throughout Praepositinus's prologue. The opening quotation is directed at lettered and contemplative men, who ought to be daughters of Zion. They are called daughters and not sons for an important reason, with reference not to the infirmity of the weaker sex but their ability to produce many children. Similarly, clerks ought to be prolific, of true doctrine, good deeds and holy conversation. Zion is interpreted as speculation, which consists in three things: the labour of inquiry, the devotion of prayer and the knowledge of the eternal vision.

Praepositinus then emphasises the point that, because the Bride-groom stands outside, the daughters of Zion must go out to Him to be loved with embraces. But there is a bad exit and a good exit. The bad exit is threefold: the exit from true to erroneous things, from perma-nent to transitory things, from honest to disgraceful things. The good exit is threefold also: the exit from the flesh to the spirit, from the natural to the supernatural, from the earth to God. Elaborate allegories are spun out from these and other triads.

Moving from exits to entries, Praepositinus discusses the two en-trances to the Psalter as provided by Peter of Poitiers, referred to as the 'expositor of the Psalter'. The headings *extrinsecus* and *intrinsecus* are replaced with *ingressus ad librum* and *ingressus in libro* respectively, but this is a mere change of labels, the items treated under the headings remaining the same.

In accordance with this manner the expositor of the Psalter makes a twofold entrance, namely the entrance *to* the book and the entrance *in* the book, and each contains four things in itself, as it were adorned with four colours. The entrance *to* the book contains the cause of the name, that is, why this book is said to be a psalter or soliloquy; and the cause of the quantity, that is, why it contains 150 psalms; and the cause of the distinction, that is, why it is divided into three groups of 50 psalms; and the cause of frequent use, that is, why in Church the writing of David is used more often than that of the other prophets. And this is said to be the entrance *to* the book, because, these things being known, little or nothing of the sense of the book is opened to us. The second entrance, which is *in* this book, similarly contains four things, namely the title, material, intention and mode of treatment. And this is said to be the entrance *in* the book because, these four things being known, the contents of the book are in some measure disclosed to us.[115]

For many later exegetes, Praepositinus had given the Paris Psalter *ingressus* its final form. Two amplifications of his work make this clear. The first is found in a Cambridge manuscript, Corpus Christi College MS 217, a well-written collection of 1450 *distinctiones* on the psalms[116]. The prologue is that of Praepositinus, with considerable modifications[117]. The second adaptation of Praepositinus was more important. The Psalter-commentary attributed to the great Dominican teacher, Hugh of St Cher, who lectured on the Bible 1230–5, uses an edited version of the Praepositinus prologue[118]. In this case, the com-mon phenomenon of prologue-borrowing takes on a new significance: the 'sociology' of the prologue had changed. Hugh's team of friar-scholars at the Dominican house of St Jacques stands out as one of the most remarkable of all medieval research institutes. The *Postillae* on the whole Bible which circulated under Hugh's name may be regarded as one of the cooperative works on Scripture carried out at St Jacques[119]. One can imagine a disciple of Hugh's, impressed by the Praepositinus prologue, taking it to his master Hugh, who approved it for incorporation into the St Jacques commentary.

It would seem, then, that the wish for symmetry and logical clarity has produced a highly patterned and somewhat artificial prologue to the Psalter. There is precise discrimination between the two beginnings or entrances and what is proper to each; the four headings of the extrinsic beginning or entrance to the work are paralleled with the four headings of the intrinsic beginning or entrance in the work. The ornamented quality of this excursus is striking, and it is tempting to speculate that the prologue to the Psalter-commentary of Peter the Chanter († 1197), which inveighs against superfluous glosses, is referring, at least in part, to the encrustations found in the prologues of his Parisian contemporaries[120].

The Chanter's opening text is Revelation v.4–5: St John wept because no-one was found worthy to open the book; then one of the elders said, 'Weep not; lo, the Lion of the tribe of Judah, the Root of David, has conquered, so that he can open the book with its seven seals'. The book in question is said to be the Old Testament; its seven seals have been opened by Christ[121]. Peter the Chanter's theme is that Christ incarnate is the perfect gloss for the Old Testament. He criticises those who can read but refuse to understand (illustrated by the Jews) and those who are unable to read (illustrated by the Gentiles)[122]. Whoever ignores sacred letters, of which other letters are the mere servants, is truly illiterate. The Chanter's conception of the services rendered to Scripture by secular letters is manifest in his *De tropis loquendi*, an analysis of the figures and tropes found in the Bible[123]. In his Psalter-prologue, he is concerned to emphasise the point that, by the advent of Christ, the hard hearts of the Jews were opened to the understanding of Scripture and the Gentiles were rendered literate. Despite his riches, the eunuch of the Queen of Candace read Isaiah without understanding (Acts viii.27), but when Philip told him of Christ he understood, was converted, and was baptised.

This, affirms Peter the Chanter, is the true exegesis, not superfluous glosses which escape the ears of men and fail to satisfy their souls.

Glosses are long and life is short. Why, when the advent of Christ has removed the veil from the face of Moses, do men seek to replace it, to reintroduce obscurity and deny Christ? Why do they judaise, and proudly make books just like the Pharisees, who refused to accept the unique efficacy of the decalogue? Must the face of Moses appear horned?[124] However these protestations are to be interpreted, what is abundantly clear is the practical bent of so much of Peter's exegesis[125]. He does not expound the two entrances to the Psalter, being content to retain the original idiom of Peter Lombard.

Indeed, none of the Psalter-prologues of these Paris masters go beyond Peter Lombard in terms of content: all that has changed is the presentation of material, the packaging. A neat and well-expressed *distinctio* will quickly become common property: the problem is that its repetition and refinement can become a substitute for further thought. There is no new contribution to the issue of the multiple authorship of the psalms, no new insight into the abundant literary features of the Psalter. In the beginning, doubtless, the sermon-type prologue 'gave solemnity and perhaps excitement' to the first lecture of a series[126]. Unfortunately, the choice of an opening text for one's prologue led to misplaced ingenuity and repetition, as each new generation of scholars attempted to elaborate on the prologues of their teachers and, indeed, as, with the passage of time, 'the number of suitable and hitherto unused texts sank to zero'[127]. The opening text determined the contents of the prologue, which became something of a minor literary genre in its own right. As a consequence, the prologue's self-generating literary conventions got in the way of analysis of the text itself.

The limitations of the sermon-type prologue become very obvious when a series of prologues to commentaries on the entire Bible is examined. The use of the terms *extrinsecus* and *intrinsecus* may now be discussed in this wider context, through an examination of the postils of Stephen Langton and Hugh of St Cher. Although Stephen Langton (*c.* 1155–1228) was English by birth and consecrated Archbishop of Canterbury in 1207, he was very much a product of the University of Paris. At Paris, he read both arts and theology; in theology, his teachers probably included Peter Comestor and Peter the Chanter[128]. It is, therefore, no surprise to discover that Langton was very influenced by the style of prologue which produced the Paris Psalter *ingressus*.

In the prologue to one of Langton's commentaries on Numbers, the *extrinsecus/intrinsecus* distinction is applied to the phrase *scriptus intus et foris,* which describes the book referred to in Ezechiel ii. 10 and Revelation v. 1. This phrase is supposed to signify, respectively, the allegorical and literal senses of Scripture.

> This book is written within and without. For it has intrinsic material and extrinsic material, that is, spiritual material and literal material.[129]

To the literal and spiritual *materiae* correspond literal and spiritual *intentiones.* Langton's use of the technical terms may be outlined as follows:

Materia extrinseca:	The children of Israel proceeding to the promised land and their homes.
Intentio extrinseca:	The commemoration of divine favours and the gratitude of the children of Israel.
Materia intrinseca:	The elect proceeding to their heavenly home; Noah, Daniel and Job signifying rulers, continent men and married men, respectively.
Intentio intrinseca:	To encourage us to proceed through the mansions of virtue, passing from one to the other, until we see God in Zion.

The terms *extrinsecus* and *intrinsecus* have moved far beyond their original connotations in the context of a theologian's prologue. In the Psalter-commentaries of Peter of Poitiers and his contemporaries, *extrinsecus* referred to the abstract and more general points about a book which were to be examined, whereas *intrinsecus* referred to those things which should be asked about the book itself. In Langton, the *materia extrinseca* means something like the most obvious subject-matter, while the *intentio extrinseca* denotes the most obvious significance of that subject-matter. On the other hand, the *materia intrinseca* indicates a more profound and mysterious subject-matter, while the *intentio intrinseca* indicates the deep significance thereof.

These observations based on the Numbers-commentary may be confirmed by an examination of commentaries on Exodus and the Twelve Minor Prophets. For Langton, the framework of textual analysis derived from introductions to the *artes* was a means whereby complex contours of allegorical meaning could be traced. His interest was in the rich mosaic of spiritual significance believed to be present in the Old Testament.

In the prologue to the commentary on Exodus, Langton begins with the description given therein of the construction of the tabernacle, a passage which provided many Paris theologians with the introductory

allegories for the prologues to their commentaries. The veil described
at Exodus xxxvi.35 is interpreted as evangelical doctrine, its four pillars as the Four Evangelists[130]. The five pillars of the door are the five
Mosaic books, while its curtain is the Old Law. By the silver bases of
the columns are understood the doctrine of the Old Law, by their middle sections the apostolic doctrine which rests on the Old Law as its
proper foundation, while the golden capitals represent evangelical doctrine 'which is golden because it is edited from the mouth of the
saviour'[131]. The four distinct colours in the trappings represent the
fourfold method of reading Scripture, historically or literally, allegorically, morally or tropologically, and anagogically. Then Langton proceeds to the *modus agendi, materia* and *intentio* of Exodus. In this case,
the first two headings pertain to the literal aspects of the work, while
the *intentio* is indistinguishable from a tropological reading of the text:
in the same way as the children of Israel passed from Egypt into the
promised land, so the Christian ought to relinquish vice and turn himself into a tabernacle of the Lord. The work is written *intus et foris,* and
so it must be read both spiritually and literally.

After the Psalter, the book of the Twelve Minor Prophets was one of
the most difficult Old Testament works to describe in terms of authorship. However, Langton focuses on the extrinsic and intrinsic aspects of
the *materia* and *intentio* of the Minor Prophets with a result which may
be summarised as follows:

Materia extrinseca: The twelve tribes
Intentio extrinseca: To recall the twelve tribes from idolatry
Materia intrinseca: Good and evil men
Intentio intrinseca: To unite men of God.[132]

The emphasis is on the profound cause which impelled the prophets to
write, rather than on the individual prophets themselves[133]. On the
authorship question, little is said beyond the observation that the
writings of the minor prophets are not in the same order today as they
were among the Hebrews.

Much of Hugh of St Cher's prologue-material belongs to the world
of Langton. The 'type C' headings form the basis of the intrinsic discussion in all but two of Hugh's thirty-seven major prologues, the exceptions being the prologues to the commentaries on Mark and Acts,
where the four causes appear[134]. On average, five of the 'type C' head-

ings occur. In the prologues to the Sapiential Books of the Old Testament, Hugh usually adds a third, *cui parti philosophiae supponatur*[135]. The fullest series of terms appears in the prologue to Ecclesiasticus[136].

The *extrinsecus/intrinsecus* distinction occurs throughout Hugh's postils. As in Langton, the distinction refers to spiritual sense and literal sense, respectively. Thus, we read in the prologue to Numbers:

The literal or extrinsic intention of Moses is to narrate in orderly fashion the conduct and progress of the children of Israel from mount Sinai to the plain of Moab. The intrinsic intention is, by the favours shown and by the punishments imposed to excite us to both the love and fear of God. . .[137]

Apart from the greater premium being put on the literal sense, there is little to distinguish this account from Langton's, as discussed above. The prologues to the commentaries on the Twelve Minor Prophets by Langton and Hugh provide a more interesting comparison[138]. Hugh uses *exterior* and *interior* in place of Langton's *extrinsecus* and *intrinsecus*[139]. The terms *extrinsecus* and *intrinsecus* have strayed so far beyond their original functions that they have become redundant and, not unnaturally, they are now dropped from the repertoire.

In many of Hugh's Old Testament prologues appears the figure of the curtain of the tabernacle with its four precious colours which represent the four senses of Scripture[140]. Again one is reminded of Langton[141]. Another recurring feature is the phrase *scriptus intus et foris,* which appears in each of Hugh's first nine Old Testament prologues[142]. Sometimes it appears in conjunction with[143], and sometimes instead of[144], the distinctions *extrinsecus/intrinsecus* and *litteraliter/spiritualiter*. In sum, Hugh's postils are a repository of many of the most characteristic themes and motifs of twelfth-century exegesis. The need to replace, or at least to supplement, Hugh was felt at an early stage, and this may be ascribed to a belief that his exegesis was rather old-fashioned and outmoded[145].

Our comparison of the commentaries of Langton and Hugh has revealed that, even in much of the most sophisticated and highly developed 'twelfth-century-style' exegesis, literary-theoretical idioms were regarded as useful only in so far as they illuminated the meaning hidden deep in the text. The standardised application of 'type C' headings to all the books of the Bible tended to establish the similarities between texts, rather than to provide a basis for discrimination between texts

according to different authorial purposes and different genres of writing. Despite the literary classifications of Scriptural texts provided by
Abelard, Hugh of St Victor and others[146], there was little variation in
the prologue-vocabulary employed to describe the different types of
text. Texts were seen to be very different if considered literally; if considered allegorically, the similarities emerged. The commentators were
more interested in the similarities than in the differences. After all, did
not all the books of the Bible have a single *auctor*, God? The undeniable
fact of the great *auctoritas* of Scripture fostered belief in the indivisible
unity of the Bible. Hence, technical terms derived from the study of
the *artes* were often used to bring out various senses or levels of meaning, rather than the various qualities of individual texts.

It would seem, then, that twelfth-century exegetes were interested
in the *auctor* mainly as a source of *auctoritas:* the human writer of Scripture was important in proportion to the extent to which he had provided (perhaps unwittingly) part of the vast pattern of meaning supposed to lie behind the literal sense of Scripture. It was this pattern
which the exegetes strove to describe, not the individual contribution
of any human *auctor.* Discussions of authorship hurried past personal
factors to discover what riches God, the source of *auctoritas,* had hidden
in the text. The notion of the *auctor* as an agent engaged in literary
activity was submerged; the truth of the Bible was maintained at the
expense of its human contributors.

But the prologues to Hugh of St Cher's commentaries on St Mark
and the Acts of the Apostles, which are elaborated on the four causes of
Aristotle, point the way towards future developments. Aristotelian
epistemology, as interpreted by thirteenth-century scholars, gave the
human faculties and human perception a new dignity; the Scriptural
exegetes of that period afforded the 'body' of Scripture, its literal sense,
a corresponding dignity[147]. Meaning was no longer believed to have
been hidden by God deep in the Biblical text: it was expressed by the
human *auctores* of Scripture, each in his own way or ways. As we shall
see, these new attitudes proved very propitious for the development of
literary theory.

3

Authorial Roles
in the 'Literal Sense'

IN THE MOST CHARACTERISTIC and representative of the Scriptural exegesis produced in the thirteenth and fourteenth centuries, the respective roles of God and man in producing Holy Scripture were described precisely. According to St Thomas Aquinas, God is the sole *auctor* of things and can use things to signify, whereas human *auctores* are *auctores* of words and use words to signify[1]. When things are used significatively in Scripture, allegorical senses arise; when words are used significatively, we have the literal sense[2]. The literal sense was believed to express the intention of the human *auctor*. As St Thomas's teacher Albert the Great put it (writing shortly after 1270), 'the intention of the speaker as expressed in the letter is the literal sense'[3]. In his commentary on Romans, St Thomas rejected those received interpretations which do not pay sufficient attention to the *intentio auctoris* ('this response seems not at all to be in accordance with the intention of the Apostle') but accepted those which keep close to the letter ('this exposition is literal and according to the intention of the Apostle'[4]).

A more rigorous logical method was being applied in the study of the Bible. St Thomas made much of Augustine's remark that an argument can be drawn only from the literal sense of Scripture, and for Thomas, 'argument' in this context meant strictly logical argument, proceeding by means of premiss and syllogism[5]. Allegorical senses which involve significative things, are of no use to the logician, who is confined to the literal sense[6]. 'From the literal sense alone can arguments be drawn, and not from the things said by allegory'[7].

But there are various kinds of literal sense: sometimes, the *auctor* may speak plainly and directly; sometimes, he may employ figurative expressions. All kinds of figurative language, including metaphors, parables and similitudes, involve significative words and are, therefore, part of the literal sense.

Although spiritual things are set forth under the figures of corporeal things, yet those things which are intended by sensible figures to concern spiritual things do not pertain to the mystical sense, but to the literal; because the literal sense is that which is first intended by the words, either speaking properly or figuratively.[8]

As a result, the exegete has the task of sifting the literal sense of the human *auctor,* deciding when his meaning is expressed 'properly speaking' *(proprie dicta)* and when it is expressed figuratively *(figurate)*[9].

The commonplace nature of this approach is indicated by the fact that it was restated in the early fourteenth century by the controversial Nominalist philosopher, William of Ockham (*c.* 1285–1347), who argued that the statements of *auctores* cannot always be taken 'according to the propriety of speech' *(secundum proprietatem sermonis)*[10]. Many figurative expressions were employed by philosophers, by saints and by Scriptural *auctores,* and they are to be found even in everyday speech. According to the grammarians, 'transferences' *(translationes)* from 'proper' to 'improper' speech are made for three reasons: for the sake of metre, as in poetry; for the sake of ornament, as in rhetoric; and for the sake of necessity, either brevity or utility, as in philosophy. In all of these ways, Ockham concludes, 'transferences' occur in Scripture. Unfortunately, many errors originate among the simple-minded who wish to accept all the statements of the *auctores* 'according to the propriety of speech' when they ought to be understood 'in accordance with authorial intention'.

Because of such procedures as these, the fact of the divine inspiration of Scripture no longer interfered with thorough examination of the literary issues involved. The roles played by the human *auctores,* and the literary forms and devices which they had employed in their works, were established as features of the literal sense, as facets of their personal purposes in writing. The ideas concerning literary style and structure which emerged from theologians' discussions of 'formal causes' will be considered in the following chapter. Our present chapter has as its subject their discussions of the inspired authors as 'efficient causes'.

At the outset, something must be said about the impact of the Aristotelian 'four causes' on Scriptural exegesis, with particular reference to the 'efficient cause'. It will be argued that the Aristotelian theory of causality helped to bring about a new awareness of the integrity of the individual human *auctor*. We shall then turn our attention to the connection between the individuality of the human *auctor* and the 'literal sense' which he was supposed to express. In particular, the influence of Jewish scholarship, which emphasised the 'literal sense' of Scripture, encouraged a more precise discrimination between the inspired authors. The major exegetes of the thirteenth and early fourteenth centuries, it would seem, were not prepared to submerge their *auctores* in the amorphous ocean of *auctoritas*. This is borne out by our examination of the way in which these new attitudes to authorship resulted in a transformation of exegesis of the Psalter—one of the Scriptural texts which, as was suggested in the previous chapter, medieval theologians found particularly difficult to describe in terms of authorial role and literary form.

All these ideological and procedural changes having been illustrated, we shall be able to analyse in more depth the diverse authorial roles and functions that were then being found in the literal sense of Scripture. These roles seem to fall into two main groups, in accordance with two types of personal activity which (in the opinion of the commentators) the human *auctores* had practised, namely, their individual literary activity and their individual moral activity.

The late-medieval interest in the individuality of the human *auctor* extended to pagan *auctores*. Writers from both camps, the Scriptural and the secular, were being credited with comparable literary and moral achievements. Moreover, Old Testament *auctores* and pagan *auctores* were held to possess comparable degrees of *auctoritas* in common subject-areas. The final section of this chapter, therefore, will consider the extent to which the new attitudes to authorship contributed to a general reconciliation, within late-medieval scholarship, of sacred and profane *auctores*.

THE HUMAN *AUCTOR* AS EFFICIENT CAUSE

The single most important impulse behind the new conceptions of authorial role and literary form was the new method of thinking and techniques of study which late-medieval scholars derived from Aristotle. Among many other influences and implications, commentators were encouraged to adopt and develop a prologue based on Aristotelian theories of causality.

The technical philosophical details of these theories were worked out in generations of commentaries on Aristotle's *Physica* and *Metaphysica*. For example, in expounding the *Metaphysica* (after 1270) Albert the Great had contrasted 'certain ones who said there were five kinds of causes' with others who believe in only four causes[11]. It would appear that he regarded 'Plato and his followers' (perhaps including Avicenna) as the thinkers who had arrived at a five-fold division of causes by distinguishing between an 'efficient cause' of being and a 'moving cause' of generation and change. The partisans of the four-cause theory were identified as 'Aristotelians' for, according to Albert, Aristotle did not posit an efficient cause that was not also a moving cause and, therefore, maintained that there were four main causes: the efficient and moving cause, the material cause, the formal cause and the final cause. Albert seems to have considered himself to be a member of the latter camp, for he is quite consistent in identifying the efficient cause with the moving cause.

This was the view which had won wide acceptance. The four causes as explained by Aristotle provided the paradigm for the 'Aristotelian prologue' to commentaries on *auctores*. Between 1235 and 1245, it became popular among lecturers in the arts faculty at the University of Paris. For example, in 'Master Jordan's' commentary on *Priscianus minor* (written *c*. 1245), Priscian's *modus agendi* and the form in which his materials were arranged were described as two aspects of a single thing, the formal cause *(causa formalis)*:

The formal cause of this science is the form of treatment and the form of the treatise. The form of treatment is the mode of proceeding which is principally definitive, divisive, probative, improbative, and applies examples; the form of the treatise is the form of the thing produced which consists in the separation of books and of chapters and the order thereof.[12]

The efficient cause *(causa efficiens)* had two aspects also, the external *(extra)* and the internal *(intra)*. The external efficient cause was identified with the author, as in the logical commentaries of Robert Kilwardby, who lectured in the Parisian arts faculty (*c*. 1237–*c*. 1245) before his entry into the Dominican Order. In expounding the *Isagoge,* Kilwardby remarks, 'concerning the efficient cause which is altogether external, much solicitude need not be taken'[13]. Similar comments are found at the beginnings of his commentaries on Aristotle's *Praedicamenta* and *Peri hermeneias,* the anonymous *Liber sex principiorum* and

Boethius's *Liber divisionum*[14]. In an anonymous commentary on the *Praedicamenta,* the internal efficient cause is identified with the internal formal cause and the internal final cause, on the authority of a passage in Aristotle's *Physica:*

The external efficient cause of this book, which is first within the whole of logic, was Aristotle. The internal efficient cause is the same as the internal final cause and formal cause, according to what Aristotle says in the *Physics,* that three causes coincide in one.[15]

In this anonymous commentary, the external final cause is in its turn divided into the immediate cause *(causa propinqua)* and the remote cause *(causa remota):*

The external final cause is twofold, namely immediate and remote. The immediate cause is to know the predicaments; the remote cause is demonstration and those things which avail for demonstration like definition and division.

The immediate cause was the specific didactic aim of the text, while the remote cause was the more general way in which it could instruct and improve the human mind, as is made clear by the description of the final cause of Aristotle's *Topica* provided by a master 'Elyas' who may be the Dominican Elias Brunetti:

The final cause is double, internal and external. The internal is the same as the form; the external is twofold, namely immediate and remote. The immediate cause is artificially to construct syllogisms concerning both parts of a problem; the remote cause is the whole of philosophy, and as a result the perfection of the rational soul by virtue, for which science finally exists.[16]

These attempts to impose dichotomies on the efficient and final causes probably reflect the continuing influence of the *extrinsecus/intrinsecus* distinction[17].

The prologues of *artistae* usually began with a discussion of the material cause, their main interest being in comprehensive definition, subdivision and analysis of the subject-matter[18]. The efficient cause was usually discussed last, receiving cursory treatment. After the *auctor* of one's textbook had been identified as Priscian, Aristotle or whoever else, there seemed to be little more to say. A concomitant of this was that, while the *artistae* were very concerned with the formal cause of the science in question (in particular, with its proper modes of procedure and the correct order of study), they paid little attention to the specific formal cause which the *auctor,* in writing his book, had brought into being[19]. By contrast, the theologians—because they were dealing with divinely-inspired texts—had a special interest in the efficient and formal causes of the books of the Bible, and adapted the 'Aristotelian prologue' accordingly. As we shall see, this resulted in discussions of authorial role and literary form which possess a degree of complexity and sophistication not found in prologues to the textbooks of the arts faculty, works which had been produced by merely human agency.

Between 1223 and 1227, the Franciscan Alexander of Hales had substituted Peter Lombard's *Libri sententiarum* for the Bible in his lectures in the Parisian faculty of theology[20]. The four causes are not invoked in the prologue to his *Sentences* commentary[21]; neither do they appear at the beginning of his commentary on St John's gospel (written before 1236)[22]. However, the influence of artists' discussion of the four causes is manifest in Alexander's later *Summa theologiae,* completed by his disciples after his death in 1245 (see pp. 119 *et seq.*).

In the first *Sentences* commentary to issue from Oxford (c. 1241–8), the Dominican, Richard Fishacre, distinguished between the diverse instrumental efficient causes of theology, namely, its human *auctores,* and its principal efficient cause, namely, God[23].

Although therefore some part of sacred Scripture seems to have been written by Moses, and similarly some part by the prophets, some by the Evangelists, and some by the Apostles, yet not they themselves but God both wrote and spoke by them, as the principal efficient cause by the instrument.[24]

A similar distinction is found in Robert Kilwardby's *Sentences* commentary (written sometime between 1248 and 1261), which has a much more elaborate introduction. The framework of Kilwardby's Aristotelian prologue' is as follows:

'Wisdom has built her house, she has set up her seven pillars'. [Proverbs ix. 1] In these words can be considered the four causes of this doctrine and indeed of the whole of sacred Scripture. The efficient cause, by the name 'wisdom' . . . The material cause is indicated in the signification of the statement. For in the name 'wisdom' the material or subject of the first book of *Sentences* is intimated . . . The formal cause for its part is obvious from the order of the words in the foresaid authoritative statement. The order of the books also is according to the order of the words . . . The final cause can in a certain manner be considered in that it is said, 'has built her house'.[25]

As has already been mentioned, the 'Aristotelian prologue' made its appearance in Scriptural exegesis in the commentaries on St Mark and the Acts of the Apostles which Hugh of St Cher produced at St Jacques,

Paris, between 1230 and 1236. St Mark's gospel is described as a summary of what was said more fully in St Matthew's gospel; in his first nine chapters Mark employed an abbreviating style (*modus abbreviationis*). Then, the 'introductory causes' are explained:

The efficient cause is Mark himself, or the grace of God, or the request of the disciples of Peter, on whose petition the Evangelist wrote, as Peter confirmed. . . . The material cause is Christ and his works. The formal cause or the mode of treatment has few words but many profundities. The final cause is indicated by John xx.[31], where it is said, 'these things are written that you may believe, and that believing you may have life'.[26]

Hugh's younger contemporary, Guerric of St Quentin (who held the second chair of theology at St Jacques between 1233 and 1242), was perhaps the first exegete to apply the four causes in exegesis of the Old Testament[27]. Guerric began his commentary on Isaiah by quoting Ecclesiasticus xlviii.27, 'in the power of the spirit he saw the last things, he comforted the mourners of Zion'. Here one may perceive the text's two levels of authorship, the human and the divine, which Guerric describes as the 'twofold efficient cause' (*duplex causa efficiens*):

The efficient cause is twofold, namely moving and operating. The operating cause is Isaiah, which is understood by the supposition of this word, 'he saw'. But there is also a cause which is efficient and not operating, which is noted here: 'by the spirit', namely by the Holy Spirit, which moved Isaiah that he should write. The Holy Spirit itself did not write, which is noted in that it says 'by the spirit'.[28]

In other words, the Holy Spirit may be regarded as the 'moving' efficient cause which motivated the 'operating' efficient cause, namely the prophet Isaiah, to write.

This idea of the *duplex causa efficiens* became popular as a useful formula for summary description of the inspired authorship of Biblical texts. God was regarded as the first *auctor* or the unmoved mover of such a book, whereas the human *auctor* was both moved (by God) and moving (in producing the text). This is the point made in prologues to the Psalter and the Apocalypse wrongly ascribed to Albert the Great:

From these statements it is clear what are the efficient causes of this book, because the cause which is moving and not moved is the holy Spirit, while the cause which is moving and moved is David himself.[29]

The efficient cause which is moving and not moved was the entire Trinity, revealing to Christ the man . . . The cause moving and moved was the man Christ, and the angel, and John.[30]

The same basic distinction between types of efficient cause occurs, for example, in the Psalter-commentaries of Nicholas Gorran (written in the period 1263–85) and Nicholas of Lyre[31].

Human feelings and emotions could also play a part in this causal system. In the prologue to his commentary on Romans, St Thomas Aquinas analysed the emotions of fear and love as possible motivating forces[32]. What did St Paul mean when he described himself as a servant (*servus*) of Jesus Christ (Romans i. 1)? Whoever is the cause of his own actions is free; whoever is another's cause, in the sense of being directed by another, is a servant. But there are two kinds of servitude, the servitude of fear and the servitude of love. The servitude of fear forces a man to act against his will; on the other hand, if someone acts as another's cause in accordance with a chosen end or objective, this is the servitude of love. As 'the philosopher' (Aristotle) says in his *Ethica* concerning friendship, one should benefit a friend and submit oneself to him on his account. It would seem, then, that there was nothing abject or degrading in St Paul's role as a servant of Christ, since he served out of love and in accordance with his final end.

The idea of complex motivation also comes out in the heading 'causes moving to write' (*causae moventes ad scribendum*), a heading which could designate some or all of the four causes, or a causal system in which the four causes were said to play a major part. In his commentary on Peter Lombard's prologue to the *Libri sententiarum* (written *c.* 1245–50), St Albert the Great distinguished between the *auctor* and the *causae moventes* (final cause, material cause and formal cause) which moved the *auctor* to write[33]. When analysing the same prologue, St Thomas Aquinas provided a similar explanation of the *causae moventes*[34]. Writing much later (*c.* 1332), the Oxford Dominican, Thomas Waleys, divided the efficient cause of *De civitate Dei* into the *causa effectiva librorum* and the *causa movens ad scribendum*[35]. The first is St Augustine, the second consists of the saint's personal reasons for writing, what he hoped to achieve in his work.

Other texts were believed to have had an even more complex motivation and, in these cases, commentators were not content to speak of a merely double *causa efficiens*. In his commentary on St Luke's Gospel (written between 1254 and 1257), the great Franciscan theologian, St Bonaventure, defined a triple efficient cause (*triplex causa efficiens*): the Holy Spirit, divine grace and the evangelist.

And so in this work there was a triple efficient cause, namely the supreme, which is the person of the Holy Spirit; the lowest, the evangelist himself; and the intermediate, namely the grace of the Holy Spirit . . .[36]

The Paris Dominican, Nicholas Gorran, and the Cambridge Dominican, John Russel (a little-known theologian who flourished at the turn of the thirteenth century) believed that a quadruple efficient cause *(quadruplex causa efficiens)* was at work in the Apocalypse: God, Christ, the angel who visited St John on Patmos, and St John himself[37]. Here is Russel's version:

Indeed, the efficient cause is quadruple in this book, namely God, Christ, the angel and John. God is the principal and primary efficient cause; Christ, the secondary; the angel, the mediate; and John, the immediate . . .[38]

The element of comparison suggested by these accounts of double, treble and quadruple efficient causality is important in so far as it manifests the exegetes' belief in the essential unity and rapport of the roles of God and man in the production of Scripture. But the element of distinction also suggested therein is far more important from our point of view. Discrimination between the primary efficient cause and the secondary or instrumental efficient causes meant that all contributors to Scripture, both divine and human, received due attention, with important consequences for the development of literary theory. These two elements will now be considered in turn.

Late medieval theologians, of course, accepted unquestioningly the fact of the divine authorship of the Bible, a fact which guaranteed its authority. As St Bonaventure put it in his commentary on the *Sentences,* if we wish to prove that the human *auctores* of Scripture told the truth, the short answer is that we know this to be the case because the Holy Spirit inspired them[39]. It is the faith which the *auctores* received from God which makes their writings authentic. In one of the ordinary disputations which he held at Paris between 1276 and 1292, Henry of Ghent made the same point by reference to artistic skills[40]. Where there is a craftsman *(artifex)* who directs and guides a work and another who works with his hands in accordance with rules conveyed from the craftsman, the latter is not said to be the *auctor* of the work but rather the former. Similarly, although the science of theology is described by men, it is directed and guided by God, who alone can properly be called its *auctor*. The *auctoritas* of this science is reducible to divine *auctoritas;* its sole source was God. By contrast, philosophy, which in its first invention involved the cooperation of human ingenuity, is, to that extent, fallible.

Similar confirmations of authority are found in the prologues of the Bible-commentators. For example, Albert the Great distinguished between the human *auctor* and the *auctoritas* of the Book of Baruch:

> Psalm cxvii. 26, 'Blessed is he who comes in the name of the Lord'. In this statement the author and the cause of the following work is demonstrated, and the authority of this Scripture. The author, because the 'blessed' man may be interpreted as Baruch . . . The authority of the Scripture is noted in that it is said, 'in the name of the Lord'. For a name is applied from knowledge, and knowledge of God, who is truth alone, supplies the authority of the words. For the authority [of the Book of Baruch] is revelation, and revelation is the most firm foundation which is to be had.[41]

The human *auctor* of the text is Baruch, but its *auctoritas* came from God. In a commentary on St John's Gospel attributed to Albert, God is designated as the 'interior' *auctor* while the human writer is the 'exterior' *auctor*[42]. From the former derives the authenticity of the text; from the latter derives its fidelity. Giles of Rome went so far as to remark that it was superstitious to inquire about the human *auctor* of Scriptural text when one knew very well that its *auctoritas* was vouched for by the God who had inspired His instrumental causes to write (see p. 38).

But, by the same token, the great *auctoritas* of Scripture could be taken for granted, and this is precisely what happened in many late-medieval prologues to Biblical commentaries. God was invoked as ultimately being responsible for all that was written in Scripture because He was its primary efficient cause. The point required little elaboration or substantiation. In the world of the 'Aristotelian prologue', the divine omnipotence no longer interfered with the integrity of the human *auctor*.

The Aristotelian theory of causality, as interpreted by many late-medieval scholars, made careful provision for the integrity of instrumental efficient causes. God was the first mover or primary efficient cause, who moved inferior causes from potentiality to act. The primary efficient cause divulged power to instrumental efficient causes, each of which set in motion those parts of creation which were under its jurisdiction.

Truly, mediate causes between the primary efficient cause and the ultimate effect have purposes (*intentiones*) proper to them, as is the case with intelligences and celestial bodies and corruptible corporeal agents . . .[43]

This statement by Robert Grosseteste (Bishop of Lincoln 1235–53) concerns the movement of the heavens, but the general principle contained therein was so fundamental to thirteenth-century Aristotelian science that it is relevant to the literary theory which this science fostered. The intermediate causes were allowed a certain amount of individual power; they were not mere cogs in a smoothly-running divine machine[44]. In the same way an *auctor* of Scripture, being a cause which existed between the first efficient cause (God) and the effect (the text), was granted his personal purpose.

A similar conclusion emerges from an examination of the relevant passages in the *Summa theologiae* of St Thomas Aquinas. There is a unique first cause of all things, to be identified with God; its activity is the universal cause of all other activity. But, Aquinas assures us, this is not to deny a measure of independence and individuality to created things: on the contrary, each thing has its proper and inalienable operation.

If the active powers that are observed in creatures accomplished nothing, there would be no point to their having received such powers. Indeed, if all creatures are utterly devoid of any activity of their own, then they themselves would seem to have a pointless existence, since everything exists for the sake of its operation.[45]

But what happens to these proper operations when creatures are brought under the direct control of the first cause, thereby becoming divine tools or instruments? The status of the instrumental efficient cause, as understood by Aquinas, is well summed up by T. Gilby:

Instrumental secondary causes act in virtue of a causality passing through them from a higher principal cause, and produce an effect of an order higher than their own proper order: a man is the instrumental secondary cause of a miracle.[46]

In Biblical inspiration, God inspires an *auctor* to write with a sublimity which far exceeds his normal powers. But this does not mean that the normal powers of the human instrument are thereby either destroyed or disregarded. As Aquinas says, when discussing the causes of the sacraments, an instrumental cause has two actions[47]. First, there is its instrumental action, according to which it acts not by any virtue of its own but by virtue of the principal agent of which it is an instrument. Then there is its proper action, which was fully taken into account by the superior agent who sought to utilise this property. Hence, the water of baptism, which washes the body according to its proper operation, also washes the soul in so far as it is an instrument of the divine power. Applying this theory to Biblical inspiration, it would seem that a writer's diverse talents are presupposed and exploited by God. As a result, the differences between the personalities and the various *modi agendi* of the human *auctores* of Scripture can be fully recognized. Peter is not Paul; neither are they alike in style. Moreover, a single *auctor* can express himself in different ways in different books, as was the case with Solomon and St John.

From all this it would appear that the influence of Aristotle's theory of causality as understood by late-medieval schoolmen helped to bring about a new awareness of the integrity of the individual human *auctor*. Henceforth each and every inspired writer would be given credit for his personal literary contribution. Different levels of authorship had been identified: the efficient cause could be double, triple or quadruple, depending on the particular causal process. Different types of motivation had been recognised: personal reasons could have played a significant part, working in harmony with the crucial (but rarely overbearing) factor of divine direction.

The impression we have gained from the sources cited above, of a change of attitude to the human *auctor* of Scripture, seems to be confirmed by the material brought together in the following section, which attempts to illuminate the relationship between the individual human *auctor* and his intended meaning, i.e. the 'literal sense' of holy writ. The way in which two highly articulate commentators, Nicholas Trevet and Nicholas of Lyre, justified their use of literalistic Jewish exegesis will make abundantly clear the high value which was being placed on the literal sense as the expression of the human *auctor*. Then, in the Psalter exegesis provided by these scholars and by a distinguished predecessor who influenced them considerably, Thomas Aquinas, we shall see, as it were, the new attitude in action, producing new solutions to old problems concerning the literary form of the Psalter and the authorship of the various psalms.

THE 'LITERAL SENSE' OF THE HUMAN *AUCTOR*

With the decline of interest in the allegorical senses of Scripture corresponded an increase of interest in a Jewish tradition of exegesis which emphasised the importance of the literal sense. In general, it was believed that the Jews did not fully understand the Old Testament, that their understanding of it was limited to the literal sense; Christian exegetes accepted their learning on these conditions[48]. The thirteenth century was the age of the expert[49], and the 'Hebrew doctors' were believed to possess a considerable, if limited, expertise.

By the early fourteenth century, Hebrew studies were firmly established as an essential part of exegesis[50]. Nicholas Trevet, the greatest scholar among the English 'classicising friars' of the early fourteenth century, broke with convention in writing a commentary (completed between 1317 and 1320) on Jerome's Hebraica instead of his Gallican Psalter; herein, constant reference is made to the new translation which Grosseteste had made from the Hebrew[51]. The dedicatory letter to John of Bristol which is prefixed to Trevet's Psalter-commentary castigates, as two extremes, excessive allegorical interpretation on the one hand and, on the other, that pernicious Jewish literalism which denies Christ[52]. The ancient commentators, Trevet claims, concentrated on the profound mysteries found in allegories and, as a result, they rejected or treated perfunctorily the literal sense, in the mistaken belief that they were throwing away the rind and securing the sweet kernel. Now, the blessing of his Provincial is sought for a commentary which concentrates on the solid base of the letter and provides an historical and literal exposition. Trevet assures John of Bristol that his use of Jewish learning has not led him into error: he has studiously avoided those 'Jewish fables' which treacherously exclude Christ from their understanding of Scripture.

Trevet then affirms that he is concerned with whatever offers itself as being from the primary intention *(prima intentio)* of the words of the *auctor,* and with 'what kind of foundation the holy Ghost, speaking through the mouth of the author, first laid for the mystical senses'[53]. The literal sense, it would seem, is the expression of the *prima intentio;* it was provided by the inspired human *auctor,* while the mystical senses were the work of the Holy Spirit. Considered as a whole, Trevet's

Psalter-commentary manifests the conviction that the Jews were, and are, adept at expounding the words of the human *auctor*, even though they fail to grasp the spiritual significance intended by the divine *auctor*.

Nicholas of Lyre (*c.* 1270–1340), widely regarded as the best-equipped Biblical scholar of the Middle Ages, made more extensive use of rabbinic tradition in general and of the opinions of Rashi in particular[54]. The second prologue to his *Postilla litteralis* on the whole Bible (completed 1331) stresses the importance of the literal sense, and justifies his use of Jewish exegesis in explaining it[55]. Lyre complains that the *sensus litteralis*, the foundation of all the other senses of Scripture, has been much obscured. This is partly the fault of scribes, who corrupt the text, and partly the fault of would-be correctors, who do not place punctuation marks where Lyre thinks they should be. Then, he raises the problem that Latin often does not translate the Hebrew idioms as well as one would wish. Jerome advocated the use of Hebrew codices in order to gain an accurate literal sense, but Lyre complains that this advice has fallen on deaf ears.

Another kind of obscurantism is then discussed, that practised by previous generations of Christian commentators. Although the *antiqui* said many good things, they spent little time on the literal sense but multiplied the spiritual senses to such an extent that the literal sense was partly suffocated. Lyre, therefore, proposes to concentrate on the literal sense, only occasionally inserting short spiritual expositions. He intends to explain the literal sense, not only with the help of the opinions of the Catholic doctors but also with reference to the opinions of the Jews.

With the exegetes' two major new interests in mind—the human *auctor* as efficient cause and the literal sense as the personal meaning of the human *auctor*—we may proceed to examine the way in which interpretation of the Psalter was transformed in the thirteenth and fourteenth centuries. The attitudes and approaches of Thomas Aquinas, Nicholas of Lyre and Nicholas Trevet often contrast strikingly with those of the twelfth-century commentators discussed in our previous chapter.

In the Psalter-commentary of Aquinas, written at Naples 1272–3, there is little left of the old *extrinsecus* headings:

Three things in general are to be considered. The first is the translation of this work. The second is the method of expounding it. The third is its distinction.[56]

The last of these headings is a variant of the *causa distinctionis,* but Aquinas sought a principle of division which works at the literal level and not at the allegorical[57]. The one hundred and fifty psalms which comprise the Psalter do not follow the chronology of history, but in so far as some of them touch on historical events, they can be compared and related accordingly. For St Thomas, the basic order or structure of the Psalter consisted in relationships existing between the various psalms understood in their literal sense: although he did briefly paraphrase an account of number-symbolism from the *Glossa ordinaria,* he was not interested in systematically pursuing an underlying and mystical principle of structure[58]. Moreover, whereas twelfth-century exegetes had, through allegorical interpretation, emphasised the similarities between the various books of the Bible, Aquinas was very aware of their differences. There is a multiform mode or *forma* in Holy Scripture, he claims[59]. The narrative mode is found in the historical books; the admonitory, exhortative and preceptive mode in the books of the Law and the prophets and in Solomon's books; the disputative mode, in Job and in the Apostle Paul. But the deprecative or praising mode is used in the Psalter: although other modes are found in other books, the Psalter has a special *modus agendi* which consists of the mode of praise and oration *(modus laudis et orationis).*

The headings 'translation of this work' *(translatio huius operis)* and 'mode of exposition' *(modus exponendi)* are new, and indicate new interests. Under the former, Aquinas provides a short account of the three translations made by St Jerome, the Roman Psalter, the Gallican Psalter and the Hebraica. The Gallican Psalter is the basis of Aquinas's commentary, while constant recourse is made to the Hebraica which, he declares, 'is used by many' although it is not employed in the liturgy. Under the latter heading, an orthodox literalism is advocated, the errors of Theodore of Mopsuestia being singled out for special censure. St Thomas's concern for the literal sense intended by the human *auctor* (which has been discussed above) here extends to include the intentions of the translator and the commentators who follow in the author's footsteps. This concern was shared by the Psalter-commentators who followed Aquinas, notably Nicholas Trevet and Henry Cossey (regent master at Cambridge *c.* 1325–6), both of whom discuss the translation of the Psalter and the correct method of expounding it[60].

For Aquinas, the case of Theodore of Mopsuestia epitomised the problems faced by commentators who wished to provide a literal in-

terpretation of the Psalter. Aquinas believed that Theodore, in rejecting the Christological interpretation of the Old Testament, had
claimed that therein nothing had expressly been said about Christ: the
writers in question were speaking of other things, though it was possible to adapt their statements to apply to Christ[61]. St Thomas cites, as
an example of this error, Psalm xxi.18, 'They divide my garments
among them', which according to Theodore does not refer to Christ but
was literally said about David. This method of exegesis was condemned
by 'the Fifth Synod' (the Council of Constantinople in 553); whoever
follows it is a heretic.

St Thomas sought his solution in a development of St Jerome's
theory of prefiguration: the psalms at once designate events which were
actual to the psalmist (res gestae) and prefigure or foreshadow various
things concerning Christ or the Church[62]. As St Paul says in I Corinthians x. 11, 'all these things concern us in figure'. When the prophets
spoke of events which occurred in their day, they were writing, principally, not about these events themselves but in so far as they were
figurae of future and fulfilling events. The Holy Spirit ordained that, in
speaking of things which were contemporaneous to them, they added
certain features which transcended the immediate historical context,
thereby encouraging the soul to rise to a Christological understanding[63]. Therefore, in the Psalter, we read certain things concerning the
reign of David and Solomon which were simply not implemented in
that historical period, but which were to be implemented in the reign
of Christ, in figure of whom they were written. Psalm lxxi provides a
good example. According to its title, Aquinas explains, it concerns the
reign of David and Solomon. Yet it includes references to things ex-
ceeding the capability of those men: 'In his days may righteousness
flourish, and peace abound, till the moon be no more' (verse 7), and
'May he have dominion from sea to sea, and from the river to the ends
of the earth' (verse 8). Aquinas concludes that this psalm is to be expounded of the reign of Solomon, in so far as he is a figura of Christ the
King, in whom all the things here stated will be completed and
fulfilled.

Erich Auerbach has discovered in 'figural' mimesis a means whereby
the concrete particulars of Old Testament history could be preserved,
even while the spiritual significance which it carried was manifest. In
the process of foreshadowing and fulfilment, the historical reality of

both the foreshadowing type (the Old Testament character or event) and the fulfilling type (its New Testament counterpart) were accommodated.

Figura is something real and historical which announces something else that is also real and historical. . . . Real historical figures are to be interpreted spiritually . . . , but the interpretation points to a carnal, hence historical, fulfilment—for the truth has become history in flesh.[64]

These remarks certainly apply to St Thomas's exposition of the psalms. His theory of prefiguration provides the occasion for comprehensive retailing of much *historia David,* history concerning the life and times of David and his people.

This quest for an orthodox literalism helps to explain the peculiar blend of tradition and originality in St Thomas's commentary. If Psalm xxi must be interpreted as designating Christ in its literal sense, other psalms are literally about the personal achievements and tribulations, the virtues and the vices, of King David. Understood literally, Psalm vii tells how David felt when he fled from the face of his son Absalom (cf. II Kings xvii); Psalm viii indicates David's special devotion to the 'feast of weeks' (cf. Deuteronomy xvi); Psalm ix records David's thanksgiving on being delivered from Absalom (cf. II Kings xviii–xxix), and so on[65]. The second part of the second decade of psalms fits into the period in which, after Saul's death, David became King, while Psalm l tells of David's repentance for his two great sins, the adultery with Bathsheba and the murder of her husband Uriah[66].

Such literal expositions are balanced by extensive figural interpretations, and by the occasional moralisation from the *Glossa ordinaria.* The following schemata are applied in glossing Psalms x and xx respectively:

This psalm can be expounded literally of David, but mystically or allegorically of Christ. But morally it can be interpreted of the just man and heretics, as the *Glossa* expounds it.[67]
This Psalm is related of Christ who is 'the king' and David who was his figure, and therefore it can be expounded of both: of Christ according to truth, of David according to figure.[68]

Sometimes Aquinas will declare his preference for the figural aspect: for example, because Psalm xxxix speaks in the person of the Church, it is better understood as referring to mankind awaiting the grace of the New Testament[69]. But in general he seems to want to reduce the amount of allegorical interpretation. Peter Lombard had claimed that Psalm xxvii treats briefly of the passion and resurrection of Christ[70]. In St Thomas's gloss the stress is rather on the fact that, according to 'the letter', certain psalms relate to the person of David, and this is one of them[71].

On some occasions, Aquinas's awareness of the humanity of the psalmist extends to an interest in the rhetorical style of his orations. The Psalter has as its special *modus agendi* the 'mode of praise and oration', and this may be analysed with the help of Ciceronian oratory[72]. David composed his work in the *modus orantis,* which does not follow a single method but adapts itself to the diverse dispositions *(affectus)* and motions. Therefore, the first psalm expresses the disposition of the man raising his eyes to the whole state of the world, and considering the way in which some advance while others fail; the tenth psalm is spoken in the person of a man desiring the benefits of God and the security which they bring, and so on[73]. Elsewhere, the continuing influence of twelfth-century exegesis is manifest, as when, for example, the *persona* in question is the mystical body of Christ, head and members[74].

But the most conservative facet of St Thomas's exegesis surely must be his championship of the theory that David was the single *auctor* of all the psalms. Asaph, Itamar, Idithun and the others recited the psalms, but the credit must go to the poet and not to the reciter[75]. The stock allegorical interpretations of the names in the *tituli psalmorum* are briefly reiterated[76]. It would appear, then, that St Thomas was prepared to follow St Jerome, whom he admired so much, only part of the way.

Nicholas Trevet went much further, by reiterating the possibility that certain psalms were the work of writers other than David. In the discussion of the efficient cause of the Psalter provided in his prologue, we are informed that David composed either every psalm (according to Augustine) or at least the greater part of them (according to the Jews)[77]. When expounding the *titulus* of Psalm xxviii, which cites the sons of Core, Trevet suggests that this poem could pertain to these men in one of four different ways, 'either because they were the authors of the psalm, or because they were the subject of the psalm, or because this psalm was allotted to be sung by one of them, or because it concerned them in some manner'[78]. Trevet constantly refers back to this account when analysing the other psalm-titles which refer to the sons of

Core. Asaph is afforded similar treatment: Psalm xlix is described as the first psalm in which this personage is represented, indicating that either he was its *auctor* or he had the task of singing it[79].

However, Nicholas of Lyre, who was indebted to Aquinas for many of his basic theological ideas, went all the way; indeed, one could say that he went the second mile. The magnificent 'Aristotelian prologue' to his Psalter-commentary constitutes one of the major landmarks of late-medieval discussion of authorial role[80]. Lyre's concern was with the 'mind of the prophet' *(mens prophetae)*, the inspired mind of David. Whereas twelfth-century commentators had devoted much space to the 'kind of prophecy' *(genus prophecie)* which God had granted to David, Lyre believed that the prophet had a mind of his own: when God uses human beings as instruments, He must make use of the mental equipment which men actually have. Divine inspiration works on and through the human *mens*. The man who sees visions or dreams dreams is now much more than a mere 'sleeping partner' of God.

But Lyre was careful to make it clear that his distinction between the two efficient causes of the Psalter does not imply any disharmony between the intentions of the two *auctores*. In the act of divine inspiration, the mind of God and the mind of man concur.

In the act of prophesying, God (touching or elevating the mind of the prophet to supernatural knowledge) and the mind of the prophet (touched or illuminated in this way), concur. It is necessary that the moving action and the thing moved should coincide . . . God concurs as the principal agent, and the mind of the prophet as the instrumental agent.

God revealed the mysteries which are contained in the Psalter, and David expressed them. Or did he? Certainly this was the opinion of St Augustine, but St Jerome thought otherwise. According to Jerome, Hilary and the 'Hebrew doctors', David did not compose all the psalms, though he was certainly responsible for many of them. Jerome named no less than ten *auctores:* David, Moses, Solomon, the three sons of Core, Asaph, Etham, Heman and Idithun. He also suggested that there were others whose names have been lost to us. Some names have been preserved in the *tituli psalmorum,* but certain psalms are without titles, while others have titles which do not give the authors' names. 'Rabbi Solomon' agrees with Jerome that there were ten *auctores* involved, but his list is not identical with Jerome's: Melchisedec, Abraham, Moses, David, Solomon, Asaph, the three sons of Core and

Idithun. Lyre was concerned to give each contributor to the Psalter his due and, where authorities differed concerning the names of the *auctores*, he recorded the differing opinions, lest a name be lost. The opinions of the 'Hebrew doctors', functioning within the framework of the Aristotelian causes, encourage an emphasis on the identity of individual *auctores*.

Lyre also discusses Esdras, the person responsible for the form of the Psalter as we now have it[81]. Much weight is given to the view of Jerome that Esdras, scribe and prophet, or perhaps some other holy prophet, collected the psalms together and placed them in a single book. Lyre points out that the fact that Esdras collected psalms 'made by diverse people' does not make him the human *auctor* or instrumental efficient cause of the book: Esdras engaged in a literary activity which was different in kind from David's.

The psalms made by David and others were collected and assembled in one book, which is called the book of psalms: and this was done by Esdras the scribe and prophet, or by some other holy prophet, as Jerome says . . . But it is commonly held by our doctors, that Esdras, who recovered the law burnt by the Chaldeans, assembled the psalms made by diverse people in this volume. However, he is not called the author or instrumental efficient cause of the book, but rather David himself, who made the major part of the psalms.

A whole takes its name from the major part, and David wrote most of the psalms: therefore we may speak of 'the psalms of David', fully aware that there were other *auctores* involved. Esdras, the *collector*, provided the first psalm as the prologue to his collection. Lyre has distinguished between the individual *auctores* of the psalms and also between two kinds of literary activity involved in the production of the Psalter. The activity of an *auctor* is different from that of a *collector*.

The measure of autonomy which the Aristotelian efficient cause has provided here for the human contributors to the Psalter may be better understood if it is related to the other causes which, together with the efficient cause, comprised the analytical framework of the 'Aristotelian prologue'. The distinctions which (according to late-medieval scholars) Aristotle had posited between the four causes were of course reflected in the prologues which commentators elaborated around the causes. In his commentary on the *Metaphysica*, Aquinas explained that the final cause is the goal or end (*finis*) of every process and motion: the goal of motion is something sought for outside 'the thing moved'[82]. These ideas being applied in literary analysis, 'the thing moved', the text, was considered apart from the terminus of motion, the final cause. Because the ultimate reason 'for the sake of which' the text came into existence was thereby regarded as a distinct though related aspect of analysis, the allegorical justification which had permeated the typical twelfth-century type of analysis was, as it were, channelled away from the discussion introduced by the other headings. The exact differentiation between causes which was a requirement of Aristotelian science encouraged exact differentiation between the *auctor, materia, modus agendi* and *utilitas,* within the prologue which this science fostered.

For example, in the prologue to his Psalter-commentary, Aquinas stated that the end *(finis)* of the text is oration, which he defined as the 'elevation of the mind in God', then proceeded to discuss four ways in which the soul may be raised in God[83]. Nicholas of Lyre explained that man is 'ordained to a certain supernatural end' and that, in the pursuit of this goal, he must be helped by the revealed truth which is expressed in Scripture[84]. The Psalter expresses, 'by the mode of praise', truths which are expressed in other ways in other parts of Scripture, and so it has great utility *(utilitas)* in the inculcation of hope and the pursuit of this final goal. Such ultimate justifications of the Psalter, as aspects of the final cause, no longer impinge on the discussion of more literary issues (including authorship, structure, style of writing and the work's effect) which is to be found under the other headings.

But the relationship between analysis of *finis* and analysis of literary features was not merely one of non-interference. The former provided a theoretical basis on which the latter could rest. The efficient cause and the final cause were not alternative aspects of analysis which competed for the attention of the commentator: they were complementary, and the one supported the other within a hierarchical system of analysis[85]. This may be illustrated from Lyre's Psalter-prologue. The *causa efficiens principalis* is God; the *intentio libri* is divine praise, the *causa finalis* indicates how efficacious the Psalter is in leading men to salvation[86]. Paralleling this abstract justification is a concrete procedure of literary analysis. Lyre discusses the diverse *intentiones* and activities of all the contributors to the Psalter; his definition of the *causa finalis* provides the basis for an examination of the particular literary style (the *modus laudis*) which is a means to that end. Once readers have been assured of the divine rapprochement which guarantees the Psalter's *auctoritas,* the literary issues can emerge.

We are now in a position to examine more closely the ways in which these literary issues were treated. The new interest in the integrity of the human *auctor* is manifested by two aspects of his individuality which late-medieval theologians sought to describe, the individual literary activity in which the *auctor* had engaged, and his individual moral activity. These two aspects will now be examined in turn.

THE LITERARY ACTIVITY OF THE HUMAN *AUCTOR*

In the thirteenth century, a series of terms came to be employed in theological commentaries which indicates a wish to define more precisely the literary activity characteristic of an *auctor*. The literary role of the *auctor*, considered in its widest sense, was distinguished from the respective roles of the scribe *(scriptor)*, compiler *(compilator)* and commentator *(commentator)*. St Bonaventure discussed this series of terms at the end of the elaborate 'Aristotelian prologue' to his commentary on Peter Lombard's *Libri sententiarum* (written 1250–2)[87]. Is it correct to call the Lombard an *auctor?* Bonaventure decides that this work possesses sufficient *auctoritas* by virtue of the quality of its materials. But the accuracy of the term *auctor* is also considered from a more literary point of view. There are four ways of making a book, and only one is appropriate to the *auctor:*

The method of making a book is fourfold. For someone writes the materials of others, adding or changing nothing, and this person is said to be merely the scribe. Someone else writes the materials of others, adding, but nothing of his own, and this person is said to be the compiler. Someone else writes both the materials of other men, and of his own, but the materials of others as the principal materials, and his own annexed for the purpose of clarifying them, and this person is said to be the commentator, not the author. Someone else writes both his own materials and those of others, but his own as the principal materials, and the materials of others annexed for the purpose of confirming his own, and such must be called the author.

The *auctor* contributes most, the *scriptor* contributes nothing, of his own. The scribe is subject to materials composed by other men which he should copy as carefully as possible, *nihil mutando*. The *compilator* adds together or arranges the statements of other men, adding no opinion of his own *(addendo, sed non de suo)*. The *commentator* strives to explain the views of others, adding something of his own by way of explanation. Finally and most importantly, the *auctor* writes *de suo* but draws on the statements of other men to support his own views. Applying this schema to the case of Peter Lombard, Bonaventure concludes that, since he offers certain profound statements of his own and supports them with the *sententiae* of the fathers, he may rightly be called the *auctor* of the *Libri sententiarum*.

Bonaventure employed these definitions throughout his commentaries on Scripture. For example, in his commentary on the Book of Wisdom attributed to Solomon (written 1254–7), he distinguished between three degrees or levels of authorship[88]. At the highest level is the efficient cause 'by the mode of inspiring', namely, God. By inspiration, the omnipotent gives understanding to the human *auctor:* all wisdom comes ultimately from God. Then, there is the efficient cause 'by the mode of devising', which is Solomon, for Solomon is commonly held to be the *auctor* of all the Sapiential Books. Solomon can be regarded as the *auctor* of Wisdom because this book was compiled from his sayings. The proximate efficient cause is 'by the mode of compiling', and this is identified with Philo the Jew. In reiterating the views of Hraban Maur, Bonaventure is careful to provide the correct technical term for Philo's literary activity:

Hraban asserted that the book was more likely to have been written (i.e. compiled) not by Solomon, as is reputed, but by Philo the most wise Jew.

God is the source of all *auctoritas;* after Him comes the human *auctor* who is responsible for what is actually said in a given text, and finally there is the person who compiles the sayings of the human *auctor.*

A more detailed and critical discussion of the authorship of Wisdom is found in the enormously popular commentary on that book written *c.* 1333–4 by the Oxford Dominican, Robert Holcot[89]. Holcot assembles numerous *auctoritates* on the subject. Jerome said that Philo the Jew, writing in Greek, compiled this book from the sayings of Solomon. Hence, the book can be said to be Philo's and not Solomon's and, for this reason, the Jews do not number the book among their sacred Scriptures. But there are evident arguments against this opinion. The *Ecclesiastica historia* says that Solomon was the *auctor,* and Matthew xxvii refers to a prophecy from the Book of Wisdom: therefore, Wisdom must have been edited before the passion of Christ, whereas Philo flourished at the time of the Apostles. Moreover, at Wisdom ix.7 we read, 'you have chosen me to be a king of your people', words which accord not with Philo, an Alexandrine Jew living in Egypt, but with Solomon.

Augustine, Holcot continues, inclined to the opinion that Jesus, the son of Sirach, made both Wisdom and Ecclesiasticus, and that his style of writing had certain similarities with Solomon's. But Augustine went back on this opinion in his *Retractiones:* obviously, the Saint had doubts on the issue. Holcot himself is convinced that Solomon is the 'principal author' of Wisdom, but he admits that it is possible that Philo, a good Greek scholar, could have known the Hebrew Book of Solomon or the 'profound sayings of the book' and edited Solomon's sayings in Greek. When these sayings were translated into Latin, naturally they were associated with Philo. What, then, about the opinion of Jerome? Holcot argues that Jerome did not assert that the book was Philo's, but merely reported the opinion of the Jews on the matter. Therefore, this book may be numbered among the canonical Scriptures, as Augustine explicitly says in *De doctrina christiana.* The fact that Wisdom prophesies of Christ gives it great *auctoritas* among the faithful, though naturally the Jews do not accept this point.

A similar treatment of this same problem is provided in Nicholas of Lyre's Wisdom-commentary (1330). According to Lyre, Solomon is the 'principal author' of Wisdom, but the book was compiled from the profound sayings of Solomon by Philo[90]. In an aside, Lyre makes it clear that, in this context, he is thinking only of the human *auctores* involved ('but, speaking of the human authors . . .') and not of the divine *auctor.* In his commentary on Ecclesiasticus (1331), Lyre gives an explanation of the translation of the work, concluding that Jesus, the son of Sirach, was, under God, the chief writer involved[91]. Throughout his commentaries on the Sapiential Books, Lyre is mainly concerned with the 'human authors' who work 'under God'.

All the exegetes cited above were consistent in regarding the Book of Wisdom as a compilation (*compilatio*). The second book of Machabees was also described as a *compilatio* by late-medieval exegetes, and this marks a distinct break with the typical twelfth-century way of describing the work. In a passage subsequently incorporated into the *Glossa ordinaria,* Peter Comestor described II Machabees as a recapitulation (*recapitulatio*) of I Machabees, an interpretation which was echoed by Stephen Langton: 'This volume [i.e. of Machabees] is divided in two books. The second is a recapitulation and a following up of the first[92].

But both Hugh of St Cher and Nicholas of Lyre described II Machabees as a *compilatio*[93]. Here is part of Lyre's commentary on the text:

This second book of Machabees is in some measure an abbreviation of a certain large volume, written by Jason Cyrenaeus, having five constituent books in which the deeds of Judaeus Machabaeus and his associates were diffusely treated; in this book they are set forth briefly and succinctly . . . To read this compendium can be done easily and without tedious scanning while reading.

Such an interest in Scriptural *compilationes* may be related to the fact that, by the thirteenth century, medieval techniques of compilation had reached a high level of sophistication, as may be gathered from a reading of two impressive examples, the *Speculum maius* of Vincent of Beauvais and the *De proprietatibus rerum* of Bartholomew the Englishman[94].

Nicholas of Lyre regarded Wisdom and II Machabees as *compilationes*[95]. Moreover, he regarded the Psalter, Proverbs, and the Book of the Twelve Minor Prophets as collections, *collectiones*[96]. The difference which Lyre saw between a *compilatio* and a *collectio* seems to have been that, whereas a *compilatio* had an orderly arrangement of materials, a *collectio* had not—a point to which we shall return. Lyre regarded the Psalter as such an excellent example of a *collectio* that he referred to it when describing other Biblical collections. For example, at the beginning of his Proverbs-commentary, he points out that those responsible for this *collectio* were not responsible for the collected items, just as Esdras was not the *auctor* of the psalms he collected in one volume:

The people responsible for this collection are not nor cannot be said to be the authors of this book, but rather Solomon, who composed the parables; just as Esdras, or whoever else collected the psalms in one book, is not said to be the author of the book of psalms, but rather David, who composed the greater part of the psalms . . .[97]

Lyre proceeds to say that the collectors of Solomon's parables wrote a prologue to Proverbs, just as Esdras provided the first psalm as a prologue to the Psalter.

The vocabulary employed in describing the various literary roles performed by the human *auctores* of Scripture was also used to clarify the issue of the respective roles of God and man in producing inspired Scripture. Our concern with the former must involve us in a brief consideration of the latter, since the technical meanings of the terms were common to both contexts.

In the *Sentences* commentaries of Fishacre, Kilwardby and Bonaventure, there is disagreement concerning the degrees of responsibility to be allotted to the primary efficient cause and the instrumental efficient causes. For Fishacre, the human writer played the role of mere scribe (*scriptor*) to God's *auctor;* the divine instruments were given little credit[98]. By contrast, Kilwardby was concerned at once to give the human *auctores* of the Bible their due, and to describe the human literary activity of the Lombard[99]. Like Fishacre before him, he argued that neither men nor angels can be the *auctores* of the science of theology, because they are too limited; only God has the necessary qualifications. But Kilwardby affirms that men and angels have their roles to play. They are the promulgators or scribes of sacred doctrine; indeed, they may be called compilers, just like the master of the *Sentences,* Peter Lombard.

The analogy with what Kilwardby regarded as the compiling activity of the Lombard is neatly applied. There is no attempt to belittle human achievement: quite the contrary. The Holy Spirit set the assignment; the human *auctores* carried out the work of God. Their names appear in the titles of their books through the divine ordination, so that we might imitate them, and partake of the grace which God gives to those who produce literature for His benefit. And so, the Lombard must be allowed his reward. God may be responsible for the truth contained in the *Sentences,* but the Lombard is responsible for the compilation:

Note too, that although God is the author of the truth transmitted in the sentences, yet the efficient cause of the compilation, or the author to the extent that it is a compilation, is well and truly said to be the Master.

The Lombard carried out the literary work, moved (as he says in his prologue) by the love of Christ. Therefore, God is the primary efficient cause of the *Libri sententiarum,* while Peter Lombard is its secondary efficient cause.

Bonaventure's neat series of definitions of the terms *scriptor, compilator, commentator* and *auctor,* as quoted above, occurs in the prologue to his *Sentences* commentary as part of an excursus on the scientific nature of theology. This venture into the realm of literary theory may have been occasioned by a desire to improve on the way of assessing Peter Lombard's contribution favoured by previous schoolmen[100]. Fishacre, Kilwardby and, apparently, Alexander of Hales, had merged the Bible and the *Sentences* together as the textbooks of theology; their discussions of causality and scientific procedure concerned theology in the abstract. Bonaventure was more discriminating. First, he treats of God as the *auctor* of wisdom and of the science of theology; then, he moves to consider the *Sentences* on its own and not in conjunction with the Bible[101]. It is because of this clear distinction between the two major textbooks of theology that Bonaventure can describe the Lombard, and not God, as the *auctor* of the *Sentences*. The *auctoritas* of the Bible is, of course, much greater, and in this case one must admit divine responsibility, but the *Sentences* is a book for which a human *auctor* can be given the responsibility and the credit.

Similar depictions of the roles of God and man are found in commentaries on the other base-text of theology, the Bible. In his commentary on Baruch (written sometime between 1270 and 1280), St Albert the Great carefully distinguished between the *auctor* Jeremiah and the compiler Baruch[102]. Baruch wrote down the words which he took from the erudite sayings of Jeremiah, just as God put His words in the mouth of Jeremiah. Psalm xliv.2 is invoked, 'my tongue is as ready as the pen of a busy scribe'. Baruch was a busy scribe; Jeremiah was as ready as the pen of a busy scribe. St Albert then puns his way to the theological point. Baruch would not have been one of the Lord's blessed (*benedictus Domini*) if he had not written down the blessed statement (*benedictio*) of the Lord. Everything which proceeds from the mouth of a blessed man must be well said (*benedictus*).

Albert proceeds to justify the collection and compilation (the verbs *colligo* and *compilo* are used) of scraps of truth. After the feeding of the five thousand, Jesus said, 'Collect the scraps . . . so that nothing is wasted' (John vi.12). No scrap of inspired Scripture must be wasted for, as St Paul says, 'all that is written is written for our doctrine' (Romans xv.4).

On the other hand, those most authoritative of *auctores*, the Four Evangelists who had recorded the life and deeds of Christ, could be described as having practised a sort of compilation. For example, the Carmelite, William of Lidlington (†1310), explained how the Evangelists had compiled the eloquence of Christ:

Truly, the efficient cause is double, the principal and the secondary. The principal agent is the son of God Himself, namely Christ, who is the sole master of all the most sound doctrine . . . The secondary agents are the Evangelists inspired by the Holy Spirit, who are the agents compiling eloquence as the instrument of Christ.[103]

But the most elaborate discussion of this type known to me occurs in the famous *Summa in questionibus Armenorum* of Richard FitzRalph, who was Chancellor of Oxford University in 1332 and, subsequently, Archbishop of Armagh. This work (written shortly after 1349) takes the form of a dialogue between 'Ricardus' and 'Joannes', and FitzRalph's views must be inferred from their consensus of opinion. In the opening debate, which develops the theory of exegesis found in the prologues to Nicholas of Lyre's *Postilla litteralis,* Joannes complains that he sometimes finds it difficult to see to what extent a Scriptural utterance expresses the mind of the author *(mens auctoris)*[104]. For example, if Moses affirmed as *auctor* the books of the Pentateuch (and tradition believes this to be so), then it would appear that Moses was the *auctor* of lies and falsehoods. For example, at Genesis iii.4, a lie is expressed by the statement of the serpent to Eve, 'you shall not surely die'. And at Genesis xxvii.24, when Isaac asks Jacob, 'Are you my son Esau'? the reply is, 'I am'—behold, another lie! If one suggests that persons other than Moses (namely, the serpent and Jacob) are the *auctores* in these problem-passages, it would appear that there are many *auctores* in a single book. If, on the other hand, one states that neither Moses nor the speakers concerned possess authorship, these passages are left without an *auctor*. Both these conclusions are untenable.

FitzRalph's Ricardus then suggests a solution. Joannes, he claims, is having trouble with the term *auctor* because, 'according to the usage of speech', the notion of authorship can be understood in three different ways. Either an *auctor* is

1 himself the person who asserts a passage, its *assertor,*
2 its 'editor or compiler' *(editor vel compilator),* or
3 he is both together. And this is the correct sense of *auctor.*

In the problem-passages, Moses is not the *assertor* but the *editor* or *compilator* of lies. Moses described the sequence of events, while the serpent and Jacob were the assertors and *auctores* of the lies. Thus, Moses and no one else fulfils both criteria laid down for the third and correct sense of the term *auctor*. And so, the truth of sacred Scripture is saved. Moses is personally responsible for what he asserts of himself, not what he asserts others to have said or done.

The theological implications of this analysis are then outlined. No prophet can be called an *auctor* in the third and correct sense of the term, because a prophet does not assert the revelation he has received as his own property but claims God as its *auctor*. A comparison is made with Baruch. Baruch wrote from the mouth of Jeremiah; Jeremiah wrote from the mouth of the Lord. Baruch fulfilled the roles of *scriptor* and *compilator* in relation to the *auctor* Jeremiah; the prophet fulfilled the roles of *scriptor* and *compilator* in relation to the *auctor* God. Therefore, no prophet can be praised or blamed for what he asserts to be from God. The thorny problems of prophecy and predestination relate not to the human prophet but to the divine will; in this case, the onus of responsibility is God's and His alone.

Ricardus illustrates this point with examples of prophecies that were not fulfilled in the way in which the prophets claimed they would be. 'Yet forty days and Nineveh will be overthrown', Jonah had claimed (Jonah iii.4). However, this catastrophe was averted because God Himself 'repented' of His wrath, having been moved by the repentance of the townspeople (Jonah iii.10). There is no question of calling the prophet a liar, since he wrote and spoke in accordance with the divine will. Jonah's action of warning was exactly what God willed him to do.

Two major literary points have been clarified by the series of discussions summarised in this chapter-section. The first is that, in opposition to the legalistic connotation of *auctor* which suggested responsibility for an act or a piece of writing, has emerged a term, *compilator*, which connotes absence or indeed denial of responsibility for such things. The responsibility lacked or denied by the *compilator* is both literary and moral, as FitzRalph's discussion shows. A writer who plays this role cannot take the credit for the value of a piece of writing; neither can he be blamed for any harm it might cause.

Two of Fitzralph's technical terms, *affirmator* and *assertor,* have their source in logic. He uses them to spell out the juridic connotation of the term *auctor,* to stress that the *auctor* is the person who bears the responsibility. In the schools, the activity of 'asserting' was usually contrasted with that of 'repeating' (*recitatio*) or 'reporting' (*reportatio*)[105]. A twelfth-century *locus classicus* for the basic notions involved, if not for the terms themselves, was the prologue to Peter Abelard's *Sic et non*[106]. Here it is suggested that a writer can sometimes report the opinions of others, or make some concession to current opinion. Such statements are to be distinguished from the writer's statements of his personal opinions. M.-D. Chenu has given several examples of the application of this principle by St Thomas Aquinas, one of which will suffice here:

> In many things which pertain to philosophy, Augustine makes use of the opinions of Plato, not asserting them but repeating them (*non asserendo sed recitando*). [107]

It is often found in the prologues to late-medieval compilations. Vincent of Beauvais justified the inclusion of passages from the Apocrypha in his *Speculum maius* on the grounds that he was not asserting them to be true or false, but simply repeating them (*recitando*)[108]. This distinction was also a commonplace of Scriptural exegesis. In the Lollard prologue to the English Bible we are told that 'ofte in storial mateer scripture rehersith the comune opynyoun of men, and affirmeth not, that it was so in dede'[109]. In sum, an *auctor* 'asserts' while a *compilator* 'repeats' or 'reports' what others have said or done, not adding anything 'of his own' (*de suo*). In FitzRalph's example, Moses, as the editor or compiler of the lies of Jacob and the serpent, only 'reported' those things.

The second major literary point to be clarified above is that analysis of the *duplex causa efficiens* by several generations of theologians produced a highly sophisticated theoretical model for assigning degrees of responsibility to the writers of a given text, or to the literary roles which they perform. This may be summarised as follows. The *auctor* is twofold, double or, as it were, bilocated: there is a primary efficient cause or 'far cause' and an instrumental efficient cause or 'near cause'[110]. In relation to the 'far cause', the 'near cause' may be called a *compilator*. But the 'near cause' may, in his turn, have put yet another cause into operation: he may have a person working under him (either under his direction or, if dead, in his footsteps!), and thus may, in turn, play the role of *auctor* to this person's *scriptor* or *compilator*.

The issue of which *auctores* were believed to be responsible for which meanings and which activities in the textbooks of theology had this question as its counterpart: does responsibility for sin affect the meaning of an *auctor* or in any way detract from his *auctoritas* as a writer? In the late Middle Ages, there was a new awareness of the sins of the *auctores*. Interest in the integrity of the human *auctor* seems to have taken two main channels: he was considered as an agent in both literary and moral activity. The commentator's new-found ability to empathise with his author's humanity produced discussion, on the one hand, of the kinds of literary activity which the *auctor* had practised, and on the other, of the kinds of deed, both good and evil, which he had performed during his life. Now we may proceed to investigate the moral activity of the human *auctor* as regarded by medieval theologians.

THE MORAL ACTIVITY OF THE HUMAN *AUCTOR*

Of course, the sins of the Scriptural *auctores* had always been known, but the early-medieval stress on the allegorical senses of Scripture had ensured that the problem never arose in an acute form. However, when late-medieval commentators came to concentrate on the literal and historical sense of Scripture, they had to recognise the problem as a serious one. Their method of coping with it may be better understood by reference to changing attitudes to one great saint and sinner, the psalmist, David.

In II Kings xi–xii, the story is told of how David saw, from the roof of his house, Bathsheba bathing, and how he desired this woman and soon committed adultery with her. Subsequently, David arranged that her husband Uriah should be placed in the forefront of the hardest fighting against the Ammonites, and killed. This being done, David took Bathsheba as his wife. But the Lord was displeased and sent the prophet Nathan to David. Nathan told the parable of the rich man who, when a guest came to his house, refused to kill any of his own sheep but, instead, took from a poor man his only lamb and prepared it for his guest. David's anger being aroused against the rich man, Nathan drove the point home: 'You are the man' (II Kings xii.7); despite all the prosperity that he had received from God, he nevertheless had taken away Uriah's wife. Whereupon, David admitted his great sin, repented, and regained his position of favour with the Lord.

In *De doctrina christiana*, St Augustine interpreted the 'guest' of Nathan's parable as David's passion for Bathsheba[111]. This lust was not a lasting disposition but a passing one; as it were, a guest. By contrast, Augustine continued, in the son of David and Bathsheba, King Solomon, this disposition did not pass on, like a guest, but took posses-

sion of his kingdom. Holy Scripture has, according to Augustine, condemned Solomon as a lover of women. The beginning of his reign
glowed with his desire of wisdom yet, when he had obtained wisdom
through spiritual love, he lost it through carnal love. It is then argued
that nearly all of the deeds recorded in the Old Testament should be
understood not only in their literal sense but figuratively as well, Augustine's precedent being St Paul's justification of prefiguration in I
Corinthians x. But the other side of the coin is important as well:

On the other hand, when one reads of any sins of noble men, even though he
can observe and verify in them some figures of future events, he may still apply
the proper meaning of the action to this end, namely, that he will by no means
venture to boast about his own virtuous deeds, nor, because of his own up-
rightness, look down upon others as if they were sinners, when he sees in such
noble men the storms of passions that must be shunned and the shipwrecks
that must be lamented. The sins of those men have been written down for a
reason, and that is that the following passage of the Apostle might be formidable everywhere: 'Therefore let him who thinks he stands take heed lest he fall'
[I Cor. x. 12].

Similarly, in his two great *apologiae* for the prophet David, St Ambrose
had stressed the exemplary, prefigural and allegorical implications of
David's sins of adultery and murder[112].

These accounts showed medieval theologians a way of reconciling the
individuality of the human *auctores* of Scripture with the supreme ob-
jectivity of their divine authority but, until the thirteenth century, the
latter tended far to outweigh the former. This may be demonstrated by
a comparison of glosses from different periods on the major penitential
psalm *Miserere mei, Dei,* the title of which directed the commentators to
the history *(historia)* of David and Bathsheba: 'A Psalm of David, when
Nathan the prophet came to him, after he had been with Bathsheba'.

The gloss on Psalm 1 attributed to Remigius of Auxerre focuses on
its warning and advising aspects[113]. The *exemplum* of David warns us
not to revel in prosperity; the fact that he received divine pardon
teaches us never to despair, no matter how great the sin. Similarly,
Letbert of Lille (whose Psalter-commentary was published in 1125)
remarked that many want to fall with David, but not to recover with
him[114]. The psalm provides an example not of lapse but of resurgence.
Divine grace was restored to David; he is, therefore, put forward as an
exemplar of the just man, not the sinner. Peter Lombard commended

the way in which David, on being accused by Nathan, did not excuse himself, but publicly confessed his sin[115]. The kind of humility which is appropriate to penitents is thereby shown. And this, claims the Lombard (echoing Cassiodorus), is why Psalm l is sung in Church more often than any of the other penitential psalms.

In these expositions, the general moral implications of the *historia* are emphasised; elsewhere, the allegorical and prefigural aspects are at the centre of attention. Pseudo-Bede, writing in the early twelfth century, moved from an affirmation of the cautionary value of David's misfortunes to describe David as a figure of Christ[116]. In this analysis, Bathsheba is said to signify the Church, and the hapless Uriah, the devil! The same procedure was followed by Honorius 'of Autun' (writing, perhaps, between 1151 and 1158), who added that Bathsheba's bathing, which was so pleasing to David, signifies the washing of baptism undergone by the congregation of the faithful to make them fit for association with Christ[117]. Just as Bathsheba did not sleep with Uriah after having had intercourse with David, so the Church is not joined to the devil after having gone to the desirable Christ. The prophet Nathan does not fit into this allegorical scheme, so he is left uninterpreted.

Honorius was at pains to reassure the puzzled reader. One should not marvel, he claimed, that Christ should be prefigured by an adulterer and the Church by an adulteress or that, by a chaste man, the devil should be designated. Such is the special quality of the Bible, written as it were in golden letters (indicating, presumably, its uniqueness and essential purity). The influence of Augustine is manifest in Honorius's interpretation of the 'guest' of Nathan's parable as illicit love. Lechery was a guest, as far as David was concerned, but it took possession of Solomon's kingdom. The lapses of the saints were written down, Honorius explained, so that the power of the medicine (of genuine repentance) in curing the desperately sick should be commended; through this example, the lapsed are given hope. Then the question is raised, since David's sin was such a major one, why is he employed as a prefiguration of Christ? This may seem less surprising when it is realised that the whole Israelite nation was used to foreshadow the Christian people. Like Augustine before him, Honorius claimed the precedent of St Paul: 'All these things concern us in figure' (i Corinthians x. 11).

The general moral implications of David's *historia* continued to be expounded in later exegesis. For example, the Oxford Dominican, Thomas Waleys, writing in the early fourteenth century, described David and St Paul as Scriptural *auctores* who had passed through a state of sin[118]. For Waleys, the fate of each *auctor* is an *exemplum* of the penitent man who receives divine mercy. Not only did David obtain remission of sin, but he also turned his mind to the contemplation of divine mysteries. The Holy Spirit uses sin to obtain repentance in the same way as a doctor of medicine uses a poison to effect a cure. Waleys quoted Albert the Great as saying that the bile of a viper is the best possible eye-lotion. As Albert himself admitted, it is marvellous that the eye is not harmed in the process but is, instead, purged. Scripture often links the viper with sin, and so Waleys moralises this piece of medical lore into a parallel with the divine process in which the mind's eye of his *auctor* was cleansed.

However, by the time of Waleys, the elaborate allegorising of David, Bathsheba and Uriah had ceased to be popular. The incredulity which it occasioned was fully recognised in the treatise *De legibus,* which forms part of the vast *Magisterium divinale* written by William of Auvergne between 1223 and 1240. Is it possible, William asks, that Uriah, a holy and just man, should represent the devil, while the adulterous copulation of David and Bathsheba represents the most immaculate conjunction of Christ and the Church?[119] The deeds recorded in II Kings do not seem to have such a significative function; verisimilitude is lacking in many things. However, it can be pointed out that David loved Bathsheba deeply and for her love procured the death of a man, then honoured her with regal marriage and elevated her to the royal throne. Likewise, the King of Heaven loved deeply the synagogue and, having procured the demise of its Jewish magistrate, honoured it with spiritual marriage and elevated it to the kingdom of heaven. If a similitude of this sort is decently expounded, William assures us, the audience will not be offended. However, he soon proceeds to echo Jerome's warning against tropological exegesis which violently conflicts with the literal sense of a passage.

Similar reservations were expressed in one of the ordinary disputations which Henry of Ghent held at Paris between 1276 and 1292[120]. Is it possible to allegorise evil deeds in a good sense? Henry replies by distinguishing between the manner in which something is done and the substance of the deed. Regarding the former, David's manner of acting was reprehensible, and no good interpretation is possible. Regarding the latter, it may be pointed out that a prince can justly have a certain soldier killed, and take his wife for himself. Considered in this light, it is not incongruous that a bad deed should have a good allegory and be expounded in a good sense.

This kind of special pleading is notably absent from the glosses on Psalm l by Hugh of St Cher, Nicholas Gorran, Thomas Aquinas, Nicholas Trevet and Nicholas of Lyre, all of whom provide interpretations which are thoroughly literal and historical. Neither is there any attempt to identify David as a figure of Christ, for a reason clearly indicated by Hugh of St Cher and Gorran. Gorran refers back to Psalm xlix, verses 16–17, where it is stated that divine praise from the mouth of a sinner is not acceptable to God[121]. Therefore, Gorran claims, it is fitting that Psalm l should follow, in which is exemplified repentance, the means whereby sin is removed and divine praise is rendered acceptable to God. Hugh of St Cher is concerned with the problem of why Psalm l is not included in II Kings xi–xii, where the full story behind its composition is told[122]. His solution is that this was not possible because the passage in II Kings is to be interpreted allegorically of Christ, and penitence, the subject of the fiftieth psalm, is not accordant with Christ. The implication of both these comments is that, because Psalm l treats of penitence, it cannot be said to prefigure Christ and, therefore, a literal reading is the correct response. Some of this literal reading may now be examined.

It has been mentioned above how Aquinas, conscious of the condemnation of Theodore of Mopsuestia, had felt obliged to assert that the passion of Christ was treated in the literal sense of Psalm xxi: although this psalm speaks figuratively of David, it also refers specially to Christ[123]. Commenting on Psalm l, Aquinas stated that, while in other psalms David spoke of other things (as, in Psalm xxi, he spoke of Christ), he made this psalm about himself[124]. A copious paraphrase of the *historia* of II Kings xi–xii is provided, and Aquinas explains that in the *Miserere* David declares his guilt, which he made manifest to all and, similarly, his remission[125]. It would seem that Psalms xxi and l are at the opposite ends of St Thomas's exegetical spectrum. If, in Psalm xxi, Christ, the fulfilling type, reigns supreme, in Psalm l, David, the prefiguring type, may be described in rich historical detail.

Aquinas's gloss on Psalm l verse 14, 'deliver me from bloodguiltiness', is revealing[126]. Two explanations are given, the first being the statement in the *Glossa ordinaria* that 'bloodguiltiness' refers, in general terms, to the concupiscence of the body, which is flesh and blood[127]. The second explanation is Aquinas's own. The term could refer to the adultery and murder committed by the historical David, because blood is involved in both sins: in murder, blood is shed, whereas adultery proceeds from a passion of the bood[128]. It would seem that St Thomas's concern for *historia* encouraged him to relate as much textual detail as possible to David's personal situation.

This practice is even more apparent in Lyre's *Postilla litteralis* on the Psalter, the fiftieth psalm meticulously being placed in its full historical context as the psalm which David wrote, not immediately after his adultery with Bathsheba, but after Nathan had accused him[129]. David is, therefore, at once the *auctor* and the subject *(materia)* of this psalm. Hence, his plea (in verse 1) that the multitude of God's tender mercies might blot out his transgressions is supposed to indicate the multitude of David's transgressions, which Lyre carefully enumerates. David sinned, in the first instance, by committing adultery; secondly, by wishing to conceal his sin; and thirdly, by the attempted method of concealment: he wanted Uriah to sleep with Bathsheba, so that the child which he had engendered would be ascribed to Uriah. Fourthly, he sinned in so far as he had his most faithful soldier treacherously killed and, fifthly, because, in the process, many of David's other servants were killed. Explaining the reference (in verse 14) to David's 'bloodguiltiness', Lyre argues that this was incurred by the shedding of the blood of Uriah and those others who died on the same occasion.

Lyre also displays a concern for exact temporal chronology. The time between David's adultery and Nathan's declaration must have been one year or thereabouts, he reckons, because Nathan refers to the child of David and Bathsheba as having already been born. The long duration of David's sin is thereby indicated, which Lyre understands as the explanation of verse 2, 'Wash me thoroughly from my iniquity, and cleanse me from my sin'. When clothes are cleaned those stains which have recently been made are washed away easily, while the inveterate stains are removed only with thorough washing.

However, most of Lyre's moralising was reserved for the *Postilla moralis,* a brief supplement to the *Postilla litteralis,* written in 1339 'for the readers of Bibles and preachers of the word of God'[130]. Taken to-

gether, these two commentaries by Lyre present a picture of the psalmist which is a substantial development of the views of St Thomas.
David is still, on occasion, a figure of Christ, and the spokesman of the
Christian Church, but he can also be an ideal king and prelate, as it
were complete in himself, with admirable abilities and virtues which
constitute a model of behaviour for his successors. In twelfth-century
exegesis, what may be called David's personal 'good character' (as opposed to his divinely-ordained function as a *figura*) was established
mainly by brief reference to his sin and repentance. By contrast, Lyre
was much more aware of the good qualities possessed by David in his
historical context. Medieval kings and prelates, in similar historical
contexts and faced with similar problems, would do well to follow the
psalmist's example. This interest in common humanity and common
problems is a most striking development of the exemplary aspect of
David's authorial role[131].

For example, in the *Postilla litteralis,* Lyre described Psalm v as having arisen out of the tribulation suffered by David at the hands of Saul
and his other enemies[132]. In the *Postilla moralis,* this psalm is allegorically interpreted as a prayer of the Church against the infidels who
occupy the Holy Land[133]. Because of this significance, Lyre claimed,
the psalm ought to be pronounced intently and with great devotion by
priests. It is not fitting that Saracens should live next to Christ's tomb,
that unbelievers should remain in the land on which His eyes once
gazed. The Saracens falsely say that the most vile Mohammed was a
prophet of the great Lord. Having lived by the sword, the followers of
this false prophet will die by it. The obligation placed on contemporary
kings, the successors of David, is obvious.

In the Psalter-commentaries examined above, the problem of the
sins of the Scriptural *auctor* was resolved through description of the
total situation in which those sins occurred. Exegetes became progres-
sively more aware of the historical details of that situation, but the
central tenet remained unchanged, namely, that David was to be regarded, not as a sinner, but as a true penitent and, indeed, a just man.

Another method of coping with the problem was to stress the importance of correct understanding of the intention of the author (*intentio
auctoris*). While the *auctor* is responsible before God for his sins he is
not responsible for a reader's misinterpretation of his work: if the reader
does not get the moral point this is the fault of the reader and not of the

auctor. There is a right way and a wrong way of interpreting authorial intention, and each reader should be careful to choose the right way. The theologians' general attitude to the interpretation of authorial intention is well expressed by the Paris master Raoul Ardent (†c. 1200) in a dominical sermon on Romans xv.4, 'all that is written is written for our doctrine, that by patience and by the consolation of the writings we may have hope'. Raoul asked, how can one reconcile this text with the sins of the *auctores*, such as the adultery of David, the pride of Saul and the womanising of Solomon? The answer is that such passages do pertain to doctrine if one reads them with correct understanding of the *intentio* in each case:

They are pertinent, my brothers, if we should consider the intention of the writer. For in sacred Scripture four things are written with diverse intentions: evils, good things, punishments and rewards. Evils are written to be feared, good things to be imitated, punishments to be discouraging, rewards to be encouraging. Therefore the adultery of David and other sins are written for the purpose of warning. And if perchance it transpires that we should fall into such sins, we should not despair but, by the example of David, revert to the remedy of repentance. In what way do those things which are written avail for our doctrine? 'That by patience', it is said, 'and the consolation of the writings', i.e. those things which are read in the Scriptures, 'we may have hope'.[134]

In this way, the exegetes of the later Middle Ages could reconcile the problem of the sins of their *auctores* with the fact of their authority as writers. A more elaborate example is found in the prologue to St Bonaventure's very popular commentary on Ecclesiastes (written 1254–7), where it is asked if Solomon can properly be called the *auctor* of this book[135]. Solomon was certainly a sinner, and God demands of the wicked man at Psalm xliv.17, 'what business have you reciting my statutes . . . since you detest my discipline?' Perhaps Solomon sinned again by speaking of the divine justice. Only a good writer is capable of sustaining faith, for only the work of a good writer or *auctor* has *auctoritas*. If Solomon was a wicked man, can his work be said to have any authority?

The answer is 'yes' because, according to Jerome and Hebrew tradition, the Book of Ecclesiastes was composed not by a man in a state of sin, but by a repentant man who regretted his sins. Bonaventure claims that the epilogue of Ecclesiastes, in which worldly vanity is renounced, makes this clear. Moreover, it may be argued that the Holy Spirit sometimes uses a bad man to express true and good things. Solomon did not sin in what he said but in so far as he failed to put his preaching into practice. Besides, God stands as the guarantor of the truth in Ecclesiastes.

But Bonaventure was not content merely to invoke God and leave it at that. He provides a literary answer as well, by examining Solomon's *modus agendi*[136]. The Book of Ecclesiastes has, he says, a singular *modus agendi* among the works of Solomon because it proceeds in the manner of an orator propounding diverse *sententiae*, sometimes in the person of a wise man, sometimes in the person of a foolish man, so that in the mind of the reader a single truth may be gleaned from the divers sayings. But it may be objected that this *modus agendi* will create enormous problems for the reader. One should pay heed to the things which a wise man says, but not to what a foolish man says: yet how can the reader be sure when the *auctor* is speaking in his own person *(in propria persona)* and when he is speaking in the person of others *(in persona aliorum)*? Bonaventure replies that when Solomon speaks *in persona aliorum*, for example in the person of the foolish man, he does not approve of the foolishness but abhors it. The *sententia* found at the end of Ecclesiastes makes clear the good *intentio auctoris:*

Thus I say, that Ecclesiastes proceeds like disputation right to the end of the book and at the end he provides a profound statement, when he says, 'Let us all together hear the end of that which is to be spoken: fear God, and know that on account of every error God will bring you into judgment'. In which statement he condemns all the sayings of the fatuous, the carnal and the worldly. Whence, whatever concurs with that profound statement, he says in his own person; whatever indeed disagrees with it, he says in the person of others: and therefore this book cannot be understood, unless it is examined as a whole.[137]

Therefore, Solomon's epilogue provides us with a measure with which to judge the ways in which doctrine is being communicated in the other parts of the book. Bonaventure also takes the opportunity to uphold Solomon as an *exemplum* of the penitent sinner[138]. Solomon sinned and repented; he received divine grace. His life is an example for us sinners, who may imitate the repentance of Solomon and hope for a corresponding grace. The analogy with the experience of David, as described in the glosses on Psalm l, is quite obvious. This seems to be Bonaventure's general precedent, and not the harsh judgment of Solomon made by St Augustine in the passage from *De doctrina christiana* quoted above (p. 104). In sum, it would appear that both David and Solomon have become men writing to men. 'Modern' men may read of the personal lives of these *auctores* and relate that 'ancient' experience to their own lives.

This completes our illustration of the manner in which Bible-commentators of the thirteenth and early fourteenth centuries described two aspects of the individuality of the human *auctor*, his individual literary activity and his individual moral activity. It seemed to them that the inspired *auctores* had engaged in a series of literary roles (*auctor, compilator, collector, editor*, etc.) and a series of moral roles, one of the most important of which was (in the cases of David and Solomon) the role of penitent sinner and ethical example. One result of the new literalistic exegesis of Scripture was that the *auctor*, as it were, came closer to the reader. David and Solomon, for example, had adopted certain literary stances and employed certain styles and structures which a modern writer could imitate; the moral reform of these same 'ancients' was held up to the 'moderns' as a model of self-improvement. This awareness of common humanity meant that the gap between the *auctor* and his medieval audience had narrowed somewhat.

Our next section is concerned with the narrowing of another traditional gap, the gap between Scriptural *auctores* and pagan *auctores*. The new attitudes to authorship which we have been examining helped to create the conditions necessary for their 'coming together' on certain definite terms. Pagan authority remained subservient to Scriptural authority, but the comparisons between the two groups of writers had become (at least) as important as the contrasts.

SCRIPTURAL AUTHORITY AND PAGAN AUTHORITY

The discussions of the role of the *auctor* which have been described above have important implications for our understanding of the way in which late-medieval scholars approached their pagan *auctores*. It has been suggested that the new emphasis on the integrity of the individual *auctor* produced two main effects, an interest in the *auctor* in so far as he performed various literary roles, and an interest in the exemplary 'life of the author' (*vita auctoris*). In the thirteenth and fourteenth centuries, all kind of *auctores*, whether Christian or pagan, were being examined in terms of both moral and literary activity. The life of a pagan *auctor* could furnish many moral points which would not discredit the life of a Christian *auctor*. Evidence collected by F. Ghisalberti suggests that the late Middle Ages saw a great development of the moralistic lives of Ovid which formed part of the prologues to the works of that pagan poet, a trend which Ghisalberti regards as the antecedent of the production of humanistic lives of the poets[139]. Corresponding to this in the commentaries of the theologians was the new kind of interest in the sins of the *auctores* which has been illustrated in the previous section.

The literary activities of Christian and pagan *auctores* were comparable also; a pagan writer could be an *auctor, compilator, commentator* or whatever. For example, the compiling activity of Virgil and Horace was cited in justifying Christian compilation. In the prologue to his *Polychronicon* (finished *c.* 1352), the English Benedictine, Ralph Higden, told a 'pagan' tale which Isidore of Seville was supposed to have told of Virgil and which Hugutio of Pisa was supposed to have told of Horace[140]. Accused of being a mere 'compiler of old things', the hero of the story replied that it was a sign of great strength to take the mace from the hand of Hercules[141]. Obviously, Higden regarded *compilatio* as a positive and important literary activity, but one which required an elaborate justification. Not all his precedents are pagan; he cites the Scriptural story of Ruth gleaning the ears of corn (Ruth ii). Although she followed after powerful men, the lord Boas ordered them not to despise her. The implication is that the Lord God does not despise the humble *compilator* who follows in the footsteps of the powerful *auctores*[142]. Defending the inclusion of 'gentile figments and pagan sayings' in his work, Higden argues that these have been incorporated in order that they may serve the Christian faith. After all, it was lawful for Virgil to seek out the gold of wisdom in the clay of Ennius, and for the children of Israel to despoil the Egyptians.

Once all *auctores* were regarded as efficient causes, the ways in which they moved and were moved could be compared. The theologians, who provided the most sophisticated discussions of multiple and diverse efficient causality, were most aware of this basis of comparison. The consequence for exegesis seems to have been a more precise calibration of *auctoritas*.

Pagan and Christian writers differed in degrees of *auctoritas*. Traditionally, the Christians knew more than the pagans. In the thirteenth century, this distinction was placed on both an epistemological and an historical footing. In twelfth-century divisions of the sciences, the term *philosophia* could denote the whole spectrum of knowledge and inquiry, including theology, which was classed as theoretical or speculative philosophy (see above, pp. 23–5). However, thirteenth-century school-men drove a wedge between theology and philosophy, the latter being regarded as the inferior of the former[143]. This development was probably due, in part, to the more rigorous definition of subject-areas made possible by the assimilation of Aristotle's *libri naturales* (and, later, his *Politica, Ethica, Rhetorica* and *Economica*) and, in part, to a desire to dissociate Christian learning from the heresies, blasphemies and errors which could be found in the works of Aristotle and his Arabian com-mentators[144]. Roland of Cremona, the first Dominican master at the University of Paris (1229), described philosophy as the handmaid *(an-cilla)* of theology, and theology as 'the ruler and queen of all the sci-ences which must wait upon it as servants'[145]. For Roland, theology was 'the science of sciences, which is raised above all philosophical speculation and surpasses all others in dignity'. Similar statements were made by St Albert the Great and St Thomas Aquinas[146].

One concomitant of this dichotomy was a distinction between the supreme Scriptural authority and the more specialised and limited au-thorities of the ancillary disciplines. St Albert emphasised that, in theology, an authoritative source is inspired by the spirit of truth, whereas the authorities of the other sciences are much weaker[147]. Simi-larly, St Thomas believed that the argument from authority based on divine revelation is the strongest possible, whereas the argument from authority based on human reason is the weakest[148]. The main principle underlying these statements is that the superior science, theology, is based on revelation, whereas all the other sciences are based on human reasonings.

The 'philosophers', who had relied on their natural reason, were mainly pagans. Hence, there was an historical aspect to this distinction between theology and philosophy. Most of the great pagan philoso-phers had lived before the advent of Christ and, therefore, were ignorant of divine revelation. However, they may have had certain inklings and intimations of the truth to come, as Virgil had in his *Eclogues*[149]. Many late-medieval thinkers were interested in pagan fore-runners and prophets[150].

It was generally agreed that pagan *auctores* and the writers of the Old Testament were similar in several important ways. First, pagan writers and Old Testament writers had lived before the time of Christ; the *auctoritas* of their work was thereby limited in relation to the great *auctoritas* of the New Testament[151]. Old Testament writers had a greater degree of *auctoritas* than pagan writers, but these two classes of writers were, as it were, close together on the scale of authorities. Pagan and Old Testament *auctores* were similar in the extent of their limitations.

Secondly, they were similar also in the nature of their limitations, in the basis of the *auctoritas* they possessed in the eyes of their readers. Both Solomon and Aristotle, for example, had used their natural reason[152]. Of course, Solomon had sometimes been aided by divine inspiration whereas Aristotle had not but, in other contexts, there often seemed to be very little between them[153]. When the *auctoritas* of Solomon consisted in inspirations, Aristotle had to defer to him. But when Solomon's *auctoritas* consisted in human reasonings, he was supposed to be operating on the same wavelength as Aristotle, whose *auctoritas* consisted solely in rationalisation[154].

Thirdly, pagan and Old Testament *auctores* were experts in the same areas of study; they were believed to have been interested in the same things[155]. The juxtaposition of Solomon and Aristotle in late-medieval exegesis is more understandable if one remembers that Aristotle was considered to possess a considerable *auctoritas* in many of those matters raised by Solomon[156]. The assertions of an *auctor* with a limited degree of *auctoritas* could be supplemented with the assertions of other *auctores* with limited degrees of *auctoritas*. Solomon was supported by the pagan philosophers and poets[157].

There was an increasing recourse to secular *auctoritates* (i.e. extracts) in commentaries on the Sapiential Books of the Bible, what Miss Smalley has called a 'secularisation of sources'[158]. The assumed justification for this seems to have been that these books discussed pagan beliefs which had to be clarified from pagan sources, and that they taught philosophy, natural science, politics and ethics, subjects in which pagan writers were held to have *auctoritas* by reason of their acknowledged experience[159]. In the twelfth century, pagan writers were read by theologians mainly to be 'despoliated'[160]; in later centuries, they were recognised as being the experts in certain areas of study and, hence, they became a source of *auctoritas*. Not only did the pagans supply material for many of the glosses, they also supplied many of the working assumptions about method. Commentaries on the Sapiential Books were introduced with elaborate extrinsic prologues which discuss wisdom or 'sapience' in the Aristotelian sense of the term (see p. 32). It may have seemed appropriate that Scriptural books which pertained to philosophical subjects should be prefaced with descriptions of philosophical principles vouched for by 'the philosopher' himself.

The Sapiential Books were susceptible to such treatment because they were believed to possess a limited degree of *auctoritas*. In his *Generalis introitus ad sacram Scripturam,* John of Rochelle (master of theology by 1238) divided the books of the Law into works 'of primary authority' and works 'of secondary authority'[161]. The Sapiential Books were placed in the latter category because they were not among the Hebrew books. This topic of the degree of *auctoritas* possessed by the Sapiential Books was also related to the issue of whether Solomon had indeed written all or any of the books traditionally ascribed to him. Hugh of St Cher regarded as 'sapiential' those books of uncertain authorship which contained sound but limited doctrine:

All books of which the authorship is not certain, or of which the sanctity is not evident, are, when they are read in Church, entitled with the name of 'Wisdom', because all truth is from Wisdom.[162]

Because Solomon occupied this somewhat ambiguous position, medieval commentators felt freer to discuss his personal activity (both moral and literary) than they ever did to discuss, for example, the personal activity of the Four Evangelists. Even in the fourteenth century, commentaries on the Evangelists remained quite conservative, relying heavily on received interpretations derived mainly from the Fathers and Saints[163]. Hence, it is no accident that most of the major discussions of human literary activity which have been examined in this chapter appear in analyses of Old Testament books, and that many of the very best examples occur in commentaries on the Sapiential Books. Elaborate discussions of authorial role were provided in intrinsic prologues to commentaries on books of limited *auctoritas,* whereas the extrinsic prologues to those same books provided the rationale for the support of this *auctoritas* with quotations *(auctoritates)* from pagan writers, writers who were well aware of the truth that came from sapience[164].

Our conclusions so far may be summarised as follows. The late-medieval concern for the integrity of the individual *auctor* produced new principles, both for the analysis of those authorial roles which were being discovered in the literal sense of Scripture, and for the grouping of *auctoritates* from different types of source. In the eye of the beholder, a rapport existed between the Christian and pagan authorities in certain areas of study. Scholars saw such assorted *auctores* as Solomon and Aristotle as possessing a comparable degree of *auctoritas*. Moreover, resemblances were being seen in the literary and moral activities of Scriptural and pagan *auctores*. Some 'efficient causes' appeared to have moved in similar ways. These conclusions may now be substantiated further by an examination of the 'formal causes' which the human *auctores* had implemented, within the literal sense of Scripture, in expressing and organising their divine revelations.

4

Literary Forms
in the 'Literal Sense'

IN TWELFTH-CENTURY PROLOGUES to Scriptural commentaries, the heading 'mode of proceeding' *(modus agendi)* had usually introduced discussion, conducted with limited interest in literary issues, of the way in which the deep divine meaning of the work had been formulated. The *modus* was regarded as the property of the Holy Spirit rather than that of the human *auctor*. In the related sphere of literary construction, commentators had searched the books of the Bible for hidden principles of order and form. According to Honorius 'of Autun', 'each book of sacred Scripture has its special divisions and its special significations of number'[1].

The thirteenth century saw a major change of attitude to the concept of form: form came to be regarded as a function of the literal sense of Scripture. According to the Aristotelian theories of causality promulgated by late-medieval thinkers, the form *(forma)* was the pattern aimed at in a process of generation[2]. In a literary context, the *auctor*, the agent responsible for the generation of the text, was believed to have brought the text's formal cause from potentiality to act. The human *auctor*, writer of the literal sense, produced the *forma* of his text.

The commentators who employed the 'Aristotelian prologue' spoke of the form of a work as being twofold *(duplex)*. First, a work is composed in a certain form of writing: the *auctor* uses a certain literary style or technique. Second, the work is organised in accordance with a certain form or structure. The first aspect of form was called the 'form of treatment' *(forma tractandi)*; the second was called variously the 'form of the treatise' *(forma tractatus)*, the 'division of the text' *(divisio textus)* or the 'ordering of parts' *(ordinatio partium)*. Because these two aspects of form are very different—one may compare the two very different aspects or levels of authorship brought together by the heading *duplex causa efficiens*—they will be discussed separately.

THE *FORMA TRACTANDI*

The *forma tractandi* of a given work was the 'mode of proceeding' (*modus agendi*) which the *auctor* was supposed to have used, and there were said to be two basic kinds of mode or method, because there were two basic kinds of book: the book of divine science (the Bible) and the books of the human arts and sciences (all other books). The idiom of literary theory employed in considering *formae tractandi* received its main impetus and its most comprehensive definition in the course of thirteenth-century debate on the stock question (*quaestio*) 'is theology a science?'. Because all the major theologians of the day felt obliged to pronounce on the nature of theology they had something to say about the different *formae tractandi* used in the Bible and in the textbooks of human science, and this discussion proved very propitious for the emergence of literary theory. Scriptural exegetes were thereby provided with a sophisticated and systematic idiom which did justice to the stylistic complexity of each and every sacred text, and with a theoretical justification for their sensitive analysis of literary devices.

The investigation of the nature of theology found in the *Summa theologica* attributed to Alexander of Hales (*c.* 1186–1245) was perhaps one of the first and was certainly one of the most influential[3]. Alexander begins by asking if the Bible can be classed among the books of the human arts and sciences (in this context the terms *ars* and *scientia* mean the same thing)[4]. It would appear that the Bible is not an 'artificial' or 'scientific' work, Alexander speculates, because human sciences work through the comprehension of truth by human reason, whereas sacred Scripture works through the inculcation of a pious disposition (*secundum affectum pietatis*) in men. This difficulty is resolved by distinguishing between two kinds of science: human science, which involves ratiocination, and divine science, which has sacred tradition as its basis and which is the science described by St Augustine as consisting of those things which pertain to salvation. Divine science appeals to the *affectus*, which in this context means the 'affections', 'inclination' or 'disposition' of the mind. On the other hand, human science appeals to the intellect (*intellectus*), to the rational part of the mind.

Note indeed that there must be one mode of science which has to inform the affections in accord with piety, and another mode of science which has to inform the intellect alone in the learning of truth.

Robert Kilwardby, whose account of the two kinds of science was greatly indebted to Alexander's, makes the same point by stating that human science has knowledge alone as its end or objective *(finis)*[5]. This is philosophy, science considered as science *(scientia ut scientia)*. But theology, science considered as wisdom *(scientia ut sapientia)*, strives towards the love of the good and the reverence of God. Its *finis* is the inculcation of faith, hope and charity. Within the distinction between the disposition and the intellect, Kilwardby—like Richard Fishacre before him—substituted the term *aspectus* (denoting the 'gaze' or 'looking' of the reason) for Alexander's *intellectus*[6].

This complex theory of two distinct kinds of science may be better understood if the ubiquitous distinction between the disposition and the intellect is explained. It may be traced back to St Augustine, who in his *Soliloquia* introduced the metaphor of sight to describe the intellectual and rational power of the soul[7]. The senses of the soul are, as it were, the eyes of the mind, and reason is to the mind what the act of looking *(aspectus)* is to the eyes. In order that the mind's eyes may see rightly and perfectly, they must be purified from all corporeal stain and from the desire of mortal things; this may be effected by the cleansing action of faith, hope and charity. Even if the soul should attain the true vision of God, which is the objective of looking *(finis aspectus)*, while she remains in the body she will constantly require the assistance of those cardinal virtues.

Augustine's opinions were elaborated in the pseudo-Augustinian *Liber de spiritu et anima*[8]. Through the rational power, the soul may be illuminated to obtain knowledge of things above itself, near itself, in itself and below itself (i.e. God, angels, the soul itself and earthly creation). Through the powers of concupiscence and irascibility, the soul may be influenced to desire, disdain, love or fear something. From rationality, proceed all the senses of the soul; from the other powers, all the affections. The disposition *(affectus)* is fittingly fourfold, comprising the affections of delight, misery, love and fear; these four are, as it were, the fount and the common material of all the virtues and vices.

The relative functions of the *aspectus* and the *affectus* were more precisely delineated by thirteenth-century thinkers[9]. Describing Robert

Grosseteste's constant recourse to the distinction, D. A. Callus remarked that 'he was never tired of bringing it in whenever he could, in season and out of season'[10]. Callus summarised Grosseteste's understanding of the terminology in this way:

Gazing (*aspectus*) gives us the first grasp; next comes a verification of what we have contemplated or known; and when the mind is satisfied about what is attractive or noxious, then our affection (*affectus*) yearns to embrace what is attractive or withdraws within itself in flight from what is noxious.[11]

Such precision was probably due to an increase of interest in the relationship between the *aspectus* and the *affectus* occasioned by the debate (around 1220) on the powers of the soul[12]. William of Auxerre, one of the first Parisian schoolmen to make use of the new Aristotelian learning, was also one of the first to argue that the soul's faculties are distinct both from the soul itself and from each other[13]. One consequence of this was the opposition of the *affectus* to the apprehension of the intellect. In the treatise *De bono et malo* which he composed before he became Bishop of Paris in 1228, William of Auvergne defended the identity of the soul and its faculties, but William of Auxerre's opinion found favour with, among others, Alexander of Hales and John of Rochelle[14].

Alexander of Hales related the intellect and the *affectus* to human science and divine science, respectively. Human science, which depends on the intellect, pursues knowledge in accordance with truth; divine science works through the affections, seeking to move the *affectus* to goodness[15]. Theology perfects the soul according to affection, proceeding from the principles of fear and love; this, properly and principally, is wisdom. Discussing whether the method of sacred Scripture is more certain than those employed in other sciences, Alexander explains that the answer depends on what kind of certitude one is seeking: it is more certain according to the certitude of experience and of the *affectus*, but not more certain in the area of intellectual speculation[16]. The science of theology is superior because, ultimately, it is concerned with goodness rather than knowledge.

Similar solutions were put forward by Fishacre and Kilwardby who, by emphasising the differences between divine science and human science, made the gap between faith and reason even wider. In the spirit of Grosseteste, Fishacre made the unusual suggestion that one's inclina-

tion (*affectus*) ought to be fashioned by good conduct before the gaze of
the intellect (the *aspectus*) should be allowed to range over difficult
questions about the faith[17]. Kilwardby followed both Alexander of
Hales and Fishacre in arguing for the primacy of the *affectus*[18]. Whereas
human science need only illuminate the *aspectus*, theology must prepare
the affections and kindle the disposition both in accordance with ultimate truth and in love of the ultimate good. Mere ratiocination is
inadequate for the purposes of theology since this satisfies only the
aspectus, whereas precepts, exhortation, prayer and such things are necessary in theology. Therefore, the mode (*modus*) of sacred Scripture
is partly preceptive, partly exhortative, partly orative, and so on, because by such things the *affectus* is prepared and inflamed.

The basis of the common distinction between the two kinds of science having been described, we can proceed to examine in some detail
the two modes of procedure which were supposed to correspond to
these two kinds of science. Here is Alexander's version of the modes
appropriate to human science and divine science respectively:

> The first mode must be definitive, divisive and collective; and such a mode
> must exist in human sciences because the apprehension of truth through the
> human reason is unfolded by divisions, definitions and ratiocinations. The
> second mode must be preceptive, exemplifying, exhorting, revelatory and ora-
> tive, because these methods are conducive to a pious disposition; and this
> mode is in sacred Scripture . . .[19]

These two modes will now be considered in turn.

The mode of human science, the *modus definitivus, divisivus et collectivus*, consisted of the procedures characteristic of human science in
general[20]. The *auctores* of the various human sciences were supposed to
have engaged in these procedures in writing their books. *Definitio, divisio* and *collectio* are necessary procedures in human science, as Kilwardby says in his commentary on the *Sentences:*

> These sciences which diligently seek the truth by human reason, necessarily
> have to define, divide and collect. For division and definition are necessary for
> knowledge of uncomplex things . . . Collection or ratiocination is necessary
> for knowledge of complex things . . .[21]

Definitio comes first in the order of things: this is necessary in order
that a science be delimited, that its subject-area be known[22]. No science can define itself, because every definition is from things which are

logically prior (in order to define man as a 'rational animal', we must first know what 'animal' is). Subject comes first in a science, hence the subject of a science must be defined by the science which is logically prior to it. *Divisio* gives us the parts of the subject[23]. The subject or genus is divided up into its special differences or parts; these parts of species are defined by reference to ideas that are prior to themselves (the genus 'animal' is prior to the species 'horse'). *Collectio* means ratiocination, the 'gathering together' of propositions so that conclusions may be drawn from them by syllogistic method[24]. This provides knowledge of complex things, knowledge of the special attributes *(passiones)* of the parts or species of a subject: men may argue and draw conclusions about what a science really entails.

These three procedures of human science are well summed up in this passage from the renowned logician Peter of Spain (Master of Arts at Paris around 1240):

By definition is given the entire subject. Division is given to the parts of the subject; to collect or prove and disprove is due to the attributes of the parts, because the attributes are rightly proved from their subjects.[25]

Sometimes the term 'probative and improbative mode' *(modus probativus et improbativus)* was used instead of the term 'collective mode' *(modus collectivus)*, as, for example, in the prologue to the Priscian-commentary written by 'Master Jordan' at Paris about 1245: 'The form of treatment is the mode of proceeding which is principally definitive, divisive, probative, improbative, and applies examples'[26].

The 'mode of applying examples' *(modus exemplorum suppositivus)* was not a necessary procedure of human science, unlike the very essential *modus definitivus, divisivus et collectivus*. This is made clear in the commentary on the *Barbarismus* which Kilwardby wrote at Paris before his entry into the Dominican order:

The necessary mode of proceeding is threefold: namely definitive, divisive and collective, and yet the mode which is collective is not used much by Donatus in this treatise. The mode of proceeding does not necessarily apply examples.[27]

However, while examples are not absolutely necessary for a science, they are certainly useful, especially in the teaching of a science. Peter of Spain stated that 'the application of examples is useful for learners, whence Aristotle says, "We employ examples so that whoever learns may perceive by the senses" '[28].

But the 'mode of applying examples' was by no means confined to the texts of human science; Scriptural exegetes found that their *auctores* had often used examples. For instance, the Oxford Franciscan, Thomas Docking (regent master sometime between 1260 and 1265), praised St Paul for his good *modus agendi* in Galatians, which is said to consist in irrefrangible authority, efficacious reason and the application of examples *(suppositio exemplorum)*[29]. In the 'Commendation of sacred Scripture' which he delivered as part of his inception as Master of Theology in 1256, Thomas Aquinas provided a detailed analysis of the way in which *exempla* are utilised in the Apocrypha and the Hagiographia[30].

This completes our investigation of the mode of human science; we may now consider the 'multiple mode' of holy Scripture, the *modus praeceptivus, exemplificativus,* etc. This consisted at once of the procedures characteristic of divine science and the different modes of writing or *modi agendi* employed in the various books of the Bible. No two books of Scripture were believed to be exactly alike. According to Alexander of Hales, the preceptive mode *(modus praeceptivus)* is found in the Pentateuch, the historical and exemplifying mode *(modus historicus et exemplificativus)* in the Historiographic Books, the exhorting mode *(modus exhortativus)* in the Sapiential Books, the revelatory mode *(modus revelativus)* in the Prophetic Books and the orative mode *(modus orativus)* in the Psalter[31]. The books of the New Testament are different again:

Likewise, in the Gospel is the historical mode covering the narration of the life and actions of Christ, and the instructing and advising mode in the teaching of Christ; in the Epistles of Paul and in the canonical writings there is the warning mode; in Acts, the historical mode; in the Apocalypse, the revelatory mode.

Subsequent commentators refined upon Alexander's list. For example, here is part of the discussion of the Scriptural modes provided by Odo Rigaldi, Alexander's disciple and successor in the Franciscan chair at Paris (1244–7):

The orative mode is in the Psalter in order that the affections may be moved from within. There are other modes in order that they may be moved by instruction from outside. Certainly, there is the mode that moves because of power, and this mode, the preceptive, is in the Books of the Law and the Evangelists, to which is added the threatening and promising mode corresponding to the prohibitions and precepts. Or there is the mode that moves because of wisdom, and this is the revelatory mode, as in the Prophets and the

Apocalypse. There is the mode that moves because of goodness, and this is the warning mode, either by examples as in the Historical Books or by word of mouth as in Solomon's books or by writings as in the Epistles. To these modes others are reduced and are subordinated.[32]

One is reminded of Peter Abelard's synopsis of the different literary techniques employed in both Testaments (see pp. 61–2), but the thirteenth-century discussions are at once more intricate and more systematic.

The emergence of this vast repertory of modes manifests the fact that, in the later Middle Ages, analysis of Scripture involved a considerable amount of literary analysis. As M.-D. Chenu put it,

The mode of sacred doctrine is a literary method, proceeding by analysis of a text where narratives, metaphors, poetic imagery, examples and discourses require an interpretation which has nothing to do with the 'definitions, divisions and reasonings' of Aristotelian knowledge.[33]

The principles behind most of the Biblical modes described by Alexander and his successors may be traced to standard explanations of the methods of oratory. Hence, the bases for the narrative, orative and exemplary modes are found in the two main textbooks used in the medieval teaching of rhetoric, Cicero's *De inventione* and the *Ad Herennium*[34]. The modes connected with praising and blaming are derived from demonstrative rhetoric; those connected with persuading and dissuading, from deliberative rhetoric[35]. The theologians could draw on rhetorical lore in this manner because rhetoric was generally regarded as a humble handmaiden of theology and, more precisely, as a subordinate of logic[36]. The continuing influence of this view may be illustrated by reference to glosses on the recently-introduced *Rhetorica* of Aristotle. 'Dialectic is subsequent to rhetoric', declares the opening sentence of William of Moerbeke's translation of this work[37]. In the first Latin commentary thereon, written in the late thirteenth century by the theologian, Giles of Rome († 1316), the relationship between rhetoric and dialectic is explained as follows[38]. Scientific assent and dialectical assent are purely intellectual acts, while the assent of faith can be called intellectual only in so far as the intellect is open to being moved by an appetite, a desire of the will. The rhetorician generates belief by moving the will, by arousing appetites; his persuasive arguments employ enthymemes and *exempla*. In his commentary on the *Sentences* and elsewhere, Giles argued that theology is basically affective[39]. Clearly, this is of a piece with his attitude to rhetoric. Scriptural texts obtain the assent of faith by moving the reader's will and appealing to his *affectus*. The *modus sacrae Scripturae* is essentially a rhetorical mode.

Similarly, the resources of medieval poetics could be drawn upon in expounding the complex literary effects found in Scripture. The formulation of some of the Biblical modes was probably influenced by the *accessus* and commentaries on secular *auctores* produced by medieval grammarians. However, traditional rhetoric and poetics could not provide a vocabulary to cope with all the problems of description presented by divinely-inspired texts (see pp. 33–6). Clearly, the revelatory mode, as employed in the Prophets and the Apocalypse, was far beyond the terms of reference of secular learning. The theologians were concerned to establish the superior status of the Bible; the fact that it employed such a wide diversity of modes indicated its unique qualities.

The repertory of modes outlined in discussions of the nature of theology provided a framework for analysis of the individual characteristics of the different books of the Bible, as is manifested by the way in which Alexander of Hales and St Bonaventure commended the benefits accruing from the 'multiple mode' *(multiplex modus)* of Scripture. Alexander begins by asking if the multiple mode is, in fact, beneficial to the reader of Scripture or not[40]. Since 'all that is written is written for our doctrine' (Romans xv.4), a 'uniform mode' *(uniformis modus)* might convey this doctrine better. The more uniform the mode, the more plain and easy it would be for us to understand. Alexander dismisses this suggestion with a justification of the rich literary variety of the Bible. All that is written is indeed written for our doctrine, and the more varied the writing the better.

Alexander offers three reasons in support of his view: because of the *auctor,* because of the material, and because of the end *(finis).* Concerning the first, Alexander quotes Wisdom vii.22 as saying that the Holy Spirit is both single and manifold. Because the Holy Spirit was the first *auctor* of the Bible, a manifold mode must be used in order that the rich divine teaching be clearly revealed to men. Concerning the second, Alexander states that the material of Scripture is the multiform wisdom of God. Multiform material necessitates a multiform *modus.* Thirdly, Alexander explains that the *finis* of the Bible is to instruct men in those things which pertain to salvation. Because many things pertain to salvation, the method of teaching those things should not be uniform. There are many states of men—for instance, men living under the Law, after the Law, in the time of the prophets, in the time of grace. Within any one of these states further diversity may be found. Some men are good, some are bad; they live according to different mores and customs. The instruction which Scripture provides is ordained for the salvation of men, and a multiple mode must be used in order to do justice to the nobility of this *finis*.

Bonaventure's conception of the end and means of sacred Scripture is substantially in agreement with Alexander's. In his *Breviloquium* (written 1254–7), Bonaventure says that the intention (*intentio*) of Scriptural doctrine is to make us virtuous and able to attain salvation[41]. This is achieved not merely by speculation but by a disposition of the will. Hence, the divine Scriptures had to be written in whatever way would dispose us best. Our disposition (*affectus*) is moved more strongly by examples than by ratiocinative argument, by promised rewards than by reasoning, by devotion than by dogma. The Scriptures make use of their own modes, adapting themselves to the different mental states that make souls reason differently. For instance, were a man to remain unmoved by a command or prohibition, he might be moved by favours; were this again to fail, he might be moved by wise admonitions, trustworthy promises or terrifying threats, and thus be stirred, if not in one way then in another, to devotion and praise of God. Therefore, it is right and fitting that Scripture should employ a varied mode.

The Scriptural mode, Bonaventure continues, cannot proceed to certitude by way of ratiocinative argument, since the particular facts of which it treats cannot be proved formally. Consequently, lest Scripture should appear doubtful and lose some of its power to move, God has given it, in place of the evidence of demonstration through reasoning, the certitude of *auctoritas:* so absolute is this certainty that it surpasses any certainty attainable by the keenest human mind. No passage of Scripture, he concludes, should be regarded as valueless, rejected as false, or repudiated as evil, for its all-perfect *auctor,* the Holy Spirit, could inspire nothing untrue, trivial or degraded. It would seem then that, behind the great diversity and range of the styles found in the Bible, lies the singleness and security of divine authority.

Thus far the two types of science and the literary modes appropriate to each have been described, with special attention being paid to theologians' discussions of the multiple mode of Holy Scripture. Late-medieval accounts of Biblical *formae tractandi*, far from being inconsequential, or peripheral to the main concerns of the age, were in fact an integral part of a great debate, conducted among many of the greatest thinkers of that period, about the qualities of the highest and most secure form of knowledge known to man.

Indeed, the emphasis which a theologian would place on certain Scriptural modes as opposed to others would be to some extent determined by his personal opinion of the nature of theology. For example, St Thomas Aquinas made few concessions to 'modes of symbolic thought'[42]. Disapproving of the disjunction between rational science and affective wisdom advocated by Alexander of Hales and his followers, he sought to emphasise the intellectual and rational facet of the science of theology. Aquinas's vision of subordinated sciences ruled by theology depends on an acceptance of the similarities between divine science and human science[43]. This view is reflected in his exegesis: for example, the point is laboured that Job and the Apostle Paul employ the 'disputative mode' (*modus disputativus*)[44].

Much more extreme was the reaction of Henry of Ghent. Henry held that the science of theology was speculative rather than practical or affective; his unusual brand of Neoplatonism drove a wedge between divine ideas and individual reality[45]. Hence God, the primary *auctor* of Scripture, is conceived of as having inspired the human *auctores* of the Bible without seeking their cooperation or asking their leave. Henry seems inclined to deny them any meaningful contribution to sacred Scripture[46].

The conviction that there are no divine ideas of individuals, but only of species, informs Henry's attack on Alexander of Hales's account of the *multiplex modus* of Scripture (as paraphrased above)[47]. There may be multiform materials in the Bible, the divine wisdom may be multiform and there may be multiform states of mankind but, according to Henry, this does not mean that the *modus tractandi* characteristic of theology is manifold[48]. Certainly, in some places, the Scriptures admonish, in others, they prohibit, etc., but this diversity exists, not on account of the mode of treatment, but rather because of the diverse materials treated therein: hence, in one place, precepts may be propounded; in another, prohibitions, and so on.

Henry argues that divine science does not have a mode which treats of individual things singularly and distinctly. Instead, within one and the same discourse are contained diverse *sententiae* concerning diverse materials and diverse beliefs, pertinent to diverse states of men in various ways. Different men may understand this discourse according to their individual capacities: some are content with the literal surface; others look under it for the spiritual understanding. In absolute terms, the Scriptural mode is the very sum of simplicity and uniformity. But what of the objection that, in this science, God spoke in many and multifarious modes? Henry's answer is that such variety relates not to the mode of treatment or writing but rather to the various ways in which the compositions were revealed to diverse persons. For example, Daniel received his revelation by dream; Moses, by direct speech; and David, by interior inspiration. Therefore, the absolute uniformity of the *modus tractandi* of theology is unimpeachable.

The contrast with one of Henry's opponents, Giles of Rome, could hardly be greater. Giles was interested in the supra-rational properties of Biblical texts and in the ways in which inspired Scripture appealed to the individual. Lecturing on the *Sentences* (1276), he argued that the end *(finis)* of theology is love, *caritas*[49]. As *caritas* is in the power of the affection—in contradistinction to those speculative and practical questions which concern the intellect—the science of theology is therefore affective rather than intellectual. These ideas permeate the 'Aristotelian prologue' to Giles's magnificent commentary on the Song of Songs, in which the emotive and epithalamic qualities of that text, so well brought out by St Bernard and William of St Thierry, are reassessed in the light of the new Aristotelian learning[50]. Solomon's *modus agendi,* Giles explains, appeals primarily, not to the intellect, but to the will. The inspired *auctor* expressed his revelation through a *modus affectivus, desiderativus et contemplativus:*

The mode of procedure in other sciences is by positive proof or refutation: however, in sacred Scripture, and most importantly in the Canon, it is seen to be through inspiration, that is, by revelation, because such a treatise is more substantially based on revelation than on rational proof. Indeed, the mode of proceeding in this book in particular is seen to be affective, desiderative and contemplative.

The persuasive power of this style of writing plays a major part in implementing the ultimate end or final cause of the sacred book,

namely love of God. But is this not the end of all sacred doctrine? Giles
replies that the *finis* of the Song of Songs is related to the *finis* of theology just as the part is related to the whole. In general, the end of all
sacred doctrine is the love of God, but in particular Solomon's song
provokes us to the love of God and our neighbours. Solomon employed
the 'affective mode' (*modus affectivus*) in this work; the entire science of
theology is affective rather than intellectual.

It would seem, therefore, that a theologian's general approach to the
science of theology could influence considerably his particular approach
to the individual theological text. We have been concentrating on
highly theoretical and abstract discussions of the Biblical mode of procedure: it is time to investigate what was happening in the Scriptural
commentaries themselves. Many exegetes seem to have accepted (at
least tacitly) Alexander of Hales's belief in the manifold nature of the
Scriptural mode, since their commentaries contain detailed analyses of
the various *formae tractandi* used by the various *auctores*. The next few
pages will illustrate the impressive diversity and range of style being
discovered in the Bible considered as a whole, or even within a single
book of the Bible.

The beauty of the rhetorical figures and methods of expression with
which Scriptural *auctores* had adorned their works was praised often. In
his commentary on Lamentations, John Pecham (who succeeded Kilwardby as Archbishop of Canterbury in 1279), explained the workings
of the 'lamentative mode' (*modus lamentativus*) in this way:

It must be known, that this book is adorned in three ways with musical and
rhetorical elegance. First, in eloquence, because it is written metrically . . .
Moreover, secondly it is adorned with rhetorical divisions in profound sayings
. . . Moreover, thirdly this song is adorned with the arranged letters of the
alphabet, by which the individual sayings are introduced . . .[51]

Thomas Aquinas had seen Lamentations in a similar light, believing it
to be enveloped with verbal adornment, whence it is both written metrically and coloured with rhetorical ornaments[52]. In his popular commentary on the same text, the Oxford Franciscan, John Lathbury,
quoted St Fulgentius and Gilbert of Poitiers on the emotive power of
the 'song of lamentation'[53]. In short, late-medieval exegetes believed
that their *auctores* had manipulated their styles with full awareness of
the effect of rhetorical figures and (in the case of divine poetry and song)
the power of verse.

One mode of procedure in particular, the use of proverbs or parables (the *modus parabolicus*), had received considerable attention in discussions of the nature of theology. Alexander of Hales raised the problem that, while parables and proverbs are employed in sacred Scripture, it would seem that this mode is neither historical, allegorical, tropological or anagogical[54]. His answer was that the *modus parabolicus* may be reduced to the historical sense, since, in speaking of history, one can refer either to real things, as in historical events, or to the similitudes of things, as in parables. The very same problem is found at the beginning of the *Summa theologiae* of St Thomas Aquinas, where a similar solution is offered.

The parabolical sense is contained in the literal sense, for words can signify something properly and something figuratively; in the last case the literal sense is not the figure of speech itself, but the object it figures. When Scripture speaks of the arm of God, the literal sense is not that he has a physical limb, but that he has what it signifies, namely the power of doing and making. This example brings out how nothing false can underlie the literal sense of Scripture.[55]

The Scriptural exegetes were mainly interested in the efficiency of this mode as a teaching device. The fact that it taught in an apparently fictional manner and through a sort of concealment was frequently remarked upon. Developing Aquinas's theory of the *modus parabolicus,* Nicholas Trevet argued that a parable expresses one idea on the surface of the words, which is the sign and outer rind, and another in the inward understanding, which is the thing signified and inner pith. Many psalms, he claims, signify Christ in this way[56]. In his commentary on Proverbs (*c.* 1347–8 at Cambridge), the 'classicising friar' Thomas Ringstead, having quoted Papias's definition of parable, explained that this Scriptural text treats of moral *sententiae* under occult similitudes[57].

On the other hand, sometimes a more direct and straightforward style was judged to be well-suited to the matter in hand. Aquinas dismissed the idea that Job had employed the *modus parabolicus:* his story is actual fact, not signifying anything by corporeal likenesses[58]. Similarly, according to Aquinas, the mode employed by the prophet Isaiah 'is plain and open'[59]. If twelfth-century exegetes had sometimes ignored stylistic considerations in their search for allegorical meanings, their successors placed a premium on the right meaning in the right literary form.

The stylistic range achieved by a single *auctor* or group of *auctores* could now be described with considerable precision. A good example is furnished by the explanation of the formal cause of the Twelve Minor Prophets' work which was put forward by a disciple of Alexander of Hales, William of Middleton, who helped to complete the *Summa theologica* which Alexander had left unfinished at his death. William's treatment of the 'mode of prophetic speculation' brings out the stylistic similarities and differences between his *auctores*[60]. Many exegetes, including Thomas Aquinas, Thomas Docking and Peter of Tarantasia (who became Pope Innocent V in 1276), commented on the wide range of modes of procedure employed by St Paul in his Epistles[61].

Solomon also was supposed to have had a mastery of various styles. Nicholas of Lyre postulated a threefold *forma tractandi* in the Sapiential Books: Proverbs proceeds mainly by admonishing, Ecclesiastes mainly by threatening and the Song of Songs mainly by promising[62]. In his popular commentary on Ecclesiastes, St Bonaventure asked if a single *auctor* could possibly have written Ecclesiastes, the Song of Songs and Proverbs[63]. The answer is 'yes', but these books differ in *modus agendi* and *finis*. An *auctor* is under no obligation to use a particular *modus agendi* on two occasions. In Proverbs, Solomon introduces himself speaking as a wise man to a disciple, and proceeds by the 'parabolic mode' (*modus parabolicus*). By contrast, Bonaventure claims, in the Song of Songs, a groom is seen speaking to his bride. The role of the *auctor* is different here, and so is his appropriate mode. Solomon did not want us to read the Song of Songs at the literal level, as his words to his wife, but rather as the words of Christ to the Church. Therefore, he did not give his name in the book-title, as he did in the case of Proverbs: the Song of Songs was deliberately left without a named human *auctor*. Bonaventure then distinguishes between Ecclesiastes and Proverbs in terms of *finis*. In Proverbs the wise man speaks; in Ecclesiastes, we hear the penitent man: the *finis* of the former is sapience; of the latter, contempt of the world.

Stylistic differences could be made the basis of an argument about another literary issue, for example about the authorship of a text. In a commentary on the Apocalypse falsely ascribed to St Albert the Great, the 'mode or form' of this text is described as 'prophetic' (*prophetialis*)[64]. The commentator then asks if the John who wrote this text was St John the Evangelist, as was commonly supposed in the

Middle Ages. This discussion provides an interesting record of the differing views on the subject held by unnamed scholars. One of the main arguments used, it is claimed, is that the style of the Apocalypse is quite different from that found in St John's gospel:

This book [the Apocalypse] is full of obscurities and many figures, in which there is not revelation, but rather obscurity and convolution. Item, they say that John the Apostle wrote useful things, whereas in truth this book has nothing worthy of the apostolic gravity . . . Indeed, others say that this was the book of a certain Saint John who was not the Apostle; and they prove this by the fact that the mode of writing (*modus scribendi*) in this book does not resemble the style of Saint John the Apostle.

The exegetes' discussions of their authors' *formae tractandi* became more and more literary. For example, the rhetorical figures found in Scriptural works became more complex. In an anonymous Lamentations commentary which has been printed among the works of Albert the Great, Cicero's aid is enlisted in explaining the 'lamentative mode':

The mode is not indeed of dictamen, but of introduced orations taken from the two types of oration which Tully distinguished in *The Second Rhetorics,* of which one is called 'complaint' and the other 'indignation'.[65]

The commentator solemnly lists the sixteen modes of *conquestio* and the fifteen modes of *indignatio*.

The expertise of authorities on rhetoric, music and poetry was consulted more often. Nicholas Trevet made points about the Psalter by referring to Virgil's *Aeneid*[66]; he also cited the view of Boethius that music has the power to soothe savage passions

. . . by means of touch a musical sound proceeds from the psaltery in which resides a power sedative to passions, as Boethius teaches in the beginning of the *De musica*. There he tells of a certain youth of Taormina in Sicily who, when he was drunk one night and lusted to break into a certain man's house in which a courtesan was kept, was driven by such a rage that he could not be restrained even by parents or friends. However, Pythagoras, who nearby was regarding the nocturnal courses of the stars, sent a flutegirl who sounded the Phrygian mode, which is by modern singers called Bemol. Then he advised a change to the spondaic mode, which is heavy and harsh, and is designated among us Bequarre. At once the fury of the youth was soothed and he returned to his right mind.[67]

Just as, from the psaltery, by means of touch, proceeds a musical sound able to soothe passions, so, from Christ, by means of touch, has come a force capable of healing every infirmity. The touch of His passion healed mankind. Just as, by the lute's sound, David drove an evil spirit from Saul, so, at the sound of Christ's name, demons are driven from men.

Boethius's *De musica* was drawn on by Giles of Rome also, in a discussion of sacred song which forms part of the prologue to his commentary on the Song of Songs[68]. Giles suggests that, just as in 'exterior locutions' corporeal song results from melody and proportion so also, in 'interior locutions' (called by St Augustine the heart's speeches), a sort of spiritual melody or intelligible song results from that order and proportion which is directed towards God. We should not limit the term 'song' *(cantus)* to denoting a merely sensory thing, for—as Boethius says—musical proportion pertains to the form of every created thing. Since melody and proportion also attend every virtuous action, Giles proposes to describe as 'songs' the good thoughts and affections of the human soul. God has, as it were, a good ear for 'songs' like the affections, thoughts, orations and desires of devout minds. Therefore, Christ the bridegroom invites his bride (a holy soul or Holy Church) to sing, in this fashion: 'Let me hear your voice, for your voice is sweet and your face is comely' (Song of Songs ii. 14).

These changes of attitude and emphasis may also be illustrated by reference to late-medieval classifications of the books of the Bible. Jerome's classification had been accepted with little comment by, for example, Hugh of St Victor and Hugh of St Cher[69], but their successors sought to introduce new principles of division in accordance with literary criteria. Such refinements are conveniently summarised in the *principia, introitus* or inaugural lectures which Bachelors and Masters of Theology were required by statute to present[70]. These lectures were of standard format, containing a commendation of sacred Scripture and a division of its parts. For example, in his *Generalis introitus ad sacram Scripturam,* John of Rochelle divided the Old Testament into three major parts: the Law, the Prophets and the Psalter[71]. His subdivision of the Books of the Law entails a literary principle of discrimination. The Law, in the strict sense of the term, is said to comprise the five Mosaic books which are books of precepts. However, in addition, there are law-books which work through *exempla* (Joshua, Judges, Kings, Paralipomenon, Esther, Judith, Tobit, Job and Machabees) and law-books which work through exhortation (Proverbs, Ecclesiastes, the Song of Songs, Wisdom and Ecclesiasticus).

In the portion of his 'Commendation of sacred Scripture' devoted to the Old Testament, Thomas Aquinas embroidered on Jerome's classification[72]. The Books of the Prophets may be divided in accordance with the different ways in which they lead the people to observe the Law. Isaiah works mainly by blandishment, Jeremiah mainly by threatening, and Ezechiel mainly by argumentation and vituperation. Because the Apocrypha and the Hagiographia are similar in 'mode of speaking' (modus loquendi), Thomas considers them together. Within this group, he says, some books teach by actual deeds in employing exempla, while others teach by verbal means.

By the early fourteenth century, literary form could provide the main basis of classification. Peter Auriol's Compendium totius Bibliae (1319) popularised the following division of the Old Testament: politica et legislativa (Pentateuch), chronica sive historica (Historical Books), hymnidica vel decantativa (Psalter, Song of Songs, Lamentations), monastica sive ethica (Proverbs, Wisdom, Ecclesiasticus) and prophetica (the Major and Minor Prophets)[73]. Auriol's discussion of the third part of the Old Testament, the hymnological or decantative part, is particularly interesting. In describing the 'mode of sacred poetry' (modus sacrae poetriae) he distinguishes between carmina, elegia and dramatica:

It should be known that poetic song is divided into three kinds. Into Carmina, which are songs of joy. . . , Elegies, which are songs of sorrow. . . , and Dramatic poems, which are songs of love. And this should be known: the decantative part of divine Scripture with regard to the mode of sacred poetry is divided into the Book of Psalms, which contains poems of joy and sweet pleasure, and the Book of Lamentations, which contains elegies of misery and sadness, and the Song of Songs, which contains dramas of beauty and love.[74]

Auriol has applied a scheme for classifying secular poetry to the description of sacred poetry. We may compare the list of the different species of poetry (carminis species) provided in the late eleventh century Commentum in Theodulum by Bernard of Utrecht:

There is the epithalamium, so-called because it is sung over the thalamos, that is, over marital beds, as in the Song of Songs. There is the trenos, that is, a lamentation, which is recited at the funerals of the dead . . . There is festive song, and these are called hymns; there is the elegy, which is a song of grief, from elegos meaning 'miserable' or Elegia a girl's name . . .[75]

Of course, the idea of appealing to the liberal arts for aid in describing a Scriptural text was not new. As has been mentioned already, the identification of the Song of Songs as a great 'dramatic' poem goes back to Origen (see p. 58). What was new in the late Middle Ages was the systematic and exhaustive way in which the diverse *formae tractandi* found in the Bible were being analysed.

Indeed, some exegetes seem to have 'discovered' and provided the literary theory for new literary forms, forms for which there was little basis in traditional rhetoric and poetics. For example, certain commentators were so impressed with the literary features which many prophetic writings seemed to possess, that they came to regard the 'prophetic mode' (*modus prophetialis*) as a possible *forma tractandi*. The most comprehensive discussion known to me of the *modus vel forma prophetialis* occurs in an anonymous commentary on Daniel which has been printed in the Vivès edition of the works of St Thomas Aquinas[76]. The anonymous commentator explains that all the Biblical prophets aimed at improving the people through their preaching. In order to make their divine message accessible, they employed a 'mode of preaching' appropriate to the people's capacities. This *modus praedicandi* was 'vulgar' so that everyone could understand it, using only simple words, words which were familiar to ordinary people. It was also popular, making use of parables: the people of Palestine, it is claimed, were accustomed to hearing parables. By their parables, these preachers 'signified much and persuaded many'—something which, the commentator ruefully remarks, 'we do not often achieve in preaching'. Moreover, the mode was historical and narrative. Their words were discontinuous, in that they might break off in their narratives, moving from one matter to another and, afterwards, returning to the first matter. Finally, the mode was prophetic and told of the future.

Our anonymous commentator has drawn freely on medieval theory of preaching in order to elucidate the style of those 'ancient' preachers who produced the Prophetic Books. For instance, his depiction of the discontinuous nature of the prophets' words recalls the seminal statement made by St Gregory the Great in the prologue to his *Moralia in Job*:

He who treats sacred eloquence ought to imitate the way of a stream. A flowing stream, if it meets with open valleys on its side, immediately turns into them, and when it has sufficiently filled them, immediately flows back to its bed.[77]

This passage is quoted in Robert of Basevorn's *Forma praedicandi*

(1322), where it is interpreted in terms of the need for orderly procedure in preaching. The preacher, Basevorn claims,

. . . should not dwell too long on the same point nor should he repeat more
often than is right. He should hastily progress from one thing to another as the
matter allows. An exception may be made when—without deviating too far
from the matter—he finds along the way a source of edification into which, as
I might say, he turns his stream of language as into a neighbouring valley.
When he has sufficiently filled the place of added instruction he turns back
into the channel of the intended sermon.[78]

It would seem that Daniel and his fellow-prophets controlled their
streams of language in such a manner. Basevorn's subsequent definition
of preaching as 'the persuasion of many . . . to meritorious conduct'
recalls the anonymous commentator's claim that all the Biblical
prophets intended to better the people through their preaching, an
ambition achieved by means of those successful parables which 'persuaded many'[79].

   This brief comparison will serve to remind us that the friars who
produced most of the literary theory discussed in this chapter had as
their essential vocation and function the preaching of the gospel. Their
preaching mission compelled the friars to devote themselves to the
study of doctrine, a prerequisite for the fulfilment of their evangelical
purpose[80]. The debate on the nature of theology, which has been outlined above, may seem rather recherché and remote to us, but it was a
burning issue for men preparing to be preachers and, as such, had
repercussions in their preaching[81]. Significantly, the theologians' distinction between the intellect or *aspectus* and the disposition or *affectus*
was echoed in the *De modo componendi sermones* of Thomas Waleys:

The preacher's task is not only to stir the intelligence towards what is true by
means of the inevitable conclusions of arguments, but also, by means of narrative and likely persuasion, to stir the emotions to piety.[82]

Many of the literary analyses of *formae tractandi* quoted above reflect the
overriding priority of preaching. When Alexander of Hales explained
that the *modus sacrae Scripturae* had to be multiform in order to cope
with all the different states of men, he was articulating the principle
behind the production and collection of 'sermons for different states',
sermons tailor-made to fit people of all kinds, ranks, classes and

callings, from each of the 'three estates' in medieval society and every subdivision thereof[83]. The same principle is behind our anonymous commentator's statement that the Old Testament prophets suited their *modus praedicandi* to the capabilities of the people of Palestine[84].

Clerks who were at University to become qualified preachers sought in the human *auctores* of Scripture models which they could imitate: the lecturers' comments on, for example, the didactic usefulness of parables and the persuasive power of certain styles must to some extent be seen in this light. This connection is made quite clear by the classification of Christ's preaching-methods supplied in Basevorn's *Forma praedicandi*. The Saviour is supposed to have employed promises, threats and examples; sometimes to have spoken openly, sometimes profoundly and obscurely[85]. These are familiar to us as *modi agendi* expounded by Scriptural exegetes. In sum, the Scriptural *auctor* was being regarded in the role of preacher; the literary form in which his doctrine was communicated was being interpreted in accordance with the practical needs of budding preachers. As a result, Daniel and his colleagues became preacher-prophets.

The significance of our discussion so far may be summarised as follows. Medieval theologians were not interested in making theoretical distinctions between rhetoric and poetics. Their main concern was to define the nature of theology, and one by-product of this was the creation, from a diversity of sources, of an idiom of literary theory sophisticated enough to do justice to the many rhetorical and poetic effects believed to be part of the literal sense of Scripture. Different Biblical *auctores*, it was recognised, could express themselves in different ways. A single *auctor* might express himself in different ways in different places: sometimes he might speak plainly; sometimes he might speak in a metaphorical or figurative way. Preachers with practical experience of the art of polished and persuasive expression were disposed to find precedent for their stylistic stratagems in Holy Writ; Scriptural *formae tractandi* could be identified and imitated by the modern evangelist. The relationship between scholastic literary theory and actual preaching practice was, therefore, a reciprocal one, as certain passages in the *artes praedicandi* indicate.

One aspect of the increase of interest in stylistic analysis is particularly significant for the history of literary theory. Late-medieval theologians were, in effect, establishing a common ground on which sacred poetry and profane poetry could meet. The manner in which this area of possible agreement emerged will now be investigated.

The statements of such twelfth-century exegetes as Gilbert of Poitiers and William of St Thierry about the profitable and commendable affective quality of sacred poetry may be regarded in some measure as a reply to the ancient charges brought against poetry, namely, that it inflames the passions of men, that poets are liars and that poetic writings are full of falsehoods (see above, pp. 49–52). In the thirteenth century, many thinkers went much further, by claiming that theology in its entirety, and not just some books of the Bible, worked in a kinetic way by appealing to the *affectus*. The debate on the nature of theology brought many literary issues from the periphery to a point much nearer the centre of academic attention. Exegetes were thereby encouraged to analyse in detail the affective and intellectual qualities of the various *formae tractandi* in the Bible.

In discussing the *modus* of Scripture, St Albert the Great raised the second major criticism mentioned above, that poetic writings are full of falsehoods. Because the 'poetic mode' (*modus poeticus*) employs fables (*fabulae*), things which are not true but fictitious, it would appear to be the weakest of the philosophical modes:

Certainly, the poetic mode is the weakest among the modes of philosophy, because it consists of fables, which are composed of marvellous elements, as 'the Philosopher' says in the first book of *The First Philosophy*. For the marvellous elements of fables are not true, but fictitious.[86]

Albert resolves the problem by distinguishing between human poetry, which employs the fabrications of men, and sacred poetry, which communicates indubitable truths in a figurative way. St Thomas Aquinas made a similar distinction: poetry employs metaphors for the sake of representations, in which we are naturally inclined to take delight, whereas holy teaching adopts them for their indubitable usefulness[87]. Scripture rightly puts forward spiritual things under bodily likenesses, in order that the uneducated may lay hold of them the more easily. Holy Scripture cannot contain anything that is false.

In this way, Albert and Aquinas made a sharp contrast between secular poetry and sacred poetry. It was one thing for Scriptural *auctores* to communicate truths in the literal sense by various kinds of figurative language: it was quite another for the pagan poets to communicate their half-truths and lies by apparently similar means. But, in the minds of later thinkers, the gap between these two kinds of poetry narrowed considerably.

This may be demonstrated by reference to the way in which Albert's views on poetry were developed by one of his pupils, Ulrich of Strassburg, whom Albert taught in the *studium generale* at Cologne which he had left Paris in 1248 to inaugurate. Ulrich's *Liber de summo bono,* written between 1262 and 1272, begins with a discussion of the nature of theology in which it is concluded that the end of this science is 'affective knowledge'[88]. This includes an analysis of the following *modi agendi* used in Scripture: the historical, the poetic, the moral, the legal, the scientific (in the widest sense), and the sapiential[89]. Into his treatment of the poetic mode, Ulrich introduces the theory of *integumentum,* the fictional garment in which (according to twelfth-century *accessus ad auctores*) secular poets had clothed their truths concerning natural science or morality.

Whereas Albert, in the passage quoted above, had stressed that the *modus poeticus* is the weakest of the philosophical modes, his pupil was intrigued by the fact that it is indeed a philosophical mode. Albert had claimed the authority of Aristotle in the first book of the *Metaphysica;* Ulrich cites another part of this text and the recently-established *Rhetorica* as well:

It [Scripture] has as its second mode the poetic mode, when it represents truth under fictional garments, as in the parables of holy Scripture, and this mode is appropriate to this science because, as is said in the first book of the *Metaphysics,* the *philomites,* i.e. the poet loving to feign fables, is a philosopher in that the poet feigns a fable in such a way that he excites to wonder, and by wonder subsequently excites to inquiry; and thus science takes shape, as 'the Philosopher' says in his *Rhetoric.*[90]

It is clear, Ulrich continues, that the poetic mode is included within the mode of science by virtue of this wonder, whereas the other parts of logic are included therein by virtue of argumentation. With regard to intention, poetry is a part of logic, although with regard to the measure of metre it is classified under grammar.

Ulrich then assures his reader that Scripture does not contain anything fabulous in the sense of being false[91]. As Augustine says, in the case of a parable a thing is signified, and the truth or falsity of the passage in question depends on this thing and not on the words; it suffices for this 'second sense' to be true. Then Ulrich displays the knowledge of the mystical theology of Pseudo-Dionysius which he had acquired from his master Albert[92]. In the integuments employed in Scripture for representing divine things, not only are the more noble creatures used (which, in so far as they are closer to God, participate in and represent His goodness) but also the inferior and more ignoble: because of their great distance from God, He is more likely to be named symbolically, as opposed to aptly, by their names. Hence, a lamb or a stone is less likely to be understood as God than is an angel or the sun. Indeed, Ulrich continues, since God participates in diverse things in diverse ways, certain aspects of Him are more expressly represented by inferior things than they could be by noble things. For example, the perfection of the divine nature is well represented by noble things, while the fecundity of the divine nature and certain of its works are well represented by things which are born and die. Pseudo-Dionysius could be used in the commendation or denigration of poetry, depending on one's point of view. Ulrich certainly seems to have been on the side of the Muses.

Various factors may have informed the changing attitude to poetry in general, including the impact of Pseudo-Dionysius, and the influence of Aristotle's *Poetica* as interpreted by its Arabian commentators. The Arabs were champions of the view that poetry is essentially image-making; in their theories of epistemology and moral psychology, the imagination was afforded a more elevated status than it had occupied in, for example, Augustinian systems of thought[93]. The translation of Averroes' 'Middle Commentary' on the *Poetica,* which Hermann the German made in 1256, was certainly known to such schoolmen as Roger Bacon and Thomas Aquinas—indeed, it may be the source of St Thomas's statement, as quoted above, that men are born to take delight in representations[94]. But, in general, it would seem that the *Poetica* was disseminated mainly through excerpt-literature, in the form of fragments; it was chopped up into sententious gobbets rather than assimilated *in toto*[95].

What is perfectly clear is that, by the early fourteenth century, pagan and Scriptural *auctores* had come together in terms of style. This development is indicated by the great popularity of Peter Auriol's *Compendium totius Bibliae.* Auriol was inclined to regard poetry, whether sacred or profane, generically; the obvious implication of his discussion of the 'mode of sacred poetry' (as quoted above) is that the two kinds of poetry had many modes of procedure in common. Something of the prestige, the new authority, which had been afforded to Scriptural poetry in particular, and to the poetic and rhetorical modes employed throughout Scripture in general, seems to have 'rubbed off' on secular poetry. Scriptural *auctores* were read literally, with close attention being paid to those poetic methods which were part of the literal sense; pagan *poetae* were read allegorically or 'moralised'—and thus the twain could meet.

For example, in his *Fulgentius metaforalis,* John Ridevall claimed that the intention of Fulgentius was to describe, under the covering *(integumentum)* of fables feigned by the poets, the various vices and the virtues opposed to them[96]. Unless poetic fables pertain to ethics, like those in the *Mythologiae,* theologians must not concern themselves with them, but must avoid them as being vain and foolish. This type of special pleading had, of course, been well established in the twelfth century (see pp. 11, 21): what is interesting is Ridevall's assumption that theologians should concern themselves with moral fables. Ridevall was one of the English 'classicising friars' brought to our attention in Miss Smalley's *English Friars and Antiquity in the Early Fourteenth Century.* In their exegesis of Scripture, all the members of this talented group (which included Holcot, D'Eyncourt, Hopeman, Ringstead and Lathbury) made extensive use of lore derived from the *poetae*[97].

The belief that the Bible often communicated profound truths in a poetic way came to provide the precedent for mythographers to argue that various profane poets had communicated profound truths in the same way. In the moralised *Metamorphoses* which constitutes book xv of his *Reductorium morale* (second recension, 1350–62) Pierre Bersuire explained his intention of giving a moral and allegorical exposition of the *fabulae* found in Ovid's work, only very rarely touching on their literal sense[98]. Bersuire daringly justifies his procedure by the argument that, in many passages of sacred Scripture, fables are used. At Judges ix.8, we are told that the trees set out to elect a king; at Ezechiel xvii.3, we read how the eagle with great wings carried away the branch of the cedar. The *poetae,* the inventors of fables, composed in a similar way: by figments of this kind they wished truths to be understood. Bersuire takes this alleged similarity between the uses of fables by both sacred and profane *auctores* as his justification for having moralised Ovid's fables in accordance with Christian teaching. The source of his account of Scriptural *fabulae* is St Augustine's *Contra mendacium;* the relevant passage had been included in the section on fable in a popular reference-book, Thomas of Ireland's *Manipulus florum*[99]. But Bersuire has, as it were, twisted the waxen nose of his authority in a different direction[100]: Augustine was defending the truth of Holy Scripture, and certainly not interested in justifying pagan fables.

This 'coming together' of pagan and Scriptural *auctores* is also indicated by the way in which, on occasion, the methods for explicating the different types of *auctor* developed along parallel lines. Within Scriptural exegesis, Aristotelian learning seems to have contributed to an increase of interest in the literal or historical sense of Scripture and the concomitant decline in extensive allegorical exposition. A similar literalism pervades what may be loosely termed the 'Aristotelian' commentaries on the *De consolatione philosophiae* of Boethius, notably those by William of Aragon, Nicholas Trevet and Pseudo-Aquinas[101]. To take the case of Trevet, although his expositions of the pagan fables alluded to by Boethius are heavily indebted to the glosses of William of Conches[102], there is a considerable difference in their attitudes to the material. Trevet was more interested in historical exposition than was his predecessor: he consistently reduced the amount of interpretation 'by integument' and augmented the historical information provided by William of Conches[103]. For example, in explaining the labours of Hercules, Trevet claims that the second and eleventh labours pertain to 'bare history' *(nuda historia)* alone, the second and third can be regarded only as 'fictional garments', while all the others can be expounded either historically or *per integumentum*[104].

Moreover, in these Boethius-commentaries, an historical perspective operates, in which the lives and works of the pagans are often seen in terms of an enlightened philosophy that, in many respects, anticipated Christianity, the religion from which they were barred by having been born too soon. To take one example among many, William of Aragon's Socrates is put to death because he is a monotheist who refuses to worship mere created things[105]. He dies as a pagan martyr and a 'friend of God'. This is humanism of a kind.

But, of course, not all late-medieval thinkers approved of these new developments. When, in his *De veritate sacrae Scripturae* (composed 1378), John Wyclif came to catalogue the errors of his opponents, he included several literary issues with dangerous theological implications: for example, that certain parts of Scripture are false, that the Bible does not have equal authority in all its parts, that Christ often spoke in a merely figurative way (as when he called himself 'the Lamb of God'), that Christ and his prophets often told lies, etc[106]. Wyclif reacted by arguing that the Bible was written in a unique and consistently true 'divine style', that the Book of Life was entirely different in nature from all other literary works. On a different level, the Lollard criticisms of fables being used in sermons are well known[107]. But one did not have to be a Lollard to object to the new attitude towards fables[108]. In his postill on St Matthew's Gospel (c. 1336), the English Carmelite John Baconthorpe bitterly attacked those who use falsehoods to teach truth[109]. He carefully distinguished between a *fabula*, which is a falsehood, and a parable, which is an example signifying truth. Obviously, this is a thrust at those who justified their interest in the fables of the poets by appealing to Scriptural precedent.

Such opposition may be taken as a testimony to the strength of the trends outlined here, and to the way in which certain literary questions were in the very van of controversy in late-medieval scholasticism.

The substantial corpus of literary theory described in this chapter, and indeed in this book as a whole, calls for a qualification of E. R. Curtius's view that 'Scholasticism is not interested in evaluating poetry. It produced no poetics and no theory of art'[110]. In fact, thirteenth-century theologians produced a vocabulary which enabled the literary features of Scriptural texts to be analysed thoroughly and systematically, and which encouraged the emergence, in the late thirteenth and early fourteenth centuries, of a more liberal attitude to classical poetry. Once the suggestion had been made that theology might be basically affective, no theologian could avoid considering those aspects of rhetoric and poetics which Alexander of Hales and his successors had deemed appropriate to the subject.

To this extent, medieval theologians were 'interested in evaluating poetry'. They provided, at least, the foundation on which later writers could build their poetics and theories of art. In the *Epistle to Can Grande della Scala*, the modes employed in the *Divina Commedia* are listed as follows:

The form or mode of treatment is poetic, fictive, descriptive, digressive and transumptive; and moreover it is definitive, divisive, probative, refutative and exemplificative.[111]

Dante—if indeed this passage is by him—is saying that his poem combines two kinds of mode, the 'definitive, divisive and collective' mode of human science and those literary modes which were the stock-in-trade of poets both sacred and profane. Behind this statement lies a rich tradition of discussion of *formae tractandi* by medieval theologians.

THE *FORMA TRACTATUS*

Like form regarded as style, form regarded as structure was considered by late-medieval exegetes to be a facet of the literal sense of Scripture. This new attitude is succinctly expressed by a commentator on Lamentations: 'we are accustomed not to care about divisions which cannot be drawn from the letter'[112]. The 'form of the treatise' (the *forma tractatus, ordinatio partium* or *divisio textus*) had become a product of the work of the human *auctor*.

Whereas the exegetes' interest in the *forma tractandi* seems to have been stimulated by academic debate on the nature and appropriate procedures of theology, their interest in the *forma tractatus* must be seen in the light of less cerebral and altogether more pragmatic concerns. Thirteenth-century clerks, building on techniques well advanced in the twelfth century, applied high standards of textual organisation in many spheres of literary activity and creation: for example, in dividing and subdividing the works of the *auctores* to facilitate reference, in excerpting materials from *auctores* and rearranging them in convenient compilations, in supplying the preacher with numerous tools to assist him in writing his sermons, and in the orderly construction of the sermons themselves[113].

However, for the historian of today, knowledge of how men conceived of their actions must be as important as what, when the physical evidence is examined, they appear to have done. When late-medieval scholars thought about their methods for arranging books both 'ancient' and 'modern', when they came to rationalise their own practice in this area, naturally, their concepts and their idioms were, to some extent, determined by the same basic influences behind the vocabulary used in discussing the *forma tractandi*. The present section has as its subject a few of these concepts and idioms.

As our examples of discussions of the *modus* of human science reveal, thirteenth-century scholars applied a rigorously logical definition of science, and this definition put a premium on orderly procedure. Before *collectio* or ratiocination could take place, one had to engage in *definitio* and *divisio:* only then could conclusions follow logically from propositions, and points of doctrine be proved or disproved (see above pp. 122–3). Corresponding to this hierarchy of scientific activities was a hierarchy of the sciences in which the lesser science was believed to serve the greater, an idea summed up in the very influential theory of 'subordination'[114].

In his commentary on the *Sentences,* St Bonaventure argued that the Lombard's work was 'subordinate' to the Bible and should serve it[115]. There is a great difference in degree of certainty between these two texts, the Bible having greater certainty of its truth than has the *Sentences.* When a lesser science fails to reach certainty, it seeks help from the certainty of its superior science. Therefore, Peter Lombard often reverted to Scriptural *auctoritates.* Reason is 'subordinate' to faith: it enables us to understand those things which, by faith, we believe to be most certain. St Thomas Aquinas regarded theology as the queen of the sciences, and the 'subordinate' sciences as her handmaidens. In his *Summa theologiae,* he argues that theology takes its principles directly from God through revelation, and not from the other sciences[116]. On that account, it does not rely on them as if they were in control, for their role is subsidiary and ancillary, just as an architect makes use of tradesmen or a statesman employs soldiers.

Bonaventure, Aquinas and their contemporaries derived their theories of the 'subordination of the sciences' from Aristotle. In his *Metaphysica,* Aristotle had explained that a superior science comes nearer to wisdom than a 'subordinate' science. A wise man gives orders but does not receive them; he must not obey a less wise man but must himself be obeyed. Aquinas, commenting on this passage, explained how a 'subordinate' art or science is directed to the end of a superior art or science[117]. For example, the art of horsemanship is directed to the end of the military art. It is not fitting that a wise man should be directed by somebody else, but that he should direct others:

Subordinate sciences are directed to superior sciences. For subordinate arts are directed to the end of a superior art, as the art of horsemanship to the end of the military art. But in the opinion of all it is not fitting that a wise man should be ordered by someone else, but that he should order others.

'It is the function of the wise man to order' *(sapientis est ordinare)* became a catch-phrase of St Thomas's. It is used to good effect at the beginning of his commentary on the *Ethica,* where Aquinas distinguishes between the various kinds of order which he found described by Aristotle[118]. One kind of order is that which the parts of a whole have among themselves. For example, the parts of a house are mutually ordered to each other. Another kind of order is that of things to an end. Aquinas explains that this order is of greater importance than the first because, as Aristotle says in the eleventh book of the *Metaphysica,* the order of the parts of an army among themselves exists because of the order of the whole army to the commander.

With these concepts of order and ordering in mind, we may attempt to understand how a thirteenth-century commentator might have thought of *ordinatio* in a literary sense. Around 1245, a Paris master named Jordan divided the formal cause of the *Priscianus minor* into its style and its order, termed the *forma tractandi* and *forma tractatus* respectively:

The formal cause of this science is the form of treatment and the form of the treatise. The form of treatment is the mode of proceeding which is principally definitive, divisive, probative, and applies examples; the form of the treatise is the form of the thing produced which consists in the separation of books and of chapters and the order thereof.[119]

The same idiom was used by Robert Kilwardby, who made an early reputation by lecturing in the Arts Faculty at the University of Paris, *c.*1237–*c.*1245[120]. But Kilwardby substituted *ordinatio partium* for *modus tractatus,* for example, in his commentary on the *Barbarismus* of Donatus: 'the formal cause of the work consists in the mode of proceeding and the ordering of parts'[121]. Kilwardby was consistent in his use of the term *ordinatio partium* in this literary sense[122]. A generation later, Nicholas of Paris, in the prologue to his commentary on Aristotle's *Peri hermeneias,* spoke of the formal cause of this treatise as the 'organisation of the books in parts and chapters'[123].

In Kilwardby and his successors, the organisation of an author's material into books and chapters—how the text is divided up into its constituent parts, how the material is collected together—appears to be regarded as the physical manifestation and consequence of the mode of procedure relevant to the science in the text, the 'definitive, divisive and collective mode'. In the light of Aquinas's excursus, literary *ordinatio* may also be described as the disposition and arrangement of material to an end or objective (*finis*). Applying his explanation of Aristotle's two kinds of order, one can say that the parts of a text are mutually ordered to each other, but this order of the parts among themselves exists because of the order of the whole text to the *finis* intended by its *auctor*. Literary *ordinatio* involves 'subordination': the parts of doctrine are 'subordinated' to chapters, chapters are 'subordinated' to books, and individual books are 'subordinated' to the complete work. A text can be thought of as a hierarchy of superior and 'subordinate' parts.

The idiom employed in the grammatical and logical commentaries gradually crept into the works of theologians. In the *Alphabetum in artem sermocinandi* which he completed probably between 1220 and 1225, Peter of Capua explained the *modus tractandi* and the *ordo tractatus* of this collection of *distinctiones*[124]. Introducing his commentary on Proverbs (1230–1235), Hugh of St Cher distinguished between the *modus agendi* and the *ordo tractandi*[125]. In neither of these cases is the discussion of textual arrangement placed within the scheme of the four causes. However, St Bonaventure described the formal cause of St Luke's gospel as 'the ordering of the parts and the chapters *(ordinacio parcium et capitulorum)* and the mode of proceeding in following the Scriptures'[126]. The term *divisio libri* is used instead of *ordinacio* in the prologue to Bonaventure's commentary on St John, but the idea of the 'twofold form' is definitely there:

The formal cause or the mode of proceeding, although it is by the mode of narration, is however possessed of certitude; the formal cause which is the division of the book will be manifest below, because it proceeds in a very orderly fashion . . .[127]

The distinction between the *forma tractandi* and the *forma tractatus* occurs in the prologue to Giles of Rome's commentary on the Song of Songs:

A twofold form is wont to be distinguished, namely the form of treatment, which is the mode of proceeding, and the form of the treatise, which is the ordering of the chapters in relation to each other.[128]

Henry of Ghent remarked that, because in the sciences form is twofold, namely *forma tractandi* and *forma tractatus,* therefore his *quaestio* on the mode of teaching appropriate to theology must likewise be twofold[129]. By the early fourteenth century, this distinction was well established in commentaries on the Bible. It appears frequently in Nicholas of

Lyre's *Postilla litteralis,* the most intricate application being to those *auctores* with the greatest degree of *auctoritas,* the Four Evangelists[130]. Similar vocabulary occurs in the *Sentences* commentaries of some of Lyre's contemporaries, including those by Durand of St Pourçain (third version, written between 1317 and 1327) and Thomas of Strassburg (*c.* 1337)[131].

This new vocabulary was one result of a desire to conceptualise about the current techniques of meticulously dividing and subdividing a text for teaching purposes. (It should, however, be noted that in this case the development, and indeed the sophistication, of the descriptive vocabulary lagged far behind that of the techniques to which it referred.) A master would proceed from a general division by chapters or parts; these components would in their turn be subdivided into smaller sense-units. Thereby, an elaborate framework was provided for precise *explication de texte.* Students were invited to follow the twists and turns of their author's argument.

As Miss Smalley says, this procedure 'was well chosen for application to Aristotelian books: the master could combine "minute penetrating analysis with an astonishing breadth of accurate synthesis" '[132]. A good example of a penetrating *divisio textus* is provided by Kilwardby's outline of the structure of Aristotle's *Praedicamenta,* in which the author's clear 'disposition of parts' is commended:

Since we only know a composite from our knowledge of its parts, and of their nature, and since that book is composed of parts, therefore we must not be ignorant of what parts, and what sort of parts, it is composed. So it is first of all divided into three parts. In the first of these he determines the first principles of the predicable, or those things which precede the predicable. In the second . . . he determines the predicable itself. In the third . . . he determines those things which follow on the predicable. And the adequacy and the rationale of the order appear in this, that any given thing is known sufficiently only when its antecedents are known, together with its parts or species and the dispositions which are consequent upon it. That is the proper mode of understanding a thing. The disposition of parts is therefore evident.

Indeed, the first of them is divided in two: in the first he determines. . . ; in the second. . . . And the first of these is divided in three. . . . Indeed, the second of these is also divided in three: in the first. . . ; in the second. . . ; in the third . . .[133]

Holy Scripture may have 'lent itself less easily to feeding into a verbal mincing machine'[134], but at least lecturers on theology were enabled to provide their pupils with a firm literal framework for the location of doctrinal points. Careful summarising of the literal structures of the Bible became the normal preliminary to detailed exegesis. Sometimes alternative structures were outlined, as is the case in Hugh of St Cher's discussion of the *ordo tractandi* of Proverbs[135]. This book, Hugh explains, can be said to be in either three, four or five parts. According to the tripartite division, in chapters i–x Solomon disputes about the various aspects of good and evil, in chapters x–xxv he treats of good and evil acts in alternate verses, while in the final section he deliberates on truth in general. On the other hand, Hugh continues, the Jews uphold a five-part division, which reflects different stages of composition. According to their opinion, Solomon's parables are compiled in the first part, those of King Ezechiah's men in the second, and those of King Ezechiah himself in the third. The fourth part contains a few things which Solomon was taught by his mother, while the fifth part contains instruction about the good woman. Hugh then declares his personal preference for the four-part division. A prologue is followed by a section on the things from which one ought to abstain; then Solomon teaches those things to which we ought to adhere, and finally he treats of the good woman.

For Hugh it was axiomatic that inspired writing should be proved to be orderly in one way or another: if he could not find a principle of order at the literal or historical level he looked for one on the allegorical level. Hence, the apparent disorder of Isaiah is explained by the fact that it does not follow the order of history but the order in which it was revealed by the Holy Spirit:

The mode of proceeding will be made clear from the succession of the book. For he writes the history not in orderly fashion, or by sequence, but in random fashion according to the revelation of the Spirit . . .[136]

Rather amusingly, Hugh then cites the Song of Songs ii.8 in defence of the somewhat jerky movement of the text: 'see how he comes leaping on the mountains, bounding over the hills'.

The contrast with St Thomas Aquinas's exposition of the same work is striking. Whereas Hugh had invoked the Holy Spirit to support his belief in a mystical principle of literary order, Aquinas chose as his opening text a passage which, in his interpretation, summarily described the express clarity of Isaiah's writing: 'Write the vision; make it plain upon tablets . . . ' (Habakkuk ii.2)[137]. The *modus* of this prophet, claims Aquinas, is plain and open. Isaiah employed beautiful similitudes to make his teaching more appealing; Pseudo-Dionysius is quoted on the usefulness of sensible figures in Scripture. To this clear *modus agendi* corresponds an intricate but logical *divisio textus:*

This book is divided in two parts, the prohemium and the treatise. The second begins here, 'Hear, O heavens, and give ear, O earth'. The prohemium is brought in like a title, in order to make manifest the following work. It is made manifest by four things. The first is the type of the work, the second is the author, the third is the material, the fourth is the time . . . Here begins the treatise of this book, whence a division may be adopted according to the requirement of the material. For it is said that his intention is mainly to do with the advent of Christ and the vocation of the race . . . This book is therefore divided in two parts. In the first is placed the threat of divine justice for the removal of sins; in the second, the consolation of the divine mercy . . . The first is divided in three parts . . . In the first part . . . In the second . . . In the third . . .[138]

The way in which the new techniques of *divisio textus* actually fostered a sort of 'structuralist' exegesis may be illustrated by contrasting representative expositions from different periods of a work which, by its very nature, was not susceptible of division into successive parts or chapters. Use of number-symbolism to resolve the apparent disorder of the Psalter had been a common feature of the twelfth-century exegesis of that text. It was regarded as a mosaic of mysteries arranged in three large groups of fifty psalms each; these three groups were believed to form a sequence in accordance with what they taught allegorically about three related aspects of the Christian religion. For Rupert of Deutz, the first fifty psalms defined those things in which the Christian should have faith, the second fifty confirmed Christian hope, while the third fifty nourished charity[139]. Peter Lombard argued that by these three groups of psalms are signified respectively penitence, justice and praise of the eternal life[140]. The Lombard concluded an elaborate discussion of the mystical significance of the constituent numbers seventy and eighty with praise for such a significantly-organised work: 'therefore, this book is well edited in this number of psalms'.

By contrast, after a discussion of numerology, Nicholas Trevet turned to the arts of music and poetry for principles with which to justify the lack of logical order in the Psalter[141]. A musician does not pluck the strings of a psaltery one after the other: that is not how music is obtained. Likewise, the spiritual psaltery or Book of Psalms does not follow consecutive order:

Just as in making melody on the strings of a psaltery, the strings are not touched according to their natural order but diversely and in interspersed fashion, now here now there, so likewise psalms to God's praise are not placed in the Psalter according to the continuous order of history but diversely, by interspersing what deals with later events, or alternatively according to what the devotion of the psalmist will rise to in the praise of God.

It would seem that the 'mode of praise' characteristic of the Psalter is well obtained by the eclectic order of its parts. Trevet also tackles the problem of the absence of historical sequence by appealing to the principle of 'artificial' order. To write in a selective manner is, he explains, the proper mode of writers of songs. Hence, after starting in the middle of his *historia,* Virgil returned to its beginning in book iii of the *Aeneid.* The implication is that historical order need not be required of sacred poets either.

Nicholas of Lyre's discussion of the *forma tractatus* of the Psalter is more rigorously literal[142]. An impressive attempt was made to explain the process in which the psalms were brought together. Lyre shared Jerome's view that the psalms were collected together over a long period of time. A psalm was included in the collection as it was acquired, not necessarily as it was written. Therefore, a psalm composed before another psalm in point of time may occur after it in the Psalter, simply because it was incorporated at a later date.

Lyre was at pains to explain why the psalms cannot be rearranged or, to put it in the idiom of his day, why scholars cannot impose *ordinatio* on this work. Rearrangement would be difficult, he argues, because some psalms lack ascriptions to *auctores* in their titles. The psalms of any given *auctor* are scattered throughout the book. Among the psalms of David are interspersed those of other *auctores,* and vice versa. In the Hebrew Psalter, Lyre continues, a rubric indicating the end of the psalms by David occurs after Psalm lxxi but beyond this point can be found many psalm-titles which cite David as *auctor.* The present order of the psalms is simply the order in which they were collected together. The collector Esdras added items as he obtained them, mixing the old with the recent. The psalms of a particular *auctor* were not assimilated en bloc into the collection, in the order in which they were written:

several psalms written by one *auctor* could be incorporated together with several psalms which were the work of someone else.

Therefore, Lyre concludes, the Psalter cannot be reorganised 'according to the order of authors' or 'according to the order of times'. Reorganisation according to materials is impossible also because, often, a single matter is touched on in diverse psalms which are by diverse *auctores* and far apart in composition while, conversely, diverse matters are treated sometimes in a single psalm. Apparently, one must accept the Psalter as it is, while recognising the difficulties. The psalms cannot be reorganised according to individual *auctores,* or various periods of composition, or diverse *materiae.* However, the fact that these possibilities have been envisaged is a point of considerable substance. The concept of *ordinatio* has informed Lyre's analysis of his text.

This near-obsession with textual construction is also manifested by the ways in which scholars wished to improve on the organisation of the texts of the *auctores.* It is a 'truism of palaeography' that 'most works copied in and before the twelfth century were better organised in copies produced in the thirteenth century, and even better organised in those produced in the fourteenth'[143]. Earlier divisions of material (like the chapter-headings or *Breviculi* to the *De civitate Dei* and *De trinitate* of St Augustine) were resurrected; new *divisiones* were introduced into old books[144]. A chapter division of the books of the Bible (traditionally attributed to Stephen Langton) had been generally accepted at the University of Paris by the 1230's; the St Jacques Bible-concordance (associated with Hugh of St Cher) went a stage further, by subdividing the chapters into sections indicated by letters of the alphabet, a practice which enabled more precise reference to the Scriptural text[145]. Peter Lombard had employed chapter-headings *(tituli)* to facilitate the location of topics in his *Sentences;* this *divisio textus* was supplemented by a new division into *distinctiones,* perhaps the work of Alexander of Hales[146]. Along with this literary *divisio* of authoritative texts went 'collection' *(collectio).* A greater emphasis was being placed on consultation of *originalia* (the works of the *auctores* in complete form)[147]. Hence, as many works as possible of a major *auctor* like Augustine would be collected together in a single fat volume[148].

One justification for such literary division and collection seems to have been that the intentions of the *auctores* were thereby clarified: precise and complete presentation enabled an author's argument to emerge with greater ease. Exceptional scholars, like Nicholas Trevet and Thomas Waleys, would criticise a *divisio textus* which, in their opinion, obscured instead of clarified the *intentio auctoris*[149]. For example, in the prologue to his commentary on Seneca's *Declamationes*, Trevet wonders aloud if the present *divisio* is contrary to the mind of the author *(mens auctoris)*[150]. Six or eight books are the usual divisions found in medieval copies, but Trevet argues in favour of ten. In his commentary on *De civitate Dei*, Waleys goes to Augustine's *Retractationes* to discover his author's final word on the *divisio* of the work[151].

In their commentaries on *De civitate Dei*, both Trevet and Waleys made use of Robert Kilwardby's *Intentiones* or chapter-summaries for that text[152]. As Trevet tells us elsewhere, Kilwardby contributed to the study of *originalia* by summarising almost all of Augustine's writings and those of other *auctores* as well[153]. These summaries draw on the traditional prologue-vocabulary, as the beginning of Kilwardby's *Intentio Augustini de libro primo de trinitate* will illustrate:

In the first book of *On the trinity* Augustine provides a preamble about certain essentials, namely about the errors of man concerning the divine nature, and about the mode used in holy Scripture in speaking of that, about the cause of the work undertaken and its mode of procedure, about the diverse capacities of man . . .
The Chapters of the first book of Augustine, *De trinitate*.
1. Of the threefold error of men who hold false opinions about God. That holy Scripture in speaking of God more often uses words signifying creatures, and rarely words signifying things which are properly in God and not in creatures . . . [154]

In these chapter-summaries, the most comprehensive of their kind, the principle of *ordinatio* is at work: the subordinate parts of a text (the chapters) are seen to serve the superior parts (the books).

Scholars also wished to improve on the organisation of *auctoritates*, extracts culled from the *originalia*. In his *Speculum historiale* (1254), Vincent of Beauvais followed historical order, beginning with the creation; in his *Speculum naturale*, he took the third, fourth and fifth days of creation as the basis for a summary of authoritative opinion on minerals, vegetables and animals[155]. Subordinate to these superior or more general *divisiones* are the *divisiones* into books and chapters. As M. B. Parkes puts it:

By dividing his work into books and chapters he is able to include as many as 171 chapters on herbs, 134 chapters on seeds and grains, 161 chapters on birds and 46 chapters on fishes. In the *Speculum historiale* by the same process of redeployment into discrete units he includes such material as the account of the ancient gods, and the 'biographies of leading authors' of antiquity accompanied by extracts from their works—all subordinated within the framework of universal history.[156]

In this way, Vincent provided the *ordinatio partium* for a considerable corpus of material: he is estimated to have drawn upon some two thousand writings and 450 *auctores*[157].

Vincent was one among many compilers who arranged their material according to topics, indicated the topics by *tituli,* and organised the whole in accordance with a structure which, because it was logical, could easily be grasped by the reader[158]. In his *De proprietatibus rerum* (begun between 1225 and 1231 at Oxford), Bartholomew the Englishman took the logical principle (vouched for by 'the noble and expert opinion of wise and learned philosophers') that the properties of things follow their substance, and made it the principle of his arrangement[159]. In this *compilatio,* the basic organisation of material follows the order and distinction of substances; further subdivision of material follows the order and distinction of things (which are subordinate to substances).

This structure found favour with Pierre Bersuire, who adopted it in his *Reductorium morale*[160]. Another logical principle, namely the division and order of the sciences, was followed by Brunetto Latini in his *Trésor* (written *c.* 1260), which is organised in accordance with Aristotle's distinction between the three parts of philosophy, theory, practice and logic[161]. The *Tractatus de diversis materiis predicabilibus,* which Stephen of Bourbon compiled not later than 1261, is elaborately hierarchical in structure[162]. The Seven Gifts of the Holy Ghost provide the basis of the division of material. Each of the seven books is then subdivided by *tituli* which indicate the different topics *(materiae),* and each *materia* is subdivided on the principle of 'cause and effect'. The seven-part structure of the whole work is reflected by the seven-part structure of each chapter, each part of which is indicated by a letter of the alphabet. Moreover, at the beginning of each *materia et titulus,* verse-summaries of the important points are provided. Never in the twelfth century had writers professed such concern for the organisation of their works.

Most, if not all, of this organisation of *auctores* and *auctoritates* had as its professed aim a single goal and ideal—the preaching of the gospel. Richard of Bury († 1345) praised both major orders of friars, 'who devoted themselves with unwearied zeal to the correction, exposition, tabulation and compilation of various volumes'[163]. These projects must be seen in the light of the friars' evangelical activity as a whole. They needed such *originalia*, expositions, indices and compilations to equip themselves with the *auctoritates* which Humbert of Romans (Master General of the Dominican Order, 1254–63) described as the 'arms of preachers', the 'weapons whereby we defend ourselves and attack the foe'[164]. Reginald of Piperno, who completed the *Summa theologiae* after St Thomas's death, discussed the relationship between the composition and compilation of writings and the preaching and teaching of the faith, concluding that such literary activity was a form of teaching (*quidam modus docendi*)[165].

But this 'aggressive' approach to authoritative material did not herald a decline in the respect afforded to the *auctores* or *auctoritates*. Rather, the converse is true—or, better, the traditional respect assumed new shapes. The new meaning of the term *originalia* is very revealing. It had once referred to the sealed documents issued by officials but, in the late twelfth century, Ralph Niger and Stephen Langton were using it to designate the whole work of an *auctor*, as opposed to extracts from his work[166]. In the next century, Albert the Great and Thomas Aquinas spoke of the *originalia* as authoritative works in their entirety, in the course of discussions which intimate their acceptance of a related idea: the difficulties raised by a problem-passage may be resolved if the passage is studied in the full context of the work in which it appears[167].

When Niger and Langton employed the term *originalia*, they were favourably comparing the authoritative texts *in toto* with the inadequate extracts provided in the *Glossa ordinaria*. The great twelfth-century collections of *auctoritates* seem to have been the cause of many problems and complaints. Herbert of Bosham, a pupil of Peter Lombard's, put the blame on his master's *Magna glosatura* for the currency of a legend about St Anne which he found untenable[168]. When the Lombard gave an account of this legend in his commentary on Galatians, the name of Jerome was placed alongside, in the margin. Readers of the Lombard's text, Herbert complains, were thereby led to believe that the truth of the legend was attested by the great authority of St Jerome.

Likewise, Gerhoh of Reichersberg roundly condemned those 'new documents inserted in the glosses'[169]. He thought that Gilbert of Poitiers, commenting on the Pauline Epistles, had introduced a falsehood concerning Christ as man, and was also aware that Anselm of Laon had quoted the same passage, wrongly attributing it to Ambrose.

The *Sentences* occasioned similar misunderstandings. For example, Peter Lombard had followed a quotation from Augustine with a statement to the effect that first movements of the flesh are venial sins even when the lower reason is not conscious of them[170]. Alexander of Hales, Bonaventure and Albert the Great all accepted this opinion on the authority of Augustine. But when Albert discovered that the statement on which he relied was not Augustine's but the Lombard's, he promptly changed his point of view on the issue involved.

It was in order to avoid such problems that thirteenth-century scholars applied higher standards of textual organisation both in the *originalia* and in their compilations of *auctoritates*. In the prologue to his *Speculum maius,* Vincent of Beauvais complained that many manuscripts he had read were written so badly that one could not understand the *sententiae* or work out which *auctores* were being cited[171]. A saying of Augustine or Jerome might be ascribed to Ambrose, Gregory or Isidore. Moreover, the words might be changed and the 'sense of the author' *(sensus auctoris)* obscured. This is, he continues, as common in texts of philosophers, poets and historians as it is in theological texts. For these reasons, Vincent determined on clear methods of *ordinatio* which would reduce the chances of textual corruption. The names of the *auctores* are placed in the text *(inter lineas ipsas),* as in copies of Gratian, and not in the margins, where they could easily be displaced, as in the Lombard's *Magna glosatura* and *Sentences*[172]. Vincent also explains that, whenever he includes opinions of his own or of the 'modern doctors', they are introduced with the word *actor,* a term obviously chosen to contrast with the term *auctor.* As a result, magisterial statements cannot be misread as authorial statements in copies of the *Speculum*[173].

Vincent provided sufficient information about his sources to direct the reader from the excerpts to the *originalia.* In the prologue to his *Communiloquium,* the prolific Franciscan compiler, John of Wales (regent master at Oxford around 1260), actually urged his readers to consult the *originalia,* a task he had facilitated by precise source-references[174]. *Auctoritates* are more reliable, John declares, if the books and chapters from which they came are distinctly named. Anyone who wishes to consider carefully his elementary and basic points is invited to locate them in their full contexts. According to John, the solidity of *auctoritates* consists in the certain knowledge of the books from which they are excerpted. Conversely, unattached *auctoritates* seem less solid and effective against those who resist or contradict.

In sum, one may point to an emerging conviction that the thought of an *auctor* is best understood in the context of his work as a whole. This thought may be brought out by clear explanation of the *forma tractatus* or *divisio textus* and the physical manifestation of this structure in manuscript layout. Indeed, the work to be considered as a whole may be the author's total literary output. Kilwardby's *Intentiones* for most of Augustine's works stand as the vast skeleton of the saint's thought in its entirety[175]. This impression of an author's thought being regarded as an integrated whole is also substantiated by the way in which scholars like Holcot and Waleys had recourse to Augustine's *Retractiones* for his final word on certain matters[176]. Here, one may detect the recognition that the thought of an *auctor* can culminate, develop and alter—he can even change his mind.

Peter Abelard and Gratian sought the reconciliation or concordance of *auctoritates*[177]. Vincent of Beauvais and his contemporaries attempted a concordance, not of opinion, but of arrangement. Vincent explained that the *auctoritates* included in his *Speculum* are not on a par: Scripture has the greatest degree of *auctoritas*, then come the decretals and canons which have received papal approval, with the writings of the saints and fathers, then the catholic doctors and, finally, the works of the pagan philosophers and poets[178]. If twelfth-century thinkers were interested in a continuum of *auctoritas*, their successors were interested in a hierarchical calibration of *auctoritas*.

Vincent did not attempt to make his *auctores* agree with one another, to make them all speak with one voice. They differ fundamentally; the pagans need not agree with each other or with the revealed truth of Christianity. Therefore, Vincent was content to 'repeat' or 'report', and not to 'assert' as true, the views expressed in different philosophical texts and in the Apocrypha, leaving the reader to judge for himself[179]. There are many regions of the earth, he remarks; men differ in complexion and in environment[180]. For instance, medical books say that the black poppy is poisonous yet, in our region, the poppy is edible. The implication seems to be that one man's *auctor* is another's aversion, and that the reader should choose his own poison.

The human *auctor* has arrived—still lacking in personality, but possessing his individual authority and his limitations, his sins and his style. He has been met by a discriminating and sophisticated reader.

5
Literary Theory
and Literary Practice

SO FAR, we have been concerned with the historical development, mainly in French and English schools of philosophy and theology, of the theory of authorship channelled by two major types of academic prologue. The present chapter is different in nature, because it focuses on the way in which aspects of this literary theory moved beyond their initial intellectual milieu to become available to a wider range of writers and readers. What follows is essentially speculation regarding the dissemination, and to some extent the dilution and transformation, of the literary attitudes described above. A comprehensive survey of all the relevant permutations would require a book in itself. I have, therefore, decided to concentrate on the ways in which two practising poets of fourteenth-century England, John Gower and Geoffrey Chaucer, exploited a few aspects of a vast corpus of sophisticated theory of literature. Scholastic literary theory did not merely provide these poets with technical idioms: it influenced directly or indirectly the ways in which they conceived of their literary creations; it affected their choice of authorial roles and literary forms.

INTRODUCTION

A: Adaptations of the Academic Prologue
In the fourteenth century, 'Aristotelian prologues' continued to be used in commentaries on Scriptural *auctores*. Good examples were provided by the 'classicising' friars of Oxford and Cambridge. When two of these English friars, Nicholas Trevet and Thomas Waleys, introduced their commentaries on non-Biblical *auctores* with 'Aristotelian prologues'

they transferred to them the idioms of literary theory which for generations had been developed in commentaries on sacred Scripture[1]. Trevet's expositions of, for example, Livy and the two Senecas cannot be
appreciated fully unless they are placed in the perspective of the exegetical tradition of literary analysis[2].

The types of work which could be introduced with an 'Aristotelian
prologue' gradually diversified. Of fundamental importance for the dissemination of the literary theory which it channelled is the development of glosses on texts used for teaching in grammar schools, such as
the *Liber Catonis*, the *Ecloga* of Theodulus, the *Liber cartulae* or *De contemptu mundi* (falsely ascribed to St Bernard), the *Tobias* of Matthew of
Vendôme, the *Parvum doctrinale* or *Liber parabolarum* of Alan of Lille,
the *Fabulae* of Aesop and/or Avianus and the *Floretus Sancti Bernardi*[3].
Lectures on texts like these formed the basis of late medieval 'elementary' teaching. If a pupil lacked either the opportunity or the intelligence to progress much further in his studies, he had learned at
least some scholastic literary notions, albeit in simplified form. At the
other end of the intellectual scale, 'Aristotelian prologues' appeared at
the beginning of learned commentaries on works as individual and various as Ovid's *Metamorphoses*, Livy's *Ab urbe condita*, Seneca's tragedies,
Augustine's *De civitate Dei*, Walter Map's *Dissuasio Valerii*, the
prophecies ascribed to 'John of Bridlington', and Dante's *Divina commedia*[4].

Various writers took the 'Aristotelian prologue' from the context of
commentaries on *auctores* to provide the basis of introductions to their
own works. Some modification was necessary before idioms traditionally used in describing 'ancient' and authoritative writers and writings
could appropriately be applied to oneself and one's own writing, as the
following examples will illustrate.

The writers of *artes praedicandi* were especially fond of describing the
causae of their works. For example, Robert of Basevorn stated that the
four causes of his *Forma praedicandi* (completed in 1322) were intimated
by II Timothy ii. 17, 'the Lord stood with me, and strengthened me,
that by me the preaching might be accomplished'[5]. Robert's treatment
of the material and formal causes is quite traditional. The material
cause is supposed to be designated by the word 'preaching' because, in
the *Forma praedicandi*, preaching is considered as the matter. The formal cause is found in the words 'may be accomplished': something is

formally transmitted and taught when what the beginning of the work promises for investigation is continued through the work in an orderly way, and brought to a conclusion at the end. Anyone who deals with the divine word—indeed, with any orderly treatise—should make sure that, in discussing his subject, he has an organised *modus procedendi*. Robert's method of procedure is treated and taught in fifty chapters, which are outlined in a table of contents.

It is in his treatment of the final and efficient causes that Robert moves away from traditional formulae because, here, he must describe his own role and function within the causal scheme of the *Forma praedicandi*. The final cause is designated when it is said 'The Lord stood with me and strengthened me', because a right-thinking man ought to establish as his end and objective the Lord who restores consolation in tedium, provides satisfaction of desires, establishes an alliance in friendship and furthers delight in studies. In turn, the efficient cause is designated when it is said 'by me'. May God, who is the end of this work, be also the primary efficient cause who influences it in its entirety! With elaborate decorum, Robert refuses to attribute anything to himself as proceeding from himself alone: he prefers to say with the Apostle, 'I dare not speak of any of those things which Christ works in me' (Romans xv.18), and, 'And I live, now not I, but Christ lives in me' (Galatians ii.20). Robert has identified himself as a secondary efficient cause working under the primary efficient cause, God; as a humble instrument who executes a divinely-directed task.

The prologues with which certain late medieval compilers introduced their works also display the influence of the literary theory developed by scholastic commentators. Vincent of Beauvais, adapting the 'type C' prologue, systematically had explained the *causae, materia, modus agendi, titulus, utilitas* and *divisio* of his *Speculum maius*[6]. Later compilers adapted the 'Aristotelian prologue' to suit the requirements of the genre of *compilatio* and their personal purposes in writing. Ulrich of Strassburg stated that the efficient cause of his *Liber de summo bono* was the Holy Spirit who speaks in us, because 'we are not sufficient of ourselves to claim anything as coming from us; our sufficiency is from God' (II Corinthians iii.5)[7]. As the inept instrument of this Spirit, Ulrich likens himself to the 'pen of a busy scribe' mentioned in Psalm xliv.2.

Similarly, in the prologue to Pierre Bersuire's *Reductorium morale*, the *causae* function as part of an elaborate protestation of humility in which all that is useful and worthwhile in the compilation is decorously attributed to its primary efficient cause, God:

I say that in this work the properties of things, figments of the poets and enigmas of the Scriptures constitute the material, while the application to mores constitutes the form; God then constitutes the efficient cause, while the cure of souls constitutes the final cause.[8]

The same basic procedure was followed in the prologue to an Anglo-Norman compilation, the *Lumiere as lais*[9]. The anonymous writer describes himself as an instrument employed by the principal *autur,* our Lord.

More contrived and eccentric adaptation of the 'Aristotelian prologue' is found in the Middle English *Testament of Love* by Thomas Usk († 1388). There are, in fact, three prologues in this work: the prologue to the first book functions as a general prologue to the whole work, while the first chapters of books ii and iii function as prologues to their respective books. In the general prologue, a celebration of God's 'makinge'—in which Usk invokes both Aristotle and David—leads into an explanation of his own 'makinge' in the *Testament*[10]. One can move lovingly from the properties of things to knowledge of their creator (cf. Romans i.20); the causes of things are thereby comprehended. Usk's work, he tells us, is concerned mainly with the causes of love, which explains the *titulus libri.*

Whereof Aristotle, in the boke *de Animalibus,* saith to naturel philosophers: 'it is a greet lyking in love of knowinge their creatour; and also in knowinge of causes in kyndely things'. Considred, forsooth, the formes of kyndly thinges and the shap, a greet kindely love me shulde have to the werkman that hem made. The crafte of a werkman is shewed in the werke. Herfore, truly, the philosophers, with a lyvely studie, many noble thinges right precious and worthy to memory writen; and by a greet swetande travayle to us leften of causes of the propertees in natures of thinges . . . And bycause this book shal be of love, and the pryme causes of steringe in that doinge, with passions and diseses for wantinge of desyre, I wil that this book be cleped THE TESTAMENT OF LOVE.

In the prologue to the second book, Usk discusses the theory of final causality in general, then explains that the final cause of his work is to teach about love[11]. Though his book may be unlearned, it does have this noble end.

Every thing to whom is owande occasion don as for his ende, Aristotle supposeth that the actes of every thinge ben in a maner his final cause. A final cause is noblerer, or els even as noble, as thilke thing that is finally to thilke ende; wherfore accion of thinge everlasting is demed to be eternal, and not temporal; sithen it is his final cause. Right so the actes of my boke 'Love', and love is noble; wherfore, though my book be leude, the cause with which I am stered, and for whom I ought it doon, noble forsothe ben bothe.

In sum, Usk has invoked the Aristotelian causes to justify and ennoble the *Testament of Love*. His creative activity is related to God's; his writing, though imperfect, is commendable in so far as it is directed by, and towards, a noble final cause or ultimate objective, namely, love. Usk closes his work by attempting (somewhat clumsily) to identify this love with charity, the divine love.

The 'Aristotelian prologue' and the literary notions associated with it received further alteration and elaboration at the hands of fifteenth-century writers. For example, Osbern Bokenham (*c.* 1390–*c.* 1447) began his *Legendys of Hooly Wummen* with a full account of the 'two thyngys' which 'owyth euery clerk'

To aduertysyn, begynnyng a werk,
If he procedyn wyl ordeneelly:
The fyrste is 'what', the secunde is 'why'.
In wych two wurdys, as it semyth me,
The foure causys comprehendyd be,
Wych, as philosofyrs vs do teche,
In the begynnyng men owe to seche
Of euery book; and aftyr there entent
The fyrst is clepyd cause efficyent,
The secunde they clepe cause materyal,
Formal the thrydde, the fourte fynal.
The efficyent cause is the auctour,
Wych aftyr his cunnyng doth hys labour
To a-complyse the begunne matere . . .
Certyn the auctour was an austyn frere,
Whos name as now I ne wyl expresse,
Ne hap that the vnwurthynesse
Bothe of hys persone & eek hys name
Myht make the werk to be put in blame . . .[12]

The fourteenth-century belief in the idea of the *duplex causa efficiens* as a means whereby writers could decorously describe themselves as mere instruments of the divine will, has now been lost. Bokenham gives himself all the credit for his work. His refusal to reveal his name in the 'Aristotelian prologue' does not strike one as a particularly modest gesture, in view of the amount of autobiographical detail which is provided in the *Legendys* and other works[13]. There is something mechanical in Bokenham's application of the four causes; the life seems to have gone out of the traditional idioms[14].

By contrast, the exploitations of scholastic literary theory by Chaucer and Gower were altogether more imaginative. But, before we proceed to investigate them, something must be said about the wider context in which they occur, namely, the changing attitudes to literature which characterise the later Middle Ages.

B: Changing Attitudes to Literature

In Italy, a clear line of development may be traced from the early glosses on profane *auctores,* like Ovid, to the humanistic commentaries on 'modern authors', like Dante[15]. But conditions in Italy, when compared with those prevailing elsewhere in medieval Europe, may be seen to be unique and, therefore, it is impossible to transfer insights gained in studying Italian commentaries to the very different English scene. There is nothing in fourteenth-century England to correspond to such a work as Guido da Pisa's magnificent commentary on Dante's *Inferno* (perhaps written between 1328 and 1333)[16]. But there was, in fourteenth-century England, a rich tradition of 'classicising' Scriptural exegesis. It must be emphasised that such commentaries as Holcot on Wisdom and Ecclesiastes, Lathbury on Lamentations and Ringstead on Proverbs were among the 'best-sellers' of their day[17]. One must also take into account those Scriptural commentaries which, although not written in England, were very popular there, Bonaventure's commentary on Ecclesiastes being a good example[18].

While poets like Chaucer and Gower were not trained theologians, they certainly had some interest in the major theological issues of the day. Chaucer seems to have made use of Holcot's Wisdom-commentary when writing his *House of Fame* and the Nun's Priest's Tale[19]. Holcot's theology would have interested Chaucer: Chaucer's translation of Boethius, and other writings, attest his interest in predestination and related subjects, and the person responsible for *Troilus and Criseyde* could have appreciated and would have approved of what Holcot had to say about the salvation of the 'good pagan'[20]. There is evidence that Gower also was aware of theological commentaries[21].

Quite apart from the theology, these 'classicising' commentaries were of interest to practising poets because they contained many extracts from pagan writers, both philosophers and poets. In his poem *La Male regle* (1406), Thomas Hoccleve took the story of Ulysses and the Mermaids from Holcot's commentary on Wisdom:

Holcote seith vp-on the book also
Of sapience / as it can testifie,
Whan þat Vlixes saillid to and fro
By meermaides / this was his policie . . .[22]

Writing in the later fifteenth century, Robert Henryson took the *moralitas* of his *Orpheus and Eurydice* from Trevet's commentary on the *De consolatione philosophiae* of Boethius:

maister trivat doctour nicholass,
quhilk in his tyme a noble theologe wass,
Applyis it to gud moralitie,
rycht full of fructe and seriositie.[23]

The 'classicising' commentaries are major repositories of scholastic literary theory. To obtain examples of this theory in practice, Chaucer and his contemporaries need have read no further than the prologues. In the prologues and in the commentaries themselves, they would have found pagan *auctoritates* being employed in the elucidation of pre-Christian ideas and mores, and the expertise of pagan sages constantly being drawn on in the interests of Christian learning. These are aspects of a general 'coming together' of sacred and profane *auctores* in the minds and treatises of late-medieval academics. The sharp distinction made by Albert the Great and others between Scriptural and pagan uses of similar literary devices, was gradually eroded away in subsequent scholarship (see pp. 139–43). The late medieval compilers also contributed to this process, through their juxtaposition of pagan and Christian *auctoritates* on common subjects. It was generally conceded that many pagan writers possessed considerable *auctoritas* in such subjects as natural science, ethics and politics. Moreover, styles as well as subjects were regarded as common to both camps. Peter Auriol believed that songs of joy, love and sorrow had been composed by both pagan and Scriptural poets (see p. 135). Ulrich of Strassburg emphasised the importance of the *modus poeticus* or fabulous mode as a Biblical *forma tractandi,* while Pierre Bersuire offered examples of Scriptural *fabulae* (see pp. 140–3).

In such an intellectual climate, a writer could justify his own literary procedure or *forma tractandi* by appealing to a Scriptural model, without in any way offending against the great *auctoritas* of the Bible. We have seen above how Thomas Usk invoked both Aristotle and David in describing his own literary activity. When Chaucer justified his practice of speaking 'rudeliche and large' after the manner of the Canterbury pilgrims, he was able to cite the precedent of a *modus loquendi* found in the writings of those *auctores* with the greatest possible degree of *auctoritas,* the Four Evangelists who had recorded the life of Christ:

Crist spak hymself ful brode in hooly writ,
And wel ye woot no vileynye is it.[24]

(General Prologue, lines 739–40)

When defending his translation of *Melibee* on the grounds that it preserved the *sententia* of the original text, Chaucer could refer to the fact that, although the words of the Four Evangelists often differ, their profound meaning is single and uniform:

. . . ye woot that every Evaungelist,
That telleth us the peyne of Jhesu Crist,
Ne seith nat alle thyng as his felawe dooth;
But nathelees hir sentence is al sooth,
And alle acorden as in hire sentence,
Al be ther in hir tellyng difference.
For somme of hem seyn moore, and somme seyn lesse,
Whan they his pitous passioun expresse—
I meene of Mark, Mathew, Luc, and John—
But doutelees hir sentence is al oon.   (VII, lines 943–52)

This argument had been reiterated in generations of commentaries on the Evangelists[25]. To have obtained all the ideas contained in his passage, Chaucer need have looked no further than the general prologue to Nicholas of Lyre's commentary on the gospels[26].

Discussions of the formal causes of literature by commentators, compilers and others provide a major source for the ideas of literary role, style and structure which were available to English writers. Scholastic writers had 'discovered' and provided the literary theory for forms or genres of writing for which there was little basis in classical rhetoric and poetics (cf. pp. 126, 136–9). We are now in a position to examine the extent to which some of these genres affected the way in which Gower and Chaucer conceived of their literary roles and literary forms.

THE *FORMA PROPHETIALIS* IN GOWER'S *VOX CLAMANTIS*

Generations of Scriptural exegetes found in prophetic writings certain literary properties which, in their opinion, constituted a literary form (cf. pp. 136–8). Such discussion of the *forma prophetialis* appears to have influenced commentaries on non-Biblical writings. Hence, the 'Aristotelian prologue' which begins a commentary on the prophecies attributed to John of Bridlington draws heavily on exegetical terms of reference:

The second notable thing is about the formal cause of this book, concerning which it must be noted that the author's mode of procedure is the form of this book which consists in three things. First, in the mode of writing, which is metrical. . . . Secondly, in the mode of understanding, which is obscure and prophetic, because he gives to be understood things other than what the terms signify according to the common usage of speech. Third, in the mode of organising the parts of this prophecy, because he orders the parts according to the order of events which were done in the past and which will be done in the future . . .[27]

Exegetical discussion of that most enigmatic of all prophetic writings, the Apocalypse, influenced the way in which Gower regarded the final recension of his extensive Latin poem, the *Vox clamantis*. In the general prologue to this work, Gower appeals to his namesake, St John, for guidance:

Insula quem Pathmos suscepit in Apocalipsi,
Cuius ego nomen gesto, gubernet opus.[28]

(prologus libri primi, lines 57–8)

[May the one whom Patmos received in the Apocalypse, and whose name I bear, guide this work.]

There is similar word-play with names in the Dedicatory Epistle to Archbishop Arundel, where Thomas Arundel is hailed as successor to Thomas Becket[29]. But Gower believed that he shared with St John not only a name but also a *forma tractandi:* both men composed works in the form of visions. Naturally, Gower does not presume to claim the same *auctoritas* as that enjoyed by the *auctor* of the Apocalypse, but he does suggest a similarity of literary procedure—a perfectly decorous suggestion in an age which, as we have seen, appreciated the literary virtuosity of the human *auctores* of Scripture.

In the early thirteenth century, an Apocalypse prologue attributed to Gilbert of Poitiers became one of the standard set of prologues in the 'Paris Bible'[30]. It received the attention of generations of commentators, and was translated into several languages, including English[31]. Gilbert's prologue and Gower's general prologue are alike in basic structure. Both begin with the definition of vision, then move to examine the human writer and his mode of writing. Gilbert distinguishes between three kinds of vision as follows:

One kind of vision is corporeal, when we see something by corporeal eyes. Another is spiritual or imaginary, when, sleeping or indeed waking, we discern the images of things by which something else is signified, just as Pharaoh saw ears of corn, and Moses saw a burning bush, the former while asleep and the latter while awake. Another kind of vision is intellectual, when by the revelation of the Holy Spirit, we grasp by the intellect of the mind the truth of mysteries as it really is, in which manner John saw those things which are reported in the book. For he not only saw figures with his spirit but also understood the things they signified with his mind.[32]

Gower is concerned with the second and third kinds of vision. While asleep, a man may see with the mind's eye significant images of things, what Gower calls *signa rei*. Like Gilbert, Gower cites the example of Pharaoh's dream, to which he adds the examples of the dreams of Joseph and Daniel:

Ex Daniele patet quid sompnia significarunt,
Nec fuit in sompnis visio vana Ioseph:
Angelus immo bonus, qui custos interioris
Est hominis, vigili semper amore fauet;
Et licet exterius corpus sopor occupet, ille
Visitat interius mentis et auget opem;
Sepeque sompnifero monstrat prenostica visu,
Quo magis in causis tempora noscat homo.
Hinc puto que vidi quod sompnia tempore noctis
Signa rei certe commemoranda ferunt.

(prologus libri primi, lines 7–16)

[From Daniel it is clear what dreams can mean, and Joseph's vision in his dream was not meaningless. Indeed, the good angel who is the custodian of the inner man always guards him with vigilant love; and, although sleep may occupy the outer body, the angel visits the inside of his mind and advances its work; and often, in sleep, it provides prognostications in a vision, so that the man may know better the time by its causes. Hence, I reckon that those things I saw in sleep at night-time furnish the memorable signs of actual events.]

Perhaps this introduction of the 'good angel' who guards the inner man was influenced by the traditional view of the angel who inspired St John on Patmos. Gilbert of Poitiers had claimed that the truths contained in the Apocalypse had been revealed by the whole Trinity acting through Christ[33]. Christ had revealed them to St John through the agency of the angel who visited the saint on his island and, in his turn, John had made them known to the Church. Later exegetes interpreted his statement as referring to the 'fourfold efficient cause' of the Apocalypse, namely, God, Christ, the angel and St John. The instructing angel was described as the mediate efficient cause, as in John Russel's gloss (cf. p. 81).

Indeed, the efficient cause is quadruple in this book, namely God, Christ, the angel, and John. God is the principal and primary efficient cause; Christ, the secondary; the angel, the mediate; and John, the immediate . . .

Gower uses a much more general version of the idea found in the theologians. Decorum required that he should be more indirect than the commentators who, after all, were discussing a Scriptural *auctor*. He does not claim that he received a vision through a major gift of grace, which included a visitation by an angel. His point is made in an impersonal and indirect manner: the guardian angel who watches over everyone sometimes helps a man to understand the future by a special gift of insight. John Gower, it is strongly implied, is such a man.

In the second part of his general prologue, Gower discusses the *nomen scribentis, intentio* and *materia* of the *Vox clamantis*[34]. The name of the writer is given in the form of an acrostic, a practice favoured by fourteenth-century commentators on theological texts[35] and by writers of *artes praedicandi*[36]. Certain basic similarities exist between the way in which Gower describes his *intentio* and *materia* and the way in which Gilbert had described the *intentio* and *materia* of St John. Here is the relevant part of Gilbert's prologue:

Therefore, the material *(materia)* of John in this work is in particular the state of the Church of Asia, and moreover the state of the whole Church, namely those things that it suffers in the present life and what it will receive in the future life. His intention *(intentio)* is to advise patience, which is to be maintained because brief labour is followed by great reward. The mode of treatment *(modus tractandi)* is such that, first he sets in front a prologue and salutation, where he causes the hearers to be benign and attentive. This being done, he proceeds to the narration. . . . Subsequently, proceeding to the narration he distinguishes *(distinguit)* seven visions . . .

Gower's *materia* also involves contemporary events. The Apocalypse was concerned with the sufferings and corruption of the Church in general and of the Churches of Asia in particular; the *Vox clamantis* is concerned with the general sufferings and corruption of the three estates (one of which is the Church) and with the sufferings and corruption of England in particular[37]. Both writers write in sorrow rather than in anger; both encourage patience and warn of impending divine vengeance. The Apocalypse predicts the age of Antichrist; Gower believes he is living in it[38].

It may be added that the chapter-summary (*capitulum*) which is placed at the head of Gower's general prologue explains the *intentio*, *materia* and *modus* of the *Vox clamantis* in a manner reminiscent of Gilbert's 'type C' prologue[39].

In the beginning of this work, the writer intends (*intendit compositor*) to describe how the lowly peasants violently revolted . . . And since an event of this kind was as loathsome and horrible as a monster, he narrates that in a dream he saw different throngs of the rabble transformed into different kinds of domestic animals. He says, moreover, that those domestic animals deviated from their true nature and took on the barbarousness of wild beasts. According to the distinctions (*distincciones*) of this book, which is divided into seven parts (*dividitur partes*), he treats furthermore of the causes for such enormities taking place among men.

The mode of treatment is said to take the form of a narrative about beasts which—like the beasts seen in the vision of St John—have an allegorical function. Gower's basic *divisio textus* is into seven parts, and one wonders if his final choice of this number of books was influenced by the seven seals on the book depicted by St John (Apocalypse v. 1; vi. 1–viii. 1), and the resultant seven major divisions in the structure of the Apocalypse which were expounded by exegetes.

The prologue to the second book of the *Vox clamantis* discusses not merely the second book but the work in its entirety: in an earlier recension, it probably constituted the introduction to the entire work[40]. The *nomen voluminis* is given:

Vox clamantis erit nomenque voluminis huius,
Quod sibi scripta noui verba doloris habet.   (lines 83–4)

[The name of this volume will be 'The Voice of One Crying', because it contains written words about the present sorrow.]

The *materia libri* is discussed in lines 1–2 and 77–82. Gower says that he has seen and noted many things which his reminiscent pen is now eager to write. As the honeycomb is gathered from the buds of various flowers and as the sea-shell is found and gathered from many a shore, so many different mouths have furnished the writer with the *materia* for his work. The *causae libri* (presumably Gower is thinking of the discussions of causality found in 'Aristotelian prologues') have been many. Lines 3–10 contain a discussion of the work's *finis*. Gower refuses to sacrifice to the muses: his sacrifice is to God alone, who is asked to fire the innermost depths of His servant's breast. In Christ's name, Gower will spread his net so that his mind may thankfully seize upon the things which it requires. May this book, begun with God's help, achieve a fitting end:

Inceptum per te perfecto fine fruatur
Hoc opus ad laudem nominis, oro, tui.   (lines 9–10)

[I pray that this work, begun with your help for the praise of your name, may attain a fitting end.]

Thus, the final cause of the *Vox clamantis* is established as being divine praise. One is reminded of exegetical discussions of the final cause of sacred poetry (cf. pp. 93, 124–5).

   This prologue also contains a complex examination of *intentio*, first, in relation to Gower's *materia* and then, in relation to his mode of treatment. The reader is asked to forgive the writer's faults; to embrace the matter, not the man; to think of the intention *(mens)* and not the bodily form *(corpus)* in which it is expressed:

Rem non personam, mentem non corpus in ista
Suscipe materia, sum miser ipse quia.
Res preciosa tamen in vili sepe Minera
Restat, et extracta commoditate placet . . .   (lines 13–14)

[In this matter, take the product, not the person; the intention, not the bodily form: because I, myself, am a worthless man. But a precious thing often resides in a vile mineral, and the commodity, on being extracted, is valued . . .]

Gower proceeds to apologise for the inadequacy of the *corpus,* a profession of humility which actually provides the occasion for a discussion of the relationship between his *materia* and *modus agendi*. The reader is asked to take what the writer's honest ability offers him and to refrain from demanding anything further (lines 17–18). If the writer does not use well-chosen words to embellish his verses, at least the reader should notice what they mean (lines 21–2). Whatever formalities of rhetoric the pages may lack, the fruit of the *materia* will not be the less for that (lines 27–8). Outwardly, the verses may be of moderate worth; their inner worth is the greater (lines 29–30). In this way, Gower implies that anyone who fails to appreciate the quality of his *materia* is at fault, and draws attention to his skill in style and rhetoric.

Gower seems to be identifying himself as an instrumental *causa efficiens* working under the primary *causa efficiens,* God. Although these technical academic terms are not used, the idea of the *duplex causa efficiens* is there, lending substance and structure to the rhetoricians' 'modesty formulas'. It is explained that the man whom Christ's grace enriches will never be poor, that the man for whom God provides will possess quite enough. Sometimes, thanks to divine grace, lofty things are achieved by a quite ordinary intelligence, and a weak hand frequently manages great affairs.

Gracia quem Cristi ditat, non indiget ille;
Quem deus augmentat possidet immo satis:
Grandia de modico sensu quandoque parantur,
Paruaque sepe manus predia magna facit . . .   (lines 67–70)

[Whoever Christ's grace enriches does not lack anything; whoever God provides for possesses quite enough: sometimes great things are accomplished by someone of average ability, and a puny hand often manages great feats . . .]

The elaborate nature of Gower's protestations of humility may be better understood if one is aware of the delicacy of his self-appointed position as instrumental efficient cause. He did not wish to appear to have made a personal claim for divine inspiration. This was the property of those writers with the greatest degree of *auctoritas,* the *auctores* of Scripture and the saints. Hence, Gower ascribes any *auctoritas* his work may have, in the first instance, to the primary *auctor,* God and, in the second instance, to the ancient *auctores* who have disseminated truth. Many things in the *Vox clamantis* are, Gower explains, not written out of his personal experience but are derived from writers of the past (lines 75–82). However, what comes across most strongly from the prologue to book ii is the implication that Gower has not only channelled truth but also has contributed some personal, though God-given, insights to it.

The idea of the *duplex causa efficiens* seems to lie behind the prologue to the third book of the *Vox clamantis* also. In Aristotelian fashion, Gower says that everyone ought to consider happenings in the light of their causes (lines 5–6). The causes of his work are stated to be reprehensible faults of people of all three estates. Then, Gower disavows personal responsibility for the truths contained in his work: the voice of the people has reported them to him (lines 11–13); he writes what others say and does not wish anyone to assume that this is a work of his own originality (lines 27–8). Yet this disavowal of responsibility is balanced by the indirect claim for a degree of *auctoritas* which is made in the remainder of the prologue. Gower's procedure here is very reminiscent of a technique found in prologues to *artes praedicandi,* and so we must digress to discuss the delicate balance between the indirect claim of *auctoritas* and the ostentatious refusal of personal credit which is a feature of these works.

Humbert of Romans, defending and commending the evangelical function of the Order of Preachers, claimed that the office of preacher is the most excellent possible for man[41]. The apostles are the most excellent among the saints, the angels are the most excellent among creatures, God is the most excellent being in the universe. How excellent, then, is the office of preacher, which is apostolic, angelic and godly! Humbert proceeds to extol the excellence of Scripture, which is said to be superior to all other sciences from the point of view of its *auctor, materia* and *finis.*

From the author, because while other sciences were invented from human ingenuity, although not without divine assistance, this is immediately infused from God by inspiration. II Peter i.21, 'the holy men of God spoke, inspired by the Holy Spirit'.

Since the *materia* of the preacher is derived from Scripture, it is bound to be excellent; the preacher is the proper instrument of God.

Such high ideals were not confined to the Dominicans. In general, the writers of *artes praedicandi* claimed a degree of *auctoritas* on behalf of their office. In the prologue to his *Ars componendi sermones,* Ralph Higden employed the term *duplex causa efficiens* in attempting to explain the relationship between the office of the preacher and the authority of God: 'The efficient cause is twofold, God Himself originating and the preacher himself ministering'[42]. A similar explanation is provided in

John of Wales's *De quattuor praedicabilibus*. After explaining that God is the prime mover of preaching, John turns to the human preacher:

The efficient cause which is moving and moved is any preacher who is devoted and imbued by the holy Spirit to the office of such great dignity, apt and suitable as much in manner of life as in science.[43]

Robert of Basevorn seems to have conceived of a threefold *causa efficiens* for his *Forma praedicandi:* God, the various friends for whom the work was written, and Robert himself.

Secondly, the efficient cause is designated when it is said 'by me'. May God, who is also the end *(finis),* be principally the efficient cause as universal influence, and you, my friend, be the efficient cause as a special attracting force, and the insistence of my associates be as a certain continual driving force, whereas I am the more immediate instrument, putting the task into execution.[44]

Robert explains that he had been moved by doubts about his ability to bring to perfection what he had begun. Then he thought of II Timothy iv. 17 ('The Lord stood with me, and strengthened me, that by me the preaching might be fully accomplished'), and a great part of his sadness was dispelled. When he realised that the first part of this passage was fulfilled in him, i.e. that the Lord stood with him, strengthening him, he had no doubts about the remaining part, and undertook to complete the work. Indeed, because he regards himself as an instrument of God, Robert can to some extent disavow responsibility for what he has written.

However, because the primary cause has more influence, I do not dare to attribute anything to myself as proceeding from me; but I say with the Apostle, Romans xv. 18, 'I dare not speak of any of those things which Christ works by me', and, Galatians ii. 20, 'And I live, now not I, but Christ lives in me'.

But then the reader is informed that, if he wishes to know the writer's name, it can be found in an acrostic. Robert has managed to combine decorous self-abnegation with an explanation of how he came to compose his work.

In the prologue to the second book of the *Vox clamantis,* Gower compares himself to an 'ancient' preacher-prophet, St John the Baptist, the original 'voice crying in the wilderness' (lines 83–4). In the prologue to the third book, Gower assumes the office of preacher and, by implication, claims that degree of *auctoritas* which—according to the writers of *artes praedicandi*—that office entailed. Like these 'modern' preachers, Gower describes himself in terms which enable us to identify him as an instrumental efficient cause. He prays that merciful Christ may grant favour to the undertaking of His servant:

Si qua boni scriptura tenet, hoc fons bonitatis
Stillet detque deus que bona scribat homo:
Fructificet deus in famulo que scripta iuuabunt,
Digna ministret homo semina, grana deus.   (lines 39–42)

[If a piece of writing contains something good, may the fount of goodness distil it and may God grant that a man should write good things. May God make fruitful in His servant those writings which will be of benefit: let man provide the worthy seeds, and God the grain.]

May God make fruitful in His servant those writings which will be of use; where the *sensus* of the human writer is too weak, may God impart His *sensus:*

Quo minor est sensus meus, adde tuum, deus, et da,
Oro, pios vultus ad mea vota tuos . . .   (lines 49–50)

[Where my wit is too small add yours, O God, and I pray that you should turn your benevolent face towards my prayers.]

Gower is implying that the *Vox clamantis* is the result of cooperation between himself and the primary efficient cause 'as universal influence' (to use Robert of Basevorn's idiom). God is addressed as ultimate wisdom, without whom the wisdom of the world is nothing. May the writer become wise in order readily to compose his verses and to write only the truth:

O sapiens, sine quo nichil est sapiencia mundi,
Cuius in obsequium me mea vota ferunt,
Te precor instanti da tempore, Criste, misertus,
Vt metra que pecii prompta parare queam;
Turgida deuitet, falsum mea penna recuset
Scribere, set scribat que modo vera videt.   (lines 83–8)

[O Wise One, without whom the wisdom of the world is nothing, into whose allegiance my prayers bring me, I pray to you at this instant of time, O merciful Christ, to grant that I am able to compose promptly the verses I have striven after. Let my pen avoid what is turgid, refuse to write what is false, but write those things which it sees now to be true.]

May the meaning of the writer be true to God, who is absolute truth. In this way, Gower, like the writers of *artes praedicandi*, stressed the *auctoritas* of the office of preacher and so avoided making a direct claim for personal authority.

Gower's attitude to the authorial role and literary form he adopted in the *Vox clamantis*, an attitude which is expressed clearly in the academic prologues in this work, may now be summarised. Late-medieval exegetes had come to regard many a Scriptural *auctor* in the role of preacher; in their eyes, Daniel and his colleagues were preacher-prophets (see pp. 136–8). The *Vox clamantis* represents a further stage in the dissemination and development of such theory: therein, a 'modern' writer adopts the stance of the preacher-prophet, likening his moral position and righteous indignation to those of the two 'ancient' preacher-prophets who are his namesakes, St John the Baptist and St John the *auctor* of the Apocalypse. Commentators on the prophetic books of the Bible expounded the *forma prophetialis* as a literary form; practising poets recognised this as a literary model to be imitated. Hence, Gower's 'self-commentary' on the *Vox clamantis* invites comparison between his mode of stylistic and didactic procedures and the procedures found by exegetes in prophetic works of great authority, notably in St John's Apocalypse.

GOWER'S ROLE AS *SAPIENS* IN THE *CONFESSIO AMANTIS*

In the *Confessio Amantis* Gower set out to produce 'a bok for Engelondes sake': a veritable English classic, complete with extrinsic and intrinsic prologues in which a claim to a limited *auctoritas* was implied, and an elaborate apparatus of glosses and summaries which affirm the unifying moral intention of the work[45]. If, in the *Vox clamantis*, Gower portrayed himself as a preacher-prophet, in the *Confessio amantis*, he assumed the role of the philosopher who was wise in the secular sciences of ethics and politics.

In order to mount this argument fully and clearly, it will be necessary to examine, at the outset, some of the fourteenth-century permutations of extrinsic and intrinsic pairs of prologues. Nicholas of Lyre began his *Postilla litteralis* with an Aristotelian extrinsic prologue which discusses the relationship of wisdom and science (*sapientia* and *scientia*), the hierarchy of the sciences, and the corresponding hierarchy of the books which teach the various sciences[46]. Lyre states that the philosophers' knowledge pertains only to this present life, whereas sacred Scripture directs us to that blissful afterlife of which the philosophers are ignorant. A science can be said to be more eminent than another in two ways. According to Aristotle's *De anima,* these are the greater nobility of one subject as opposed to another, and the greater certainty of one mode of procedure *(modus procedendi)* as opposed to another. Sacred Scripture, the basis of theology, clearly excels all other knowledge on both these counts. The Bible has as its subject God, the sum of nobility. It also excels in mode of procedure because, in theology, the first principles from which one proceeds are immutable truths: such certainty is not to be had in the methods of any other science. Theology, the science which seeks the highest wisdom, is most properly called *sapientia.* The *sapientia* of catholics and saints, which is holy Writ, is to be distinguished from the lesser wisdom of the philosophers (also called *sapientia,* but less correctly). What may be concluded manifestly from Scripture is to be accepted as true; what is repugnant to it is simply false.

Then Lyre supplies an intrinsic prologue in which he describes his personal purpose and his *modus procedendi* in writing the commentary[47]. He has provided us with parallel discussions of the *intentio* and *modus* of the divine *auctor,* God, and the human writer, himself. The intrinsic aspects of the various books of the Bible are analysed in the prologues which introduce the commentaries on individual books.

Whereas Lyre, in this general introduction to his complete *Postilla,* was concerned with *sapientia* as theological truth, commentators on the Sapiential Books of the Old Testament had as their subject the *sapientia* of the philosophers, whose authority rested on human reasonings rather than on divine inspirations (cf. pp. 113–15). Solomon was held to be a wise man *(sapiens)* in such philosophical disciplines as ethics, politics and natural science and, in the commentaries on his works, this wisdom was related to an Aristotelian definition of *sapientia.* For example, in the extrinsic prologue to his commentary on Wisdom, Robert Holcot explained how all the human arts contribute to God's glory[48]. He lists the four virtuous dispositions which God, the divine *auctor,* requires in his audience. The first is simplicity of heart. A man cannot serve two masters; therefore, in the words of Matthew iv. 10, 'praise the Lord and seek Him alone'. The second virtue is humble judgment. *Sapientia* puffs up, if charity does not assist. Third, the divine *auctor* requires in a listener the virtue of accurate reporting: what is said without fiction must be repeated without malice (Wisdom vii. 13). Solomon and Seneca agree on this point. As Seneca puts it, wisdom is a noble possession of the soul which enables its owner to scorn greed and, when it is distributed, it grows and increases. Holcot adds that it is the office of the wise man *(sapiens)* to instruct the less wise and courteously support the uninformed. Fourth, the listener must practise what he hears in the proper fashion. Once again, *auctoritates* from both pagan and Scriptural sources are quoted to prove the point. Holcot then moves to state the supremacy of sacred Scripture over philosophical wisdom. This done, he feels obliged to concentrate on philosophical wisdom.

Holcot's intrinsic prologue focuses on the Book of Wisdom itself:

Concerning this book, which is called the Book of Wisdom, there are in the beginning three things to be noted. The first is about its name, the second about its author, and the third about its end. [49]

The *nomen libri* is 'Wisdom', and this means many things to many men. The differing views of the peripatetics, of moral philosophers such as Socrates, Seneca and Boethius, and of theologians, are summarised, their opinions being compared and contrasted with those of Solomon. Under the second intrinsic heading, Holcot discusses the problem of authenticity: was Solomon indeed the *auctor,* or was it Philo Judaeus? Concerning the third intrinsic heading *(finis),* Holcot explains that Solomon's ultimate objective was the encouragement of a particular disposition in men. The first facet of this disposition concerns civil government. Cicero is quoted on the bestial life of men before the establishment of good laws; the Orpheus myth, as recounted in Boethius's *De consolatione philosophiae,* points the same moral. Wisdom is the basis of any good state, so Plato argued that philosophers should be kings, and kings, philosophers. The second facet of Solomon's intended disposition concerns the expulsion of one's enemies and the fortification of one's cities. Because old men are wise, the great Alexander had no nobleman in his army under the age of sixty years; they seemed to be senators rather than soldiers. Aristotle and Solomon agree that wisdom is better than strength, and that a prudent man is better than a powerful man. The third and final aspect of the recommended disposition concerns correction. Proverbs xxix. 15 states that reproof and the rod teach wisdom: a child left to himself will bring his mother to shame.

In his commentary on Ecclesiasticus, Holcot follows the same basic method, a general discussion of *sapientia* preceeding an excursus on the *auctor* and the *divisio libri*[50]. Other 'classicising friars', like Thomas Ringstead and John Lathbury, employed similar introductions[51].

This practice of treating wisdom in extrinsic and intrinsic prologues influenced the way in which Gower introduced his *Confessio amantis:* he may have got the idea from Holcot's commentary on Wisdom, which he seems to have known. The beginning of the *Confessio amantis* resembles a commentary on a Sapiential Book, which first treats of the extrinsic aspects of the book in the context of a discussion of wisdom in general, and then proceeds to discuss the book itself under such headings as *intentio auctoris, nomen libri, materia* and *utilitas*.

The *Prologus* to the *Confessio amantis* is, in fact, an extrinsic prologue about *sapientia;* the treatise which follows it is about human love, *amor:*

For this prologe is so assised
That it to wisdom al belongeth . . .
Whan the prologe is so despended,
This bok schal afterward ben ended
Of love . . .   (*Prologus*, lines 66–75)

Gower links *sapientia* and *amor* through the donnish joke that love 'many a wys man hath put under'. Hence it seems fitting that the *Prologus* on wisdom should be followed by a treatise on love. Gower's declared intention is 'in som part' to advise 'the wyse man': hence the *Prologus* warns of the ways in which the Church, the commons and the earthly rulers have ceased to follow wisdom. Gower admits that only God has the wisdom necessary for full understanding of worldly fortune:

. . .this prologe is so assised
That it to wisdom al belongeth:
What wysman that it underfongeth,
He schal drawe into remembrance
The fortune of this worldes chance,
The which noman in his persone
Mai knowe, bot the god al one.   (*Prologus*. lines 66–72)

This point is echoed at the end of the *Prologus:*

. . . And now nomore,
As forto speke of this matiere,
Which non bot only god may stiere.   (*Prologus*. lines 1086–8)

By contrast, in his intrinsic prologue (i, lines 1–92), Gower explains what is within his personal compass:

I may noght strecche up to the hevene
Min hand, ne setten al in evene
This world, which evere is in balance:
It stant noght in my suffiance
So grete thinges to compasse,
Bot I mot lete it overpasse
And treten upon othre thinges.
Forthi the Stile of my writinges
Fro this day forth I thenke change
And speke of thing is noght so strange,
Which every kinde hath upon honde,
And wherupon the world mot stonde,
And hath don sithen it began,
And schal whil ther is any man;
And that is love, of which I mene
To trete, as after schal be sene. (i, lines 1–16)

Thus, Gower admits that he cannot solve all the problems which he canvassed in the extrinsic prologue. A human *auctor* cannot reorganise the present world in accordance with those principles of order which the divine *auctor,* God, followed in His creation, but he can impose an appropriate order on his own creation, his treatise on love. The way in which Gower explains what is within his compass parallels the way in which a commentator like Holcot would move from wisdom in general to the particular branch of wisdom pertinent to the text, from the *causa causarum,* God, to the causes of the text.

The English text of the *Confessio amantis* is accompanied by a Latin commentary which appears in many of the manuscripts, some of which are contemporary with Gower. The form of Gower's intrinsic prologue is made absolutely clear by the beginning of this commentary, where the usual intrinsic headings are employed:

Since in the *Prologus* already has been treated the way in which the divisiveness of our current state has overcome the love of charity, the author intends *(intendit auctor)* presently to compose his book, the name *(nomen)* of which is called 'The Lover's Confession', about that love by which not only human kind but also all living things naturally are made subject. And because not a few lovers frequently are enticed by the passions of desire beyond what is fitting, the matter of the book *(materia libri)* is spread out more specially on these topics throughout its length.[52]

The heading *modus agendi* is not mentioned in the Latin commentary, but the relevant literary concept is considered in the English text. Every man should take example of the wisdom that has been given him, and teach it to others. For this reason, Gower will tell of his encounter with love, thereby providing posterity with an example of that unhappy, jolly woe (i, lines 78–88). This accounts for his mode of treatment. To use the technical scholastic idiom, the *modus exemplorum suppositivus* is being employed (cf. pp. 123–4).

But, is it not incongruous that prologues designed to introduce Scriptural texts should serve as Gower's models for the prologues in the *Confessio amantis?* What has 'the clerke Ovide', Gower's main *auctor* on love, to do with the Solomon of the Sapiential Books? These questions may be answered with reference to certain attitudes to literature current in the later Middle Ages. By the early fourteenth century, commentaries on the Sapiential Books had become repositories of Scriptural and pagan *auctoritates* on common subjects (as has been illustrated by Holcot's commentary on Wisdom). Solomon was supported by the pagan philosophers and, indeed, by the pagan poets, including Ovid. These *auctores* could 'come together' in this way because they were supposed to operate on a similar plane. Solomon, Aristotle and Ovid had all used their natural reason; they were philosophers and not theologians. Moreover, they were—according to the medieval commentators—interested in basically the same things (see pp. 115–16).

The conjunction of Solomon with 'the clerke Ovide' becomes comprehensible if it is realised that the works of both these writers were believed to pertain to ethics *(ethice supponitur)*. Commentators on Ovid argued that the *intentio* of his poetry was to recommend good mores and to reprehend evil ways:

> The utility is great, since when this book has been perused thoroughly the chaste women may be eager to guard their chastity and those who are unchaste and wanton may adhere to chastity. . . . It is subjoined to ethics, because it treats of morals in teaching good mores and in blaming bad.[53]

Commentators on the Sapiential Books argued that Solomon's *intentio* was to instruct in the ethical and political virtues and vices. Therefore, Hugh of St Cher could describe Ecclesiasticus in these terms:

> The intention of the author is to instruct us about virtues and to inform us by examples of the saints, so that by imitating them, with them we might merit eternal life . . . The utility of this book is knowledge of the virtues . . . This

book pertains to moral philosophy, because it is entirely about mores or virtues.[54]

Many of Ovid's literal statements were quoted as *auctoritates* on such subjects as ethics and natural science which he was supposed to share with Scriptural *auctores,* while medieval mythographers showed how allegorical interpretation of his *fabulae* could yield profound truths which were perfectly compatible with Christian doctrine[55].

Therefore, Gower was not original in placing the *materia* of love in a moral perspective—that had already been done in the scholastic study of Ovid's love poetry[56]. His personal achievement consists rather in the fact that he widened the moral perspective found in the 'Medieval Ovid'. Scholastic commentators had formulated a rather simple classification of Ovid's love-stories: some teach about legal love, some about illegal love and some about infatuation; certain stories show us what we ought to do, while others show us what we ought to avoid. By contrast, Gower employed a more comprehensive and precise framework, by grouping his love-stories in accordance with the Seven Deadly Sins. Moreover, he managed to include *materia* relating to politics, a subject which is touched on in the *Prologus* and the epilogue, and also provides the basis of book vii[57].

The political facet of the *Confessio amantis* was so important to Gower that he drew attention to it in the Latin passage which summarises his major works in turn.

This third book, which out of regard for his most vigorous lord Henry of Lancaster . . . was written in English, following the prophecy of Daniel concerning the mutability of earthly kingships, discourses from the time of Nebuchadnezzar up to the present time. Moreover, it treats according to Aristotle of those things by which King Alexander was instructed, as much in his ruling as in other things. However, the principal matter *(principalis materia)* of this work is based on love and the foolish passions of lovers.[58]

Gower's *principalis materia* falls within the subject-area of ethics; his other material falls within the subject-area of politics which, according to Aristotle, embraces the subject-area of ethics (or vice versa). As T. A. Sinclair puts it,

For Aristotle, as for Plato, the subject of political philosophy, or politikè, embraced the whole of human behaviour, the conduct of the individual equally with the behaviour of the group. Ethics was, therefore, a part of politics; we might also say that politics was a part of ethics.[59]

Although there is no evidence that Gower knew Aristotle's *Politica* or any of the medieval commentaries on it, he was certainly aware of this belief in the link between ethics and politics. In book vii of the *Confessio* is found a scheme of the division of the sciences which Gower derived from the *Trésor* of Brunetto Latini, the teacher of Dante[60]. Brunetto was 'exceptionally well acquainted' with Aristotle's works, and his division of the sciences into the theoretical, the rhetorical and the practical is 'in effect the same as Aristotle's classification of knowledge as Theoretical, Poetical and Practical'. His division of practical philosophy into ethics, economics and politics is also derived from Aristotle. Gower put his own slant on what he took from the *Trésor*: 'etique', 'iconomique' and 'policie' are considered as aspects of 'a kinges Regiment' (vii, lines 1649–83).

Book vii of the *Confessio* contains a veritable 'de regimine principum', a little treatise on the proper methods of ruling a country. Both the English text of book vii and its Latin commentary ostentatiously refer to Aristotle as the great authority on politics, although Gower's information concerning Aristotle's views seems to be limited to the account found in Brunetto's *Trésor* and to the Pseudo-Aristotelian *Secreta secretorum* (supposed to have been written by Aristotle for the instruction of King Alexander), which Gower accepted as genuine. From these sources, Gower derived much of the 'policie' which he sought to relate to the love-lore which was his *principalis materia*:

To every man behoveth lore,
Bot to noman belongeth more
Than to a king, which hath to lede
The poeple; for of his kinghede
He mai hem bothe save and spille.
And for it stant upon his wille,
It sit him wel to ben avised,
And the vertus whiche are assissed
Unto a kinges Regiment,
To take in his entendement:
Wherof to tellen, as thei stonde,
Hierafterward nou woll I fonde.   (vii, lines 1711–22)

Pagan and Scriptural *auctoritates* on politics are grouped together. The sage Daniel is quoted alongside the sage Aristotle; King Alexander alongside King Solomon. In Solomon, one may see the things most necessary for a worthy king, namely, wisdom (see vii, lines 3891–904). Gower could have found such assimilation of pagan and Scriptural *auctoritates* in any of the 'classicising' commentaries on Solomon's Sapiential Books, as well as the models for his extrinsic and intrinsic prologues to the *Confessio amantis*.

In sum, Gower's *Confessio* seems to work by assimilation of materials which, although they may appear ill-assorted to us, would have been regarded as quite compatible by the learned medieval reader. Diverse *exempla* of lovers were brought together: some commended chaste love while others warned of unchaste love, thus teaching a quite consistent morality. Was there anything incongruous about a priest of Venus extolling the virtue of chastity and attacking the sin of incest, the main topic of book viii? Not to those medieval readers who believed that Ovid had taught about just love and had reprehended love which was foolish or wicked. Pagan and Christian materials on common subjects are combined, Gower's rationale being the widespread belief that 'Ovide' and 'Salomon' shared many assumptions about the classification of the sciences and modes of scientific procedure (cf. pp. 115–16). The *materia* of 'policie' is related to the *principalis materia* of love: this is acceptable, because Gower believed that his *exempla amantum* pertained to ethics, and carefully widened his moral perspective to include politics. Those virtues necessary for 'a kinges Regiment' are necessary for the moral 'regiment' of any man.

We are now in a position to assess the nature of Gower's claim to *auctoritas* in the *Confessio amantis*. This may be effected by a comparison of its epilogue with the ending of the *Vox clamantis*. At the end of the *Vox clamantis*, Gower was concerned to disavow responsibility both for what he had said in his book and for what his readers might make of it. He protested that he did not assert his statements as an *auctor:*

Hos ego compegi versus, quos fuderat in me
Spiritus in sompnis: nox erat illa grauis.
Hec set vt auctor ego non scripsi metra libello,
Que tamen audiui trado legenda tibi:
Non tumor ex capite proprio me scribere fecit
Ista, set vt voces plebis in aure dabant.   (vii, lines 1443–8)

[I have brought together these verses, which a spirit uttered in me while I was asleep: that night was burdensome. But I have not written as an authority these verses in a book; rather, I am passing on what I heard for you to read. A swelling of my own head did not cause me to write these things, but the voice of the people put them in my ear.]

The *auctoritas* belongs to God or to the divine will as expressed by the voice of the people; he is a humble and unworthy minister of that doctrine. These statements should seem good to good people; what is bad can be left to the bad. The bad man should know Gower's writings in order that, with their help, he may become good; the good man should seek them out in order to become better (vii, lines 1443–81). Through these fulsome professions of humility, Gower draws attention to his creativity and, in an indirect and impersonal way, claims a degree of *auctoritas*–'impersonal' because the emphasis is placed, not on Gower's personal achievement, but rather on his assumed office as prophet, preacher and transmitter of truths.

In the ending of the *Confessio amantis,* there is neither the same evasion of responsibility for what has been said nor the same conviction, underlying all the effusions of humility, of the unquestionable worth of the work in leading men to salvation. Gower assures us that his 'entente' is a good one (a point which did not have to be laboured in the prophetic *Vox clamantis*) and claims that he cannot be blamed for the sad but true fact that some men will read his work simply for what it says of love. The different versions of the epilogue make this point in different ways.

In the first recension both 'pleye' and 'wisdom' are offered:

In som partie it mai be take
As for to lawhe and forto pleye;
And forto loke in other weye,
It may be wisdom to the wise:
So that somdel for good aprise
And eek somdel for lust and game
I have it mad . . .   (Macaulay, viii, lines 3056*–62*)

According to this version of Gower's poem, the *Confessio* is all things to all men. With considerable bravado, Gower refuses to be responsible for the readers' various interpretations of his work and appears to be quite unconcerned about the possibility of misinterpretation.

The revision shifts attention away from the possibility of different interpretations and focuses attention on the response that Gower would wish from his discerning reader. He asks to be excused for having composed a work 'in englesch' which 'stant betwene ernest and game' (lines 3106–11) and expresses the hope that his work will not be despised by learned men. Both versions of the epilogue contain a protestation that the poet has used 'no Rethoriqe', but the revision is more fulsome, suggesting that Gower had become more concerned to hint 'to the wise' that, in fact, he had used a lot of rhetoric.

The essential differences between the endings of the *Vox clamantis* and the *Confessio amantis* depend on the different authorial roles adopted by Gower. One had to be more circumspect in assuming the role of preacher-prophet than in assuming the role of *sapiens* in ethics and politics: the theological truths expressed in St John's Apocalypse ranked far higher than the philosophical truths expressed in Solomon's Book of Wisdom. The less the degree of *auctoritas* claimed, the less was the need for elaborate evasions in the shape of disavowals of responsibility and protestations of humility. But if, in the *Vox clamantis*, Gower had to evade the possible charge of spiritual arrogance, in the *Confessio amantis* he had to evade the possible charge of levity in his choice of main subject, namely, love. One of the functions of Gower's epilogue is to protect himself from this charge.

In the first recension *Prologus*, Gower had referred to a proverb about beginnings and endings: 'who that wel his werk begynneth / The rather a good ende he wynneth . . .' (lines 87*–8*). Presumably this means that whoever begins a work well will finish it well: the *Prologus* is about wisdom, and the epilogue returns to the subject of wisdom. In viii, lines 2908–40, Venus tells Amans that he is too old for love, and that he should, therefore, go where moral virtue dwells—where, in fact, certain of Gower's previous works are to be found. What better way to remind us that Amans is a fiction than to refer to Gower's reputation for moral and didactic works?

Venus finishes her speech with the ambiguous lines:

'Now have y seid al that ther is
Of love as for thi final ende'   (viii, lines 2938–9)

This could refer simply to the ending of the *Confessio amantis*, where Gower wanted to emphasise 'vertu moral', in order to establish that his treatise on love had moral *utilitas*. Alternatively, it could refer to the 'final ende' of Gower in particular and man in general, in the sense of that divinely-ordained end of man, namely, salvation, to which all men aspire through performance of moral actions. Or, it could refer to the *finalis causa* of the poem, namely, its efficacy in encouraging 'vertu moral' in the reader. These senses of 'ende' were probably related in Gower's mind.

Gower wished to leave his readers with an assurance about the way in which his *principalis materia* had been handled, about the sapiential context in which *amor* had been placed. Therefore, after Venus takes her leave, the narrator proceeds to pray for the state of England, to warn against the evils of disunity in the state and to summarise the duties of a king. We have returned to the concerns of the *Prologus* and the 'de regimine principum' which is book vii. The voice of 'moral Gower' is speaking, affirming that his work contains some unambiguous 'lore'. Then he reminds us that his 'lust' had been examined from a moral standpoint. The intrinsic prologue is echoed in the statement that love can encourage a man to act contrary to reason and prohibit him from acting wisely (viii, lines 3143–51). This is not to say that *amor* and 'vertu moral' are incompatible. Gower has taken pains to teach about 'just love' (as understood by the Ovid-commentators), to praise chaste married love and to condemn vicious love. Some kinds of human love can be unwise and irrational. By contrast, charity, the divine love, is wholly consonant with wisdom (see viii, lines 3162–72). Gower is not retracting his concern with *amor* (as C. S. Lewis suggested[61]), but is merely accepting that *amor* is limited, and that *caritas* is intrinsically superior to *amor*. The precise nature of the *utilitas* or final cause of the *Confessio amantis* has been clarified: *ethice supponitur*.

In spelling out the moral *utilitas* of his poem and suggesting that it pertained to ethics, Gower was aspiring to the same limited degree of *auctoritas* which contemporary commentators allowed to Ovid. This is the reason why tact was required at the end of the *Confessio amantis*, a reason very different from that which explains Gower's behaviour at the end of the *Vox clamantis*. St John, the *auctor* of the Apocalypse, did not have to be 'moralised' to be believed—Ovid did. Gower had to provide for his *Confessio amantis* what medieval commentators had provided for Ovid, a clear statement of the didactic utility or *finalis causa* of love-poetry.

Gower's claim to a limited *auctoritas* was implied rather than made explicitly, but I doubt if any learned reader of the *Confessio amantis* could have failed to appreciate the significance of either the sapiential extrinsic and intrinsic prologues with which Gower introduced his poem, or the clear moral note on which he 'ended' it. Anyway, the person who provided the Latin commentary was concerned to make sure that the implications of the English text should not be missed. He

says, in the third person, what Gower could not have said with decorum in the first person, thereby making his would-be *auctor* an actual
auctor.

After discussing the *intentio auctoris, nomen libelli* and *materia libri* (cf.
p. 181), the commentator signals the beginning of Gower's *tractatus* in
this way:

Here as it were in the person of other people *(in persona aliorum)*, who are held
fast by love, the author *(auctor)*, feigning himself to be a lover, proposes to
write of their various passions one by one in the various distinctions of this
book.[62]

This derives from a long-established method of defending the good
character of a work through reference to authorial use of *personae*, a good
example of which is St Bonaventure's treatment of Solomon's role in
Ecclesiastes (cf. pp. 110–12). Only the work of a good man has authority, Bonaventure explains: if Solomon was a wicked man, can his
work be said to have any authority? It is explained that Ecclesiastes was
written by a penitent man who looks back over his sins and regrets
them. Sometimes he speaks in his own person, sometimes in the persons of others *(in persona aliorum)*. When, for example, he speaks in the
person of the foolish man, he does not approve of this foolishness but
abhors it; when he speaks as a wise man his words are directly conducive to correct behaviour. The reader must appreciate the work in its
entirety; if so, he will find that his *auctor* has been entirely consistent.
Similarly, the commentator on the *Confessio amantis* was determined to
prove that Gower, though live, was a good *auctor*. A clear distinction is
therefore made between what Gower says in his own person (the *sapiens*
of the *Prologus*) and what he says in the persons of those that are subject
to love (including Amans and Confessor) in the course of the treatise.

At the end of the treatise, the commentator heralds the return of the
auctor in his own person:

Here at the end he recapitulates concerning that which at the beginning of the
first book he promised for the sake of love that he would treat more specially.
Truly, he concludes that the delight of all love apart from charity is nothing.
For whoever abides in charity, abides in God.[63]

In claiming that the pleasure of every kind of love except charity
amounts to nothing, the commentary goes further than the English
text which, as has been suggested above, recognises the limitations of

earthly love and the vices which its abuse can bring, but certainly does not condemn it outright. The commentator seems zealous to assure the reader that, although Amans and Confessor are the servants of love, John Gower is interested in both love and wisdom; that while the work is mainly about love, love has been placed in the context of wisdom.

The Latin commentary is, therefore, less subtle than the English text, and more explicitly moral. It serves to substantiate the claim of limited *auctoritas* which Gower had implied through his skilful manipulation of certain literary notions which, as we have seen, were developed by medieval scholars in their attempts to cope with the problems of interpretation encountered in reading 'ancient' *auctores*. The Latin commentary is an important feature of the *Confessio amantis:* when read with the English text, it emphasises the singleness of the writer's purpose and the essential unity of his materials. Indeed, the commentary is in such complete sympathy with the moral *intentio* professed in the poem that one is emboldened to believe that Gower himself provided it to accompany his 'modern English classic'.

CHAUCER'S ROLE AS 'LEWD COMPILATOR'

It would seem, then, that academic prologues provided Gower with models for the composition of his own prolegomena; the literary theory channelled through these same academic prologues provided him with principles for the description and justification of his own works. By contrast, Chaucer did not employ any of the traditional prologue-paradigms, although many of his literary attitudes seem to have been influenced by scholastic literary theory.

Chaucer's knowledge of the Aristotelian causal scheme is indicated by a passage in the Tale of Melibee[64]. While he never discusses the four causes in a specifically literary context, he does seem to have known various literary terms which occur both in the 'type C' prologue and in the later 'Aristotelian prologue'. This point may be made clearly by a comparison of some of Chaucer's literary terms with Richard Rolle's translations of several Latin words into English.

When, in the early fourteenth century, Rolle provided glosses to his English Psalter, he rendered in English a simplified version of the 'type C' prologue to that text which had been developed by such twelfth-century exegetes as Gilbert of Poitiers and Peter Lombard (cf. pp.

45, 52–4). Rolle describes the Psalter's 'mater' (= *materia*), 'entent' (= *intentio*), and 'maner of lare' (= *modus agendi*) as follows:

þe *mater of* þis boke es Crist and his spouse. þat es, haly kirk, or ilke a rightwys mans saule. þe *entent* es to confourme þo þat ere fyled in Adam tille Crist in newnes of lyf. þe *maner of lare* es swilke: vmstunt he spekys of Crist in his godhede, vmstunt in his manhede, vmstunt in þat þat he vses þe voyce of his servauntes. Als so he spekys of haly kirk in thre maners: vmwhile in þe persone of parfite men, summe tyme in persoun of vnparfit menne, summe tyme of ille menne, þe whilke are in haly kirk be body noght be thoght, be name noght be dede, in noumbyr noght in merite [italics mine].[65]

Chaucer also employs 'entente' in the sense of *intentio auctoris*[66]. Examples of his use of 'mateere' in the sense of *materia libri* are legion[67]. 'Maner' is used in the sense of *modus agendi* (to designate literary form or style) when, in the Monk's Tale, the 'maner of tragedie' is discussed[68]. Chaucer may have picked up this term from a gloss on one of the *auctores* generally described as tragedians by medieval commentators, namely 'Virgile, Ovide, Omer, Lucan and Stace'[69]. Moreover, in the Merchant's Tale, he speaks of a letter written 'in manere of a compleynt or a lay'[70].

But of much greater significance is the apparent influence of an offshoot of scholastic literary discussion, namely, the theory developed by medieval compilers in describing and defending the genre of *compilatio*.

Of Chaucer's debt to several of the great medieval compilations there can be no doubt. R. A. Pratt has argued that he took material for the Wife of Bath's Prologue and Tale, the Summoner's Tale and the Pardoner's Tale from the *Communiloquium sive summa collationum* of John of Wales[71]. In a series of articles, P. Aiken claims that Chaucer made use of Vincent's *Speculum maius* in a number of ways: as a source for the Legend of Cleopatra and the Monk's Tale, and for scientific lore about dream-visions, medicine, demonology and alchemy, which appears in the *Canterbury Tales*[72]. My point is a different one, namely, that Chaucer was indebted to the compilers not only for source-material and technical information but also for a literary role and a literary form. Chaucer seems to have exploited the compilers' typical justification of their characteristic role as writers, and to have shared, to some extent, the compilers' sense of *ordinatio partium*.

When reading the prologue to a major compilation, one is immediately struck by the care with which the writer defines his special literary activity and his distinctive literary role or function as *compilator*. Whereas an *auctor* was regarded as someone whose works had considerable authority and who bore full responsibility for what he had written, the *compilator* firmly denied any personal authority and accepted responsibility only for the manner in which he had arranged the statements of other men. For example, Vincent of Beauvais stated that he had added 'little and almost nothing of my own' to the authorial statements he had excerpted[73]. The *auctoritas* involved belongs to the *auctoritates* themselves, while the credit for the *ordinatio partium*, the organisation and structuring of the diverse extracts, goes to the compiler. The same method of professing personal humility, the same ostentatious deference to sources, occur in the prologue to Brunetto Latini's *Trésor:*

And I do not say that the book is drawn from my poor wit or my scanty learning; but it is like a honeycomb gathered from different flowers, for this book is compiled exclusively from the marvellous sayings of authors who before our time treated of philosophy, each according to the part of it that he knew; for no earthly man can know it all, for philosophy is the root from which grow all the kinds of knowledge that man can know.[74]

The *compilator* has a *forma tractandi* all of his own, what Vincent called the 'mode of the excerptor' (*modus excerptoris*)[75].

In the prologue to *De proprietatibus rerum*, Bartholomew the Englishman explained his intention in words very similar to Vincent's, protesting that he had included 'little or nothing of my own'[76]. John Trevisa, who completed his translation of Bartholomew in 1398, rendered the relevant passage in English as follows:

In þis work I haue iput of myne owne wille litil oþir nouȝt, but al þat schal be seid is itake of autentik bokes of holy seyntes and of philosophres and compile schortliche witoute idilnesse . . .[77]

A similar idiom is found in an original Middle English compilation, the short treatise on 'Actijf Lijf 7 contemplatijf', which forms one component within the larger compilation known as *The Poor Caitiff*. The anonymous writer declares that

Alle þese sentencis bifore goynge I haue gaderid of hooly writt 7 of dyuerse seyntis 7 doctouris 7 no þing of myn owne heed to schewe to my pore briþeren 7 sustren . . .[78]

By the mid-fifteenth century, this type of protestation had deteriorated into cliché, something to be reiterated mechanically. For example, Osbern Bokenham concludes his *Mappula angliae* (a brief work drawn from the first part of Higden's *Polychronicon*) with this over-elaborate statement:

I of no þynge seyde þere-yn chalenge ne desire to be holdyn neythur auctour ne assertour, ne wylle aske no more but to byn holdyn oonly the pore compilatour and owte of Latyne in to ynglyssh the rude and symple translatour . . .[79]

He proceeds to explain that he has supplied his name in an acrostic.

Fundamental to all these definitions of literary role is the distinction between *assertio* and *recitatio* which, since the time of Vincent, was a common feature of the literary theory disseminated with compilations. An *auctor* was supposed to 'assert' or 'affirm', while a compilator 'repeated' or 'reported' what others had said or done (cf. pp 100–2). According to FitzRalph's intricate excursus on authorial responsibility, Moses, as the editor or compiler of the lies told by Jacob and the serpent, only reported these things without asserting or affirming them.

When justifying his inclusion of the sayings of pagan philosophers and poets, and also of extracts from the Apocrypha, Vincent of Beauvais had warned his readers that he was only reporting such materials. Moreover, he carefully labelled those few assertions for which he was prepared to accept personal responsibility with the term *actor*. Vincent's successors were at once more aggressive and more defensive. Ralph Higden, who believed that the mighty compiler had taken the mace from the hand of Hercules, continued the martial metaphor by claiming that the names of his *auctores* formed his 'shield and defence' against detractors[80]. Personal responsibility was admitted only for those statements which Higden had indicated with his initial, 'R'. Trevisa, who completed his translation of the *Polychronicon* in 1387, was even more on the defensive than Higden had been; he had a firmer grip on the protective 'schelde' of the compiler:

þe auctores þat in the firste bygynnynge of þis book I take for schelde and defens, me for to saue and schilde aзenst enemyes þat me wolde despise strongly and blame; first for my self and for myn owne name I write þis letter [R].[81]

This desire to avoid 'blame' is manifest throughout Trevisa's translation, though there is usually little basis for it in Higden's Latin. For example, after Higden told the story about the mace of Hercules, he expressed the hope that the reader would not be offended by his literary efforts. This is the sense which is brought out in the anonymous fifteenth-century English translation of the *Polychronicon*[82]. But Trevisa renders the passage as 'þerfore I pray þat no man me blame . . .'[83].

Trevisa was also acutely aware of the *assertio/recitatio* distinction. He uses the English verb *aferme* in a technical sense, namely, the sense carried by the Latin verb *affirmare* as used by such writers as Vincent of Beauvais, Thomas Aquinas and FitzRalph.

I take nouȝt vppon me to *aferme* for sooþ all þat I write, but such as I haue seie and i-rad in dyuerse bookes, I garede and write wiþ oute envie, and comoun to oþere men.[84]

Trevisa translates the Latin verb *recitare* with the English *reherse,* for example, in the course of a reaction against Higden's use of a story about the philosopher Diogenes[85]. Diogenes was told that a friend had slandered him. His reaction was to doubt whether his friend had said such things about him, but it was quite clear that his informant had said them. Trevisa complains that, here, no clear distinction is made between the assertor and reporter, between the liar and the person who reveals him as such. Cases from the Bible are cited to prove the point:

Seint Iohn, in his gospel, seiþ nouȝt þat þe devel was in Crist; but Seint Iohn seiþ þat þe Iewes seide þat þe devel was in Crist: and Crist hymself despisede not God; but he reherseþ hou me bere hym on honde þat he despisede God: þat it followeþ in the storie.

It is little wonder that Trevisa, so aware of the distinction between assertion and reporting in the treatment of problem-passages of Scripture, should carefully label his personal *assertiones* in the text of the *Polychronicon* with his name, 'Trevisa'[86].

Sometimes, the highly controversial nature of the 'rehearsed' materials led the compiler to adopt a defensive position and to exploit the conventional idioms for disavowing responsibility. A major case in point is the one in which the 'rehearsed' materials concerned the 'judicial art' of making particular predictions, i.e. predictions about a particular human personality or about the fate of an individual[87]. Such material was potentially dangerous because it consisted of, or depended on, the opinions of pagan philosophers who—according to their medieval critics—had advocated a strict determinism in which divine

3 THE WRITER AS REPORTER (see pp. 193–204). Oxford, Bodleian Library, MS Douce 213, fol. 1ʳ. Lawrence of Premierfait, French translation of Boccaccio's *Decameron*.

grace could play no part[88]. The ubiquitous late-medieval criticisms of the *ars judicialis* make it perfectly clear that any writer who wished to handle this subject had to do so with considerable delicacy and diplomacy.

For example, although the Oxford astrologer, John Ashenden, was not a determinist, he felt obliged to guard against misinterpretation of his work[89]. In a short treatise found in Oxford, Bodleian Library, MS Digby 176, a formal protestation is made concerning the contingency of his predictions. The predicted effects, Ashenden explains, will not inevitably or necessarily occur in consequence of the predicted conclusions. He has merely described the signs of future events, 'in accordance with astronomy and the opinion of those astronomers whom I have cited in this treatise'[90].

Ashenden attributed to himself a similar role in his famous *Summa judicialis de accidentibus mundi* (completed December 1348), which became a standard reference-book on astrology. He complains that his science has often been misunderstood[91]. Besides, he, himself, is not an *auctor:* 'My intention is to compile the wise sayings of astrologers concerning the prognostication of occurrences which happen in this world by dint of the volubility of superior bodies. . . ' . Ashenden will add nothing out of his own head to the compiled rules and *sententiae,* apart from what seems to follow from the authoritative sayings; his expressed wish is to 'by no means be reputed to be an author but only a compiler in this work'. The compiler's typical disavowal of responsibility is functioning here as a defence against those who distrust certain aspects of astrology. As a compiler dependent on his authors' statements, Ashenden cannot be blamed for the truth or falsity of the contents of his book.

This same kind of defence is found in the *Liber judiciorum* preserved in Oxford, Bodleian Library, MS Bodley 581. In its prologue, we learn that the compiler prepared this book of divinations for the consolation of King Richard II, but he does not want to be regarded as its *auctor*[92]. A good example of the corresponding idiom in Middle English is provided by Chaucer's *Treatise on the Astrolabe*. Higden and Trevisa had regarded the compiler's typical disavowal as a shield against detractors: for Chaucer, it was a sword to slay envy.

But considre wel that I ne usurpe not to have founden this werk of my labour or of myn engyn. I n'am but a lewd compilator of the labour of olde astrologiens, and have it translatid in myn Englissh oonly for thy doctrine. And with this swerd shal I sleen envie.[93]

Chaucer calls himself a 'lewd' or unlearned compiler, presumably to make the point that he is not a learned compiler like Vincent of Beauvais or John Ashenden. Within the treatise itself, Chaucer's objective role as a 'rehearsing' compiler is illustrated by an important comment about the pagan practice of casting personal horoscopes:

Natheles these ben observaunces of judicial matere and rytes of payens, in whiche my spirit hath no feith, ne knowing of her *horoscopum*.[94]

Another highly controversial subject was human love: like judicial astrology, it was supposed to be potentially dangerous and conducive to sin, and many of its acknowledged *auctores* were pagans. The greatest medieval compilation of *auctoritates* on love is perhaps Jean de Meun's *Roman de la Rose* (written between 1275 and 1280). Jean's compiling activity is one of the main thirteenth-century testaments to the flexible nature of the literary form of *compilatio*. He was one of the first writers to make a fictitious narrative, namely, the pursuit of the Rose, the occasion for compilation of diverse *materiae* on a grand scale.

C. W. Dunn writes of the *Roman*,

the age of Jean de Meun was animated by the Aristotelian dictum, *sapientis est ordinare*. As a man of learning he instinctively ordered his theme and related love to the whole scheme of things. . . . Reason reveals love's folly, Genius argues its necessity, the Duenna describes the sordidness of its strategems, Forced Abstinence suggests the unhealthiness of its renunciation, and so on, until every aspect of love has been ordered within the totality.[95]

What this account misses is that the lover's pursuit of the Rose provides the opportunity and the rationale for the inclusion of material relating to 'the whole scheme of things'. Jean's basic *ordinatio partium* consists of the various stages in the pursuit of the Rose, stages which enable Jean's characters to discuss diverse aspects of love, until every aspect has been ordered with the overall structure. Within this general arrangement, other *materiae* are subordinated: for example, when treating of lovers' misfortunes, Jean's 'Raison' provides a description of the Wheel of Fortune, a discussion of Wealth and Justice, and stories 'of the cases of illustrious men' (see lines 4837–6900).

Jean exploits the compiler's typical defence in his *apologia* for the *Roman*, a statement which has long been recognised as an influence on the General Prologue to Chaucer's *Canterbury Tales.* The noble women in Jean's audience are asked not to blame the writer for the derogatory things he has said about women, for all that was written was written for their doctrine (lines 15195–203). If any reader thinks that Jean is telling lies about love, she should consult the *aucteurs* who are his sources: he is dependent on his authors and, if they told the truth, then so has he.

S'il vous semble que je di fables,
Pour menteeur ne m'en tenez,
Mais aus aucteurs vous en prenez
Qui en leur livres ont escrites
Les paroles que j'en ai dites,
E ceus avec que j'en dirai;
Ne ja de riens n'en mentirai,
Se li preudome n'en mentirent
Qui les anciens livres firent.   (lines 15216–24)

[If you think I tell untruths, do not hold me a liar, but search the authors who in their books have written the things that I have said and will say. I shall not lie in any respect as long as the wise men who wrote the ancient books did not lie.]⁹⁶

   All Jean's *aucteurs* agree with him, and he should not be blamed for reporting or repeating their words:

Par quei meauz m'en devez quiter:
Je n'i faz riens fors *reciter* . . .   (lines 15233–4: Italics mine)

[So you should pardon me: I do nothing but report their words . . .]

He has made additions (as all the poets have been wont to do) to order the *matire* taken from his sources (lines 15235–9).
   Obviously, deference to *auctores* could become a 'shield and defence' for the personal opinions and prejudices implied by a compiler's very choice of excerpts and for the way in which he had handled them. In Jean's *apologia,* the traditional protestation of the compiler is well on its way to becoming a 'disavowal of responsibility' trope.
   We are now in a position to examine the role of 'rehearsing' compiler which Chaucer assumed in the *Canterbury Tales,* wherein the fictitious narrative of a pilgrimage to Canterbury provides the rationale for the compilation. As compiler, Chaucer proposes to 'rehearse' the words of other men as accurately as he can, without being responsible for what they say:

But first I pray yow, of youre curteisye,
That ye n'arette it nat my vileynye,
Thogh that I pleynly speke in this mateere,
To telle yow hir wordes and hir cheere,
Ne thogh I speke hir wordes proprely.
For this ye knowen al so wel as I,
Whoso shal telle a tale after a man,
He moot *reherce* as ny as evere he kan
Everich a word, if it be in his charge,
Al speke he never so rudeliche and large,
Or ellis he moot telle his tale untrewe,
Or feyne thyng, or fynde wordes newe . . .
Also I prey yow to foryeve it me,
Al have I nat set folk in hir degree
Heere in this tale, as that they sholde stonde.
My wit is short, ye may wel understonde.

(General Prologue, lines 725–46: Italics mine)

The idiom in which this self-depreciation is couched displays the influence of the compiler's stock disavowal of responsibility. One may compare Vincent's remark, 'I added little, or almost nothing, of my own', or Ashenden's expressed desire 'to compile sentences, adding nothing out of my own head' or, indeed, Chaucer's own protestation that his *Treatise on the Astrolabe* was not 'founden of my labour or of myn engyn'. In the General Prologue, Chaucer the compiler seems to be protesting that he has not 'founden' the *Canterbury Tales* 'of my labour or of myn engyn'.

As compiler, Chaucer cannot be held responsible for, for example, the words of the churlish Miller:

    . . . this Millere
He nolde his wordes for no man forbere,
But tolde his cherles tale in his manere.
M'athynketh that I shal *reherce* it heere.   (I, lines 3167–70: Italics mine)

What he is doing, in the technical sense, is 'rehearsing' the *materia* ('mateere') of the pilgrims; the *intentio* ('entente') of the compiler is stated to be a good one:

. . . demeth nat that I seye
Of yvel *entente,* but for I moot *reherce*
Hir tales alle, be they bettre or werse,
Or elles falsen som of my mateere.   (I, lines 3172–5: Italics mine)

A reporter deserves neither thanks nor blame for what he repeats without fabrication or alteration: 'Blameth nat me . . . ' .

But, of course, many medieval compilers were accustomed to including something out of their own heads, of adding some personal assertion to their reportage. Vincent appeared in his *Speculum maius* as the *actor;* Ralph Higden indicated personal assertions within his work by the initial 'R'; in the passages marked with his name, the more aggressive John Trevisa delivered his own opinions and sometimes criticised his sources. The most ostensibly personal assertions of Chaucer the pilgrim are the two tales he tells, namely, Sir Thopas and Melibee.

Chaucer's sense of combining and organising diverse materials may owe something to the compilers' theory and practice of *ordinatio partium*. The major medieval compilations were compendious, containing *materiae* to cater for a wide range of demands and tastes. Vincent of Beauvais prided himself on the amount of diverse materials he had managed to include in his *Speculum maius* [97]. Brunetto Latini explained that his *Trésor* combined both teaching and delight:

This book is called 'Treasury'. For, just like the lord who wishes in one small place to collect something of great worth, not only for his delight, but to increase his power and protect his position in both war and peace, places in it the most valuable things and the most precious jewels that he can, to the best of his ability; just so is the body of this book compiled from wisdom, as one which is drawn from all the parts of philosophy concisely into one digest. [98]

Brunetto's practice may have influenced Gower's conception of the scope of his *Confessio amantis,* which comprises both 'lust' and 'lore': certainly, the Latin commentary stresses the point that Gower compiled extracts from chronicles, histories and the sayings of the (pagan) philosophers and poets[99]. When Higden described the *ordinatio* of his *Polychronicon,* he explained how he had taken various things from various sources and had reorganised them in accordance with new principles[100]. His fifteenth-century translator renders the relevant passage as follows:

In whom alle things excerpte of oþer men ar broken in to smalle membres, but concorporate here liniamentally; thynges of disporte be admixte with saddenes, and dictes ethnicalle to thynges religious, that the ordre of the processe may be obseruede . . .[101]

In the *Canterbury Tales* also, 'thynges of disporte be admixte with saddenes, and dictes ethnicalle to thynges religious'. Chaucer aimed at

being compendious, at providing 'Tales of best sentence and most sol-
aas', 'cherles tales' and noble tales, 'myrie' tales and 'fructuous' tales,
pagan tales and Christian tales[102]. When the host stops Chaucer the
pilgrim from completing the Tale of Thopas, he urges him to tell
something 'in which ther be som murthe or som doctryne' (VII, line
935), making it clear that different standards apply to different types
of tale. The major reference-books of the day may be regarded as having
provided the general precedents for the combinations of 'murthe' and
'doctrine', of 'lust' and 'lore', practised by Chaucer in the *Canterbury
Tales* and, indeed, by Gower in the *Confessio amantis* and Jean de Meun
in the *Roman de la Rose*.

Of course, the nature of Chaucer's diverse *materiae* is not identical
with the nature of the diverse *materiae* of a compiler like, for example,
Vincent of Beauvais[103]. The point is rather that both writers drew on a
common corpus of literary theory; they described their different diver-
sities in a similar way. Moreover, Vincent 'ordinated' materials in relation to chapters, books and *tituli*, whereas Chaucer 'ordinated' materials in relation to tales and tellers; both writers shared basic principles of
hierarchical or 'encapsulating' structure[104]. It is as if Chaucer derived
certain principles of order from compilations and from the explanations
of *ordinatio* which accompanied them, principles which he chose to
apply in his own way.

Moreover, Chaucer and Vincent (among other compilers) shared the
principle of the reader's freedom of choice *(lectoris arbitrium)*. In the case
of Vincent, this means that the reader can isolate and believe whatever
things he wishes to believe: no attempt has been made to force the
auctores to speak with one voice, and it is up to the reader to make his
own choice from the discordant *auctoritates* offered to him[105]. Chaucer
also is interested in the freedom of the reader. If a reader does not want
a tale like the Miller's Tale, there are many other types of 'mateere' on
offer:

. . . whoso list it [the Miller's Tale] nat yheere,
Turne over the leef and chese another tale;
For he shal fynde ynowe, grete and smale,
Of storial thyng that toucheth gentillesse,
And eek moralitee and hoolynesse.   (I, lines 3176–80)

The common principle involved is that a compiler is not responsible for
his reader's understanding of any part of the *materia*, for any effect

which the *materia* may have on him and, indeed, for any error or sin
into which the *materia* may lead a reader. 'Blameth nat me if that ye
chese amys', warns Chaucer; 'Avyseth yow, and put me out of blame'
(I, lines 3181, 3185).

But perhaps the most intriguing facet of Chaucer's exploitation of
the principles of *compilatio* is the way in which he seems to have transferred the compiler's technique of authenticating sources to his
'sources', the Canterbury pilgrims. All the major compilers habitually
authenticated their sources by stating that the 'rehearsed' words were
the proper words of their *auctores,* and by carefully assigning the extracted *auctoritates* to their respective *auctores* (see pp. 157–8). Likewise,
Chaucer has his narrator explain that the words he 'rehearses' are the
proper words of the fictitious pilgrims. In order to 'speke hir wordes
proprely', he must give 'everich a word' that each pilgrim uttered, 'al
speke he never so rudeliche and large' (General Prologue, lines 725–
42). The 'wordes' of a churl like the Miller are proper to the Miller,
who

. . . nolde his wordes for no man forbere,
But tolde his cherles tale in his manere . . .
The Millere is a cherl, ye knowe wel this;
So was the Reve eek and othere mo,
And harlotrie they tolden bothe two.   (I, lines 3167–84)

The device of organising diverse *materiae* by distributing them amongst
diverse fictional characters was not new: we have already noted its use
by Jean de Meun. What was new was the kind of attention paid to what
the fictional characters said.

Chaucer's professed concern for the *ipsissima verba* of his pilgrims
seems to parallel the concern of a compiler like Vincent of Beauvais for
the actual words of his *auctores.* For example, in the first chapter of his
apologia, Vincent complains bitterly about textual corruptions in manuscripts, which make it difficult to understand the authors' meanings
and, indeed, to know which *auctor* is responsible for whatever
sententia[106]. Moreover, he feels obliged to point out that he has used
not the *originalia* of Aristotle but collections of 'flowers' extracted from
the *originalia* by brother friars who could not always follow the order of
the words in Aristotle's text, although in every case they tried to follow
the meaning[107]. Merely to preserve the meaning is not good enough for
Chaucer the compiler, who is determined to preserve the proper words
of each pilgrim without 'feigning' anything or adding 'wordes newe':

Whoso shal telle a tale after a man,
He moot reherce as ny as evere he kan
Everich a word, if it be in his charge,
Al speke he never so rudeliche and large,
Or ellis he moot telle his tale untrewe,
Or feyne thyng, or fynde wordes newe.
He may nat spare, althogh he were his brother;
He moot as wel seye o word as another.

(General Prologue, lines 731–8)

In sum, it may be argued that Chaucer treats his fictional characters with the respect that the Latin compilers had reserved for their *auctores*. The 'lewd compilator' has become the compiler of the 'lewd'.

The distinctive quality of Chaucer's exploitation of the conventions of *compilatio* may further be illuminated by contrasting it with the more avant-garde practice of Giovanni Boccaccio (1313–75). In the prologue to his *Decameron*, Boccaccio explains that he has narrated a hundred stories to provide 'succour and diversion' for women in love.

In reading them, the aforesaid ladies will be able to derive, not only pleasure from the entertaining matters therein set forth, but also some useful advice. For they will learn to recognise what should be avoided and likewise what should be pursued, and these things can only lead, in my opinion, to the removal of their affliction.[108]

This idiom is familiar to us from the *accessus Ovidiani* (see pp. 55–6), but its significance has been altogether altered by the force of Boccaccio's appeal to the pleasure-principle. The *Conclusione* places a similar emphasis[109]. Like Jean de Meun and Chaucer, Boccaccio protests that it is no more indecent for him to have written certain vulgar expressions than it is for people to use them in their everyday speech. But there the similarity with the other writers ends. He proceeds to insist that his stories were told neither in a church nor in the schools of philosophers, nor in any place where either churchmen or philosophers were present. They were told in gardens, in a place designed for pleasure, among mature people who were not to be led astray by stories. So forceful is this appeal to the principle of 'literature for refreshment' that Boccaccio comes close to claiming a large measure of autonomy for pleasurable fiction[110]. Jean de Meun's *apologia* and Chaucer's General Prologue are quite different in spirit.

Boccaccio also claims—rather half-heartedly—that he should be regarded as the mere scribe and not as the inventor of the stories in the

Decameron. Because he was constrained to transcribe the stories just as
they were told, he cannot be blamed for any of their shortcomings:

> There will likewise be those among you who will say that some of the stories
> included here would far better have been omitted. That is as may be: but I
> could only transcribe the stories as they were actually told, which means that if
> the ladies who told them had told them better, I should have written them
> better. But even if one could assume that I was the inventor (*lo'nventore*) as well
> as the scribe (*lo scrittore*) of these stories (which was not the case), I still insist
> that I would not feel ashamed if some fell short of perfection, for there is no
> craftsman other than God whose work is whole and faultless in every respect.[111]

This passage clearly demonstrates knowledge of the technique for disavowing responsibility as employed in compilers' prologues, but
equally clear is Boccaccio's impulse to discard the convention and come
out in the open as the unashamed inventor of his stories, the self-
confessed craftsman whose creativity parallels (in so far as is humanly
possible) the perfect creation of God. By comparison, Jean de Meun
and Chaucer appear quite conservative. They were content to adopt the
role of the reporter who cannot be blamed for what his sources say, to
peer out from behind the 'shield and defence' of the compiler.

It remains to assess the extent to which Chaucer was influenced by
one of the standard 'final causes' or ultimate justifications of *compilatio*.
The wish to justify their special literary activity had encouraged some
compilers to think not only of the practical *utilitas* of *compilatio* (its
efficacy in providing doctrine in a convenient and predigested way) but
also of its *utilitas* in a more absolute sense—it is the function of doctrine to bring us eventually to salvation. Each of the *formae tractandi*
discussed by commentators on *auctores* had its characteristic *finalis causa*
or noble end; why not the *forma tractandi* characteristic of collection and
compilation, the *modus excerptoris?* Certain fourteenth-century compilers therefore took from the exegetes a sophisticated *finalis causa:* 'All
that is written is written for our doctrine, that by the steadfastness and
by the encouragement of the scriptures we might have hope' (Romans
xv. 4).

The exegetes had produced the *finalis causa* of *compilatio* in expounding Scriptural texts which (perhaps due in part to the large number of
compilations being written by their contemporaries) they had come to
describe as 'ancient' collections and compilations of material. Defending the compilation of scraps of truth in the Book of Baruch, Albert the

Great had cited the words of Jesus after the feeding of the five thousand: 'Collect the scraps . . . so that nothing gets wasted' (John vi. 12)[112]. We must, Albert insists, not only pick up the books of the prophets but also collect with diligence their fragments or scraps for, as Deuteronomy viii. 13 says, 'man does not live by bread alone but by every word that proceeds from the mouth of the Lord'. All that is written in Scripture, however fragmentary or trivial it may seem, is written for our doctrine.

Nicholas of Lyre adopted Romans xv. 4 in expounding the final cause of his archetypal *collectio,* the Psalter[113]. Man, he explains, is ordained to a supernatural end, but he would not be aware of this end nor of the means of knowing it through praise and love, were it not for the divinely-inspired Scriptures. As St Paul says, 'all that is written is written for our doctrine, that by steadfastness and by the encouragement of the Scriptures we may have hope'. This hope is the sure expectation of future beatitude. Because the Psalter proceeds 'by the mode of praise', it has great utility in the encouragement of this hope.

In these two examples, the materials in question are divinely-inspired writings, and the stress falls on the second part of St Paul's statement ('. . .that by steadfastness and by the encouragement of the Scriptures we may have hope'). The compilers who adopted this final cause shifted the stress to the first part of the statement ('All that is written is written for our doctrine . . .'), and the 'all' came to mean 'almost anything', writings of all kinds. For example, Ralph Higden cited Romans xv. 4 in defence of his juxtaposition of pagan and Christian *auctoritates* on common subjects[114]. Isidore of Seville is quoted as saying that we should not condemn 'ancient' commentators and historians for speaking diversely, for things written in the past are full of errors by reason of their antiquity. The pagans who lived before Christ had a limited *auctoritas,* and therefore Higden must disclaim responsibility for their views. St Paul did not say that all that is written is true: he said that all that is written is written for our doctrine. The onus is therefore placed on the discriminating reader.

From this it was but a short step to enlisting 'All that is written . . .' as a justification of the compilation of pagan *fabulae.* Between 1316 and 1328 an anonymous Franciscan took the existing structure of Ovid's *Metamorphoses* and recompiled its constituent parts, inserting explanations of the moral significance of each part. At the beginning of this work, the *Ovide moralisé,* the anonymous friar justifies his procedure by appealing to the final cause of *compilatio:*

Se l'escripture ne me ment,
Tout est pour nostre enseignement
Quanqu'il a es livres escript,
Soient bon ou mal li escript.[115]   (lines 1–4)

[If the Scriptural passage does not lie to me, whatever is written in books is all for our doctrine, be the writings good or ill.]

All that is written is written for our doctrine, whether what is written is good or bad.

A similar idiom is employed much later than Chaucer, by William Caxton in the prologue to his English 'Moral Ovid' (1480). Here, Romans xv.4 is related to the principle (which is a commonplace of the *accessus Ovidiani*) that evil is described so that one might beware of it, while good is described so that one may follow it:

Alle scriptures and wrytyngis ben they good or evyll ben wreton for our prouf-fyt and doctrine. The good to thende to take ensample by them to doo well. And the evyll to thende that we shoulde kepe and absteyne vs to do evyll.[116]

Caxton also applied this argument to a collection of prose tales, the *Morte Darthur* (printed 1485):

I . . have doon sette it in enprynte to the entente that noble men may see and lerne the noble actes of chyvalrie . . . and how they that were vycious were punysshed and ofte put to shame and rebuke; humbly bysechyng al noble lordes and ladyes wyth al other estates . . . that shal see and rede in this sayd book and werke, that they take the good and honest actes in their remem-braunce, and to folowe the same . . . Doo after the good and leve the evyl, and it shal brynge you to good fame and renommee.

    And for to passe the tyme thys book shal be plesaunte to rede in, but for to gyve fayth and byleve that al is trewe that is conteyned herin, ye be at your lyberté. But al is wryton for our doctrine, and for to beware that we falle not to vyce ne synne, but t'exersyse and folowe vertu . . .[117]

By this stage, Romans xv.4 could be used to justify practically everything.

We may now proceed to examine Chaucer's two applications of Romans xv.4. The first of these, which occurs at the end of the Nun's Priest's Tale, need not detain us long. However one wishes to interpret the Nun's Priest's Tale, its debt to the genre of moralised *fabula* is incontrovertible[118]. Therefore, it is quite fitting that Chaucer should end his tale by echoing the justification of *moralisatio* found in one of the greatest compilations of moralised *fabulae,* the *Ovide moralisé.*

Chaucer could have extended this kind of justification to cover most of the *Canterbury Tales;* however diverse the parts may be, he could have argued that, ultimately, they serve truth, although not by the same method. But there is no systematic appeal to these terms of reference throughout the fragments of the *Canterbury Tales* which we have—a point of some substance when we come to consider Chaucer's other use of 'All that is written . . .', in the 'retracciouns' which follow the Parson's Tale and conclude the entire work. The text of the tales found in the Ellesmere Chaucer and subsequent manuscripts may be provided with this final cause, but it is very doubtful if Chaucer himself provided it as such.

At the beginning of the 'retracciouns', Chaucer expresses the hope that, if there is anything in his 'litel tretys' which appeals to his readers, they should thank Jesus Christ, 'of whom procedeth al wit and al goodnesse',

And if ther be any thyng that displese hem, I preye hem also that they arrette it to the defaute of myn unkonnynge, and nat to my wyl, that wolde ful fayn have seyd better if I hadde had konnynge. For oure book seith, 'Al that is writen is writen for our doctrine', and that is myn entente.[119]

The 'litel tretys' to which he refers must be the treatise on penitence now known as the Parson's Tale, for the *Canterbury Tales* considered as a whole is not a treatise in the technical sense of the term, and it could hardly be called little (though it should be remembered that Chaucer calls his *Troilus and Criseyde* a 'litel bok' at v, line 1789). 'All that is written . . .' provides a transition point in the 'retracciouns', the point at which Chaucer moves from speaking of his treatise on penitence to discuss his 'collected works'. In the vast majority of the applications of Romans xv.4 known to me, a grouping together or collection of diverse materials is described or presupposed. For this reason, it seems altogether appropriate that Chaucer, having introduced St Paul's words by way of *apologia* for any inadequacies in the work we know as the Parson's Tale, should proceed to apply these words in an *apologia* for his writings considered as a whole.

First, the 'translacions and enditynges of worldly vanitees' are re-

voked, including those *Canterbury Tales* 'that sownen into synne'. Then
Chaucer moves from the bad to the good, including his *Boece* and sun-
dry 'bookes of legendes of seintes, and omelies, and moralitee, and
devocioun'. Perhaps the way in which numerous compilers had described and justified their *ordinatio* of 'lust' and 'lore' influenced the way
in which Chaucer conceived of his total output. The 'entente' of a
writer can be good, he may write with the commendable purpose of
providing doctrine, but it is up to the reader to 'doo after the good and
leve the evyl'.

The Yet Chaucer chose not to exploit the compiler's traditional defence
in this manner, the manner of the *Ovide moralisé* prologue and Caxton's
preface to Malory: in the 'retracciouns' Romans xv.4 is *not* used to
justify practically everything. The fact that many of Chaucer's idioms
are conventional should not disguise the fact that he is not using them
conventionally. Although Chaucer had exploited several aspects of the
theory of *compilatio* in several works, in his 'retracciouns' he was not
prepared to assume the role of the 'lewd compilator' to whom no blame
could accrue. On the contrary, he takes the blame for the sinful material that he wrote—the fact that some of it was 'rehearsed' is now
irrelevant—and hopes that Christ in his mercy will forgive his sins.
The 'shield and defence' of the compiler has slipped, and for once we
see Chaucer as a writer who holds himself morally responsible for his
writings.

The 'retracciouns' seem to be linked to the Parson's Tale but not to
the *Canterbury Tales* as a whole; the Parson's Prologue promises a moral
tale (a 'meditacioun', to be exact), but not necessarily the penitential
treatise we end up with. In the 'retracciouns' Chaucer is concerned
with his 'collected works' in their entirety and not just with those
works which he had compiled as the *Canterbury Tales*. I suspect that,
had Chaucer himself expounded Romans xv.4 as the final cause of the
Canterbury Tales, he would have related it quite specifically to the *forma*
of this work in the manner of, for example, Nicholas of Lyre and the
Ovide moralisé compiler, as cited above. For these reasons I incline to
the view that the 'litel tretys' on penitence and the 'retracciouns' (form-
ing one unit) were added to the Canterbury Tales—probably by Chaucer but possibly by someone else—in keeping with the usual practice
of *compilatio*. (After Chaucer's death, the compilation of the Canterbury
Tales continued, with non-Chaucerian items being incorporated within
Chaucer's structure.)

After the 'retracciouns' in the Ellesmere manuscript, the following colophon occurs:

Heere is ended the book of the tales of Caunterbury, compiled by Geffrey Chaucer, of whos soule Jhesu Crist have mercy. Amen.[120]

The phrase 'of whos soule Jhesu Crist have mercy' suggests that it could be posthumous, but the tone does fit in with the pious language of the 'retracciouns'. Maybe the technical term 'compiled' was designed to fit in with Chaucer's use of Romans xv.4 in the 'retracciouns', which the person responsible for the colophon (perhaps one of Chaucer's 'literary executors') recognised as a standard final cause of *compilatio*. That is, it may have been realised that Chaucer's *apologia* for his 'complete works' served admirably as an *apologia* for the diverse *materiae* which he had brought together in the *Canterbury Tales:* Chaucer had even specified the 'tales of Caunterbury . . . that sownen into synne', and implicitly had referred to the virtuous tales in his mention of 'bookes of legendes of seintes, and omelies, and moralitee, and devocioun'. Such a (hypothetical) response to Chaucer's text could be regarded as an important literary judgment on it: the *Canterbury Tales* may have been interpreted, and edited, as a *compilatio*.

Finally, we must pose the question, did Chaucer ever think of himself as an *auctor*, of his work as possessing some limited degree of *auctoritas?* My impression is that whereas Gower was interested in presenting himself as a 'modern author', Chaucer was not. Chaucer was fond of assuming self-depreciating literary roles, and the role of compiler would have been particularly congenial to him.

Yet perhaps there is one exception, namely the claim which Chaucer made for *Troilus and Criseyde*. This little tragedy is ordered to

. . . kis the steppes, where as thow seest pace
Virgile, Ovide, Omer, Lucan, and Stace.   (v, lines 1791–2)

But this claim is different in nature from those made by Gower. Whereas Gower claimed a limited *auctoritas* for his major works by assuming the functions of certain kinds of 'ancient' *auctores,* the basis of Chaucer's commendation of *Troilus* consists rather in his profession that this work is dependent on 'ancient' literature—indeed, at one point he presents himself as a mere translator (ii, lines 12–18).

The 'modern' writers who were his main sources (Boccaccio, Benoît, Petrarch) would not serve this purpose, so Chaucer did not acknowledge them, but ascribed material taken from their works to 'ancient' *auctores*. Chaucer did not much care what 'Omer, Dares and Dite' had actually said; he did not bother to verify the existence of his 'auctour Lollius': he wished to use the names of the *auctores,* to 'cash in' on their antiquity and *auctoritas*[121]. Thus, he created the illusion that his 'storie' was indeed 'ancient', and established himself as the objective historian who sought to describe how certain pagans had lived and loved. The comments on his literary activity which Chaucer provided in the prohemium to book ii and at the very end of *Troilus* have more in common with the prologues of compiling historians like Vincent of Beauvais and Ralph Higden than they have with Gower's prologues[122].

It would seem, then, that Chaucer and Gower held rather different conceptions of the role of the *auctor* and of the literary forms which should be their models. Gower presented himself in authorial roles and employed authorial *formae,* methods which were substantially in line with contemporary Italian practice though, of course, the scale was very different[123]. Moreover, he ensured that his works were provided with that *apparatus criticus* (commentary, summaries, etc.) which the discerning reader had come to expect in copies of many 'ancient' works. The difference between the sporadic and superficial commentary on the *Confessio amantis* and the comprehensive commentary which Boccaccio supplied for his own *Teseida* is a difference of degree rather than of kind[124]. By contrast, for the most part, Chaucer was content to assume the role of compiler and to exploit the literary form of *compilatio*. Indeed, so deliberate was he in presenting himself as a compiler that one is led to suspect the presence of a very self-conscious author who was concerned to manipulate the conventions of *compilatio* for his own literary ends. If Gower was a compiler who tried to present himself as an author, Chaucer was an author who hid behind the 'shield and defence' of the compiler.

Epilogue:
The Familiar Authors

ONE OF PETRARCH'S *Litterae de rebus familiaribus* contains the following assessment of Cicero:

. . . though nearly everything pleases me in Cicero—a man whom I cherish beyond all my other friends—and though I expressed admiration for his golden eloquence and divine intellect, I could not praise the fickleness of his character and his inconstancy, which I had detected in many instances.[1]

In this short passage are illustrated many of the features of a theory of authorship usually associated with the Renaissance. Cicero is at once someone to be respected and a 'familiar' or friend[2]. Yet, this reverence and assumed acquaintance do not entail uncritical admiration: Petrarch is acutely aware of the sins and shortcomings of his *auctor*.

The precedent for Petrarch's radical approach to authorship was provided, paradoxically enough, by rediscovered authoritative texts, namely, Cicero's letters to Atticus, Quintus and Brutus, which Petrarch himself had recovered in 1345[3]. On reading these 'quarrelsome letters', Petrarch tells us, he was 'soothed and ruffled at the same time': the style was delightful, but the facility with which Cicero shifted from commending illustrious men to condemning them was offensive.

I could not restrain myself, and, indignation prompting me, I wrote to him as a friend of my own years and time, regardless of the ages which separated us. Indeed, I wrote with a familiarity acquired through an intimate knowledge of the works of his genius, and I pointed out to him what it was that offended me in his writings.[4]

Disregarding the distancing and aggrandising power of time, a 'modern' has claimed a close proximity of relationship, a high degree of familiarity, with an 'ancient', on the basis of their common literary, intellectual and moral concerns. The style of Cicero's letters provided Petrarch with a new literary form; their content provided him with the new information necessary for the placing of Cicero's life and literature in a genuine historical perspective.

Cicero, for Petrarch, was a model of eloquence and a brilliant thinker, a monotheistic philosopher who 'never wrote one word that would conflict with the principles of Christ'[5]. Nevertheless, he had failed often to practise what he preached, turning a deaf ear to his own doctrines. Both these sides of the author's character are described in the two 'familiar letters' which Petrarch addressed to him: the first censures Cicero's life; the second praises his genius[6]. Cicero's inconstancy is gravely censured, yet Petrarch writes out of 'sincere love' and empathises with his author: 'I feel that I know you as intimately as if I had always lived with you'[7].

I grieve at your lot, my friend; I am ashamed of your many, great shortcomings, and take compassion on them.[8]

Some aspects of his author's life arouse Petrarch's compassion, although he can rejoice freely in the mental abilities and powers of expression which Cicero possessed in such abundance.

You indeed, O Cicero (speaking with your leave), did live as a man, speak as an orator, and write as a philosopher. It was your life that I found fault with, not your intellectual powers, nor yet your command of language. Indeed, I admire the former, and am amazed at the latter. And, moreover, in your life I feel the lack of nothing except the element of constancy, and a desire for peace that was to have been expected of a philosopher.[9]

The philosophical wisdom of this *auctor* may be respected, his eloquence may be admired and imitated, and his moral shortcomings may be censured.

But not everyone was prepared to accept this point of view. When debating with an opponent who refused to believe ill of Cicero, Petrarch had regaled him with the two letters to Cicero, but to no avail[10]. The 'venerable gentleman' persisted in admiring everything indiscriminately about Cicero, 'lest he might seem to cast even the slightest aspersions on so praiseworthy an author': his only defence was the 'mere splendour of Cicero's name'. 'Authority had driven out reason', was Petrarch's tart conclusion.

This last statement could well serve as a motto for earlier 'lives' of Cicero. Views similar to those held by Petrarch's 'venerable gentleman' lie behind the eulogistic accounts found in works like the *Speculum maius* of Vincent of Beauvais, the *Compendiloquium de vitis illustrium philosophorum* of John of Wales, and the *Liber de vita et moribus philosophorum* of Walter Burley (*c.* 1275–*c.* 1345). These accounts shall be paraphrased briefly, since they at once recapitulate the attitudes to authorship which have been described in the above chapters, and illustrate the fixed assumptions that Petrarch was up against.

Vincent of Beauvais's contribution consists of a mere *cathena* or 'chain' of *auctoritates* derived from Cicero's works, linked together in a sententious sequence[11]. On the face of it, Burley's compilation looks more promising: the prologue declares his intention of bringing together in one volume the sparse information about their lives which the philosophers and poets recorded in their works[12]. Moreover, he has included many of their 'notable responses and elegant sayings', so that the reader might be consoled and morally informed. However, all Burley tells us about the life of Cicero is that he was the most noble among the Roman consuls: he illuminated the time of Julius Caesar, when he was by far the greatest and most studious philosopher[13]. Having repudiated his wife, Cicero was offered a prince's sister in marriage, whereupon he said that he could not serve both a wife and philosophy together. This trivial anecdote is followed by a list of Cicero's writings and a collection of *sententiae* excerpted from them. Burley, like Vincent of Beauvais before him, seems to have felt that Cicero's true character was revealed by his most sententious statements. The account provided by John of Wales is similarly eulogistic, but at least he could offer two moralistic *exempla* featuring Cicero, one from Seneca and one from Aulus Gellius[14]. This depiction of Cicero is wholly in keeping with the principle, outlined in the prologue to the *Compendiloquium*, that certain gentiles lived a life so good that they put Christians—who ought to know better and do better—to shame. John cites Isaiah xxiii.4, 'Be thou ashamed, O Zidon, for the sea has spoken', then proceeds to paraphrase St Gregory's interpretation of this text, as found at the beginning of the *Moralia in Job* (see p. 37). 'Zidon' signifies the stable New Law under which Christians live, while the 'sea' signifies the life of the gentiles. Well may Zidon be ashamed, for the life of virtuous pagans reproves life under the present regime, and the deeds of secular men confound the deeds of the religious. For these reasons, John explains, he thought fit to collect the notable sayings of the philosophers and the imitable examples of virtuous men, in order to stimulate the young and put would-be philosophers to shame, to repress arrogance and encourage humility.

These compilers were interested in Cicero mainly as an authority in moral philosophy and rhetoric. By contrast, Petrarch's interest comprised both the achievements and the limitations of his favourite author, the 'ancient' whom he presumed to address—in the most familiar of tones—as his friend. Clearly, there are outstanding differences between the respective theories of authorship held by Petrarch and, for example, Thomas Aquinas[15]. Yet some of Petrarch's attitudes can, as it were, be regarded as imaginative extensions of ideas which had emerged in scholastic literary theory. When coming to terms with the 'literal sense' of sacred Scripture, late medieval exegetes had been obliged to adopt fresh positions concerning the achievements and limitations of Biblical authors (see pp. 103–12). Authors like David and Solomon had on occasion been divinely inspired, but they had sinned as well; yet respect for their authority had come to be regarded as perfectly compatible with recognition of the shortcomings of their humanity. David was esteemed to be the greatest of the prophets: he was also a pattern of penitence, a man whom every sinner was urged to identify with and emulate. In approaching Cicero, Virgil and Seneca with a similar reverence, awareness of faults and sense of common humanity, Petrarch attained a new view of the pagan author.

In the writings of Petrarch, one can see the barriers coming down between various kinds of author, whether between pagan and Christian or 'ancient' and 'modern'. Many of the *Litterae de rebus familiaribus* record the activities and misfortunes of Petrarch and his 'modern' friends among contemporary Italians; for this, he claimed the precedent of Cicero's letters. Petrarch's letters to Cicero were the first in a series of letters to his 'ancient' friends among the classical authors.

In Boccaccio's *Life of Dante,* a 'modern author' is treated with a degree of familiarity similar to that with which Petrarch had treated Cicero. Boccaccio had learnt from Petrarch that one could find fault with an author's life without calling in question his intellectual powers or command of language. The great poet's scholarship and genius are praised while his faults are censured, although it is quite clear that, in

Boccaccio's view, Dante was more sinned against than sinning. Boccaccio demonstrates his awareness of Dante's pride, tactfully remarking that the great poet 'did not deem himself worth less than in truth he was'[16]. When Dante's involvement in petty political squabbles is described, one is reminded of Petrarch's criticisms of the way in which Cicero had demeaned himself in 'wrangles and frays' which could bring no relief to the state but only harm upon himself. Boccaccio is 'ashamed' to record his author's fierce partisanship: 'any feeble woman or child, in speaking of parties and condemning the Ghibellines, could move him to such rage that he would have been led to throw stones if the speaker had not become silent'[17]. Reverence for a great writer cannot blind us to his faults.

I am ashamed to sully the reputation of so great a man by the mention of any fault in him, but my purpose to some extent requires it, for if I am silent about the things less worthy of praise, I shall destroy much faith in the laudable qualities already mentioned. I ask, therefore, the pardon of Dante, who perchance, while I am writing this, looks down at me with scornful eye from some high region of heaven.

One of Dante's main faults, Boccaccio continues, was his licentiousness. Although this vice may be natural, common and even, in a certain sense, necessary, it cannot be decently excused. But what mortal shall be the just judge to condemn it? 'Not I', answers Boccaccio. Women have great power over men, as is illustrated by what Jupiter did for the sake of Europa, Hercules for Iole and Paris for Helen. But these are matters of poetry, which men of little judgment would dismiss as lies. Therefore, Boccaccio turns to more authoritative *exempla*, beginning with Adam and Eve and proceeding to the love-affairs of David and Solomon:

David, notwithstanding the fact that he had many wives, no sooner caught sight of Bathsheba than for her sake he forgot God, his own kingdom, himself, and his honour, becoming first an adulterer and then a homicide. What may we think he would have done, had she laid any commands upon him? And did not Solomon, to whose wisdom none ever attained save the Son of God, forsake Him who had made him wise, and kneel to adore Balaam in order to please a woman?[18]

Dante may not be excused but, at least, he is not alone among authors. Boccaccio has placed him in good company, by bracketing him with authors of sacred Scripture. Similarly, the Dante-commentators could claim that their 'modern author' shared literary roles and forms with Scriptural authors[19]. If, at the end of the Middle Ages, *auctores* became more like men, men became more like *auctores*.

Equally striking is the way in which, in the writings of Petrarch and Boccaccio, the barriers have come down between pagan and Christian authors. Albert the Great and Thomas Aquinas had firmly distinguished between secular poetry and sacred poetry. It was one thing for Scriptural *auctores* to communicate truths in the literal sense by various kinds of figurative language: it was quite another for the pagan poets to communicate their half-truths and lies by apparently similar means (see pp. 139–40). When expounding Aristotle's remark in the *Metaphysica* about the 'theologising poets' who were the first philosophers, Aquinas averred that the philosopher is, in a sense, a lover of myths or *fabulae*[20]. But this opinion was not germane to Aquinas. By contrast, Petrarch and Boccaccio seized upon it eagerly: in it, they found a justification for their comparisons of secular poets with sacred poets in terms of style and, indeed, in terms of subject.

In a 'familiar letter' to his brother Gherardo, Petrarch invoked Aristotle in support of his contention that poetry is very far from being opposed to theology: indeed, 'one may almost say that theology actually is poetry, poetry concerning God'.

To call Christ now a lion, now a lamb, now a worm, what pray is that if not poetical? And you will find thousands of such things in the Scriptures, so very many that I cannot attempt to enumerate them. What indeed are the parables of our Saviour, in the Gospels, but words whose sound is foreign to their sense, or allegories (to use the technical term)? But allegory is the very warp and woof of all poetry. . . . Why, even the Old Testament fathers made use of poetry, both heroic song and other kinds. Moses, for example, and Job, and David, and Solomon, and Jeremiah. Even the psalms, which you are always singing, day and night, are in metre, in the Hebrew; so that I should be guilty of no inaccuracy or impropriety if I ventured to style their author the Christian's poet.[21]

In Boccaccio's *Life of Dante*, Aristotle's statement is cited in support of the claim that 'theology is simply the poetry of God'[22]. When their subject is the same, Boccaccio explains, theology and poetry can be considered as almost one and the same thing. When their subject is not the same, theology and poetry at least agree in their method of treatment *(forma dell'operare):*

Holy Scripture—which we call theology—sometimes under the form of history, again in the meaning of a vision, now in the signification of a lament, and in many other ways, designs to reveal to us the high mystery of the incarnation of the divine Word, . . . so that, being thus taught, we may attain to that glory which He by his death and resurrection opened to us. . . . In like manner do poets in their works—which we term poetry—sometimes under fictions of various gods, again by the transformation of men into imaginary forms, and at times by gentle persuasion, reveal to us the causes of things, the effects of virtues and vices, what we ought to flee and what we ought to follow; in order that we may attain by virtuous action the end that they, although they did not rightly know the true God, believed to be our supreme salvation.[23]

Apparently, the end (fine) of poetry is not incompatible with the superior end of theology, although it is, of necessity, limited by the pagans' ignorance of Christ and their subsequent failure to understand the nature of our supreme salvation.

Similar views are expressed in Boccaccio's *Genealogia deorum gentilium,* written between 1350 and 1374 under Petrarch's influence. Here it is argued that the 'mode of composing' (modus componendi) was the same for pagan and Old Testament poets[24]. Analysing the device of employing figurative forms and epithets to describe mystical and heavenly things, Boccaccio comments that this procedure is found in Scripture as well as in pagan poetry[25]. When he contrasts the poet's appropriate mode (modus poeticus) with the philosopher's characteristic mode of syllogistic argument[26], one is reminded of the theologians' stock distinction between the basically affective mode of sacred Scripture and the basically ratiocinative mode of human science (see pp. 119 et seq.)

It would seem that, by the time of Petrarch and Boccaccio, both 'ancients' and 'moderns', and pagans and Christians, could freely be compared in terms of styles and structures, of authorial roles and degrees of authority, and of shortcomings and sins. The *auctores* are now 'familiar authors'—'familiar' to the reader and, as it were, to each other. We have come a long way from Albert and Aquinas.

Notes

INTRODUCTION

1   Cf. P. Dronke, *Fabula: Explorations into the Uses of Myth in Medieval Platonism*, Mittellateinische Studien und Texte, ix (Leiden, 1974), p. 13.

2   R. Wellek and A. Warren, *Theory of Literature*, 3 ed. (Harmondsworth, 1963), p. 39. For this reason such treatises on the art of poetry as Geoffrey of Vinsauf's *Poetria Nova* and John of Garland's *Poetria Parisiana* fall outside the scope of this study—they represent a tradition of 'writing about writing' which is different in kind from the commentary-tradition discussed here. Arts of preaching are mentioned only to the extent that some of them contain literary theory derived from commentary-tradition.

3   Dronke, *Fabula*, p. 13.

4   The oft-repeated comments summarised here are conveniently brought together in the introduction to *Arnulfi Aurelianensis Glosule super Lucanum*, ed. B. Marti, Papers and Monographs of the American Academy in Rome, xviii (Rome, 1958).

5   This particular cliché has been refuted convincingly by L. R. Lind in the introduction to his edition of *The Ecclesiale of Alexander of Villa Dei* (Lawrence, Kansas, 1958), p. 3.

6   *Platonism, Scholastic Method, and the School of Chartres*, the 1979 Stenton Lecture (University of Reading, 1979). The work of R. H. and M. A. Rouse offers a similar conclusion: see especially their 'Florilegia and Latin Classical Authors in Twelfth- and Thirteenth-Century Orléans', *Viator*, x (1979), 131–60.

7   *Latteburius in threnos Ieremiae* (Oxford, 1482), unfol.

8   In a paper entitled 'Chaucer and Comparative Literary Theory' which I gave at the Second International Congress of the New Chaucer Society, I emphasised the 'alterity' or 'surprising otherness' of scholastic literary theory and advocated the comparative study of late medieval literary the-

ory and modern literary theory. This usage of the term 'alterity' is derived from H. R. Jauss, who has defined the 'alterity' of medieval literature in terms of the essential differences between the world which it opens up and the world in which we live, the extent to which old texts make us aware of the 'otherness' of a departed past. See his *Alterität und Modernität der mittelalterlichen Literatur* (Munich, 1977), and 'The Alterity and Modernity of Medieval Literature', *New Literary History*, x (1979), 385–90. Paul Zumthor defines 'blind modernism' as the unthinking imposition of modern principles of literature on medieval writings: 'Comments on H. R. Jauss's Article', *ibid.*, pp. 367–76 (p. 371).

9   For a succinct account of 'defamiliarization', which in a literary context involves deliberate deviation from the norms of writing and of audience expectancy, see R. H. Stacy, *Defamiliarization in Language and Literature* (Syracuse University Press, 1977).

CHAPTER 1

1   Cit. H. F. Sebastian, *William Wheteley's commentary on the Pseudo-Boethius' tractate De disciplina scolarium and medieval grammar school education* (unpub. Ph.D. Thesis, Columbia University, 1970), p. 300.

2   An almost identical statement is found in the prologue to Wheteley's commentary on the *De consolatione philosophiae* of Boethius: it is useful, he claims, to inquire the causes of a work, for those things which were said by 'authentic' men are the more firmly impressed on the mind of the hearer. Oxford, New College, MS C.264, fol. 11^v.

3   Cf. J. Porcher, 'Le *De disciplina scholarium*, traité du XIIIe siècle faussement attribué à Boèce', in *Positions des thèses soutenues par les élèves de la promotion de 1921 de l'École des Chartes* (Paris, 1921), pp. 91–3; also *Pseudo-Boèce: De disciplina scholarium*, ed. O. Weijers (Leiden, 1976), pp. 8–11.

4   *The Parliament of Fowls*, lines 22–5 (*The Works of Geoffrey Chaucer*, ed. F. N. Robinson, 2 ed. (Oxford, 1957), p. 311).

5   Cf. M.-D. Chenu, 'Auctor, actor, autor', *Bull. du Cange*, iii (1927), 81–6.

6   This information is taken from the major medieval dictionaries: *Papias: De linguae latinae vocabulis* (s.l., 1476), s.v. *auctor;* Hugutio of Pisa, *Magnae derivationes*, s.v. *augeo*, in Oxford, Bodleian Library, MS Bodley 376, fol. 1^r; *Joannes de Janua: Catholicon*, s.v. *auctor* (Venice, 1495), fols 73^v–74^r; *Summa Britonis sive Guillelmi Britonis expositiones vocabulorum Biblie*, ed. L. W. Daly and B. A. Daly, Thesaurus mundi, xv (Padua, 1975), i, 74. Hugutio begins by glossing *augere* as *amplificare,* 'to increase', 'to grow': hence *auctor,* written with a 'u' and a 'c', means *augmentator.* When *autentim* ('id est autoritatem') is signified, *autor* is written with a 'u' and

without a 'c'. Cf. the mnemonic verses found in the *Graecismus* of Everard of Béthune, cit. Chenu, *Toward understanding St Thomas*, p. 179, n. 1. The same verses occur in de'Balbi's *Catholicon*, s.v. *auctor*. William Brito claimed that the senses of the term *auctor* have the following order of precedence: *autentim* first, *augeo* second and *agere* third (ed. Daly, i, 74).

7   According to Hugutio, *autor*, written without a 'c' and with a 'u', may mean *ligator*, 'someone who ties together'.

8   Cf. Chenu, *Bull. du Cange*, iii, 83.

9   Cf. Chenu, *Toward understanding St Thomas*, pp. 130–2.

10 MS Bodley 376, fol. 1ʳ. This was expanded in de'Balbi's *Catholicon*, s.v. *auctoritas*. The phrase also occurs in the *Distinctiones verborum* attributed to Alexander Neckam (in Oxford, Bodleian Library, MS Hatton 101, p. 333).

11 *Catholicon*, s.v. *auctoritas* (fol. 75ʳ).

12 In late-medieval scholasticism, the term 'science' was 'used primarily of the intellectual disciplines, such as natural philosophy, ethics, metaphysics and theology, and only secondarily and infrequently of the technological arts': see J. A. Weisheipl, 'The Curriculum of the Faculty of Arts at Oxford in the Early Fourteenth Century', *Med. Stud.*, xxvi (1964), esp. pp. 143–4.

13 See M.-D. Chenu, 'Authentica et magistralia', in *La Théologie au douzième siècle*, 2 ed., Études de philosophie médiévale, xlv (Paris, 1966), 351–65; J. de Ghellinck, 'Patristique et argument de tradition au bas moyen âge', in *Beiträge zur Geschichte der Philosophie und Theologie des Mittelalters*, suppl. III. i (1935), 403–26.

14 Cf. L. J. Paetow, *The Arts Course at Medieval Universities with special reference to grammar and rhetoric* (Champaign, Illinois, 1910), pp. 11–32; Curtius, *European Literature*, pp. 452–3.

15 *Accessus ad auctores, etc.*, ed. Huygens, pp. 88–9.

16 See H. Denifle, *Die Entstehung der Universitaten des Mittelalters* (Berlin, 1885), i, 684.

17 See P. Delhaye, ' "Grammatica" et "Ethica" au XIIe siècle', *RTAM*, xxv (1958), esp. pp. 67–78; cf. the *Prae-exercitamina Prisciani grammatici*, in *Rhetores Latini Minores*, ed. C. Halm (Leipzig, 1863), pp. 551–2. The most comprehensive treatment of medieval ethical justifications of poetry is now, of course, Allen's *Ethical Poetic*.

18 See L. K. Born, 'Ovid and Allegory', *Speculum*, ix (1934), 362–79; F. Ghisalberti, 'Arnolfo d'Orléans, un cultore di Ovidio nel s.XII', *Memorie del Reale Istituto Lombardo di Scienze e Lettere*, xxiv (1932), 157–234; P. Demats, *Fabula: Trois études de mythographie antique et médiévale*, Publications Romanes et Françaises, cxxii (Geneva, 1973), 61–177.

19 See E. Jeauneau, 'L'Usage de la notion d'*integumentum* à travers les gloses de Guillaume de Conches', *AHDLMA*, xxiv (1957), 35–100; W. Wetherbee, *Platonism and Poetry in the Twelfth Century* (Princeton, 1972); P. Dronke, *Fabula: Explorations into the uses of Myth in Medieval Platonism* (Leiden, 1974).

20 On the term *authenticus*, see Chenu, *Toward understanding St Thomas*, pp. 129–32; and *La Théologie au douzième siècle*, pp. 358–65. For the authentic pagan authors, see C. Thurot, 'Documents relatifs à l'histoire de la grammaire au moyen âge', *Academie des Inscriptions et Belles Lettres. Comptes Rendus*, n.s., vi (1870), 250.

21 See, for example, the comments of St Thomas Aquinas on the *Liber de causis* and *Liber de spiritu et anima* falsely accredited to St Augustine, quoted by Chenu, *Toward understanding St Thomas*, p. 132, n. 7; cf. G. Geenen, 'S. Thomas d'Aquin et ses sources pseudépigraphiques', *Ephemerides theologicae Lovanienses*, xx (1943), 71–80.

22 See Spicq, *Esquisse*, pp. 106–8, 146–52, 156–9.

23 *Postilla super librum Paralipomenon*, prologus (pr. *Hugonis postilla*, i, 295ᵛ).

24 Pr. *PL*, xxx, 254–61.

25 *De nugis curialium*, dist. iv, cap. 5 (ed. M. R. James, Anecdota Oxoniensia, xiv (Oxford, 1914), 158; trans. F. Tupper and M. B. Ogle (London, 1924), p. 197).

26 Cf. R. J. Dean, 'Unnoticed commentaries on the *Dissuasio Valerii* of Walter Map', *MARS*, ii (1950), 128–50.

27 See E. Jeauneau, ' "Nagi gigantum humeris insidentes": Essai d'interprétation de Bernard de Chartres', *Vivarium*, v (1967), 79–99.

28 *Philobiblon*, cap. ix (trans. E. C. Thomas and ed. M. MacLagan (Oxford, 1960), pp. 98–9).

29 De Bury is restating stock twelfth-century views: cf. Jeauneau in *Vivarium*, v, 79–99; also, the statement of William of Conches cit. by Jeauneau, 'La Lecture des auteurs classiques a l'École de Chartres durant la première moitie du XIIe siècle', in *Classical Influences on European Culture a.d. 500–1500*, ed. R. R. Bolgar (Cambridge, 1971), pp. 95–6.

30 *Philobiblon*, cap. ix (ed. MacLagan, pp. 98–101). Other writers identified the 'ancients' and 'moderns' more precisely than de Bury. The term *antiqui* could designate the 'ancient' writers of Greco-Latin antiquity as opposed to 'modern' Christians, or the 'ancient' Church Fathers as opposed to 'modern' medieval writers, or those 'ancient' men who lived before the advent of Christ as opposed to those 'modern' men who live after it. Cf. M.-D. Chenu, 'Antiqui, Moderni', *RSPT*, xvii (1928), 82–94; see, further, H. Zimmerman, *Antiqui und Moderni: Traditionbewusstein und Fortschrittskewusstein im späten Mittelalter* (Berlin, 1973). In the twelfth

century, a more specialised sense developed, whereby *antiqui* referred to a previous generation of scholars, while *moderni* designated the scholars of one's own generation. See L. M. de Rijk, *Logica modernorum*, Wijsgenge Teksten en Studies, vi, xvi (Assen, 1962–7), i, 16–7; cf. Chenu, *Toward understanding St Thomas*, pp. 137–8.

31 Cf. Alexander Neckam's *Sacerdos ad altare*, ed. C. H. Haskins, *Studies in the History of Mediaeval Science* (Cambridge, Mass., 1924), pp. 372–6; see, further, the summary description of the lecture *(lectio)* by P. Glorieux, 'L'enseignement au moyen âge: techniques et méthodes en usage à la faculté de théologie de Paris au XIIIe siècle', *AHDLMA*, xxxv (1968), 108. For the introduction of the Lombard's *Sentences* as a main teaching text, see above, p. 78.

32 See H. Marrou, *S. Augustin et la fin de la culture antique* (Paris, 1938), p. 11, and *Histoire de l'éducation dans l'antiquité*, 6 ed. (Paris, 1965), pp. 400–1.

33 See P. Riché, *Education and Culture in the Barbarian West*, trans. J. J. Contreni (Columbia, S. Carolina, 1976).

34 *Metalogicon*, i.24 (ed. C. C. I. Webb (Oxford, 1929), pp. 53–7); cf. Quintilian, *Institutio oratoria*, I.v.11, I.viii.8, I.viii.13 (ed. H. E. Butler (London and New York, 1921–2), i, 82, 148–50, 152).

35 John of Salisbury described William as 'the most accomplished grammarian since Bernard of Chartres': *Metalogicon*, i.5 (ed. Webb, pp. 16–17).

36 *Guillaume de Conches: Glosae super Platonem*, ed. E. Jeauneau, Textes philosophiques du moyen âge, xiii (Paris, 1965), p. 57.

37 *Didascalicon*, iii.8 (ed. C. H. Buttimer, Catholic University of America, Studies in Medieval and Renaissance Latin, x (Washington, 1939), p. 58). Similarly, William of Conches distinguished between syntactical structure *(continuatio)*, exposition of the letter *(expositio litterae)* and profound meaning *(sententia)*: *Glosae super Platonem*, ed. Jeauneau, p. 67; also, his commentaries on Priscian and Macrobius, cit. by E. Jeauneau, 'Deux rédactions des gloses de Guillaume de Conches sur Priscien', *RTAM*, xxvii (1960), 234–6. Hugutio incorporated William's distinction in his *Magnae derivationes*: see G. Robert, *La Renaissance du XIIe siècle: les écoles et l'enseignement*, Publications de l'Institut d'Études Médiévales d'Ottawa, iii (Paris and Ottawa, 1933), 55, n. 2. This was reiterated by Giovanni de'Balbi, *Catholicon*, s.v. *commentum* and *glosa* (fols 101^r, 153^v).

38 Glorieux, *AHDLMA*, xxxv, 108.

39 Cf. Marrou, *Histoire de l'éducation*, p. 407.

40 *Metalogicon*, i.24 (ed. Webb, p. 54).

41 *Accessus ad auctores, etc.*, ed. Huygens, pp. 2–6; E. A. Quain, 'The Medieval *Accessus ad auctores*', *Traditio*, iii (1945), 228–42. The term

introitus was used by Peter Comestor in the prologues to his commentaries on the Psalter and St Matthew's gospel: see the extracts printed in Stegmüller, *Bibl.*, 6564/1 and 6575. Peter of Poitiers employed the term in his Psalter-commentary: see P. S. Moore, *The Works of Peter of Poitiers* (Washington, 1936), pp. 95–6, 178. The term *ingressus* was used, for example, by Praepositinus of Cremona in his Psalter-commentary: ibid., pp. 95–6. Cf. the prologue to an anonymous collection of *distinctiones* on the Psalter found in Cambridge, Corpus Christi College, MS 217, described on p. 65 above, and the prologue to Hugh of St Cher's Psalter-commentary, printed *Hugonis postilla*, ii, 2ʳ–3ᵛ. This application of *ingressus* may have originated in scholarship within the trivium; see, for example, the beginning of Thierry of Chartres' commentary on the *Rhetorica ad Herennium:* 'Ingressum facit ad artem in quo captat Gaii Herenii benivolentiam'. Quoted by K. M. Fredborg, 'The Commentary of Thierry of Chartres on Cicero's *De inventione*', *CIMAGL*, vii (1971), 232.

42 Hunt, 'Introductions to the *Artes*', p. 94.

43 *Vitae Vergilianae*, ed. J. Brummer (Leipzig, 1912), p. 11. The introduction to the commentary on the *Aeneid* by Donatus's namesake, Tiberius Claudius Donatus (*fl.* late fourth century), does not employ this schema: *Tiberi Claudi Donati interpretationes Vergilianae*, ed. H. Georgii (repr. Stuttgart, 1969), i, 1–7.

44 *Servianorum in Vergilii carmina commentariorum*, Harvard edition, ii (1946), 1–5. On the use of the ancient kinds or modes of speaking *(genera dicendi)* in lives of Virgil, see F. Quadlbauer, *Die antike Theorie der genera dicendi im lateinischen Mittelalter*, Sitzungsberichte der österreichischen Akademie der Wissenschaften, phil.-hist. klasse, Bd. cclxi, 2 Abk. (Wien, 1962), 23–6.

45 *Accessus ad auctores, etc.*, ed. Huygens, pp. 58–65.

46 Ibid., pp. 28–9.

47 See G. Przychocki, 'Accessus Ovidiani', *Rozprawy Akademii Umiejetnosci*, wydzial filologiczny, serya III, tom. iv (1911), 108.

48 *Vitae Vergilianae*, ed. Brummer, p. 60.

49 Ibid., p. 62.

50 Cf. C. Lutz, 'One formula of *accessus* in Remigius's Works', *Latomus*, xix 1960), 774–80, who compares the Remigian prologue based on the *circumstantiae* with the discussion of the *circumstantiae* found in Erigena's commentary on Martianus Capella. Elsewhere, Erigena claimed that the province of rhetoric comprises those hypotheses or finite issues determined by the seven circumstances: see *PL*, cxxii, 475; cf. R. McKeon, 'Rhetoric in the Middle Ages', in *Critics and Criticism, Ancient and Modern*, ed. R. S. Crane (Chicago, 1952), pp. 276–7.

51 For discussion, see Lutz, *Latomus,* xix, 774–80; also J. Brummer, 'Zum Überlieferungegeschichte der sogenannten Donat-Vita des Vergil', *Philologus,* lxxii (1913), 288; J. J. Savage, 'The Scholia in the Virgil of Tours, Bernensis 165', *HSCP,* xxxvi (1925), 163–4.

52 This is the opinion of M. Cappuyns, *Jean Scot Erigène* (Paris, 1933), p. 74. See further, Lutz, *Latomus,* xix, 774–80, who believes that Remigius was the source of the *accessus* to Virgil found in a Munich MS of the twelfth century, Monacensis 18059; cit. in the edition of Servius by G. Thilo and H. Hagen (Leipzig, 1881), i, pp. lxxxiv–lxxxv, and also by Przychocki, *Roz. Akad. Umiejet.,* III.iv, 112.

53 The theory of *circumstantiae* may be traced back to Hermagoras, *Fragmenta,* ed. D. Matthes (Leipzig, 1962), pp. 13 *et. seq.* Cf. the treatments by Fortunatianus, *Ars rhetoricae,* ii.1; Augustinus, *De rhetorica,* vii; Victorinus, *In rhetorica Ciceronis,* and the anon. *Excerpta rhetorica* (all in *Rhetores minores,* ed. Halm, pp. 103, 141, 226, 586); also, Boethius, *De differentiis topicis,* iv (pr. *PL,* lxiv, 1214); *The Rhetoric of Alcuin and Charlemagne,* ed. W. S. Howell (Princeton, 1941), p. 6. For applications of the *circumstantiae* in analyses of moral behaviour by late-medieval schoolmen, see J. Gründel, *Die Lehre von den Umständen der menschlichen Handlung im Mittelalter,* Beiträge zur Geschichte der Philosophie und Theologie des Mittelalters, xxxix.5 (1963).

54 Hunt, 'Introductions to the *Artes*', p. 94. Huygens often has argued that Remigius, adapting the model provided by Servius and providing a precedent for subsequent practice, was the first person to apply the *circumstantiae* in literary explication. A brief note in his 1970 revised ed. of the *Accessus ad auctores, etc.,* p. 66, makes it clear that his opinion has not altered substantially. But this view of Remigius as innovator requires considerable modification. For uses of the *circumstantiae* which antedate Remigius, see M. Silvestre, 'Le Schéma "moderne" des *accessus*', *Latomus,* xvi, (1957), 684. Especially significant are the sophisticated introductions by Sedulius Scotus, who taught at Liège from 848 and died after 858: see *Sedulius Scotus in Donati artem minorem, etc.,* ed. B. Löfstedt, CCCM, xle (1977), 3; *Commentum Sedulii Scotii in maiorem Donatum grammaticum,* ed. D. Brearley, Pontifical Institute of Mediaeval Studies, Studies and Texts, xxvii (Toronto, 1975), 31.

55 *Remigii Autissiodorensis commentum in Martianum Capellam,* ed. C. Lutz (Leiden, 1962), i, 65. On the debt of Remigius's commentary to Erigena's commentary on the same work, see C. Lutz, 'The Commentary of Remigius of Auxerre on Martianus Capella', *Med. Stud.,* xix (1957), 137–56.

56 *Remigii Autissiodorensis in artem Donati minorem commentum,* ed. W. Fox (Leipzig, 1892), p. 6; M. Manitius, 'Remigius von Auxerre und Mico von St Riquier', *Neues Archiv,* xxxvi (1911), 46.

57 R. B. C. Huygens, 'Remigiana', *Aevum,* xxviii (1954), 331–2; A. Man-

cini, 'Un commento ignoto di Remy d'Auxerre ai *Disticha Catonis'*, *Rendiconti della R. Accademia dei Lincei*, ser. v, xi (1902), 179.

58 *PL*, lxxvi, 795; *PL*, xciii, 195B.

59 *PL*, cvi, 1264B.

60 *PL*, clxxv, 74B–C, 87–8, 115. See, further, the elaborate use of the headings in Hugh's *De tribus maximis circumstantiis gestorum*, ed. W. M. Green in *Speculum*, xviii (1943), 484–93.

61 See the prologues to his commentaries on Baruch and Ezechiel, for *locus* and *tempus* respectively (pr. *Hugonis postilla*, iv, 124ᵛ, 134ʳ).

62 This commentator discussed instead Virgil's *intentio, modus agendi, utilitas* and *ordo*: *Commentum quod dicitur Bernardi Silvestris super VI libros Eneidos*, ed. J. W. Jones and E. F. Jones (Lincoln, Nebraska, and London, 1977), pp. 1–3. For a powerful argument against the attribution of this work to Bernard Silvester, see Christopher Baswell, 'The Medieval Allegorization of the "Aeneid": MS Peterhouse 158', *Traditio*, xli (1985), 199–221.

63 Hunt, 'Introductions to the *Artes*', pp. 94–6. Cf. Quain, *Traditio*, iii, 242–52; P. Courcelle, *Late Latin Writers and their Greek Sources*, trans. H. E. Wedeck (Cambridge, Mass., 1969), esp. p. 286.

64 *In Isagogen Porphyrii commenta*, ed. S. Brandt, *CSEL*, xlviii (1906), 4–5. Boethius was generally recognised as the instigator of the 'type C' prologue: see, for example, the twelfth-century *accessus* to Persius cit. Kristeller, *CTC*, iii, 226.

65 *Traditio*, iii, 261–4. Quain was arguing against Przychocki's opinion that the source of the 'type C' headings was the *circumstantiae* as expounded by ancient Greek and Latin rhetoricians. Cf. Przychocki, *Roc. Akad. Umiejet.*, III. iv, 106–20.

66 Quain, *Traditio*, iii, 243–56.

67 *Anonymous Prolegomena to Platonic Philosophy*, ed. L. G. Westerink (Amsterdam, 1962), pp. xxvi–xxvii; cf. William of Moerbeke's translations of the commentaries by Ammonius and Simplicius: *Ammonius: Commentaire sur le Peri hermeneias d'Aristote, traduction de Guillaume de Moerbeke*, ed. G. Verbeke, Corpus latinum commentariorum in Aristotelem graecorum, ii (Louvain and Paris, 1961), 1–15; *Simplicius: Commentaire sur les Categories d'Aristote, traduction de Guillaume de Moerbeke*, ed. A. Pattin, CLCAG, v.i (Louvain and Paris, 1971), 10–11.

68 *Anonymous Prolegomena*, ed. Westerink, p. xxviii.

69 Ibid., p.xxix.

70 Ibid., pp. xxxiii–xli, for a summary description of the eleven headings used in the text edited by Westerink: the life of Plato, the distinctive characteristics of Platonic philosophy, the justification for Plato's writing, the dialogue-form, the elements of each dialogue, the titles of the

dialogues, the principle in accordance with which Plato's doctrine is divided, the method of presentation, the rules for establishing his central purpose or intention, and the order of his dialogues.

71 Thus, the headings used by William of Conches in introducing Plato's *Timaeus* were derived from the standard 'types A and C': see *Glosae super Platonem*, ed. Jeauneau, p. 58.

72 Quoted from Rouen MS 1470 (s. x–xi) by Manitius, *Neues Archiv*, xxxvi, 49; cf. Silvestre, *Latomus*, xvi, 689. One of the 'modern' requirements listed here, the life of the poet, indicates the influence of a 'type B' prologue-heading on the 'type C' paradigm. Cf. the practice of including a life of Juvenal in 'type C' prologues to his satires, e.g. in Oxford, Bodleian Library, Auct. F.6.9 (s. xii), cit. Kristeller, *CTC*, i, 198.

73 *Accessus ad auctores, etc.*, ed. Huygens, pp. 66–7.

74 Ibid., p. 78.

75 *In artem primam Donati*, ed. Fox, p. 2. Remigius's statement concerning *titulus* is cited by Pseudo-Aquinas (perhaps a fifteenth-century German writer) in his discussion of the title of Boethius's *Consolatio philosophiae* (pr. *Aquinatis opera*, xxx, 3).

76 *Accessus ad auctores, etc.*, ed. Huygens, p. 60; cf. Dominicus Gundissalinus, *De divisione philosophiae*, ed. L. Baur (Munster, 1903), p. 141.

77 Remigius, *In artem primam Donati*, ed. Fox, p. 1; cf. *Accessus ad auctores, etc.*, pp. 29, 60–1.

78 *Arnulfi Aurelianensis glosule super Lucanum*, ed. B. M. Marti, Papers and Monographs of the American Academy in Rome, xviii (Rome, 1958), 3.

79 *Accessus ad auctores, etc.*, ed. Huygens, p. 48.

80 Cf. Hunt, 'Introductions to the *Artes*', p. 95.

81 *De divisione philosophiae*, ed. Baur, p. 140.

82 Cit. N. M. Häring, 'Thierry of Chartres and Dominicus Gundissalinus', *Med. Stud.*, xxvi (1964), 286.

83 Ed. H. Fitting as *Summa codicis des Irnerius* (Berlin, 1894), pp. 4–5. Cf. the prologue of Bulgarus (fl. mid-twelfth century) printed by H. Kantorowicz, *Studies in the Glossators of the Roman Law* (Cambridge, 1938), pp. 233–9. See, further, the similar treatments of Gratian and the canon law by Sicardus of Cremona and Rufinus, cited by Quain, *Traditio*, iii, 239–40, who provides a useful chart of the prologue-headings used by canon lawyers. The schema of Rufinus (writing 1157–9) is very elaborate, comprising the *iuris intentio, iuris utilitas, canonum intentio* and *canonum utilitas*, as well as the *materia, intentio, modus tractandi, utilitas* and *titulus* of Gratian: see the *Summa decretorum des Magister Rufinus*, ed. H. Singer (Paderborn, 1902), pp. 3–5.

84 On the practice of 'pious and reverent exposition' see Spicq, *Esquisse*, pp. 10–4; Chenu, *Toward understanding St Thomas*, pp. 144–9; J. de Ghellinck, *Le Mouvement théologique du XIIe siècle*, 2 ed. (Bruges, 1948), pp. 233–4.

85 See the references given in notes 18 and 19 above.

86 *Accessus ad auctores, etc.*, ed. Huygens, pp. 26, 29, 30, 32; H. S. Sedlmayer, *Prolegomena critica ad Heroides Ovidianas* (Vienna, 1878), pp. 96–8; F. Ghisalberti, 'Medieval Biographies of Ovid', *JWCI*, ix (1946), 44–6; *Arnulfi Aurelianensis glosule super Lucanum*, ed. Marti, p. 3.

87 See esp. Conrad of Hirsau, *Accessus ad auctores, etc.*, ed. Huygens, p. 119.

88 See, for example, the *materia* of Bulgarus, pr. Kantorowicz, *Glossators of the Roman Law*, pp. 233–9. The even wider concept of the 'general' material and intention may have been introduced by Johannes Bassianus (writing *c.* 1180): ibid., p. 45.

89 See Quain, *Traditio*, iii, 239–40.

90 Cit. from Bern, Burgerbibliothek HS 539b (s. XIII) in *Die Persius-Scholien nach den Berner Handscriften*, ed. E. Kurz (Burgdorf, 1875), p. viii. On the literary theory in introductions to the satirists, see Miller, 'John Gower, Satiric Poet', pp. 80–8.

91 London, British Library, MS Royal 15 B.III, fol. 2^r–2^v. This text represents a later recension of William's commentary.

92 *PL*, cxci, 630–1; cf. Servius, *In Vergilii carmina commentarii*, ed. Thilo and Hagen, iii, 1.

93 *Comment. sup. VI libros Eneidos*, ed. Jones, pp. 1–2. 'Natural order' was discussed by Donatus in his life of Virgil, ed. Brummer, p. 18; the distinction between the two kinds of order was elaborated in the *Scholia Vindobonensia ad Horatii artem poeticam*, ed. J. Zechmeister (Wien, 1877), pp. 4–5 (on *Ars poetica*, lines 42–5); cf. Bernard of Utrecht in *Accessus ad auctores, etc.*, ed. Huygens, p. 64.

94 *De divisione philosophiae*, ed. Baur, p. 142. Arnulf of Orléans made sporadic reference to the *capitula* in Lucan's *Pharsalia*: *Glosule super Lucanum*, ed. Marti, pp. 229, 242, 273, 302. A more thorough approach is manifest in the commentary on Claudian attributed to a contemporary of Arnulf's, Geoffrey of Vitry: *The commentary of Geoffrey of Vitry on Claudian de raptu Proserpinae*, ed. A. K. Clarke and P. M. Giles (Leiden, 1973), pp. 29, 56.

95 MS Royal 15 B.III, fol. 3^r.

96 *Arnulfi Aurelianensis glosule super Lucanum*, ed. Marti, p. 3.

97 *Accessus ad auctores, etc.*, ed. Huygens, pp. 22, 63, 84–8.

98 See the *accessus* pr. Kristeller, *CTC*, i, 192–3, 195, 198; iii, 225–7. It

was a commonplace to remark that the satirists had begun their poems abruptly, thereby indicating their serious purpose: see Kristeller, *CTC*, i, 185; iii, 225–7.

99 *Comment. sup. VI libros Eneidos*, ed. Jones, p. 2. Cf. the similar statement in a fourteenth-century *accessus* to Juvenal pr. Kristeller, *CTC*, i, 197.

100 *Accessus ad auctores, etc.*, ed. Huygens, p. 67. Conrad's source is Isidore of Seville, *Etymologiae*, ed. W. M. Lindsay (Oxford, 1911), viii.6.

101 *Didascalicon*, ii.1 (ed. Buttimer, p. 24).

102 *The Didascalicon of Hugh of St Victor*, trans. J. Taylor (New York and London, 1961), p. 62. See, further, Taylor's excellent summary of Hugh's classification of knowledge, pp. 7–11, where the opinions of William of Conches are compared and contrasted. For William's classification of knowledge, see *Glosae super Platonem*, ed. Jeauneau, pp. 60–2; C. Jourdain, 'Des Commentaires inédits de Guillaume de Conches et Nicolas Traveth sur la Consolation de Boèce', *Notices et extraits de manuscrits de la Bibliothèque Impériale*, xx. 2 (1862), 72–4. See, also, J. A. Weisheipl, 'Classification of the Sciences in Medieval Thought', *Med. Stud.*, xxvii (1965), 65–8.

103 Kantorowicz, *Glossators of the Roman Law*, p. 51.

104 For examples, see Przychocki, *Roz. Akad. Umiej.*, III. iv, 89; also, the two *accessus* printed by K. Young, 'Chaucer's appeal to the Platonic deity', *Speculum*, xix (1944), 5, 6.

105 See the series of articles by P. Delhaye, 'L'Enseignement de la philosophie morale au XIIe siècle', *Med. Stud.*, xi (1949), 77–99; 'La Place de l'éthique parmi les disciplines scientifiques au XIIe siècle', in *Miscellanea moralia in honorem A. Janssen* (Gembloux, 1948), 29–44; ' "Grammatica" et "Ethica" au XIIe siècle', *RTAM*, xxv (1958), 59–110.

106 *Arnulfi Aurelianensis glosule super Lucanum*, ed. Marti, p. 3.

107 See the references to Ovid commentaries in note 86 above; cf. Minnis, 'Moral Gower', pp. 54–60.

108 In Paris, Bibliothèque Nationale, MS Lat. 2904, quoted by Kristeller, *CTC*, i, 193–4.

109 *Commentarium in cantica canticorum*, prologus, in *Origenes Werke*, viii, ed. W. A. Baehrens, Die griechischen christlichen Schrifsteller der ersten drei Jahrhunderte, xxx (Leipzig, 1925), 75–6.

110 For Jerome, see note 159 below; Augustine, *De doctrina christiana*, ii.17, ii.28, iv.5 (ed. G. M. Green, CSEL, lxxx (1963), 53–5, 63–5, 121–3), and *De civitate Dei*, viii.11 (ed. E. Hoffmann, CSEL, xl (1899–1900), i, 371–3); Cassiodorus, *Expositio psalmorum*, in Psalm. xxiii. 10 (ed. M. Adriaen, CCSL, xcvii–xcviii (1958), i, 219).

111 *Comment. in cant. cant.*, prologus (ed. Baehrens, pp. 75–6). The Books of

the Bible were not the only works to be credited with encyclopaedic and comprehensive scientific learning. At an early date, the works of Virgil had been praised in similar terms. See, for example, the *Vita Vossiana* printed by H. R. Upson, 'Mediaeval Lives of Virgil', *CP*, xxxviii (1943), 105, in which the *Bucolics* are supposed to pertain to physics (natural science), the *Georgics* to ethics (moral science) and the *Aeneid* to logic (rational science). Cf. Quadlbauer, *Die antike Theorie der genera dicendi*, pp. 25–7.

112 *Etymologiae*, ed. Lindsay, ii.24. Later medieval writers in the monastic tradition identified theoretical science with the contemplative life: see the discussions of *theoria* by L. Gougaud, 'La Théorie dans la spiritualité médié-vale', *RAM*, (1922), 381–94; J. Leclercq, *Études sur le vocabulaire monastique du moyen âge*, Studia Anselmiana, xlviii (Rome, 1961), 80–2.

113 *PL*, cxiii, 1127; *PL*, clxii, 1187–8 (dubious attribution); *PL*, cxcvi, 409A–D; *PL*, cxxi, 148: *PL*, clii, 638B–9A (dubious attribution); *PL*, clxxii, 270B.

114 *PL*, cxxxi, 148B–C. The authenticity of this commentary has been questioned: see p. 41.

115 *PL*, clii, 638B (dubious attribution).

116 Cit. H. E. Allen, 'The *Manuel des pechiez* and the Scholastic prologue', *The Romanic Review*, viii (1917), 457, n. 60.

117 *Expositio in Hierarchiam coelestem*, i.1 (pr. *PL*, clxxv, 927A).

118 See, especially, the ingenious adaptation by Godfrey of St Victor, who divided the tropological interpretation of Scripture into ethics, economics and politics: *Fons philosophiae*, ed. P. Michaud-Quentin, Analecta Mediaevalia Namurcensia, viii (Namur, 1956), lines 483, 485–96.

119 Oxford, Bodleian Library, MS Bodley 528, fol. 55^r; Oxford, Bodleian Library, MS Bodley 87, fol. 150^r. On these two versions of this commentary by Langton, see G. Lacombe and B. Smalley, 'Studies on the Commentaries of Cardinal Stephen Langton', *AHDLMA*, v (1931), 140–4.

120 For examples, see the prologue incorporated into the *Glossa ordinaria* on the Psalter, *PL*, cxiii, 843, and the prologue to the Psalter-commentary of Peter Lombard, *PL*, cxci, 58.

121 *Metaphysica*, i.3 (in *The Works of Aristotle*, vol. viii, trans. W. D. Ross (Oxford, 1908), 983a); *Physica*, ii.7 (ibid., vol. ii, trans. R. P. Hardie and R. K. Gaye (1930), 198a–b).

122 Bk. ii, lectio 5, 178 (in *The Commentary on Aristotle's Physics by St Thomas Aquinas*, trans. R. J. Blackwell, R. J. Spath and W. E. Thirlkel (London, 1963), p. 87).

123 See, for example, the 'Aristotelian prologues' to Ovid pr. Ghisalberti, *JWCI*, ix, 50–4.

124 *Topica*, xiv.58–xvii.65 (in *De inventione, etc.*, pp. 424–31); *PL*, lxiv, 1145–6. Moreover, writers associated with Chartres had provided elaborate analyses of divine causality in the creation of the world. William of Conches described the efficient cause as the divine essence, the formal cause as the divine wisdom, and the final cause as the divine goodness, while the material cause consisted of the four elements. *Glosae super Platonem*, ed. Jeauneau, pp. 98 *et seq*. Cf. Thierry of Chartres' *Tractatus de sex dierum operibus*, iii (in *Commentaries on Boethius by Thierry of Chartres and his School*, ed. N. M. Häring, Pontifical Institute of Mediaeval Studies, Studies and Texts, xx (Toronto, 1971), 556–7). See, also, J. M. Parent, *La Doctrine de la creation dans l'école de Chartres*, Publications de l'Institut d'Études Médiévales d'Ottawa, viii (Paris and Ottawa, 1938), 34–43, 47, 56, 59–60, 66–8, 70, 91–2.

125 For examples, see *Accessus ad auctores, etc.*, ed. Huygens, pp. 28, 30, 32, 33, 37.

126 Cf. Weisheipl, *Med. Stud.*, xxvi, 147–151, 159–61, 173–6. The literature on the impact and dissemination of the 'new' Aristotle is vast: for basic bibliography, see Chenu, *Toward understanding St Thomas*, pp. 73–5.

127 See M. Grabmann, 'Der Kommentar des sel. Jordanus von Sacshen († 1237) zum Priscianus minor', *Mittelalterliches Geistesleben*, iii (Munich, 1956), 232–42, esp. pp. 234–5; Sandkühler, *Die frühen Dantekommentare*, pp. 30–43; R. A. Gauthier in *RSPT*, lxvi (1982), 367–73.

128 For examples, see the copious quotations given by B. Nardi, 'Osservazioni sul medievale "accessus ad auctores" in rapporto all '"Epistola a Cangrande" ', in his *Saggi e note di critica Dantesca* (Milan and Naples, 1966), pp. 269–89.

129 See pp. 78–9.

130 See E. M. Sanford, 'The Manuscripts of Lucan: Accessus and Marginalia', in *Speculum*, ix (1934), 278–95; also, the prologues to humanistic commentaries on Juvenal and Persius pr. Kristeller, *CTC*, i, 205, 207, 211, 212, 213; iii, 248, 249, 258. See further the *Prohemia poetarum* attributed to Thomas Walsingham (†c. 1422) printed in *Thomae Walsingham de archana deorum*, ed. R. A. van Kluyve (Durham, N.C., 1968), pp. xii–xiii. The 'type B' or Servian prologue enjoyed something of a revival in humanistic commentaries on poets: for examples, see Kristeller, *CTC*, i, 208, iii, 250, 251, 272, 288–9, 306.

131 *Topica*, ii.8 (in *De inventione, etc.*, pp. 386–8).

132 *Comment. in De invent.*, i.4 (in *Rhetores minores*, ed. Halm, p. 170).

133 Cf. Hunt, 'Introductions to the *Artes*', p. 98.

134 Häring, *Med. Stud.*, xxvi, 281. For the debate on the dating of this com-

mentary, see J. O. Ward, 'The Date of the Commentary on Cicero's *De inventione* by Thierry of Chartres', *Viator*, iii (1972), 219–273.

135 Cit. Häring, *Med. Stud.*, xxvi, 281; cf. p. 286. This distinction, combined with the *extrinsecus/intrinsecus* distinction, was used also by Thierry's pupil, Peter Helias, in his commentary on *De inventione* (but not in his *Summa super Priscianum*); the same combination occurs in Alan of Lille's commentary on the *Rhetorica ad Herennium:* see K. M. Fredborg, 'Petrus Helias on Rhetoric', *CIMAGL*, xiii (1974), 31–3. The *extrinsecus/intrinsecus* distinction alone was used in the second redaction of the Priscian-commentary by William of Conches, a pupil of Thierry's elder brother, Bernard of Chartres. Its prologue is edited by Jeauneau, *RTAM*, xxvii, 243–7. For the relationship between commentaries by William and Petrus Helias, see Fredborg, 'The Dependence of Petrus Helias' *Summa super Priscianum* on William of Conches' *Glose super Priscianum*', *CIMAGL*, xi (1973), 1–57.

136 This schematic discussion of the art of rhetoric is more or less identical with the whole section on rhetoric in Gundissalinus, *De divisione philosophiae*, ed. Baur, pp. 63–9. Dr Hunt believed that Thierry was the source of Gundissalinus: 'Introductions to the *Artes*', pp. 91–3, 98. N. M. Häring came to the opposite conclusion: see *Med. Stud.*, xxvi, 275–80. Dr Hunt's conclusion has been supported by Ward, *Viator*, iii, 245–64, and K. M. Fredborg, 'The Commentary of Thierry of Chartres on Cicero's *De inventione*', *CIMAGL*, vii (1971), 6–12.

137 'Introductions to the *Artes*', pp. 87, 97; *De inventione*, I.iv.5 (p. 12); *PL*, lxiv, 1207A–B, cf. 1211B. See further McKeon in *Critics and Criticism*, ed. Crane, p. 271. The oldest known extant commentary on Aristotle's *De sophisticis elenchis* provides interesting evidence regarding the precedents recognised by twelfth-century commentators and followed in their prologues. The anonymous logician begins with a reference to Boethius's *De differentiis topicis*, then gives the examples of Cicero and Aristotle who, in introducing the *De inventione* and *De sophisticis elenchis* respectively, provided an outline of the extrinsic aspect relevant to each case: De Rijk, *Logica modernorum*, i, 265.

138 Cf. Hunt, 'Introductions to the *Artes*', pp. 100–5.

139 Pr. Hunt, ibid., pp. 100–1, who compares other anonymous glosses on grammar beginning *Omnia traditio* and *Tocius eloquentie principium*. Cf. the *accessus* to Priscian edited by Huygens, *Accessus ad auctores, etc.*, p. 49.

140 Hunt, 'Introductions to the *Artes*', pp. 100–5.

141 Gundissalinus, *De divisione philosophiae*, ed. Baur, pp. 19–112, 115–21. For discussion of Gundissalinus's classification of the sciences, see Weisheipl, *Med. Stud.*, xxvii, 68–72.

142 *De divisione philosophiae*, pp. 140–2.

143 For discussion, see pp. 146–7, 177–80.

144 *Alberti Magni opera omnia* (Aschendorff, 1951–), xiv, pt. 1, 1, 5.

145 *Expositio in omnes S. Pauli Epistolas*, prologus (*Aquinatis opera*, xiii, 1–3). On the first appearances of aspects of the 'new' Aristotelian learning in Scriptural commentaries, see Smalley, *Study of the Bible*, pp. 308–28.

146 *Bonaventurae opera*, i, 1; *Roberti Kilwardby, De natura theologiae*, ed. F. Stegmüller, Opuscula et textus historiam ecclesiae illustrantia, xvii (Aschendorff, 1935), 7–12.

147 Marrou, *S. Augustin et la fin de la culture antique*, pp. 9–26; on Augustine's rhetorical training, see pp. 47–83.

148 Ibid., p. 349. For discussion and examples from other theologians, see Riché, *Education and Culture*, pp. 88–95.

149 Epistola xxi.13, Epistola xxii.42, in *PL*, xxii, 385, 394. In the latter passage, *sensus* and *verba* are compared to bread and husks, respectively. False eloquence was often likened to the husks eaten by the swine in the parable of the prodigal son: cf. B. Blumenkranz, 'Siliquae porcorum: l'exégèse médiévale et les sciences profanes', in *Mélanges d'histoire du moyen âge dédiés à la mémoire de L. Halphen* (Paris, 1951), pp. 11–17.

150 *Institutiones*, I.xv.7; cf. I.xv.1, 2 and 5 (ed. R. A. B. Mynors (Oxford, 1937), pp. 45, 41–3, 44); cf. Riché, *Education and Culture*, pp. 164–9.

151 *PL*, lxxv, 515–16. Gregory is allegorically interpreting Deuteronomy xvi.21, 'you shall not plant any tree beside the altar of the Lord'.

152 Ibid., 513C. Cf. Hugh of St Victor, *Didascalicon*, v.2; vi.3 (ed. Buttimer, pp. 95–6, 113–5, and Taylor's notes to his translation, pp. 219–20, 222).

153 For Cassian, see de Lubac, *Exégèse médiévale*, i, 190–8; O. Chadwick, *John Cassian: A Study in Primitive Monasticism*, 2 ed. (Cambridge, 1968), pp. 101–2. The distich has been attributed to Augustine of Dacia († 1282): see now, F. Chatillon, 'Vocabulaire et prosodie du distique attribué à Augustin de Dacie sur les quatre sens de l'écriture', in *L'Homme devant Dieu: Mélanges offerts au père Henri de Lubac* (Lyon, Fourvière, 1963–4), ii, 17–28.

154 *PL*, clvi, 25D–26A. Trans. *Readings in Medieval Rhetoric*, ed. J. M. Miller, M. H. Prosser and T. W. Benson (Bloomington and London, 1973), pp. 170–1. Cf. Cassian, *Conlationes*, xiv.8 (ed. M. Petschenig, CSEL, xiii (1886), 404–7).

155 Cf. M.-D. Chenu, 'The Masters of the Theological "Science" ', in his *Nature, Man and Society in the Twelfth Century*, trans. J. Taylor and L. K. Little (Chicago and London, 1968), pp. 281–2.

156 Cf. de Lubac, *Exégèse médiévale*, i, 425–87; Smalley, *Study of the Bible*, pp. 1–26, 214–42, 292–308.

157 *De doctrina christiana,* ii.6 (ed. Green, p. 37). For a summary of Augustine's belief in the attractiveness of the difficulties in Scripture, see Marrou, S. *Augustin et la fin de la culture antique,* pp. 487–90.

158 *De doctrina christiana,* iii.29; cf. iv.6 (ed. Green, pp. 103, 123–4).

159 See Jerome, *Epistola* xxx.1 (pr. *PL,* xxii, 441–2); *Commentarius in Ecclesiasten,* i.1 (ed. M. Adriaen, CCSL, lxxii (1959), 250–1). For the similar statements of Augustine and Cassiodorus, see note 110 above.

160 Jerome, *Commentaria in Isaiam prophetam,* prologus (pr. *PL,* xxiv, 18B–19B).

161 Cf. Riché, *Education and Culture,* p. 167; J. M. Courtes, 'Figures et tropes dans le psautier de Cassiodore', *Revue des études latines,* xlii (1964), 361–75.

162 *De sacramentis christianae fidei,* prologus, cap.vi (pr. *PL,* clxxvi, 185C); cf. de Lubac, *Exégèse médiévale,* i, 74–94, and de Ghellinck, *Le Mouvement théologique,* pp. 93–6.

163 *Didascalicon,* praefatio (ed. Buttimer, pp. 1–3). For a lively discussion of the emergence of theology as an academic discipline and medieval views on its position within the hierarchy of the sciences, see G. R. Evans, *Old Arts and New Theology* (Oxford, 1980).

164 *Accessus ad auctores, etc.,* ed. Huygens, pp. 88–90.

165 *De trinitate et operibus eius,* vii.11 (pr. *PL,* clxvii, col. 1765).

166 Ibid.; cf. *De victoria verbi Dei,* xi.2 (pr. *PL,* clxix, col. 1444). Cf. Hugh of St Victor, *Didascalicon,* iii.2 (ed. Buttimer, pp. 49–52), and the relevant note in Taylor's translation, p. 210, n. 34; also, C. Lutz, 'Remigius' Ideas on the Origin of the Seven Liberal Arts', *Med. et Hum.,* x (1956), 32–49, and notes 110 and 159 above.

167 Cf. Smalley, *Study of the Bible,* p. xv. For the technical sense of *sacra pagina* 'sacred page' see J. de Ghellinck, *'Pagina* et *sacra pagina:* Histoire d'un mot et transformation de l'objet primitivement désigné', *Mélanges A. Pelzer* (Louvain, 1947), pp. 23–59.

168 Cf. the remark by Augustine that it is not what divinely-inspired writers have in common with pagan orators and poets that gave him more pleasure in that eloquence than he could express, but rather the extent to which those writers were eloquent in a manner all of their own. See *De doctrina christiana,* i.6 (ed. Green, p. 11). Cf. Cassiodorus, *Expositio psalmorum,* prologus, capi xv–xvi (ed. Adriaen, i, 18–22).

169 C. Thurot, 'Extraits de divers manuscrits latins pour servir à l'histoire des doctrines grammaticales au moyen âge', *Notices et extraits des manuscrits de la Bibliothèque Nationale et autres bibliothèques,* xxii, pt. 2 (1868), 103–4.

170 See p. 73, and note 1 on p. 247.

171 *Moralia in Job,* praefatio (pr. *PL,* lxxv, 515–28).

172 Ibid., 517A–B.

173 Ibid., 517C–519A.

174 For later discussions of the 'good pagan', see pp. 114, 143, 165.

175 *Epistola,* cap.iv (pr. *PL,* lxxv, 514D–515A).

176 *Goffredo di Auxerre, Expositio in cantica canticorum,* ed. F. Gastaldelli, (Rome, 1974), i, 5. Cf. F. Gastaldelli, 'L'esgesi biblica secondo Goffredo di Auxerre', *Salesianum,* xxxvii (1975), 222–3.

177 For discussion of this method of interpreting the Song of Songs, see pp. 51–2.

178 Stegmüller, *Bibl.,* 911; printed among the works of St Thomas Aquinas in the Parma edition, xiv, 387–426.

179 Ibid., p. 388.

180 Cf. Smalley, *Study of the Bible,* pp. 281–355.

181 Ibid., p. 297.

CHAPTER 2

1 See the useful list of Remigius's works in *Remigii commentum in Martianum,* ed. Lutz, i, 11–16; also Stegmüller, *Bibl.,* 7189–7247; *Bibl. suppl.,* 7194–7246.

2 See B. Bischoff, 'Living with the Satirists', in *Classical Influences on European Culture a.d. 500–1500,* ed. R. R. Bolgar (Cambridge, 1971), p. 84; cf. Smalley, *Study of the Bible,* pp. 49–51.

3 However, the position of Remigius is not so crucial as Huygens has suggested: see Chapter I, n. 54 on p. 224.

4 *PL,* cxxxi 148; cf. M. Manitius, *Geschichte der lateinischen Literatur des Mittelalters* (Munich, 1911), i, 516–7; B. Smalley, 'La *Glossa ordinaria*', *RTAM,* ix (1937), 398: P. A. Vaccari, 'Il genuino commento ai salmi di Remigio di Auxerre', in his *Scritti di erudizione e di filologia,* i (Rome, 1952), 283–329.

5 *PL,* ccvii, 361C, 819D. See also the tentative use of prologue-headings in cols 735B–C.

6 *PL,* cxvii, 11–294, 295–358, 937–1220.

7 *PL,* clii, 638B–9A.

8 See A. Stoelen, 'Les Commentaires scripturaires attribués à Bruno le Chartreux', *RTAM,* xxv (1958), 177–247, and 'Bruno le Chartreux, Jean

Gratiadei et la "Lettre de S. Anselme" sur l'euchariste', ibid., xxxiv (1967), 18–83.

9 Lottin, *Psychologie et morale*, v, 173–4; cf. N. Häring, 'Two Commentaries on Boethius by Thierry of Chartres', *AHDLMA*, xxvii (1960), 68. Anselm seems to have provided most of the glosses to the Psalter and Pauline Epistles (see Smalley, *Study of the Bible*, p. 60) but not the prologues which introduce these glosses in the early printed editions, as in *Biblia glossata*, iii, 443–8; vi, 9–12.

10 *PL*, clxii, 1187–9.

11 See J. Leclercq, 'Le Commentaire du Cantique des Cantiques attribué à Anselme de Laon', *RTAM*, xvi (1949), 23–39. The evidence for Anselm's authorship is inconclusive; Miss Smalley regards the attribution as 'doubtful, and indeed probably wrong' (personal communication).

12 *PL*, cxvi, 196–7. Cf. A. Wilmart, 'Un Commentaire des psaumes restitué à Anselme de Laon', *RTAM*, viii (1936), 325–44. His suggestion was rejected by Lottin, *Psychologie et morale*, v, 170–5; A. Landgraf, 'Die Zuweisung eines Psalmenkommentars an Anselm von Laon', *Biblica*, xxiii (1942), 170–4; D. Van den Eynde, 'Literary Note on the Earliest Scholastic *Commentarii in psalmos*', *Franciscan Studies*, xiv (1954), 121–54; W. Hartmann, 'Psalmenkommentare aus der Zeit der Reform und der Frühscholastik', *Studi Gregoriani*, ix (1972), 346–54. For a recent defence of Wilmart's opinion, see V. I. J. Flint, 'Some Notes on the Early Twelfth Century Commentaries on the Psalms', *RTAM*, xxxvii (1971), 80–5.

13 Stegmüller, *Bibl.*, 2511–32, 6374–84, 3566–75. There are no firm grounds for believing that Abelard was the innovator responsible for introducing the 'type C' prologue in Scriptural exegesis, as was implied by Hunt, 'Introductions to the *Artes*', pp. 85–112; cf. N. Häring, 'The Lectures of Thierry of Chartres on Boethius *De trinitate*', *AHDLMA*, xxv (1959), 120–1. For the dating of Honorius's commentary, see H. Menhardt, 'Der Nachlass des Honorius Augustodunensis', in *Zeitschrift für deutsches Altertum und deutsche Literatur*, lxxxix (1958), 69.

14 On the blending of old and new in medieval exegesis, see, for example, Spicq, *Esquisse*, pp. 10–15, 72–8; H. H. Gluncz, *History of the Vulgate in England from Alcuin to Bacon* (Cambridge, 1933), pp. 206–7.

15 See, especially, the principles outlined by Abelard in the prologue to his *Sic et non*, discussed on p. 59; cf. Spicq, *Esquisse*, p. 73.

16 For description of the *Glossa ordinaria*, see B. Smalley, *Study of the Bible*, pp. 52–64, and her series of articles in *RTAM*, vii (1935), 235–62; viii (1936), 24–60; ix (1937), 365–400. It must be emphasised that the text of the *Glossa ordinaria* did not achieve the state represented by the early printed editions until relatively late, perhaps in the early thirteenth century.

17 Smalley, *Study of the Bible*, pp. 64–5; *RTAM*, ix, 370–1.

18 It may be added that the stock prologue-headings were applied in expounding the prologues of Jerome incorporated in medieval Bibles. For
example, Peter Comestor discussed the *auctor, materia, locus, tempus* and
modus agendi of St John's gospel as indicated by Jerome's prologue: Oxford,
Bodleian Library, MS Bodley 494, fols 1ᵛ–2ʳ. In his commentary on St
Matthew, Peter first gave his own views on the *materia, intentio* and *modus
agendi* of his *auctor* and then discussed the *intentio, ordo* and *utilitas* which
he supposed Jerome to have found in this gospel: Oxford, Bodleian Library, MS Laud. Misc. 291, fols 1ʳ–1ᵛ, 2ᵛ–3ʳ. St Albert the Great,
explaining the *intentio, materia* and *ordo* of the prophet Zachariah, professed himself to be dependent on Jerome, just as Jerome had been dependent on others: *Alberti opera*, ed. Borgnet, xix, 518. In this way, medieval
exegetes 'read in' their own notions of literary theory into ancient prologues.

19 G. Lacombe and B. Smalley, 'Studies on the Commentaries of Cardinal
Stephen Langton', *AHDLMA*, v (1931), 83.

20 E.g. the four Psalter-prologues in Cambridge, Corpus Christi College,
MS 217, fols 21ʳ–22ᵛ. This MS is described by Moore, *Works of Peter of
Poitiers*, p. 95.

21 *De doctrina christiana*, iii.21 (ed. Green, p. 98).

22 See, especially, the statement of Thomas of Cîteaux (writing between
1175 and 1180), who distinguished between three kinds of epithalamium, the historical, philosophical and theological: *PL*, ccvi, 17D–
18A. See, further, the *Glossa ordinaria* on the Song of Songs, *PL*, cxiii,
1127; Honorius 'of Autun' (writing between 1151 and 1158), *PL*, clxxii,
349D–350A; Philip of Harvengt († 1183), *PL*, cciii, 186A, 188B; St
Bernard of Clairvaux, *Sermones super cantica canticorum*, sermo i.8 (ed. J.
Leclercq, et al., *S. Bernardi opera* (Rome, 1957–), i, 6); William of St
Thierry, quoted on p. 48; Peter the Chanter, in Paris, Bibliothèque
Nationale, MS Lat. 15565, fol. 52ᵛ.

23 See, especially, the statement of Philip of Harvengt, who asserts the
supremacy of the Song of Songs over the inane fables of the poets: *PL*,
cciii, 181B, cf. 185–6A. See, further, the *Glossa ordinaria, PL*, cxiii,
1128B; Richard of St Victor, *PL*, cxcvi, 405B, 408B; Peter the Chanter,
BN Lat. 15565, fol. 52ᵛ; and the commentary on the Song of Songs
ascribed to Anselm of Laon, *PL*, clxii, 1188B, 1189C. With this entire discussion may now be compared Jean Leclercq's lively discussion of
Solomon as 'a Biblical master of love', in *Monks and Love in Twelfth
Century France* (Oxford, 1979), pp. 27–61.

24 *Biblia glossata*, iii, 443 (= *PL*, cxiii, 842A). For St Thomas's praise of the
excellence of the Psalter, see Chenu, *Toward understanding St Thomas*. pp.
245–6.

25 For Ambrose, see *PL*, xiv, 922B, 923C, 966D, 1039, 1087B–C; for Augustine, see *De doctrina christiana*, ii.8 (ed. Green, p. 41) and *De civitate Dei*, xvii.14 (ed. Hoffmann, ii, 245–6); for Cassiodorus, see *Expositio psalmorum*, praefatio, cap. ii (ed. Adriaen, i, 10).

26 See Jerome's comments on Psalms lxxiv, lxxvii, lxxx, lxxxiii, etc. (ed. Morin, pp. 48, 64–5, 78, 95–6).

27 See his Epistola cxl, Ad Cyprianum Presbyterum (pr. *PL*, xxii, 1169); cf. the *Praefatio in librum psalmorum iuxta Hebraicam veritatem* (pr. *PL*, xxviii, 1123–8).

28 For affirmations of the excellence of David's prophecy, see Peter Lombard, *PL*, cxci, 59B; Pseudo-Haimo, *PL*, cxvi, 193–5; Letbert of Lille, *PL*, xxi, 644B; Gerhoh of Reichersberg, *PL*, cxciii, 627–8, 637–8; ?Bruno the Carthusian, *PL*, clii, 639B; Pseudo-Remigius, *PL*, cxxxi, 145–8; Honorius 'of Autun', *PL*, clxxii, 272C–3B.

29 *Biblia glossata*, iii, 443 (= *PL*, cxiii, 841).

30 See, for example, the glosses on Psalms xlix, lxxx, lxxxi, and lxxxiii, in *Biblia glossata*, iii, 797 (= *PL*, cxiii, 916D), 1065 (= 979B), 1075 (= 981A), 1085 (= 985B–D).

31 For Jerome, see note 26 above. Cf. *Cassiodori expositio psalmorum*, on Psalms lxxii, lxxiii, lxxxiii, etc. (ed. Adriaen, ii, 660, 671, 767–8); *S. Augustini enarrationes in psalmos*, on Psalms xxxviii, xli, xliii, xliv, xlv, etc. (ed. Dekkers and Fraipont, i, 401–2, 460–1, 481–2, 493–4, 517–8).

32 *Biblia glossata*, iii, 444–5 (= *PL*, cxiii, 848–4).

33 Cf. M. Pontet, *L'Exégèse de S. Augustin prédicateur* (Paris, 1946), pp. 387–91.

34 *Didascalicon*, v.2 (trans. Taylor, p. 121). For similar applications of the cithar metaphor, see H.-J. Spitz, *Die Metaphorik des geistigen Schriftsinns*, Munstersche Mittelalter-Schriften, xii (Munich, 1972), 223–31; J. Fontaine, 'Les Symbolismes de la cithare dans la poésie de Paulin de Nole', in *Romanitas et christianitas: Studia I. H. Waszink oblata*, ed. W. Den Boer, *et al.* (Amsterdam and London, 1973), pp. 123–43.

35 For the lives of Virgil, see *Vitae Vergilianae antiquae*, ed. C. Hardie (Oxford, 1966); Upson, *CP*, xxxviii, 103–11; for the lives of Ovid, see Ghisalberti, *JWCI*, ix, 10–59.

36 The Lombard's comment follows that of Remigius: *PL*, cxci, 57C–D.

37 Stegmüller, *Bibl.*, 6637. Smalley, *Study of the Bible*, p. 64.

38 *PL*, cxci, 55A.

39 Ibid., 58.

40 Cf. Cassiodorus, In psalterium praefatio, cap. 2 (ed. Adriaen, i, 9–11).

41 *PL,* cxci, 59B. For the various series of psalm-titles that appear in medieval manuscripts, see P. Salmon, *Les 'Tituli psalmorum' des manuscrits latins,* Collectanea biblica latina, xii (Rome, 1959).

42 Cf. the statement by Honorius at the beginning of his *Expositio psalmorum* (*PL,* clxxii, 271B). See, also, Letbert of Lille, *PL,* xxi, 644D; the preamble to Pseudo-Remigius on the Psalter and the commentator's own opinion, *PL,* cxxxi, 137–8, 147C; Pseudo-Haimo, *PL,* cxvi, 195D.

43 Cf. the cursory treatment afforded this historical context by Philip of Harvengt, *PL,* cciii, 85C–D; Honorius, *PL,* clxxii, 349A, 352. Honorius systematically describes Solomon's verses literally, allegorically, tropologically and anagogically, the literal readings being very brief. St Bernard was not interested in the literal sense of the work, spending most of his time in 'the shadowy wood where allegories lurk unseen': Sermo xvi.1 (ed. Leclercq *et al.,* i, 90–1).

44 *Guillaume de St Thierry, Exposé sur le cantique des cantiques,* ed. J.-M. Dechanet and M. Dumontier, Sources chrétiennes, lxxxii (Paris, 1962), 82.

45 *De doctrina christiana,* iv.12 (ed. Green, pp. 137–9). Cf. Cicero, *Orator,* xxi.69 (in *Brutus, Orator,* ed. H. H. Hubbell (London and Cambridge, Mass., 1939), pp. 356–7; *De oratore,* II.xxvii.115, II.xxviii.121, II.lxxvii.310 (ed. H. Rackham (London and Cambridge, Mass., 1942), i, 280, 284, 434).

46 See, for example, Cicero's *Orator,* xxi.69 (ed. Hubbell, pp. 356–7); *De optimo genere oratorum,* i.3 (in *De inventione, etc.,* pp. 356–7.)

47 Cf. Cicero, *De oratore,* II.lxxvii.310 (ed. Rackham, i, 434); *Brutus,* xxiii.89 (ed. Hubbell, pp. 82–3); also, Augustine, *Contra Cresconium,* I.xiii.16 (ed. M. Petschenig, CSEL, lii (1909), 338–40). See, further, E. de Bruyne, *Études d'esthétique médiévale* (Brugge, 1946), i, 47–8, 58.

48 Cf. *De oratore,* III.lv.210–2 (ed. Rackham, ii, 166–9); Quintilian, *Institutio oratoria,* XII.x.69 (ed. Butler, iv, 488–9).

49 *Ad Herennium,* IV.viii.11 (pp. 252–4). Cf. Chapter I, n. 44, on p. 223.

50 *De doctrina christiana,* iv.7 (ed. Green, p. 143).

51 Ibid., iv.7, iv.18 (pp. 124–5, 144–6).

52 M. Dickey, 'Some Commentaries on the *De inventione* and *Ad Herennium* of the Eleventh and Early Twelfth Centuries', *MARS,* vi (1968), 14–15; K. M. Fredborg, 'The Commentaries on Cicero's *De inventione* and *Rhetorica ad Herennium* by William of Campeaux', *CIMAGL,* xvii (1976), 31–2.

53 Gilbert the Universal (Bishop of London 1128–34) was very interested in the rhetorical qualities of Lamentations: see, for example, his discussion of Jeremiah's use of complaint and indignation (cf. *Ad Herennium,*

III.xiii.24, IV.xv.22), incorporated in the *Glossa ordinaria*: *Biblia glossata*, iv, 908). Gerhoh of Reichersberg's elaborate exposition of the Psalter's *modus tractandi* has already been cited, on p. 22. Even more impressive is the commentary on the Song of Songs by Philip of Harvengt, who demonstrates an extensive knowledge of classical *auctores*: *PL*, cciii, 181–490.

54   There were supposed to be four basic emotions or *affectus* out of which all human emotions are composed, namely, love, fear, delight and misery: cf. E. Gilson, *The Mystical Theology of St Bernard*, trans. A. H. C. Downes (London, 1940), p. 101. The Augustinian theory of the *affectus* is discussed above, p. 120.

55   See, for example, *De inventione*, I.ii.3, I.v.6, I.xvi.22–5 (pp. 6–7, 14–15, 44–51); *De optimo genere oratorum*, i.3–ii.5 (ibid., pp. 356–9); *Ad Herennium*, I.iv.7–v.8 (pp. 12–16); Quintilian, *Institutio oratoria*, XII.x.58–60 (ed. Butler, iv, 482–5).

56   See, especially, Plato, *Republic*, x, 603–7 (in *Ancient Literary Criticism, The Principal Texts in New Translations*, ed. D. A. Russell and M. Winterbottom (Oxford, 1972), pp. 71–4).

57   *Accessus ad auctores, etc.*, ed. Hugyens, p. 67.

58   Stegmüller, *Bibl.*, 2511. In a unique colophon in Oxford, Balliol College, MS 36, we are told that Gilbert read his glosses to Anselm 'causa emendationis': see the *Catalogue of the Manuscripts of Balliol College, Oxford*, compiled by R. A. B. Mynors (Oxford, 1963), p. 26; cf. Smalley, *Study of the Bible*, p. 64. For Gilbert's links with Chartres, see N. Häring, 'Chartres and Paris Revisited', in *Essays in Honour of A. C. Pegis*, ed. J. R. O'Donnell (Toronto, 1974), esp. pp. 299–313.

59   Intendit enim propheta non solum de Cristo que proponit docere, verum in docendo affectum carnalium hominum ad eandem laudem trahere (Balliol MS 36, fol. 2^r).

60   Unde et metrice scripsit et diversis loquendi generibus opus ornavit et ante archam voce et instrumentis et maxime cum psalterio ipse cum multis et coram multis cantavit.

61   For William's theory of the affections, see M. M. Davy, *Théologie et mystique de Guillaume de St Thierry, i, La Connaissance de Dieu*, Études de théologie et d'histoire de la spiritualité, xiv (Paris, 1954), 146, 220–1; E. R. Elder, 'William of St Thierry: Rational and Affective Spirituality', in *The Spirituality of Western Christendom*, ed. E. R. Elder (Kalamazoo, Michigan, 1976), pp. 85–105.

62   *Exposé sur le cantique*, p. 74.

63   St Bernard, *In cant. cant.*, sermo xxxvii, 1–2 (ed. Leclercq, ii, 9–10).

64   *De natura et dignitate amoris*, i.1 (pr. *PL*, clxxxiv, 379C).

65 See esp. ibid., 381A; see further Gilson, *Mystical Theology of St Bernard*, pp. 200; 230–1, n. 82; 247, n. 261, and Leclercq, *Monks and Love*, pp. 62–85.

66 *Exposé sur le cantique*, pp. 76–8.

67 Ibid., pp. 88–102; cf. the argument of William's *De nat. et dig. amoris*, summarised by Gilson, *Mystical Theology of St Bernard*, pp. 200 *et seq.*

68 Cristus integer caput cum menbris est materia huius libri, de qua agit propheta hoc modo. Loquitur enim aliquando [simul de toto, id est Cristo et ecclesia; aliquando] de singulis, id est Cristo vel ecclesia. De Cristo autem tribus modis: aliquando enim de divinitate ut ibi, 'tecum principium', aliquando de humanitate proprie ut ibi, 'desiderium cordis eius tribuisti ei', aliquando transsumptione, dicendo de eo quod solis convenit membris ut ibi, 'longe a salute mea verba delictorum meorum'. De ecclesia vero duobus modis: aliquando secundum perfectos, aliquando secundum inperfectos. De perditis autem aliquando interserit propter bonos. De hac autem materia et hoc modo agit hac intentione, ut perditi in Adam Cristo per quem solum peccata dimittuntur et immortalitas redditur, conformentur, id est sicut portaverunt imaginem terreni, portent imaginem celestis. Titulus libri est: incipit liber ymnorum. Ymnus est laus Dei cum cantico . . . (Balliol MS 36, fol. 2ʳ).

69 In Oxford, Bodleian Library, MS Auct. D.2.1, Gilbert's headings for the Psalter as a whole are written neatly in the left-hand margins of the prologue, in coloured inks: *materia, modus, intentio, titulus, genus prophetiae, nomen libri* and *numerus psalmorum*. The names of the *auctores* from which the glosses are derived are placed in the right-hand margin. A similar method is followed in the presentation of individual psalms; e.g. the first psalm is accompanied by the following headings: *nullus titulus, materia, intentio* and *partitio psalmi*. See, further, plate 2, p. 53.

70 Herbert of Bosham, who corrected and edited Peter Lombard's commentary, tells us that the Lombard undertook an expansion of Anselm's commentary to render it less obscure: see J. de Ghellinck, 'La Carrière de Pierre Lombard: Nouvelle précision chronologique', *RHE*, xxx (1934), 98.

71 See *PL*, cxci, 57–9, 69, 77–8, 81–3, etc.

72 Ibid., 60.

73 *PL*, cxvi, 196C–D. Wilmart thought this commentary was by Anselm of Laon: see note 12 above. Its prologue has many resemblances to the prologue which introduces a Psalter-commentary recently restored to Letbert of Lille (who died in 1110, although his commentary was not published until 1125): see A. Wilmart, 'Le Commentaire sur les psaumes imprimé sous le nom de Rufin', *Rev. bén.*, xxxi (1914/9), 258–76. Letbert's prologue—if it is indeed his work—is one of the most elaborate of all twelfth-century introductions to the Psalter, comprising discussion of the Psalter's *titulus, causa inscriptionis, finis, materia, pars philosophiae, intentio* and *modus:* see *PL*, xxi, 641–6.

74 *Accessus ad auctores, etc.*, ed. Huygens, p. 32. The earliest extant MS of this *accessus* is Munich, Bayerische Staatsbibliothek, Clm. 19475 (XIIs., from Tegernsee): see Huygens, pp. 2–6. With our discussion here cf. Minnis, 'Moral Gower', pp. 55–8.

75 Similar vocabulary is employed in prologues to commentaries on the Pauline Epistles: see pp. 62, 242 n. 97. In his commentary on the Four Evangelists, Peter the Chanter provides a description of the *communis materia, intentio* and *utilitas omnium:* London, British Library, MS Royal 10.C.V., fol. 172ʳ. Cf. the descriptions of the common and special intentions of classical satires: Kristeller, *CTC*, i, 188, 195–6; iii, 224–5, 227. See, further, the similar vocabulary in legal *materiae* cited on p. 21 above.

76 *Accessus ad auctores, etc.*, ed. Huygens, p. 32. This relationship between praise and censure derives from ancient rhetorical theory: see, for example, Cicero, *De inventione*, II.lix.177–8 (pp. 342–5); *Ad Herennium*, III.vi.10–viii.15 (pp. 172–85).

77 For use of the related terms *prodesse* and *delectare*, or *utilitas* and *delectatio*, in commentaries on secular *auctores*, see *Accessus ad auctores, etc.*, ed. Huygens, pp. 22, 26, 36, 45, 63, 84, etc.; Ghisalberti, *JWCI*, ix, 42–3, 46, 58; Kristeller, *CTC*, i, 197. Horace's injunction to 'mix grave and gay' was well known: see, for example, the statements by Stephen Langton and Robert Holcot quoted by Smalley, *English Friars and Antiquity*, p. 158. See, further, Curtius, *European Literature*, pp. 417–35, and the extensive discussions of *delectatio* in Glending Olson, *Literature as Recreation in the Later Middle Ages* (Ithaca and London, 1982), and J. Suchomski, *'Delectatio' und 'Utilitas': Ein Beitrag zum Verständnis mittelalterlicher komischer Literatur* (Bern, 1975).

78 *Exposé sur le cantique*, pp. 80–2. Cf. Philip of Harvengt's statement about Greek comedy, *PL*, cciii, 186A; also, the commentary on the Song of Songs ascribed to Anselm of Laon, *PL*, clxii, 1189B–C. For a general survey of the limited notions of Roman drama current in the Middle Ages (which, however, ignores Scriptural exegesis), see M. H. Marshall, 'Theatre in the Middle Ages: Evidence from Dictionaries and Glosses', *Symposium*, iv (1950), 1–39.

79 *De arte metrica*, ed. H. Keil, *Grammatici Latini*, vii (Leipzig, 1880), p. 259.

80 *Accessus ad auctores, etc.*, ed. Huygens, p. 65.

81 *Comment. in Buc.*, prologus (ed. Thilo and Hagen, iii, 1–2); *Etymologiae*, ed. Lindsay, viii.7.11; *Accessus ad auctores, etc.*, ed. Huygens, pp. 32, 44.

82 *Origen: The Song of Songs, Commentary and Homilies*, trans. R. P. Lawson, Ancient Christian Writers, xxvi (Westminster, Maryland, and London, 1957), 21–2.

83   See, for example, the anonymous commentary cit. Spicq, *Esquisse*, p. 245.

84   *PL*, clxxviii, 1339–49. For a useful discussion, see J. Cottiaux, 'La Conception de la théologie d'Abélard', *RHE*, xxviii (1932), 247–95, 533–51, 788–828. Abelard's methods have been interpreted as a development of techniques used by canon lawyers in their reconciliation of discordant canons: see M. Grabmann, *Die Geschichte der scholastichen Methode* (Freiburg, 1909–11), i, 234–46. Abelard was by no means the only theologian to employ these techniques, and he was certainly not the first, but he was one of the most articulate: see E. Bertola, 'I precedenti storici del metodo del *Sic et non* di Abelardo', *RFN*, liii (1961), 255–80.

85   *PL*, clxxviii, 1343B.

86   Ibid., 1347C–D.

87   *Petri Abaelardi opera theologica*, ed. E. M. Buytaert, CCCM, xi–xii (1969), i, 44–6.

88   Cf. the material cit. Bertola, *RFN*, liii, 271–2.

89   *Biblia glossata*, vi, 12 (= *PL*, cxiv, 469–70); *PL*, cxci, 1299D–1300C. For the dating of the Lombard's commentary on the Pauline Epistles, and his various other works, see, now, I. Brady's prolegomena to *Petri Lombardi sententiae in IV libros distinctae*, i, pars 1, Spicilegium Bonaventurianum, iv (Grottaferrata, 1971).

90   *Abaelardi opera*, ed. Buytaert, i, 47–8. Cf. quaestio 98 of the *Sic et non* (*PL*, clxxviii, 1486–8).

91   *PL*, cxci, 1302–3.

92   *Historia calamitatum*, ed. J. Monfrin, 2 ed. (Paris, 1962), p. 68; *Biblia glossata*, vi, 13A–B (= *PL*, cxiv, 469B).

93   The importance of knowing an author's intention is, of course, one of the principles explained in the *Sic et non* prologue: *PL*, clxxviii, 1345–6.

94   See Lottin, *Psychologie et morale*, i.1, 22–4; *Peter Abelard's Ethics*, ed. D. E. Luscombe (Oxford, 1971), pp. xxxii–xxxiii; D. E. Luscombe, *The School of Peter Abelard* (Cambridge, 1969), pp. 19, 79, 139–40, 151–2, 174–7, etc.

95   *Abaelardi opera*, ed. Buytaert, i, 41. Cf. the anonymous follower of Abelard, now known as the 'Cambridge commentator', *Commentarius Cantabrigensis in epistolas Pauli*, ed. A. Landgraf, Notre-Dame University Publications in Medieval Studies, ii (Notre Dame, Indiana, 1937–45), i, 1–2.

96   *De inventione*, II.lvi.168–9 (pp. 334–7).

97   Cf. the *Glossa ordinaria* on the Pauline Epistles, *Biblia glossata*, vi, 9 (not in *PL*, cxiv); Peter Lombard, *PL*, cxci, 1302B. These analyses of general and special materials and intentions parallel the representative analysis of

Ovid's *Heroides* quoted on pp. 55–6. It would have been logical to transfer a technique of analysis from study of a pagan collection of letters, the *Heroides*, to study of a sacred collection of letters, the Pauline Epistles, especially in view of the then-current interest in letter-collections, *ars dictaminis* and epistolary style.

98 *Abaelardi opera*, ed. Buytaert, i, 47. Cf. the *Glossa ordinaria* (*Biblia glossata*, vi, 9–10. Not in PL, cxiv). See, further, the similar comments on other Pauline Epistles: *PL*, cxiv, 551A, 587D, 601B, 609A–B, 623D, 633A. Cf. also the *Comment. Cantabrig.*, i, 6; the beginning of Gilbert of Poitiers' commentary on Romans, in Oxford, Magdalen College, MS 118, fol. 33ʳ; Peter Lombard, *PL*, cxci, 1302B, 1534B; *PL*, cxcii, 9C, 95A, 169D, 223B, 259B, 289B–C, 312C, 326C–D, 363C, 384B, 395B. In these glosses, the Ciceronian objectives of an exordium (to render an orator's hearers attentive, docile and benevolent) are applied in describing the letter-writer's appeal to his readers. This is a common feature of the theory of letter writing; e.g. it appears in one of the earliest treatises on the subject, written *c.* 1087 by Alberic of Monte Cassino: *Alberici Casinensis flores rhetoricii*, ed. D. M. Inguanez and H. M. Willard, Miscellanea Cassinese, xiv (Montecassino, 1938), 38. Cf. Cicero, *De inventione*, I. xv.20 (pp. 40–3); *Ad Herennium*, I.iii.5–vii.11 (pp. 10–23). According to Alberic, the salutation *(salutatio)* with which a letter begins should identify both the sender and the recipient, and it must be appropriate to the recipient, the subject and the intention of the writer. Theory of this kind seems to lie behind the theologians' descriptions of St Paul's salutations.

99 J. W. Baldwin, *Masters, Princes, and Merchants: The Social Views of Peter the Chanter and his Circle* (Princeton, 1970), i, 44.

100 Cf. Hunt, 'Introductions to the *Artes*', pp. 105–6.

101 Cf. Moore, *Works of Peter of Poitiers*, pp. 95–6.

102 These works, together with Peter the Chanter's *Summa Abel*, are the earliest extant collections of *distinctiones:* see Moore, p. 78; G. Lacombe, *La Vie et les oeuvres de Prévostin*, Bibliothèque Thomiste, ix (Le Saulchoir, 1927), 112–30.

103 Cf. R. H. Rouse and M. A. Rouse, 'Biblical Distinctions in the Thirteenth Century', *AHDLMA*, xli (1974), esp. p. 28; also, Moore, pp. 78–82; J. B. Allen, *The Friar as Critic* (Vanderbilt, Nashville, 1971), pp. 102–112.

104 See the examples from Peter of Poitiers' *Summa super psalterium*, pr. Moore, pp. 79–81, and Rouse, *AHDLMA*, xli, 28. Distinction collections were employed in the writing of sermons: ibid., p. 30; cf. the enthusiastic reaction of Peter of Aldgate to a sermon by Gilbert Foliot which employed *distinctiones*, cit. R. W. Hunt, 'English Learning in the Late Twelfth Century', in *Essays in Medieval History*, ed. R. W. Southern (London, 1968), p. 120.

105 Cf. B. Smalley, 'Peter Comestor on the Gospels and his Sources', *RTAM*, xlvi (1979), 109–10.

106 Ibid., p. 110. The earliest-known Paris lecture-course on a Gospel (in Oxford, Bodleian Library, MS Lat. th.d.45) begins with a passage from the Old Testament, the description of the ark in Exodus xxv. 12–14. St Luke's *materia, intentio, causa scribendi* and *modus agendi* are then explained. See B. Smalley, 'An Early Paris Lecture Course on St Luke', in *Sapientiae Doctrina: Mélanges offerts à Dom H. Bascour*, Réch. de théol. anc. et méd., numéro spécial, i (Leuven, 1980), 305.

107 See the *Allegoriae super tabernaculum Moysi*, ed. P. S. Moore and J. A. Corbett (Notre Dame, Indiana, 1938), p. xvii.

108 Smalley, *RTAM*, xlvi, 110.

109 'Facies michi tentorium in introitu tabernaculi quatuor preciosis coloribus contextum'. Tabernaculum quo Deus in nobis habitat, in quo nos reficit et saginat, divina pagina est. Nam sicut ingrethientibus tabernaculum duo occurrebant introitus qui per duo tentoria distinguebantur, ita accedentibus ad sacre Scripture paginam duo occurrunt principia scilicet intrinsecus et extrinsecus. Et sicut illa tentoria quatuor preciosis coloribus erant distincta, ita et hec principia in quatuor partes sunt divisa. Nam principium extrinsecus distinguitur in causam nominis et causam quantitatis et causam distinctionis et causam frequentationis. Principium intrinsecus in titulum, materiam, intentionem et ordinem (Oxford, Corpus Christi College, MS 48, fol. 59^r). The text from Paris, Bibliothèque Nationale, MS Lat.425, fol. 1^r, is pr. Moore, pp. 95–6, 178. Cf. the very similar prologue to an anonymous Psalter-commentary found in Paris, Bib. Nat., MS Lat. 455, cit. Moore, p. 178.

110 Cf. Hunt, 'Introductions to the *Artes*', pp. 105–6.

111 Cf. the similar use of headings in Peter of Corbeil's gloss on the Pauline Epistles, cit. ibid., p. 106, n. 1.

112 See Stegmüller, *Bibl.*, 6564. 1. The terms *extrinsecus* and *intrinsecus* are not used in Peter's commentaries on the Gospels: cf. Smalley, *RTAM*, xlvi, 110.

113 Praepositinus seems to have produced two versions of his prologue: the first, to introduce his glosses on the first 50 psalms; the second, being a slightly modified version of the first, to introduce his *distinctiones* on the entire Psalter. We are concerned with the later commentary, Stegmüller, *Bibl.*, 6987.

114 Paris, Bibliothèque Nationale, MS Lat. 454, fol. 73^r.

115 Iuxta huc modum expositor psalterii duplicem facit ingressum, scilicet ingressum ad librum et ingressum in libro, et uterque quatuor continet in se quasi quatuor coloribus distinguatur. Ingressus ad librum continet

causam nominis, id est, quare psalterium vel soliloquium liber iste dicatur; et causam quantitatis, id est, quare CL psalmos contineat; et causam distinctionis, id est, quare in tribus quinquagensis distinguatur; et causam frequentationis, id est, quare ab ecclesia scriptura David plusquam aliorum prophetarum frequentatur. Et dicitur iste ingressus ad librum, quia, hiis cognitis, parum vel nichil de sensu libri nobis aperitur. Secundus ingressus, qui est in libro, similiter quatuor continet, scilicet tytulum, materiam, intentionem et modum agendi. Et hoc dicitur ingressus in libro quia, hiis quatuor cognitis, ea que in libro continentur aliquatenus nobis reserantur (Ibid., fol. 73ᵛ). A prologue bearing certain resemblances to that of Praepositinus is found in Cambridge, Pembroke College, MS 7, fol. 1ʳ *et seq*. This commentary, falsely attributed to Stephen Langton (cf. Stegmüller, *Bibl.*, 7799), is probably by Hilduin, Chancellor of Notre Dame in 1160 or 1189. See B. Smalley, 'A Collection of Paris Lectures of the Later Twelfth Century in the MS Pembroke College, Cambridge 7', *Camb. Hist. Jour.*, vi (1938), 103, 113.

116 For a description of this MS, see Moore, *Works of Peter of Poitiers*, pp. 92–3.

117 Cambridge, Corpus Christi College, MS 217, fols 21ʳ–22ᵛ.

118 Pr. *Hugonis postilla*, ii, 2ʳ–3ᵛ; Stegmüller, *Bibl.*, 3675.

119 These comprehensive commentaries seem to have been completed during Hugh's first five years of teaching at St Jacques, a formidable task for one man: see Smalley, *Study of the Bible*, pp. 272–4. On the Bible-concordance produced at St Jacques see R. H. Rouse and M. A. Rouse, 'The Verbal Concordance to the Scriptures', *AFP*, xliv (1974), 5–30.

120 Cf. Hunt, 'Introductions to the *Artes*', p. 107. Peter makes the same basic point at the beginning of his commentary on Genesis, when expounding Jerome's preface: superfluous glosses are to be avoided, because Christ is the best gloss for the Old and New Testaments. London, British Library, MS Royal 2.C.VIII, fol. 1ᵛ.

121 Oxford, Corpus Christi College, MS 49, fol. 4ʳ.

122 Here, Peter is elaborating on Isaiah xxix. 11–12.

123 Here, we are assured that the liberal arts are the seats and, as it were, the substructures, of theology: Paris, Bibliothèque Nationale, MS Lat. 14892, fol. 123ʳ.

124 Cf. Peter of Poitiers' elaborate allegorisation of the veiled and horned face of Moses, in *All. sup. tab. Moysi*, ed. Moore and Corbett, pp. 193–7.

125 This feature of the Chanter's theology in general is stressed throughout Baldwin's book, *Masters, Princes and Merchants*.

126 Smalley, *RTAM*, xlvi, 110.

127 Ibid.

128 Baldwin, *Masters, Princes and Merchants,* i, 25–6; ii, 16.

129 Oxford, Trinity College, MS 65, fol. 214^v. Stegmüller, *Bibl.,* 7747.

130 Trinity, MS 65, fol. 86^r. Stegmüller, *Bibl.,* 7745.

131 Cf. the similar statements by Rupert of Deutz in his commentary on Genesis, cit. Spitz, *Die Metaphorik,* pp. 194, 196. Rupert uses the terms *extrinsecus* and *intrinsecus* to refer to literal sense and spiritual sense respectively.

132 Oxford, Bodleian Library, MS Rawlinson, G.427, fol. 69^r. Stegmüller, *Bibl.,* 7843.

133 See the quotation from this MS by Hunt, 'Introductions to the *Artes*', pp. 106–7, n. 3.

134 Stegmüller, *Bibl.,* 3719, 3725. Texts in *Hugonis postilla,* v, 82^r; vi, 151^v.

135 As in the prologues to the commentaries on Ecclesiastes and Ecclesiasticus: ibid., iii, 62^v, 153^v. Cf. the prologue to the Song of Songs: ibid., iii, 93^v.

136 Unde more doctorum primo videndum est, quis auctor, quae sit libri materia, quis modus agendi, quis finis, quae intentio, quae utilitas, et cui parti philosophiae supponatur, quis titulus, quot libri partes, quis expositor, quis translator (ibid., iii, 153^v).

137 Ibid., i, 121^v.

138 For the relevant Langton passage, see Hunt, 'Introductions to the *Artes*', pp. 106–7, n. 3; for Hugh's prologue, see *Hugonis postilla,* iv, 283^r.

139 Ibid., iv, 283^r.

140 It appears in the prologues to the commentaries on Genesis, Exodus, Leviticus, Numbers and the Psalter: ibid., i, 2^r, 71^v, 99^v, 121^v; ii, 2^v.

141 See, for example, the prologue to Langton's commentary on Exodus, cit. pp. 69–70. Langton also allegorises the tabernacle in the prologue to his commentary on Genesis where (as in the prologue to his Exodus-commentary) the four colours are interpreted as the four senses of Scripture: Trinity, MS 65, fol. 1^r. The tabernacle also appears in the prologue to Langton's commentary on Leviticus: ibid., fol. 176^r.

142 See the prologues to the commentaries on Genesis, Exodus, Leviticus, Numbers, Deuteronomy, Joshua, Judges, Ruth and Kings: *Hugonis postilla,* i, 2^r, 71^v, 99^r, 121^v, 145^r, 171^v, 188^v, 207^v, 210^v. Cf. Langton's use of *intus et foris* in e.g. his commentary on Deuteronomy: 'Hic autem liber scriptus est intus et foris, intus quia addit, foris quia recapitulat, vel litteraliter et spiritualiter' (Trinity MS 65, fol. 254^v).

143 In the prologue to Hugh's commentary on Numbers, the terms *foris* and

intus are used in conjunction with both the *extrinsecus/intrinsecus* and *litteralis/spiritualis* distinctions: *Hugonis postilla*, i, 121^v. In the prologue to Hugh's commentary on Leviticus, *foris* and *intus* are related to the *litteralis/spiritualis* distinction: ibid., i, 99^r.

144 As in the prologue to Hugh's Exodus-commentary: ibid., i, 71^v.

145 Smalley, *Study of the Bible*, p. 274.

146 For Abelard's classification, see pp. 61–2; for Hugh's see *Didascalicon*, iv.2 (ed. Buttimer, pp. 71–2). See, further, Spicq, *Esquisse*, pp. 147–8.

147 Smalley, *Study of the Bible*, pp. 292–3.

CHAPTER 3

1 *Summa theologiae*, I^a 1, 10, responsio (Blackfriars ed. (London and New York, 1964–81), i, 36–9). Cf. Augustine, *De doctrina christiana*, i.2, ii.1, iii.5ff. (ed. Green, pp. 9, 33–4, 84ff.); Hugh of St Victor, *Didascalicon*, v.3 (ed. Buttimer, pp. 96–7). Aquinas's version of the distinction between significative words and significative things was incorporated in the first prologue to Nicholas of Lyre's *Postilla litteralis* (pr. *Biblia glossata*, i, unfol.) and repeated in the prologue to his subsequent *Postilla moralis* (ibid.). From Lyre's *Post. litt.* it was taken to be included in the Lollard prologue to the English Bible: see *The Holy Bible made from the Latin Vulgate by John Wycliffe and his Followers*, ed. J. Forshall and F. Madden (Oxford, 1850), i, 52–3. The whole of the present chapter may now be compared with G. R. Evans, *The Language and Logic of the Bible: The Road to Reformation* (Cambridge, 1985), esp. pp. 7–19 (on the divine and human authorship of holy Scripture).

2 Cf. the somewhat different formulation of this theory by Henry of Ghent, *Summa quaestionum*, art. 16, qu.3 (pr. *Summae quaestionum ordinariarum Henrici a Gandavo* (Paris, 1520), fol. 105^v). Stegmüller, *Sent.*, 318.

3 *Summa theologiae*, I^a P. tract. 1, qu.5, m.4, ad 3um (*Alberti opera*, ed. Borgnet, xxxi, 28). See, further, Albert's Bible-glosses in *Opera*, xxii, 312, 324, 481. Cf. Aquinas, *Quodlibetum septimum*, qu.6, art.2 (pr. *S. Thomae Aquinatis quaestiones quodlibetales*, 8 ed., ed. R. Spiazzi (Marietti, 1949), p. 155), and Nicholas of Lyre, in the prologue to his commentary on Job (*Biblia glossata*, iii, 12). Richard FitzRalph defined the literal sense of a Scriptural passage as 'that sense which the human author immediately understands of the passage': *Summa Ricardi Radulphi in quaestionibus Armenorum* (Paris, 1512), fol. 2^v.

4 *Super epistolam ad Romanos*, cap.iv, lect.1, 331 (pr. *S. Thomae Aquinatis, super epistolas S. Pauli lectura*, ed. P. R. Cai (Marietti, 1953), p. 59); cf. Spicq, *Esquisse*, p. 251.

5 *Summa theologiae*, I^a 1, 10, ad 1um; cf. ad 3um (Blackfriars ed., i, 38, 40) Cf. Augustine, Epistola xciii.8 (pr. *PL*, xxxiii, 334). On the demon-

strative capability of the *sensus litteralis*, see Spicq, *Esquisse*, pp. 279–81; also, Smalley, *Study of the Bible*, pp. 300–1.

6   But, of course, they were of considerable use to the preacher. The 'spiritual' exposition was supposed to train students of theology to preach and, in lecture-courses, it was often preserved—in full or in extracts—as an aid to sermon-making. For example, most Psalter-commentaries from the late twelfth and early thirteenth centuries belong to this particular genre: see B. Smalley, 'Robert Bacon and the Early Dominican School', *TRHS*, 4 ser., xxx (1948), 1–19.

7   *Summa theologiae*, Iᵃ 1, 10. ad 1um (Blackfriars ed., i, 38). But St Thomas was not altogether consistent: see B. Smalley, 'William of Auvergne, John of La Rochelle and St Thomas Aquinas on the Old Law', in *St Thomas Aquinas 1274–1974, Commemorative Studies*, ed. A. Maurer *et al.*, Pontifical Institute of Mediaeval Studies (Toronto, 1974), ii, 11–71. Cf. the ambivalent attitude to the spiritual sense held by a pupil of St Thomas's, Remigio dei Girolami of Florence: *Contra falsos ecclesie professores*, cap. xcix, ed. E. Panella, Memorie Domenicane, n.s., ix (Pistoia, 1979), pp. 173–4. I am grateful to Dr Smalley for this reference.

8   *Expositio in librum B. Iob*, cap.i, lect.2 (*Aquinatis opera*, xiv, 4); cf. Spicq, *Esquisse*, p. 255.

9   On the notion of 'properly speaking' see Chenu, *Toward understanding St Thomas*, pp. 167–8. The premises of a syllogism must be unequivocal and unambiguous; hence the logician cannot base an argument on metaphorical expression: cf. Spicq, *Esquisse*, p. 281; T. Gilby, *Barbara celarent: A Description of Scholastic Dialectic* (London, New York, and Toronto, 1949), pp. 77–95, 253–8.

10   *William of Ockham: De sacramento altaris*, ed. and trans. T. B. Birch, Lutheran Literary Board (Iowa, 1930), pp. 40–5.

11   W. B. Dunphy, 'St Albert and the Five Causes', *AHDLMA*, xxxiii (1967), 7–21; cf. E. Gilson, 'Notes pour l'histoire de la cause efficiente', *AHDLMA*, xxix (1962), 7–31, esp. p. 18.

12   Quoted from Leipzig University Library, MS Lat. 1291 by Grabmann, *Mittelalterliches Geistesleben*, iii, 234; transcription partially corrected by Sandkühler, *Die frühen Dantekommentare*, pp. 31–2. For the dating of this commentary between 1240 and 1250, and the argument that its author cannot be identified with Jordan of Saxony, see, now, R. A. Gauthier, 'Notes sur les débuts (1225–1240) du premier "averroïsme" ', *RSPT*, lxvi (1982), 367–73.

13   Text ed. O. Lewry, *Robert Kilwardby's Writings on the Logica vetus studied with regard to their teaching and method* (unpub. D. Phil. thesis, Oxford, 1978), p. 359.

14   Ibid., pp. 368, 382, 392.

15   Cit. Lewry, ibid., p. 91, who proceeds to dismiss the suggestion that this was the work of Kilwardby.

16 Cit. Grabmann, *Mittelalterliches Geistesleben,* iii, 148. Cf. the commentary attributed to a Robert of Paris (not Kilwardby), cit. Lewry, p. 169.

17 Cf. the elaborate application of the *extrinsecus/intrinsecus* distinction in the prologue to Peter of Tarantasia's commentary on II Thessalonians, 2nd redaction: 'In quolibet opere concurrunt quatuor causae: duae extrinsecae que sunt de fieri, scilicet efficiens et finis; duae intrinsecae quae sunt de esse, scilicet materia et forma. In fieri rei, efficiens inchoat et finis consummat; in esse rei, materia inchoat et forma consummat . . .'. Pr. under the name of Nicholas Gorran, in *In omnes d. Pauli epistolas elucidatio, authore Nicolao Gorrano* (Antwerp, 1617), p. 498. In Peter's commentary on the *Sentences* (1256–8), he distinguishes between the *causae moventes ab intrinseco* and the *causae moventes ab extrinseco: In prolog. Lomb., divisio textus* (pr. *Innocentius V sententiarum commentaria* (Toulouse, 1652), i, fol. 7ʳ). Cf. the prologue to Bonaventure's commentary on St Luke, *Prooemium commentarii in Lucam (Bonaventurae opera,* vii, 3).

18 This is evident from the prologues cit. Lewry, *Kilwardby's Writings on the Logica vetus,* esp. pp. 44, 222, 359, 369, 382, 408. Cf. S. Harrison Thomson, 'Robert Kilwardby's Commentaries *In Priscianum* and *In Barbarismum Donati', New Schol.,* xii (1958), 52–65.

19 For examples, see Lewry, pp. 135, 169, 358, 367, etc.

20 See I. Brady in *Magistri Alexandri de Hales, Glossa in quattuor libros sententiarum Petri Lombardi,* Bibliotheca Franciscana scholastica medii aevi, xii–xv (Quaracchi ed., 1951–7), i, 102–3.

21 Ibid., i, 1–4. Stegmüller, *Sent.,* 62.

22 Paris, Bibliothèque Nationale, MS Lat. 14438, fol. 1ʳ. Alexander refers to the principle of 'efficient causality' in expounding St John's opening statements, but the schema of the four causes does not provide the basis of Alexander's prologue.

23 For this dating, see J. A. Weisheipl, *Friar Thomas d'Aquino* (Oxford, 1975), p. 69. Stegmüller, *Sent.,* 718.

24 R. J. Long, 'The Science of Theology according to Richard Fishacre: An Edition of the Prologue to his Commentary on the *Sentences', Med. Stud.,* xxxiv (1972), 88. For other examples of 'Aristotelian prologues' to *Sentences* commentaries, see V. Doucet, 'Quelques commentaires sur les "Sentences" de Pierre le Lombard', in *Miscellanea Lombardiana* (Novara, 1957), pp. 276, 279, 283, 288.

25 *De natura theologiae,* ed. Stegmüller, pp. 7–12. Stegmüller, *Sent.,* 742.

26 *Hugonis postilla,* v, 82ʳ; cf. the prologue to Hugh's commentary on the Acts of the Apostles (ibid., vi, 252ᵛ). For the term 'introductory causes' *(causae introductoriae),* see John of Rochelle's *principium,* ed. M. Delorme, 'Deux leçons d'ouverture de cours biblique données par Jean de la

Rochelle', *La France franciscaine,* xvi (1933), 351; cf. Peter of Tarantasia's general prologue to his commentary on the Pauline Epistles (pr. *In omnes d. Pauli epist.,* p. 1).

27 See Smalley, *Study of the Bible,* pp. 272, 296–8; also 'A Commentary on Isaias by Guerric of St-Quentin O.P.', *Studi e testi,* cxxii (1946), 383–97.

28 Pr. from Oxford, New College, MS 40, by Smalley, ibid., pp. 388–9.

29 *Alberti opera,* ed. Borgnet, xv, 5. Stegmüller, *Bibl.,* 1023.

30 Ibid., xxxviii, 468. Stegmüller, *Bibl.,* 1040.

31 Gorran, in Oxford, Bodleian Library, MS Bodley 246, fol. 1^v; Stegmüller, *Bibl.,* 5750; Lyre, *In postillam super Psalterium praefatio* (pr. *Biblia glossata,* iii, 431); Stegmüller, *Bibl.,* 5853.

32 *In epistolam ad Romanos,* cap. i, lect. 1 (*Aquinatis opera,* xiii, 4). Stegmüller, *Bibl.,* 8028.

33 *Commentarii in lib. I sententiarum,* in prologum magistri expositio (*Alberti opera,* ed. Borgnet, xxv, 6). Stegmüller, *Sent.,* 51.

34 *Commentum in lib. I sententiarum,* divisio textus prologi (ed. P. Mandonnet, *T. Aquinatis scriptum super libros sententiarum* (Paris, 1927–47), i, 19).

35 *Thome Valois et Nicolai Triveth in libros b. Augustini de civitate Dei commentaria* (Toulouse, 1488), unfol.

36 *Bonaventurae opera,* vii, 5. Stegmüller, *Bibl.,* 1776.

37 *In acta Apostolorum et singulas Apostolorum, authore Nicolao Gorrano* (Antwerp, 1620), p. 178. Stegmüller, *Bibl.,* 5810.

38 Oxford, Merton College, MS 172, fol. 52^r. Stegmüller, *Bibl. suppl.,* 4920. For Russel, see B. Smalley, 'John Russel O.F.M.', *RTAM,* xxiii (1956), 277–320.

39 III Sent., dist. 23, dub. 5, cit. J. G. Bouregol, *Introduction to the Works of Bonaventure,* trans. J. de Vinck (Paterson, New Jersey, 1963), p. 24.

40 Art. 9, qu. 2 (*Summa quaestionum,* fol. 71^v).

41 *Alberti opera,* ed. Borgnet, xviii, 355. Stegmüller, *Bibl.,* 977.

42 *Alberti opera,* xxiv, 8. Stegmüller, *Bibl.,* 1001.

43 Cit. D.E. Sharp, *Franciscan Philosophy at Oxford in the Thirteenth Century,* British Society of Franciscan Studies, xvi (Oxford, 1930), 22, n. 1. For Grosseteste's theory of causality, see A. C. Crombie, 'Grosseteste's position in the history of science', in *Robert Grosseteste, Scholar and Bishop: Essays in Commemoration of the Seventh Centenary of his Death,* ed. D. A. Callus (Oxford, 1955), pp. 98–120, esp. pp. 106–7.

44 'Grosseteste is aware that Aristotle's metaphysics is faulty, that in particular it has no systematic theory concerning the relation of the first cause to
the secondary causes . . . The real problem concerning causality lies in
proving that secondary causes have real, and not simply instrumental
causal efficacy. Grosseteste decided that they have, because efficient causes
intervening between the first cause and the last effect possess an *intentio
prima*, which makes them agents rather than instruments'. J. McEvoy,
Man and Cosmos in the Philosophy of Robert Grosseteste (unpubl. D.Phil.
thesis, Louvain, 1974), p. 254.

45 *Summa theologiae*, I^a qu.105, a.5, responsio (Blackfriars ed., xiv, 77).

46 'Appendix 13: Biblical Inspiration', ibid., i, 145. This whole paragraph
is indebted to Gilby's discussion.

47 *Summa theologiae*, III^a 60, 6, and 7; 62, 1, 2 and 4 (ibid., lvi, 20–9,
50–9, 60–5).

48 Smalley, *Study of the Bible*, pp. 295–6, 303–8, 329–55.

49 Hence, St Albert the Great could say that in matters of faith and morals
one should follow Augustine rather than any philosopher, when both are
in disagreement. But in medical matters, he preferred to follow Galen or
Hippocrates, and in natural science, Aristotle or some such expert. See
Chenu, *Toward understanding St Thomas.* p. 43.

50 Smalley, *Study of the Bible*, pp. 346–55; H. Hailperin, *Rashi and the
Christian Scholars* (Pittsburg, 1963), pp. 103–5.

51 Smalley, *Study of the Bible*, pp. 346–7.

52 Ed. B. P. Shields, *A Critical Edition of Selections from Nicholas Trevet's
Commentarius literalis in Psalterium iuxta Hebreos S. Hieronymi* (Ph.D.
thesis, Rutgers, 1970), pp. 57–9; also pr. as an appendix by R. J. Dean,
The Life and Works of Nicholas Trevet (unpub. D.Phil. thesis, Oxford,
1948), pp. 103–5.

53 In his Psalter-commentary itself (Stegmüller, *Bibl.*, 6038), Trevet ex-
pands on his theory of 'literal sense' and 'primary intention' by stating
that, when certain psalms refer parabolically to Christ, the words are
spoken of Christ according to the 'primary intention': see the exegesis of
Psalm xix (ed. Shields, pp. 40–1, cf. pp. 36–7). This may be a conflation
of two ideas of Aquinas's: many psalms refer literally to Christ; the
parabolic and metaphoric sense of Scripture is a facet of the literal sense.
Aquinas's Psalter-exegesis is discussed above, pp. 86–90.

54 Hailperin, *Rashi and the Christian Scholars,* pp. 137–246.

55 Prologus secundus de intentione auctoris et modo procedendi (pr. *Biblia
glossata,* i, unfol.).

56 *In psalmos Davidis expositio,* prologus (*Aquinatis opera,* xiv, 149). Stegmül-
    ler, *Bibl.,* 8028.

57 Ibid., pp. 149–50; cf. pp. 179, 217, 309, etc.

58 Ibid., pp. 149–50; cf. the *Glossa ordinaria,* in *PL,* cxiii, 843–4.

59 Ibid., p. 148. The Scriptural modes are discussed above, pp. 124 *et seq.*

60 See, especially, Trevet's exposition of Psalm i (ed. Shields, pp. 88–9). In
    his list of the 'ten things required', Cossey included the *nomen inter-
    pretatoris* and the *modus legendi:* Cambridge, Christ's College, MS 11, fols
    5ᵛ–6ʳ. Cossey's Psalter-glosses are heavily dependent on those of Lyre and
    Trevet, whom he cites by name: e.g., his account of the *nomen inter-
    pretatoris* is a paraphrase of Trevet's.

61 *In psalm. David. exposit.,* prologus (*Aquinatis opera,* xiv, 149); cf. Com-
    ment. in Ps. xxi (ibid., p. 217). According to R. A. Greer, Theodore
    firmly believed that the Old Law foreshadowed Christ, but his sense of
    history encouraged him to reduce the amount of allegorical interpreta-
    tion, to be sparing in his figural interpretation of the Psalter and other
    works: *Theodore of Mopsuestia, Exegete and Theologian* (London, 1961), pp.
    107–110.

62 *Aquinatis opera,* xiv, 149.

63 Ibid. This approach was adopted by Trevet. Citing Maimonides, he ex-
    plains that, in parables, certain words are always inserted or omitted, so
    that we may see (as through a kind of gate) what is hidden in the parable,
    i.e. its Christological significance. See Shields, *Selections from Trevet's
    Comment. lit. in psalterium,* pp. 36–7, 41.

64 E. Auerbach, 'Figura', *Scenes from the Drama of European Literature,* trans.
    R. Manheim and C. Garvin (New York, 1959), pp. 29, 39.

65 *Aquinatis opera,* xiv, 167, 167 (incorrect pagination), 170.

66 Ibid., pp. 179, 344. For full discussion of the latter *historia,* see above,
    pp. 103–9.

67 Ibid., p. 177. By contrast, Trevet provided a literal exposition: Oxford,
    Bodleian Library, MS Bodley 738, fol. 21ᵛ.

68 *Aquinatis opera,* xiv, 214. For Trevet's literal exposition, see MS Bodley
    738, fol. 39ʳ.

69 *Aquinatis opera,* xiv, 300. For Trevet's literal exposition, see MS Bodley
    738, fol. 73ʳ.

70 *PL,* xcxi, 277.

71 *Aquinatis opera,* xiv, 241.

72 Ibid., pp. 148, 150; cf. pp. 163, 194, 260, 315 (for appeal to *affectus*).

73 Ibid., p. 177; cf. pp. 225, 234, 270 (for theory of *persona*).

74 In Ps. xxx (pr. *Opera,* xiv, 250); cf. In Ps. xxxix (p. 300).

75 In Ps. xxxviii (ibid., p. 295).

76 For examples, see In Ps. xli (ibid., p. 309); In Ps. xliii (p. 314); In Ps. xlv (pp. 326–7); In Ps. xlix (p. 339). Cf. the similar comments by two other Psalter-commentators, Hugh of St Cher and Nicholas Gorran, both of whom regarded David as the single *auctor* of the psalms. See, for example, Hugh's glosses on Psalms xl, xli and lxi. (*Hugonis postilla,* ii, 96ʳ, 98ᵛ, 188ᵛ); also, Gorran's glosses on Psalms xl, xli, xlvi, xlviii, xlix (in Oxford, Bodleian Library, MS Bodley 246, fols 71ʳ, 73ʳ, 82ʳ, 85ʳ, 87ʳ).

77 Ed. Shields, *Selections from Trevet's Comm. lit. in psalterium,* p. 72.

78 MS Bodley 738, fol. 76ᵛ.

79 Ibid., fol. 90ᵛ.

80 In Postillam super Psalterium praefatio (pr. *Biblia glossata,* iii, 431–6).

81 In Post. sup. Psalt. praef. (ibid., iii, 431); cf. In Primo psalmo (449–50).

82 *In Metaphysicam,* i, lect. 4, C70 (trans. J. P. Rowan, *St Thomas Aquinas: Commentary on the Metaphysics of Aristotle* (Chicago, 1961), i, 30).

83 *Aquinatis opera,* xiv, 148.

84 In Post. sup. Psalt. praef. (pr. *Biblia glossata,* iii, 432).

85 According to Aquinas, at the lowest level is the material cause, which exists as the matter receiving the effect of the action. The end, agent and form together constitute the principle or beginning of action, but in a certain order. The final cause has precedence, since it moves the agent to act. In his turn, the agent brings the formal cause into being. See *Summa theologiae,* Iᵃ qu.105, art.5, responsio (Blackfriars ed. xiv, 74–9). Applied to literary craftsmanship, the final cause or ultimate objective in writing encourages the writer actually to write; in the process, he implements the formal cause by selecting an appropriate style and by structuring his writing.

86 *Biblia glossata,* iii, 431–2.

87 Prooemii qu.4, conclusio (*Bonaventurae opera,* i, 14–5). Stegmüller, *Sent.,* 111.

88 Prooemium commentarii in sapientiam (ibid., vii, 108). Stegmüller, *Bibl.,* 1774.

89 *In librum sapientiae,* cap.i, lect.2 (pr. *Roberti Holkoth Sapientiae regis Salomonis praelectiones* (Basel, 1586), pp. 6–9). Stegmüller, *Bibl.,* 7416.

90 *Postilla super libros sapientiae,* cap. i (*Biblia Glossata,* iii, 1895). Stegmüller, *Bibl.,* 5870.

91 *Postilla super Ecclesiasticum,* cap.i (*Biblia glossata,* iii, 1081). Stegmüller, *Bibl.,* 5871.

92 *Gloss. ord. sup. sec. lib. Mac.,* cap.i (*Biblia glossata,* iv, 2415); Oxford, Bodleian Library, MS Laud. Misc. 149, fol. 121^v.

93 *Hugonis postilla,* iv, 363^r; *Post. sup. sec. lib. Mac.* (*Biblia glossata,* iv, 2415).

94 For discussion, see A. J. Minnis, 'Late-Medieval Discussions of *Compilatio* and the Role of the *Compilator*', *PBB,* ci (1979), 385–421.

95 *Biblia glossata,* iii, 1895; iv, 2415.

96 In Post. sup. Psalt. praef. (ibid., iii, 431); In Primo ps. (col. 449); *Post. sup. lib. prov.,* cap.i (col. 1607); *Post. sup. lib. 12 prophet.,* praef. (col. 1699).

97 *Post. sup. lib. proverb.,* cap.i (ibid., iii, 1607).

98 See note 24, above.

99 *De natura theologiae,* qu.4 (ed. Stegmüller, pp. 32–4). The process whereby the *Sentences* came to be regarded as a *compilatio* (although the Lombard himself had not described the work as such) is discussed by Minnis in *PBB,* ci, 393–4, 413–6. The change of idiom is well illustrated by the contrast between the prologue to the *Glose super sententias* of Peter of Poitiers and the later expansion of this prologue by an anonymous theologian who, unlike Peter, referred to the *compilatio* and *ordinatio* of the *Sentences.* Several of the anonymous theologian's statements are very reminiscent of Vincent of Beauvais's *apologia* for his *Speculum maius.* For Peter's prologue, see R. M. Martin, 'Notes sur l'oeuvre littéraire de Pierre le Mangeur', *RTAM,* iii (1931), 63–4; the later expansion is cit. Lottin, *Psychologie et morale,* vi, 121–2.

100 See M.-D. Chenu, *La Théologie comme science au XIIIe siècle,* 3 ed. Bibliothèque Thomiste, xxiii (Paris, 1966), pp. 45–57, 71–85; U. Köpf, *Die Anfänge der theologischen Wissenschaftstheorie im 13. Jahrhundert,* Beiträge zur historischen Theologie, xlix (Tübingen, 1974), pp. 145–9.

101 *Bonaventurae opera,* i, 1–15.

102 *Alberti opera,* ed. Borgnet, i, 357–8, 360.

103 Oxford, New College, MS 47, fol. 3^r. Stegmüller, *Bibl.,* 2905.

104 *Summa Ricardi,* fols 2^r–3^v. For discussion, see A. J. Minnis, ' "Authorial Intention" and "Literal Sense" in the Exegetical Theories of Richard FitzRalph and John Wyclif', *Proceedings of the Royal Irish Academy,* lxxv, section C, i (Dublin, 1975).

105 Cf. Chenu, *Toward understanding St Thomas*, p. 140, n. 21; p. 143.

106 *PL,* clxxviii, 1339–49, esp. 1341D–2A.

107 *Summa theologiae* I[a] qu. 77, art. 5, ad 3um (Blackfriars ed., xi, 106); cf. Chenu, *Toward understanding St Thomas*, p. 143.

108 Apologia totius operis, cap.ix (ed. A.-D. v. den Brincken, 'Geschichts-betrachtung bei Vincenz von Beauvais: Die Apologia Actoris zum *Speculum maius', Deutsches Archiv für Erforschung des Mittelalters,* xxxiv (1978), 479; cf. Apologia, cap. viii (ibid., p. 477)).

109 *The Holy Bible by Wycliffe,* ed. Forshall and Madden, i, 56.

110 For this distinction between the 'far cause' and the 'near cause', see, for example, *Works of Chaucer,* ed. Robinson, p. 178.

111 *De doctrina christiana,* iii.21 (ed. Green, pp. 97–9).

112 *De apologia prophetae David; Apologia David altera* (ed. C. Schenkl, CSEL, xxxii, 299–408).

113 *PL,* cxxxi, 397–8.

114 *PL,* xxi, 848D.

115 *PL,* cxci, 483D–4A.

116 *PL,* xciii, 747C–D.

117 *PL,* clxxii, 283.

118 *Postilla super primos xxxviii psalmos Davidicos Thomae Iorgii* (London, 1481), pp. 1–3. Stegmüller, *Bibl.,* 8245.

119 *De legibus,* cap. xvii (pr. *Guilielmi Alverni Episcopi Parisiensis opera omnia* (Venice, 1591), p. 47).

120 *Summa quaestionum,* art. 16, qu.5 (fol. 107[v]).

121 MS Bodley 246, fol. 89[v].

122 *Hugonis postilla,* ii, 118[r].

123 Cf. Hugh of St Cher *(Hugonis postilla,* ii, 43[r]) and Nicholas Gorran (MS Bodley 246, fol. 39[v]). See, further, Trevet's gloss on Psalm xxi, where both the Christian literal interpretation and the Jewish literal interpretation are given. According to the former, this psalm literally refers to Christ; according to the latter, it literally refers to Esther's delivery of the people of Israel from persecution (MS Bodley 738, fol. 40[r]).

124 *Aquinatis opera,* xiv, 344.

125 Ibid., pp. 344–5. Cf. Trevet's gloss (ed. Shields, *Selections from Trevet's Comm. lit. in psalterium,* pp. 121–31).

126 *Aquinatis opera*, xiv, 349.

127 *PL*, cxiii, 920A. Expanded by Hugh of St Cher (*Hugonis postilla*, ii, 120ᵛ), and Gorran (MS Bodley 246, fol. 92ʳ).

128 Aquinas is followed by Trevet (ed. Shields, p. 129).

129 *Biblia glossata*, iii, 805–16.

130 Prologus N. de Lyra in moralitates Biblorum (ibid., i, unfol.).

131 Cf. E. A. Gosselin, *The King's Progress to Jerusalem: Some Interpretations of David during the Reformation Period and their Patristic and Medieval Background*, Humana Civilitas, ii (Malibu, 1976), pp. 28–9.

132 *Biblia glossata*, iii, 483–90.

133 Ibid. Cf. Gosselin, *The King's Progress to Jerusalem*, p. 30.

134 *PL*, clv, 1675–8.

135 Prooemium commentarii in Ecclesiasten, qu. 4 (*Bonaventurae opera*, vi, 8). Stegmüller, *Bibl.*, 1773.

136 Prooemium, qu. 3 (ibid., p. 8); cf. the *Commentarius in librum Ecclesiastes*, cap. i, qu. 1 (pp. 9–10). This examination was heavily influenced by Gregory the Great, *Dialogorum lib. IV*, iv.4, pr. *PL*, lxxvii, 321–5.

137 Prooemium, qu. 3, solutio oppositi (ibid., p. 8).

138 *In lib. Eccles.*, cap. i, qu. 1 (ibid., pp. 9–10).

139 Ghisalberti, *JWCI*, ix, 10–59. In this context one should also consider the production of lives of the 'modern' Italian poets, including Dante. Boccaccio's life of Dante is discussed above, pp. 216–17.

140 *Polychronicon Ranulphi Higden*, ed. C. Babington and J. R. Lumby, Rolls Series (London, 1865–86), i, 10–12. Cf. the version of this story told by Jerome, *Liber Hebraicarum quaestionum in Genesim*, praef., in *PL*, xxiii 935.

141 For other so-called pagan compilers see Minnis, *PBB*, ci, 420–1.

142 Higden may have derived this description of compiling as gleaning from the prologue to Thomas of Ireland's *Manipulus florum* (1306): for the relevant passage see R. H. and M. A. Rouse, *Preachers, Florilegia and Sermons: Studies on the Manipulus florum of Thomas of Ireland*, Pontifical Institute of Mediaeval Studies, Studies and Texts, xlvii (Toronto, 1979), p. 124; cf. pp. 114–7. A less precise version of the same metaphorical description is used by Chaucer, *The Legend of Good Women*, F Prologue, lines 73–7; cf. G Prologue, lines 61–5 (*Works of Chaucer*, ed. Robinson, p. 484).

143 See Weisheipl, *Med. Stud.*, xxvii, 72–90; Chenu, *La Théologie comme science*, pp. 71–80; Köpf, *Die Anfänge der theologischen Wissenschaftstheorie*,

pp. 37–44; the introduction to *Aquinas: Division and Methods of the Sciences,* trans. A. Maurer, 3 ed. (Toronto, 1963); M. Riquet, 'St Thomas et les *auctoritates* en philosophie', *Archives de philosophie,* iii.2 (1925), 117–55; M.-D. Chenu, 'Les "philosophes" dans la philosophie chrétienne médiévale', *RSPT,* xxvi (1937), 27–40; D. A. Callus, 'The Function of the Philosopher in Thirteenth-Century Oxford', *Miscellanea mediaevalia,* iii (Berlin, 1964), 153–62. See, further, D. E. Sharp, 'The *De ortu scientiarum* of Robert Kilwardby', *New Schol.,* viii (1934), 1–30, esp. pp. 5–6; *Robert Kilwardby, De ortu scientiarum,* ed. A. G. Judy, Auctores Britannici Medii Aevi, iv (Oxford, 1976), pp. 9–14.

144 For a convenient summary of the philosophers' supposed errors, see Giles of Rome, *De erroribus philosophorum* (ed. J. Koch (Milwaukee, 1944)). In 1270 and again in 1277, Stephen Tempier, Bishop of Paris, condemned the views on necessity held by such 'Latin Averroists' as Siger of Brabant and Boethius of Dacia. The influence of Aristotle, as interpreted by his Arabian commentators, had encouraged opinions which, according to the intellectual establishment, denied freedom of choice to both God and man. See P. Mandonnet, *Siger de Brabant,* Les philosophes Belges, vi–vii (Louvain, 1908–11), vi, 15–221. For the corresponding condemnations in England, see ibid., pp. 233–44, and D. L. Douie, *Archbishop Pecham* (Oxford, 1952), 272–310.

145 Cit. M. Grabmann, 'I divieti ecclesiastici di Aristotele sotto Innocenzo III e Gregorio IX', in *Miscellanea historiae pontificae,* v.7 (Rome, 1941); cf. G. Leff, *Paris and Oxford Universities in the Thirteenth and Fourteenth Centuries* (New York and London, 1968), pp. 198–9. For refs. to similar statements, see B. Baudoux, 'Philosophia "Ancilla theologiae" ', *Antonianum,* xii (1937), 293–326.

146 See M. Cuervo, 'La Teologia como ciencia y la sistematización teologica según S. Alberto Magno', *Ciencia tomista,* xlvi (1932), 173–99; Aquinas, *Summa theologiae,* Iᵃ 1, 5 (Blackfriars ed., i, 16–19); also 'Appendix 6: Theology as Science' (ibid., pp. 67–87). See, further, Chenu, *La Théologie comme science,* pp. 71–85; Köpf, *Die Anfänge der theologischen Wissenschaftstheorie,* pp. 145–9.

147 Cit. Chenu, *Toward understanding St Thomas,* pp. 138–9.

148 Ibid., p. 139, n. 19.

149 See D. Comparetti, *Vergil in the Middle Ages,* trans. E. F. M. Benecke (London, 1895), esp. pp. 219–31.

150 For the 'good pagan' Trajan, supposed to be the most virtuous of the Roman emperors, see John of Salisbury's *Policraticus,* v.8 (ed. C. C. J. Webb (Oxford, 1909), i, 318); also, R. W. Chambers, 'Long Will, Dante, and the Righteous Heathen', *Essays and Studies,* ix (1923), 50–69; for the virtuous centurion Cornelius, see Holcot, *In lib. sap.,* lect. 155 (Basel ed., p. 516). Cf. John of Wales's attitude to righteous heathen, as

described by W. A. Pantin, 'John of Wales and Medieval Humanism', in *Medieval Studies presented to Aubrey Gwynn* (Dublin, 1961), pp. 297–319.

151 For a clear statement of the late-medieval 'hierarchy of authorities', see Vincent of Beauvais, *Apologia totius operis*, esp. capi xi–xii (ed. v. den Brincken, pp. 482–5). Cf. *Polychronicon Ranulphi*, i, 16–20.

152 See Smalley, 'Sapiential Books III', pp. 267–8; Chenu, in *RSPT*, xxvi, 28–31; Chenu, *Toward understanding St Thomas*, p. 138. In the early fourteenth century, discussion of pagan reason revolved around the thorny issue of what could be known *ex puris naturalibus* (i.e. in purely natural conditions, without the aid of divine grace). Nominalist theologians, like Ockham and Holcot, argued that the virtuous pagan who exploited his natural capacities and 'did what was in him' would be saved in the normal course of events *(de potentia Dei ordinata):* see H. Oberman, *The Harvest of Medieval Theology* (Michigan, 1967), pp. 132–4, 243–8; G. Leff, *William of Ockham* (Manchester, 1975), pp. 493–5.

153 Cf. Smalley, 'Sapiential Books I', pp. 329–37; 'Sapiential Books III', pp. 267–9; 'Sapiential Books IV', p. 115; also, H. Oberman, ' "Facientibus quod in se est Deus non denegat gratiam"': Robert Holcot and the Beginnings of Luther's Theology', *Harvard Theological Review*, lv (1962), 317–42, esp. pp. 317–21.

154 Cf. Chenu, in *RSPT*, xxvi, 28–31, 37.

155 Cf. Smalley, 'Sapiential Books III', pp. 267–8. For William of Auvergne's use of pagan experts in natural science, see Smalley, 'Sapiential Books I', pp. 329–37. For politics and ethics as philosophical disciplines, see Chenu, *RSPT*, xxvi, 32–3. For Bonaventure's use of pagan experts in ethics, see Smalley, 'Sapiential Books II', p. 46; 'Sapiential Books III', pp. 268–9. The 'coming together' of pagan and Christian experts on common subjects is discussed by Miss Smalley throughout her *English Friars and Antiquity*.

156 See Smalley, 'Sapiential Books III', pp. 267–8; 'Sapiential Books IV', pp. 103, 114.

157 See notes 152, 154 and 155 above. The practice of citing pagan *poetae* in commentaries on Sapiential Books was well established by the early fourteenth century: for examples, see Smalley, *English Friars and Antiquity*, pp. 152, 156, 159, 189, 226–7, etc.

158 Smalley, 'Sapiential Books IV', p. 116.

159 See note 154 above.

160 For the concept of 'spoliation', see Quain in *Traditio*, iii, 223–4; de Ghellinck, *Le Mouvement théologique*, pp. 10–16; J. Leclercq, *The Love of Learning and the Desire for God*, trans. C. Misrahi (Fordham, 1961), pp. 55–6.

161 Ed. Delorme, *La France franciscaine*, xvi, 356–7.

162 *In Postillam super Ecclesiasticum*, prologus (*Hugonis postilla*, iii, 153^r).

163 See, for example, Nicholas of Lyre's general prologue to his commentary on the Four Evangelists (*Biblia glossata*, v, unfol.).

164 See, for example, the prologues to Holcot's commentary on Wisdom, discussed above, pp. 178–9.

CHAPTER 4

1   *Expositio in cantica canticorum*, prologus (*PL*, clxxii, 331C).

2   See, for example, Aquinas, *In Metaphysicam*, v, lect.2, C764 (trans. Rowan, i, 305).

3   Tractatus introductorius, quaestio 1 de doctrina theologiae (*Alexandri de Hales Summa theologica* (Quaracchi, 1924–48), i, 1–13). For recent assessments of the importance of this investigation, see Chenu, *La Théologie comme science*, p. 40; Köpf, *Die Anfänge der theologischen Wissenschaftstheorie*, pp. 261–75. The *Summa* ascribed to Alexander is, in fact, a compilation of the work of many theologians, including Alexander's pupil, John of Rochelle, St Bonaventure and William of Middleton: see V. Doucet's prolegomena in the Quaracchi ed. of the *Summa*, iv, pp. xiii–cclxx; also Lottin in *Psychologie et morale*, vi, 207–23. With the entire discussion of *forma tractandi* which follows may now be compared Allen, *Ethical Poetic*, 67–116.

4   Chenu, *La Théologie comme science*, p. 40, n.1.

5   *De natura theologiae*, qu.3 (ed. Stegmüller, pp. 27–9).

6   Ibid., pp. 8, 29, 34; also Kilwardby's *De ortu scientiarum*, cap. xxxv (ed. Judy, pp. 123–4). For Fishacre, see Long's edition of the prologue to his *Sentences* commentary in *Med. Stud.*, xxxiv, 96. Fishacre and Kilwardby were probably influenced by Grosseteste's practice. See D. A. Callus, 'Robert Grosseteste as Scholar', in *Grosseteste: Commemorative Essays*, ed. Callus, pp. 21–2.

7   *Soliloquia*, i.6 (*PL*, xxxii, 875–6).

8   *De spiritu et anima*, cap.i (*PL*, xl, 781–2).

9   For examples, see Köpf, *Die Anfänge der theologischen Wissenschaftstheorie*, pp. 198–205; de Bruyne, *Étud. d'esthét. méd.*, iii, 78–82.

10 Callus, *Grosseteste: Commemorative Essays*, p. 21.

11 Ibid., p. 16.

12 Lottin, *Psychologie et morale*, i, 483–4; cf. de Bruyne, *Étud. d'esthét. méd.*, iii, 78–9, 91.

13 Lottin, *Psychologie et morale*, i, 487.

14 *De bono et malo*, cap.xii (ed. J. R. O'Donnell, *Med. Stud.*, viii (1946), 274–7); Lottin, *Psychologie et morale*, i, 491, 493.

15 Tract. introduct., qu.1, cap.iv, art.1 (*Summa Alexandri*, i, 7–9).

16 Tract. introduct., qu.1, cap.iv, art.2 (ibid., pp. 9–10).

17 See Smalley, *Study of the Bible*, p. 279, n.3; also Callus, *Grosseteste: Commemorative Essays*, p. 22.

18 *De natura theologiae*, qu.3 (ed. Stegmüller, p. 29).

19 Tract. introduct., qu.1, cap.iv, art.1 (*Summa Alexandri*, i, 8).

20 For a recent account, see Köpf, *Die Anfänge der theologischen Wissenschaftstheorie*, pp. 160–86.

21 *De natura theologiae*, qu.3 (ed. Stegmüller, p. 28). Cf. Kilwardby in *De ortu scientiarum*, cap.liv (ed. Judy, pp. 179–81); also, the summary of this account by Sharp, *New Schol.*, viii, 24–5.

22 *De natura theologiae*, qu.3 (ed. Stegmüller, p. 28). Cf. the useful general explanation of the concepts involved by Gilby, *Barbara celarent*, pp. 152–70.

23 *De natura theologiae*, qu.3 (ed. Stegmüller, p. 28); cf. Gilby, *Barbara celarent*, p. 177.

24 *De natura theologiae*, qu.3 (ed. Stegmüller, p. 28); cf. Gilby, *Barbara celarent*, pp. 179–80, 203–6. See, further, M.-D. Chenu, 'Notes de lexicographie philosophie médiévale: *collectio, collatio*', *RSPT*, xvi (1927), 435–46.

25 Cit. from Munich, Clm 4603, by Sandkühler, *Die frühen Dantekommentare*, pp. 37–8.

26 Cit. from Leipzig University Library, MS Lat. 1291, by Grabmann, *Mittelalterliches Geistesleben*, iii, 234.

27 Cit. from Vatican Chigi, MS v.159, by S. Harrison Thomson, *New Schol.*, xii, 63.

28 Cit. Sandkühler, *Die frühen Dantekommentare*, p. 38.

29 Oxford, Magdalen College, MS 154, fol. 1ʳ. Stegmüller, *Bibl.*, 8101.

30 *Principium de commendatione et partitione sacrae Scripturae*, ii.1 (*St Thomae Aquinatis opuscula omnia*, vi, ed. P. Mandonnet (Paris, 1927), 487–8).

31 Tract. introduct., qu.1, cap.iv, art.3 (*Summa Alexandri*, i, 10).

32 Cit. B. Pergamo, 'De quaestionibus ineditis Fr Odonis Rigaldi, Fr Gulielmi de Melitonia et codicis Vat. Lat. 782 circa naturam theologiae deque earum relatione ad Summam theologicam Fr Alexandri Halensis', *AFH*, xxix (1937), 42.

33 Chenu, *La Théologie comme science*, p. 40.

34 For a possible basis for the *modus narrativus*, see Cicero's *De inventione*, I.xix.27 (p. 55); for a possible basis for the *modus laudis*, see *Ad Herennium*, III.vi.10 (pp. 172–5); for a possible basis for the *modus exemplorum suppositivus*, see ibid., IV.xlix.62 (pp. 383–5).

35 For the provinces of demonstrative rhetoric and deliberative rhetoric, respectively, see *De inventione*, I.v.7 (p. 16); II.iii.12 (p. 176); *Ad Herennium*, III.i–v (pp. 157–73); III.vi.10–viii.15 (pp. 172–85); Cassiodorus, *Institutiones*, ii.2 (trans. L. W. Jones, *An Introduction to Divine and Human Readings by Cassiodorus* (New York, 1946), pp. 149–50).

36 For discussion of the subordinate position of rhetoric, see McKeon in *Critics and Criticism*, ed. Crane, pp. 267–71.

37 Cit. Brother S. Robert, 'Rhetoric and Dialectic: According to the First Latin Commentary on the Rhetoric of Aristotle', *New Schol.*, xxxi (1957), p. 488.

38 Ibid., pp. 488–98. See, further, G. Bruni, 'The "De differentiae rhetoricae, ethicae et politicae" of Aegidius Romanus', *New Schol.*, vi (1932), 1–18.

39 See P. W. Nash, 'Giles of Rome and the Subject of Theology', *Med. Stud.*, xviii (1956), 66–7.

40 Tract. introduct., qu.1, cap.iv, art.3 (*Alexandri Summa*, i, 10–11).

41 Prologus S. Bonaventurae in Breviloquium, v: de modo procedendi ipsius sacrae Scripturae (*Bonaventurae opera*, v, 206–7).

42 Dronke, *Fabula*, p. 3, n.1.

43 See E. Gilson, *The Elements of Christian Philosophy* (New York, 1963), pp. 30–7; F. C. Copleston, *Aquinas* (Harmondsworth, 1955), pp. 73–80.

44 *Aquinatis opera*, xiv, 1–2, 148; cf. *S. Thomae Aquinatis opuscula omnia*, vi, ed. Mandonnet, p. 488.

45 See Nash in *Med. Stud.*, xviii, 67–8; cf. E. Gilson, *History of Christian Philosophy in the Middle Ages* (London, 1955), pp. 447–52, 759–62.

46 *Summa quaestionum*, art. 9, qu.2 (fols 71^r–72^r).

47 Cf. Gilson, *History of Christian Philosophy*, pp. 450–2.

48 *Summa quaestionum*, art. 14, de modo tradendi theologiam (fols 99^v–101^v).

49 See Nash in *Med. Stud.*, xviii, 66–7. For the disagreement between Giles of Rome and Henry of Ghent concerning the nature of theology, see ibid., pp. 67–8. The relevant differences between Giles and his former teacher, St Thomas Aquinas, are well summarised in the *Incerti auctoris impugnationes contra Aegidium Romanum contradicentem Thomae super primum*

sententiarum, ed. G. Bruni, Bibliotheca Augustiana medii aevi, ser. 1, Textus theol. et phil., i (Rome, 1942), 6–15. Subsequently, Harvey of Nedellec (who read the *Sentences* 1302–3) criticised Giles's view of theology as affective, claiming that it is basically speculative: cf. *Hervei Natalis in quatuor libris sententiarum commentaria* (Paris, 1647), pp. 10–13. However, Giles had a staunch defender in a later member of his order, Thomas of Strassburg (who read the *Sentences* 1335–7): see the prologue to *Thomae ab Argentina commentaria in IV libros sententiarum* (Venice, 1564).

50   Pr. among the works of Aquinas in the Parma ed., *Aquinatis opera,* xiv, 388. Cf. the discussion in Allen, *Ethical Poetic,* pp. 91–2.

51   Pr. among the works of St Bonaventure in, e.g., *Opera omnia* (Venice, 1751–6), v, 937–8. Stegmüller, *Bibl.,* 4847.

52   *Aquinatis opera,* xiv, 668. Stegmüller, *Bibl.,* 8041.

53   *Latteburius in threnos Ieremiae* (Oxford, 1482), fol. 19^v. Stegmüller, *Bibl.,* 4762.

54   Tract. introduct., qu.1, cap.iv, art.3 (*Alexandri Summa,* i, 10–11).

55   *Summa theologiae,* I^a 1, 10, ad 3um (Blackfriars ed., i, 41).

56   In Ps. xvi.9–10 (cit. Shields, *Selections from Trevet's Comment. lit. in Psalterium,* p. 36); cf. In Ps. xix (cit. ibid., p. 41). Shields discusses a few aspects of St Thomas's influence on Trevet on pp. 28–31.

57   Attributed to Robert Holcot or Thomas Waleys, *In proverbia Salomonis* (Paris, 1515), fol. 3^r. Stegmüller, *Bibl.,* 8172.

58   *Expositio in librum B. Iob,* prologus (*Aquinatis opera,* xiv, 1–2).

58   *In Isaiam prophetam expositio,* prooemium S. Thomae (ibid., p. 427).

60   Oxford, Bodleian Library, MS Laud. Misc. 160, fols 1^r–4^r. Stegmüller, *Bibl.,* 2942–53.

61   *Aquinatis opera,* xiii, 2–3, 157, 299, 382, 443, 505, 530, 556, 573, 585, 621, 644, 661, 666–7; for Docking, see Magdalen College, MS 154, fol. 1^r. For Peter of Tarantasia, see the commentaries falsely attributed to Nicholas Gorran, *In omnes D. Pauli ep. elucid.,* pp. 1–9, 140, 235, 250, 368, 412, 443, 472, 498–9, 515, 548–9, 573, 587, 592.

62   *Postilla super libros Salomonis,* praefatio (*Biblia glossata,* iii, 1606).

63   *Commentarius in librum Ecclesiastes,* cap.i, qu.1–5 (*Bonaventurae opera,* vi, 9–10). Stegmüller, *Bibl.,* 1773.

64   *Prologus in Apocalypsim B. Joannis Apostoli* (pr. *Alberti opera,* ed. Borgnet, xxxviii, 469). Stegmüller, *Bibl.,* 1040.

65   *Praefatio in threnos Jeremiae* (*Alberti opera,* xviii, 244). The commentator is elaborating on Gilbert the Universal's gloss: see above, pp. 238–9, n. 53.

66   Shields, *Selections from Trevet's Comment. lit. in Psalterium*, pp. 71, 77.

67   Ibid., pp. 68–9, 74.

68   Pr. among the works of Aquinas in the Parma ed., *Aquinatis opera*, xiv, 387.

69   *Didascalicon*, iv.2 (ed. Buttimer, pp. 71–2); Spicq, *Esquisse*, pp. 147–8.

70   For general discussion of these lectures, see Weisheipl, *Friar Thomas d'Aquino*, pp. 71–2, 99–104; also B. Smalley, 'Wyclif's *Postilla* on the Old Testament and his *Principium*', *Oxford Studies presented to D. Callus*, Oxford Historical Society, New Series, xvi (Oxford, 1964), 253–96.

71   Ed. Delorme, *La France franciscaine*, xvi, 351–60.

72   *Principium de commendatione et partitione sacrae Scripturae*, ii.1 (pr. *Aquinatis opuscula*, vi, 487–8).

73   Cf. Smalley in *Oxford Studies presented to D. Callus*, p. 253.

74   *Petri Aurioli compendium Biblie totius* (unloc., 1514), pars iii, unfol. Stegmüller, *Bibl.*, 6422.

75   *Accessus ad auctores, etc.*, ed. Huygens, pp. 62–3.

76   *T. Aquinatis opera omnia*, ed. S. E. Frette, apud L. Vivès (Paris, 1871–80), xxxi, 196. Cf. Spicq, *Esquisse*, pp. 245–9.

77   *Moralia in Job*, praefatio (*PL*, lxxv, 513).

78   *Forma praedicandi*, prologus (ed. Th.-M. Charland, *Artes praedicandi*, Publications de l'Institut d'Études Médiévales d'Ottawa, vii (Paris and Ottawa, 1936), 235; trans. L. Krul in *Three Medieval Rhetorical Arts*, ed. J. J. Murphy (Berkeley, 1971), p. 116).

79   Cap.i (Krul, p. 120).

80   Cf. Chenu, *Toward understanding St Thomas*, pp. 39–50, 58–69; W. A. Hinnebusch, *The History of the Dominican Order* (New York, 1966–73), ii, 231–80.

81   For discussion of the way in which scholastic training prepared preachers for their evangelical mission, see Smalley, *Study of the Bible*, pp. 254–7; Rouse, *Preachers, Florilegia and Sermons*, pp. 43–90; R. H. Rouse, '*Statim invenire*: Schools, Preachers, and New Attitudes to the Page', forthcoming in *The Renaissance of the Twelfth Century*, ed. R. Benson and G. Constable; D. d'Avray, *The Transformation of the Medieval Sermon* (unpub. D.Phil. thesis, Oxford, 1976), pp. 77–80, and also his recent book *The Preaching of the Friars* (Oxford, 1985), esp. pp. 132–203.

82   Trans. G. R. Owst, *Preaching in Medieval England* (Cambridge, 1926), p. 333; Latin text in Charland, *Artes praedicandi*, p. 365. See further the entire chapter in which this passage occurs (ibid., pp. 357–68), in which Waleys discusses the *modus narrativus* and the *modus argumentativus* as used

in sermons, and stresses that the end of preaching is not only to inform the *intellectus* but also to move the *affectus*. Hence, the preacher should avoid syllogistic argument, because this is a scholastic and scientific mode of procedure. Cf. the *Ars concionandi* printed among the works of St Bonaventure, where the preacher is warned against using technical syllogistic argument in sermons which must appeal to a wide audience, including simple people: *Ars concionandi*, pars iii (*Bonaventurae opera*, ix, 18). Cf. also Basevorn's remark that in Christ's preaching no necessary subtlety or appeal to the emotions was lacking: *Forma praedicandi*, cap.viii (trans. Krul, p. 129). See further the medieval introductions to *exempla*-collections, in which the affective appeal and mnemonic power of *exempla* are identified as the bases of their usefulness in preaching: e.g., the prologues to the *Alphabetum narrationum* and *Speculum exemplorum*, both cit. T. F. Crane, *The Exempla or illustrative stories from the Sermones vulgares of Jacques de Vitry*, Folk-Lore Society (London, 1890), pp. xx–xxi.

83 Tract. introduct., qu. 1, cap.iv, art. 3 (*Alexandri Summa*, i, 11). On the *ad status* genre of sermons, see Crane, *Exempla of de Vitry*, pp. xi–xlvi, lxxiv, xc; Owst, *Preaching in Medieval England*, pp. 247–65, 304; d'Avray, *The Medieval Sermon*, pp. 134–211.

84 This general principle of suiting the style to the capacities of one's audience, which may be traced back to Ciceronian rhetoric, was fully articulated in the section on preaching in Augustine's *De doctrina christiana*, iv.7, 12, 17 (ed. Green, pp. 124–33, 137–8, 143). It became a commonplace of *artes praedicandi* and *exempla*-collections: see, for example, Waleys's *De modo componendi sermones,* cap.i (ed. Charland, pp. 337–8); the prologue to the *Alphabetum narrationum*, cit. Crane, *Exempla of de Vitry*, p. xx.

85 *Forma praedicandi*, cap.viii (trans. Krul, pp. 128–9); cf. Basevorn's description of St Paul's preaching-technique, cap.ix (ibid., pp. 129–30).

86 In I P. Summae theologiae, tract. 1, qu. 5, mem. 2 (*Alberti opera*, ed. Borgnet, xxxi, 23–4).

87 *Summa theologiae*, I^a 1, 9, ad 1um (Blackfriars ed., i, 34–5).

88 I, tr. 2, cap.ix de multis specialibus modis theologie (ed. J. Daguillon, *Ulrich de Strasbourg O.P., La Summa de bono, livre i,* Bibliothèque Thomiste, xii (Paris, 1930), pp. 36–7).

89 I, tr. 2, cap.ix de multis specialibus modis theologie (ibid., pp. 51–5).

90 My revised translation here is indebted to Peter Dronke, *Dante and Medieval Latin Traditions* (Cambridge, 1986), p. 127 n. Cf. the discussions of Aquinas, Petrarch, and Boccaccio cit. on p. 217 above.

91 Lib.I, tract. 2, cap.ix (ed. Daguillon, p. 52).

92 Cf. Albert's commentaries on the works of Pseudo-Dionysius, ed. Borgnet, *Alberti opera*, xiv. See, further, Alexander of Hales's citation of

Pseudo-Dionysius, Tract. introduct., qu. 1, cap. iv, art. 1 (*Alexandri summa*, p. 8); Boccaccio, *De genealogie deorum gentilium libri*, xiv. 18 (ed. V. Romano (Bari, 1951), p. 737); also, H. F. Dondaine, *Le Corpus Dionysien de l'Université de Paris au XIIIe siècle* (Rome, 1953).

93 For Al-Farabi's views, see J. J. Murphy, *Rhetoric in the Middle Ages* (Berkeley, 1974), pp. 91–2. Averroes, as translated by Hermann the German, stated that 'sermones poetici sunt ymaginativi' and that the art of poetry seeks the level of pleasure which moves an audience to virtue through stimulation of the imagination: *Averrois Corubensis commentarium medium in Aristoteles poetriam*, ed. W. F. Boggess (unpub. Ph.D. thesis, University of N. Carolina, 1965), pp. 3, 41, 43, etc. For Avicenna's definition of poetry as 'imaginative speech', see *Avicenna's commentary on the poetics of Aristotle*, ed. I. M. Dahiyat (Leiden, 1974), pp. 31–58, 61–4.

94 W. F. Boggess, 'Aristotle's *Poetics* in the Fourteenth Century', *SP*, lxvii (1970), 278–94, esp. 'Appendix A', p. 284. See, further, O. B. Hardison, 'The Place of Averroes' Commentary on the *Poetics* in the History of Medieval Criticism', *Medieval and Renaissance Studies 4*, ed. J. L. Lievsay (Duke Univ. Press, 1970), pp. 57–81; J. B. Allen, 'Hermann the German's Averroistic Aristotle and Medieval Literary Theory', *Mosaic*, ix (1976), 67–81. The significance of Hermann's translation is brought out well in Allen's *Ethical Poetic*. A modern translation of the Arabic text has recently been published by Charles E. Butterworth, *Averroes' Middle Commentary on Aristotle's 'Poetics'* (Princeton, 1986).

95 See Boggess, *SP*, lxvii, 278–94, esp. 'Appendices C–E' on pp. 285–90.

96 *Fulgentius metaforalis*, ed. H. Liebeschütz (Leipzig, 1926), pp. 65–6.

97 For examples, see Smalley, *English Friars and Antiquity*, pp. 152, 156, 159, 189, 226–7, etc.

98 *Petrus Berchorius, Reductorium morale, liber xv: Ovidius moralizatus, cap. i: De formis figurisque deorum*, ed. J. Engels (Utrecht, 1966), pp. 2–3. Cf. the similar use of the fable of the trees choosing a king by Boccaccio, *Genealogie deorum gent.*, xiv. 9; xv. 8 (ed. Romano, pp. 707, 769).

99 *Contra mendacium*, xiii. 28 (ed. I. Zycha, CSEL, xli (1900), 511); cf. *Flores omnium pene doctorum collecti per Thomam Hibernicum*, s.v. *fabula* (Lyon, 1555), p. 406. For discussion of this compilation, see Rouse, *Preachers, Florilegia and Sermons*.

100 Alan of Lille had said that an authority 'has a wax nose, which means that it can be bent into taking on different meanings': *PL*, ccx, 333 l; cf. Chenu, *Toward understanding St Thomas*, pp. 144–5.

101 For an account of these commentators, and bibliography, see A. J. Minnis, 'Aspects of the Medieval French and English Traditions of Boethius's *De consolatione philosophiae*', in *Boethius: His Life, Thought and Influence*, ed. M. T. Gibson (Oxford, 1981), pp. 312–61.

102 See Jourdain, *Not. et extr.*, xx.2 (1862), 40–82.

103 Cf. Allen, *The Friar as Critic*, pp. 5, 68–9; D. K. Bolton, *Manuscripts and Commentaries on Boethius, De consolatione philosophiae in England in the Middle Ages* (unpub. B. Litt. thesis, Oxford, 1965), pp. 213–4, 267–8.

104 *Comment. in Boet. de cons. phil.*, iv, met. 7, which I studied in a typescript of the (unfinished) edition of Trevet's commentary by the late E. T. Silk, kindly supplied by Professor Silk.

105 *Comment. in Boet. de cons. phil.*, i, pr.3 (Cambridge, University Library, MS Ii.3.21, part 2, fol. 17^r). For discussion of this story as told by William, see my article in *Boethius: His Life, Thought and Influence*, ed. Gibson, p. 324.

106 For discussion, see Minnis in *Proc. Royal Irish Acad.*, lxxv, sect.C, 1, pp. 13–14, 25–7.

107 J. T. Welter, *L'Exemplum dans la littérature religieuse et didactique du moyen âge* (Paris and Toulouse, 1927), p. 449, n. 62; G. R. Owst, *Preaching in Medieval England*, pp. 80–5, 236, 241; Owst, *Literature and Pulpit in Medieval England*, 2 ed (Oxford, 1961), p. 207.

108 For an instance of a congregation rejecting a preacher's use of fables see Owst, *Literature and Pulpit*, p. 179.

109 See B. Smalley, 'John Baconthorpe's Postill on St Matthew', *MARS*, iv (1958), 110–14.

110 Curtius, *European Literature*, p. 224.

111 *Dantis Alagherii epistolae*, ed. P. Toynbee, 2 ed. by C. Hardie (Oxford, 1966), p. 175.

112 Cit. from a Lamentations-commentary attributed to St Albert the Great, by Spicq, *Esquisse*, p. 212. With the entire discussion of *forma tractatus* which follows may now be compared Allen, *Ethical Poetic*, pp. 117–78.

113 See Rouse, *Preachers, Florilegia and Sermons*, esp. pp. 7–42, 65–90; Rouse, '*Statim invenire*', forthcoming in *The Renaissance of the Twelfth Century*, ed. Benson and Constable; Minnis, in *PBB*, ci, 385–421; R. H. and M. A. Rouse, 'The Texts called *Lumen anime*', *AFP*, xli (1971), 5–113; M. B. Parkes, 'The Influence of the Concepts of *Ordinatio* and *Compilatio* on the Development of the Book', *Medieval Learning and Literature: Essays presented to R. W. Hunt*, ed. J. J. G. Alexander and M. T. Gibson (Oxford, 1975), esp. pp. 115–35; R. Rouse, 'La Diffusion en occident au XIIIe siècle des outils de travail facilitant l'accès aux textes autoritatifs', *Revue des études islamiques*, xliv (1976), 115–47; d'Avray, *The Medieval Sermon*, pp. 92–110.

114 For general discussion, see Chenu, *La Théologie comme science*, pp. 71–85; Köpf, *Die Anfänge der theologischen Wissenschaftstheorie*, pp. 145–9, 168–71; 'Appendix 6: Theology as Science', in the Blackfriars ed. of St

Thomas's *Summa theologiae*, i, 67–87, esp. pp. 73–4; also, the introduction by Maurer to *Aquinas: The Division and Methods of the Sciences*, pp. vii–xxxix.

115 Prooemium in lib. I sent., qu.2, conclusio, iv (*Bonaventurae opera*, i, 11).

116 *Summa theologiae*, I^a 1, 2 (Blackfriars ed., i, 10–13).

117 In lib. i, lect.2, 41–2 (trans. Rowan, i, 19).

118 *In lib. ethicorum*, lect.1, i.1 (trans. C. I. Litzinger, *St Thomas Aquinas: Commentary on the Nicomachean Ethics* (Chicago, 1964), i, 6).

119 Cit. Grabmann, *Mittelalterliches Geistesleben*, iii, 24. On this use of terminology, see J. Pinborg, *Die Entwicklung der Sprachtheorie im Mittelalters*, Beiträge zur Geschichte der Philosophie und Theologie des Mittelalters, xlii (1967), 25. For the date of this commentary, and convincing evidence that it is not the work of Jordan of Saxony, see Gauthier in *RSPT*, lxvi (1982), 367–73.

120 For Kilwardby's early career, see Judy's introduction to his ed. of *De ortu scientiarum*, pp. xi–xvii; also E. M. F. Sommer-Seckendorff, *Studies in the Life of Robert Kilwardby, O.P.*, Institutum historicum FF. Praedicatorum, Dissertationes historicae, viii (1937).

121 Cit. from Vatican Chigi MS v.159 by Thomson, *New Schol.*, xii, 63.

122 See the extract from Kilwardby's *Notule super Priscianum minorem* cit. Hunt, 'Introductions to the *Artes*', p. 107, n.2. Elias Brunetti employed similar terminology in his commentary on Aristotle's *Topica:* see Grabmann, *Mittelalterliches Geistesleben*, iii, 147.

123 Cit. from Munich, Clm 14460 by Sandkühler, *Die frühen Dantekommentare*, p. 41.

124 Cit. Rouse, '*Statim invenire*', forthcoming in *The Renaissance of the Twelfth Century*, ed. Benson and Constable.

125 *Hugonis postilla*, iii, 2^r.

126 *Bonaventurae opera*, vii, 6.

127 Ibid., vi, 242.

128 Pr. in the Parma ed. of *Aquinatis opera*, xiv, 388. I have supplied the correct terms from the *apparatus criticus*.

129 *Summa quaestionum*, art.14 de modo tradendi theologiam (fol. 99^v).

130 See the prologue to his commentary on the Psalter (*Biblia glossata*, iii, 432), the general prologue to the Sapiential Books (ibid., 1606) and the general prologue to the commentary on the Four Evangelists (ibid., v, unfol.).

131 In Prolog. sent. divisio (*Durand de St-Pourçain, In sententias theologicas Petri Lombardi* (Venice, 1571), fol. 2^r); In prolog. sent. divisio (*Thomae ab Argentina commentaria*, fol. 5^r).

132 B. Smalley, 'The Bible in the Medieval Schools', in *The Cambridge History of the Bible, vol.ii: The West from the Fathers to the Reformation*, ed. G. W. H. Lampe (Cambridge, 1969), p. 210.

133 Ed. Lewry, *Kilwardby's Writings on the Logica vetus*, p. 371. For other examples, see Lottin, 'Deux commentaires sur l'*Ethica vetus* des environs de 1230–1240', in *Psychologie et morale*, vi, 232. The formulae used by different commentators in subdividing their authoritative texts could be very distinctive: see esp. the excellent description of St Thomas's idiom of *divisio textus* in A. Dondaine and L. J. Bataillon, 'Le Commentaire de S. Thomas sur les Météores', *AFP*, xxxvi (1966), 110–17.

134 Smalley, *Cambridge History of the Bible, ii*, 210.

135 *Hugonis postilla*, iii, 2ʳ.

136 *Hugonis Cardinalis opera omnia in universum Vetus et Novum Testamentum* (Venice, 1754), iv, fol. 2ʳ. Stegmüller, *Bibl.*, 3688. Cf. the similar means of defending the Psalter employed by Letbert of Lille: 'ut cum ordo rerum, aut ordo temporum iuxta literam non tenetur, alter ordo subtilior iuxta spiritualem intelligentiam requiratur' (*PL*, xxi, 644D–5A).

137 *In Isaiam prophetam expositio*, prooemium (*Aquinatis opera*, xiv, 427).

138 *In Is. prophet.*, cap.i (ibid., p. 430).

139 *PL*, clxvii, 1182.

140 *PL*, cxci, 56B–7A.

141 *Selections from Trevet's Comment. lit. in psalterium*, ed. Shields, pp. 71–2.

142 In Ps. i (*Biblia glossata*, iii, 449–50).

143 Parkes, in *Medieval Learning and Literature*, ed. Alexander and Gibson, p. 115.

144 See C. Lambot, 'Lettre inédite de S. Augustin relative au *De civitate Dei*', *Rev. bén.*, li (1939), 109–121; cf. Parkes, in *Medieval Learning and Literature*, ed. Alexander and Gibson, pp. 124–5.

145 See Rouse, *AFP*, xliv (1974), 5–30.

146 See I. Brady, 'The Rubrics of Peter Lombard's *Sentences*', *Pier Lombardo*, vi (1962), 5–25; also I. Brady, 'The "Distinctions" of Lombard's *Book of Sentences* and Alexander of Hales', *Fran. Stud.*, xxv (1965), 90–116. The greater ease of reference obtained by such division is mentioned by Roland of Cremona in the prologue to his *Sentences* commentary: 'In unoquoque autem volumine capitulorum distinctiones et quaestionum prolixarum, non minutarum, descripsimus, ut quid velint sine difficultate et in quo loco inveniat'. Cit. Doucet in *Miscell. Lombard.*, p. 287. On the relatively late date of this recension of Roland's commentary, see ibid.; also Lottin, *Psychologie et morale*, vi, 171–80.

147 For relevant refs. see Minnis, *PBB*, ci, 385–6; also, the Bibliography, under R. W. Hunt and D. A. Callus.

148 Cf. Parkes, in *Medieval Learning and Literature*, ed. Alexander and Gibson, pp. 123–4.

149 Even more vociferous was Dionysius the Carthusian (1402–71), who remarked that the manifold divisions which some commentators prefix to texts are seen to obscure rather than to elucidate the sense of the words: see *Enarrationes in lib.i de consolatione philosophiae*, met.i, art.3 (*D. Dionysii Cartusiani opera omnia* (Tournai, 1906), xxvi, 22).

150 Oxford, Bodleian Library, MS Rawl. G. 186, fol. 1^r; cf. Dean, *Life and Works of Trevet*, p. 212.

151 See the prologue to Waleys's commentary, pr. *Thome Valois et Nicholai Triveth in libros B. Augustini de civitate Dei commentaria* (Toulouse, 1488), unfol.

152 For Trevet's use of Kilwardby's *Intentiones*, see Smalley, *English Friars and Antiquity*, p. 62; for Waleys's own description of his use of them, see the prologue to his commentary on *De civitate Dei*, pr. in the 1488 edition.

153 See D. A. Callus, 'The "Tabula super originalia patrum" of Robert Kilwardby O. P.', *Stud. med. in hon. Martin*, pp. 243–4.

154 Cit. ibid., p. 255.

155 Cf. Parkes, in *Medieval Learning and Literature*, ed. Alexander and Gibson, pp. 128–9.

156 Ibid., p. 129.

157 See the entry 'Vincent of Beauvais' in *The Oxford Dictionary of the Christian Church*, 2 ed., ed. F. L. Cross and E. A. Livingstone (Oxford, 1974), p. 1441.

158 Cf. Minnis, *PBB*, ci, 394–5, 398, 404.

159 *De proprietatibus rerum fratris Bartholomei anglici*, prohemium (Lyon, 1481), unfol.

160 *Reductorium morale Petri Berchorii Pictaviensis* (Venice, 1583), p. 2.

161 *Li Livres dou Tresor de Brunetto Latini*, ed. F. J. Carmody (Berkeley, 1948), p. 17.

162 *Anecdotes historiques, légendes et apologues tirés du recueil inédit d'Étienne de Bourbon*, ed. A. Lecoy de la Marche, Société de l'histoire de France (Paris, 1877), pp. 9–10.

163 *Philobiblon*, ed. MacLagan, p. 93.

164 Cit. Hinnebusch, *History of the Dominican Order*, ii, 231.

165 Supplementum, qu.96, art.11, ad 5um (*S. Thomae Aquinatis summa theologiae,* Iterata editio (Madrid, 1955–8), v, 589).

166 See Rouse, '*Statim invenire*', forth. in *The Renaissance of the Twelfth Century,* ed. Benson and Constable; cf. Smalley, *Study of the Bible,* p. 226 and n.4.

167 See J. de Ghellinck, ' "Originale" and "originalia" ', *Bull. du Cange,* xvi (1939), 104–5; cf. Chenu, *Toward understanding St Thomas,* pp. 47, 48, 129, 131, 152. This insistence on knowledge of the total context is an extension of one of the recommendations made by Peter Abelard in the prologue to his *Sic et non: PL,* clxxviii, 1341–3. It is probably related to developments in grammar and in the new 'terminist' logic: see De Rijk, *Logica modernorum,* ii.1, 113–7. Similarly, in their exegeses of Scripture, Aquinas and his contemporaries insisted on the importance of careful examination of the context, of the 'circumstances of the letter' (*circumstantia litterae*) for establishing the correct literal sense of a passage and the true intention of its *auctor:* Chenu, *Toward understanding St Thomas,* p. 144; Spicq, *Esquisse,* pp. 250–1.

168 See Brady, *Pier Lombardo,* vi, 11–12.

169 *Gerhoch of Reichersberg: Letter to Pope Hadrian about the Novelties of the Day,* ed. N. M. Häring (Toronto, 1974), p. 12.

170 See Weisheipl, *Friar Thomas d'Aquino,* pp. 73–4.

171 Apologia totius operis, cap.i (ed. v. den Brincken, pp. 465–6).

172 Apologia, cap.iii (ibid., p. 468).

173 For the contrast between authorial statements and magisterial statements, see Chenu, *Toward understanding St Thomas,* pp. 134–7.

174 *Communiloquium* (Lyon, 1511), fol. 3^r, cit. Minnis, *PBB,* ci, 402.

175 Cf. note 153 above.

176 For Holcot's comment, see above, p. 96; for Waleys's, see the prologue to the 1488 ed. of *T. Valois et N. Triveth in lib. Aug. de civ. Dei comment.,* unfol.

177 For Abelard, see above, pp. 59–60. According to twelfth-century commentators, Gratian had intended to collect together diverse laws and harmonise them: the Canon lawyers conceived of a process of exposition and reconciliation of differences between laws. This explains the original title of what came to be known as the *Decretum,* namely, *Concordantia discordantium canonum.* See Minnis, *PBB,* ci, 397–8.

178 Apologia totius operis, capi xi–xii (ed. v. den Brincken, pp. 482–5).

179 Apologia, capi viii, ix (ibid., pp. 477–8). For discussion of the distinction between 'asserting' and 'reporting', see Minnis, *PBB,* ci, 389, 409–10, 419; also above, pp. 100–12, 193–6.

180 Apologia, cap.viii (ed. v. den Brincken, p. 477).

CHAPTER 5

1   Cf. Smalley, *English Friars and Antiquity*, pp. 58–60, 88–90; cf. pp. 110–21.

2   For Trevet's Livy-commentary, see R. J. Dean, 'The Earliest Medieval Commentary on Livy', *Med. et hum.*, iii (1945), 86–98; iv (1946), 110. For refs. to modern editions of Trevet's commentaries on Seneca's tragedies, see the Bibliography.

3   For the *auctores octo*, widely used on the continent until 1500, see N. Orme, *English Schools in the Middle Ages* (London, 1973), pp. 103–4. See, further, G. L. Hamilton, 'Theodulus, a Medieval Textbook', *MP*, vii (1909), 1–17; R. Hazelton, 'The Christianization of Cato', *Med. Stud.*, xix (1957), 157–73. For English 'teaching collections', see Orme, *English Schools*, pp. 104–6; E. Rickert, 'Chaucer at School', *MP*, xxix (1931/2), 257–74.

4   For refs. see Ghisalberti, 'Giovanni del Virgilio espositore delle "Metamorfosi" ', *Il Giornale Dantesco*, xxxiv, n.s. iv (1933), 1–110; Smalley, *English Friars and Antiquity*, pp. 58–60; Sandkühler, *Die frühen Dantekommentare*.

5   Ed. Charland, *Artes praedicandi*, pp. 233–5. By contrast, the writers of *artes poeticae*, while certainly aware of the schema of the four causes, made trivial use of it or ignored it. See esp. John of Garland's eccentric interpretation of the material cause, in *The Parisiana poetria of John of Garland*, ed. T. Lawlor (New Haven and London, 1974), pp. 28–31.

6   Apologia totius operis, capi i–iv, xvi–xvii (ed. v. den Brincken, pp. 465–70, 490–3).

7   Lib.I, tract.i, cap.i (ed. Daguillon, pp. 5–6).

8   *Reductorium morale*, prologus (p. 1).

9   Pr. by P. Meyer in *Romania*, viii (1879), 328–332; cf. Allen in *The Romanic Review*, viii, 434–62.

10   *The Works of Geoffrey Chaucer, vol. vii: Chaucerian and other pieces*, ed. W. W. Skeat (Oxford, 1897), pp. 2–3.

11   Ibid., p. 49.

12   *Bokenham's Legendys of Hooly Wummen*, ed. M. S. Serjeantson, EETS (OS) ccvi (Oxford, 1938), p. 1.

13   For the information about Bokenham's life which is found in his writings see Serjeantson's introduction, ibid., pp. xiii–xviii.

14   But not all fifteenth-century academic prologues are pedestrian: see the very sophisticated prologues of Reginald Pecock, in *Reginald Pecock's*

Donet, ed. E. V. Hitchcock, EETS (OS) clvi (Oxford, 1918), 1–8; *Pecock's Folewer to the Donet,* ed. E. V. Hitchcock, EETS (OS) clxiv (Oxford, 1923), 1–6; *Pecock's Reule of Cristen Religioun,* ed. W. C. Greet, EETS (OS) clxxi (Oxford, 1926), 1–30, esp. pp. 9–22, 29. See further the Messenger's introductory speech in *Everyman,* which includes brief statements concerning the *titulus* (lines 4–6), *materia* (lines 7, 16–20) and *intentio* (lines 8–15) of this morality play: *Everyman,* ed. A. C. Cawley (Manchester, 1961), p. 1.

15   Cf. Ghisalberti, JWCI, ix, 10–59. For the suggestion that the *Vita Vergilii* by Donatus influenced Boccaccio's *vita* of Dante see G. Billanovich, *Petrarca litterato, i: Lo scrittoio del Petrarca,* Storia e letteratura, xvi (Rome, 1947), p. 76.

16   *Guido da Pisa's Expositiones,* ed. Cioffari, pp. xxi–xl.

17   Smalley, *English Friars and Antiquity,* pp. 141–2, 214–5, 222–3.

18   On the popularity of this commentary, see Smalley, *Study of the Bible,* pp. 274–5; 'Sapiential Books II', p. 41; 'Sapiential Books IV'.

19   K. O. Petersen has argued that Chaucer made use of homiletic material from this commentary in the Nun's Priest's Tale: see her *Sources of the Nonnes Preestes Tale,* Radcliffe College Monographs, x (Boston, 1898), pp. 109ff. R. A. Pratt believes that Holcot provided Chaunticleer and Pertelote with much of their information about dreams: 'Some Latin Sources of the Nonnes Preest on Dreams', *Speculum,* lii (1977), 538–70. W. O. Sypherd has found echoes of Holcot in the *House of Fame: Studies in Chaucer's House of Fame,* Chaucer Society Publications, 2 ser., xxxix (London, 1907), 74–6.

20   For Holcot's view of the 'good pagan', see Smalley, *English Friars and Antiquity,* pp. 185–93; Oberman, *Harvest of Medieval Theology,* pp. 235–48. Many Middle English writers were interested in the fate of virtuous heathen: for a useful survey, see T. G. Hahn, *God's Friends: Virtuous Heathen in Later Medieval Thought and English Literature* (Ph.D. thesis, University of California, Los Angeles, 1974).

21   See H. C. Mainzer, *A Study of the Sources of the Confessio amantis of John Gower* (unpub. D.Phil. thesis, Oxford, 1967), esp. p. 84.

22   *Hoccleve: The Minor Poems,* ed. F. J. Furnivall and I. Gollancz, EETS (ES) lxi and lxxiii (Oxford, repr. 1970), 33.

23   *The Poems and Fables of Robert Henryson,* ed. H. H. Wood, 2 ed. (Edinburgh, 1958). Chaucer made use of Trevet's commentary in his translation of Boethius: see K. O. Petersen, 'Chaucer and Trevet', *PMLA,* xviii (1903), 173–93; B. L. Jefferson, *Chaucer and the Consolation of Philosophy of Boethius* (Princeton, 1917), pp. 9–15; E. T. Silk, *Cambridge Ii.3.21 and the relation of Chaucer's Boethius to Trevet and Jean de Meung* (Ph.D. thesis, Yale, 1930).

24 Cf. Boccaccio's claim that 'our Lord and Saviour' spoke 'often in parable appropriate to the style of comic poet': *Geneal. deor. gent.*, xiv.18 (ed. Romano, pp. 737–8). Chaucer's invocation of Christ in this context has no precedent in Jean de Meun's *Roman de la Rose*, 15135–302 (ed. E. Langlois (Paris, 1914–24), iv, 92–8), an excursus which has many striking parallels with Chaucer's General Prologue to the *Canterbury Tales*.

25 See, for example, Hugh of St Cher's prologue to his commentary on St Matthew's gospel (*Hugonis postilla*, v, 3ʳ), where the traditional symbols for the Four Evangelists are used to explain and justify the differences between their writings. Nicholas of Lyre also used the traditional symbols, in a discussion which emphasises the harmony of the gospels: see his Praefatio in quatuor Evangelistas (*Biblia glossata*, v, unfol.); cf. his Prooemium in Evangelicum Marci (ibid., 473–4), Prooemium super Lucam (663–4), and Prologus super Ioannem (999–1000).

26 *Biblia glossata* v, unfol. Alternatively, Chaucer could have obtained these ideas from a medieval gospel-harmony like Clement of Lanthony's *Unum ex quattuor*. For the Middle English translation of this work, see E. Salter, *Nicholas Love's 'Myrrour of the Blessed Lyf of Jesu Christ'*, Analecta Cartusiana, ix (1974), 76–7. Chaucer's discussion is so general that it is impossible to identify an exact source for it.

27 Ed. T. Wright, *Political Poems and Songs*, Rolls Series (London, 1859–61), i, 25; cf. P. Meyvaert, 'John Erghome and the *Vaticinium Roberti Bridlington*', *Speculum*, xli (1966), 656–64.

28 Ed. G. C. Macaulay, *The Works of John Gower* (London, 1899–1902), ii, 22. All references to the *Confessio amantis* are to this edition. I also employ the trans. by E. W. Stockton in *The Major Latin Works of John Gower* (Seattle, 1962), pp. 49–288.

29 *Works of Gower*, ed. Macaulay, iv, 1.

30 A convenient list of the 'Paris set' of Bible-prologues is provided in N. R. Ker, *Medieval Manuscripts in British Libraries* (Oxford, 1969–), i, 96–7.

31 *An English Fourteenth-Century Apocalypse Version with a Prose Commentary*, ed. E. Fridner, Lund Studies in English, xxix (Lund and Copenhagen, 1961). For the Old French version, see S. Berger, *La Bible française au moyen âge* (Paris, 1884; repr. Geneva, 1967), pp. 87–8.

32 Praefatio Gilberti Pictaviensis in Apocalypsim Ioannis (*Biblia glossata*, vi, 1447–52). The ultimate source of this distinction is book xii of Augustine's *De Genesi ad litteram* (ed. I. Zycha, CSEL, xxviii (1894), 380–9). It was very widely disseminated in the later Middle Ages: see esp. the extensive discussion in J.-P. Torrell, *Théorie de la prophétie et philosophie de*

la conaissance aux environs 1230: La Contribution d'Hughes de Saint-Cher,
Spicilegium Sacrum Lovaniense, Études et documents, xl (Louvain, 1977).

33   Praefatio Gilberti (*Biblia glossata,* vi, 1447–8).

34   For the *nomen scribentis,* see prologus lib.i, lines 19–24; for the *intentio* and *materia* see lines 25–8. The first person to notice the scholastic origins of Gower's prologues in the *Vox clamantis* was Maria Wickert in her *Studien zu John Gower* (Cologne, 1963), pp. 87–109. However, her main interest was in the rhetorical *topoi* found in Gower's prologues, and in how such *topoi* were (in her opinion) altered, and even atrophied, by the writers of religious treatises. My discussion and conclusions are fundamentally different from hers.

35   For example, by Holcot in the prologue to his Wisdom-commentary: see Smalley, *English Friars and Antiquity,* p. 135. For the theologians' practice of hiding their names in the text of the opening lecture, see D. Trapp, 'Augustinian Theology of the Fourteenth Century', *Augustiniana,* vi (1956), 269–72.

36   For example, by Robert of Basevorn in his *Forma praedicandi:* see Charland, *Artes praedicandi,* p. 234.

37   For the influence of medieval theory of satire (including estates satire) on Gower's description of his literary role in the *Vox clamantis,* see Miller, 'John Gower, Satiric Poet', pp. 94–9.

38   See *Vox clamantis,* iii, lines 1247–52 (ibid., iv, 140).

39   Ibid., iv, 3. '*Capitulum*' usually means 'chapter' but here it means 'chapter-summary'. For the development of techniques of chapter-summary, see Callus's discussion of Robert Kilwardby's *capitula* or *intentiones,* in *Stud. med. in hon. Martin,* pp. 243–70. Cf. note 45 below.

40   For this argument, see Macaulay, *Works of Gower,* iv, pp. xxxi–xxxii, lxvii.

41   *Liber de eruditione praedicatorum,* prima pars (in *B. Humberti de Romanis opera de vita regulari,* ed. J. J. Berthier (Rome, 1888–9), ii, 374–5.

42   Causa efficiens duplex est, ipse Deus originaliter et ipse predicans ministraliter (Oxford, Bodleian Library, MS Bodley 5, fol. 1^v).

43   Causa vero efficiens movens et mota est quilibet predicator devotus et sancto spiritu inbutus ad tante dignitatis officium tam vita quam scientia aptus et ydoneus (Oxford, Bodleian Library, MS Bodley 571, fol. 162^v).

44   *Forma praedicandi,* prologus (ed. Charland, *Artes praedicandi,* pp. 233–5).

45   Quite impressive apparatus is found in manuscripts of Gower's two major works. Oxford, All Souls College, MS 98—which, according to

Macaulay (*Works,* iv, p. lxi), Gower himself supervised for presentation to Archbishop Thomas Arundel—contains a series of *capitula* or *intentiones* for the *Vox clamantis,* which in style and in function are similar to those which Kilwardby prepared for certain authoritative texts (cf. above p. 154). In many manuscripts of the *Confessio amantis* there are Latin summaries of the English text which, although written in verse and speaking in the third person, perform the same summarising function as the prose *intentiones* in the *Vox clamantis.* These verse *intentiones,* like the Latin commentary (discussed above, pp. 181–2, 188–90), are consistently moralistic in tone and point out the 'lore' in Gower's English text. The presence of such *intentiones* in early manuscripts of the *Confessio* gives that apparatus a considerable importance: Gower probably 'passed' it for publication; he may even have written it. It would seem that Gower attempted to provide for his own works that apparatus which medieval readers believed to be appropriate to an *auctor.*

46 Generalis prologus (*Biblia glossata,* i, unfol.).

47 Prologus specialis de intentione auctoris et modo procedendi (ibid., i, unfol.).

48 *In lib. Sap.,* prologus (Basel ed., pp. 1–6).

49 Ibid., lect.i (p. 6).

50 *Ropertus Holcot super librum Ecclesiastici* (Venice, 1509), fols 2^r–4^r.

51 Ringstead, *In Prov. Sal.,* fols 1^r–3^r; Lathbury, *In Thren.Ier.,* 1^r–19^v. Indeed, the practice of prefacing a commentary with an extrinsic prologue did not end with the Middle Ages. B. Weinberg has explained that a Renaissance professor, beginning his series of lectures on a text or topic, almost invariably devoted the introductory lecture (then called the *prolusio*) to explaining the place which his subject occupied in the whole scheme of human knowledge: see *A History of Literary Criticism in the Italian Renaissance* (Chicago, 1961), i, 7.

52 *English Works,* ed. Macaulay, i, 35–6.

53 From a commentary on the *Heroides* in Cod. Laur. 91 sup. 23, cit. Ghisalberti, *JWCI,* ix, 44–5. On the importance of *Heroides* commentaries for an understanding of Gower's compilation of love-stories see A. J. Minnis, 'John Gower, *sapiens* in ethics and politics', *Medium Aevum,* xlix.2 (1980), 207–29; cf. Minnis, 'Moral Gower', pp. 55–66. For discussion of the types of *Heroides* commentary available in late-medieval England see M. C. Edwards, *A Study of Six Characters in Chaucer's Legend of Good Women with reference to medieval scholia on Ovid's Heroides* (unpub. B. Litt. thesis, Oxford, 1970).

54 *Hugonis postilla,* iii, 153^v.

55 For the use of Ovid made by 'classicising friars' see Smalley, *English Friars and Antiquity,* pp. 102, 106, 152, 155–6, 189, 226. For a general survey

see S. Viarre, *La Survie d'Ovide dans la littérature scientifique de XIIe et XIIIe siècles* (Poitiers, 1966). Cf. pp. 11, 55–7 above.

56 See, for example, the *accessus* to Ovid's *Heroides* discussed above, pp. 55–7; cf. the *accessus* transcribed and examined by Edwards, *Six Characters in Chaucer's Legend*. For a fuller version of this argument see Minnis, 'Moral Gower', pp. 51–66.

57 For full discussion, see my article in *Medium Aevum*, xlix.2, 207–29, on which the following few pages are based.

58 *English Works*, ed. Macaulay, ii, 480.

59 From T. A. Sinclair's introduction to *Aristotle: The Politics* (Harmondsworth, 1962), p. 21.

60 Cf. Macaulay, *English Works*, ii, 521–2.

61 C. S. Lewis, *The Allegory of Love* (Oxford, 1936), p. 218.

62 *English Works*, ed. Macaulay, i, 37.

63 Ibid., ii, 474–5.

64 *Works*, ed. Robinson, p. 178.

65 *English Writings of Richard Rolle*, ed. H. E. Allen (Oxford, 1931), p. 7.

66 For a particularly interesting example see the *Legend of Good Women*, F prologue, lines 466–74; cf. G prologue, lines 456–64 (pp. 493–4): discussed by A. J. Minnis, 'The Influence of Academic Prologues on the Prologues and Literary Attitudes of Late-Medieval English Writers', *Med. Stud.*, xliii (1981), 375–6.

67 See the General Prologue, I, line 727 (p. 24); the Miller's Prologue, I, line 3175 (p. 48); Prologue to Melibee, VII, line 958 (p. 167); the Parson's Prologue, X, line 38 (p. 228); *Troilus and Criseyde*, I, line 53 (p. 390), etc.

68 Monk's Tale, VII, line 1991 (p. 189). The most sophisticated fourteenth-century discussions of the *modus tragoediae* are to be found in Trevet's commentaries on the tragedies of Seneca. However, there is no evidence that Chaucer knew any of these commentaries.

69 *Troilus and Criseyde*, v, line 1792 (p. 479).

70 Merchant's Tale, iv, line 1881 (p. 121).

71 'Chaucer and the Hand that Fed Him', *Speculum*, xli (1966), 619–42.

72 'Vincent of Beauvais and Dame Pertelote's Knowledge of Medicine', *Speculum*, x (1935), 281–7; 'The Summoner's Malady', *SP*, xxxiii (1936), 40–4; 'Vincent of Beauvais and the Green Yeoman's Lecture on Demonology', *SP*, xxxv (1938), 1–9; 'Chaucer's Legend of Cleopatra and the *Speculum historiale*', *Speculum*, xiii (1938), 232–36; 'Vincent of Beauvais

and Chaucer's *Monk's Tale*', *Speculum,* xvii (1942), 56–68; 'Vincent of Beauvais and Chaucer's Knowledge of Alchemy', *SP,* xli (1944), 371–89.

73 Apologia totius operis, cap.iv (ed. v. den Brincken, p. 470).

74 *Li Livres dou Tresor,* ed. Carmody, pp. 17–18.

75 Apologia totius operis, cap.vii (ed. v. den Brincken, p. 474).

76 *De proprietatibus rerum,* prologus (unfol.).

77 *On the Properties of Things: John Trevisa's Translation of Bartholomaeus Anglicus de proprietatibus rerum,* ed. M. C. Seymour *et al.* (Oxford, 1975), i, 43.

78 Oxford, Bodleian Library, MS Rawlinson C.69, fol. 106^v.

79 Ed. C. Horstmann, 'Mappula angliae von Osbern Bokenham', *Englische Studien,* x (1887), 34.

80 *Polychronicon Ranulphi,* i, 20.

81 Ibid., i, 21.

82 Ibid., i, 13.

83 Ibid.

84 Ibid., i, 19.

85 Ibid., iii, 317–19.

86 For examples, see ibid., i, 363; ii, 61, 77, 83, 91, 121, 161, 189, 195, etc.

87 See T. O. Wedel, *The Medieval Attitude to Astrology, particularly in England,* Yale Studies in English, lx (New Haven, 1920), 11, n.2. For thirteenth-century attitudes to the *ars judicialis,* see ibid., pp. 64–75; for the views of Thomas Bradwardine (*c.* 1290–1349) and John Wyclif, see ibid., pp. 124–31.

88 See, for example, the discussion by Bradwardine in his *Sermo epinicius* (1346), ed. H. A. Oberman and J. A. Weisheipl, *AHDLMA,* xxv (1958), 295–329.

89 J. A. Robson, *Wyclif and the Oxford Schools,* Cambridge Studies in Medieval Life and Thought, New Srs, viii (Cambridge, 1966), 101–3.

90 Ibid., p. 102.

91 Oxford, Bodleian Library, MS Bodley 714, fol. 1^r–1^v; cf. MS Bodley 369, fol. 1^r–1^v.

92 See the extract pr. in *Four English Political Tracts of the Later Middle Ages,* ed. J.-P. Genet, Camden Fourth Srs (London, 1968), 22–3.

93 *Works,* ed. Robinson, p. 546.

94 Ibid., p. 551.

95 *The Romance of the Rose,* trans. by H. W. Robbins and ed. C. W. Dunn (New York, 1962), p. xx.

96 Ed. Langlois, iv, 95.

97 See esp. Apologia totius operis, cap.iv (ed. v. den Brincken, pp. 469–70).

98 *Li Livres dou Tresor,* ed. Carmody, p. 16.

99 See the gloss pr. Macaulay, *English Works,* i, 3–4. For the argument that Brunetto Latini influenced Gower, see ibid., ii, 522; cf. Mainzer, *The Sources of the Confessio amantis,* esp. pp. 38–40.

100 *Polychronicon Ranulphi,* i, 16.

101 Ibid., i, 17.

102 For these quotations see I, lines 798, 3169; VII, line 964; x, line 46 (cf. VII, lines 2790–817).

103 But there is some overlap: see note 72 above.

104 For the idea of 'encapsulating' structure cf. J. Burrow, *Ricardian Poetry* (London, 1971), pp. 57–68, 86, 92.

105 Apologia totius operis, cap.viii (ed. v. den Brincken, p. 477).

106 Apologia totius operis, cap.i (ibid., pp. 465–6).

107 Apologia, cap.x (ibid., pp. 479–80).

108 *Decameron,* introduzione (ed. C. Segre, *Opere di Giovanni Boccaccio,* 4 ed. (Milan, 1967), pp. 27–8; trans. C. H. McWilliam (Harmondsworth, 1972), p. 47).

109 *Decameron,* ed. Segre, pp. 694–7.

110 On this principle see Glending Olson, 'The Medieval Theory of Literature for Refreshment and its Use in the *Fabliau* Tradition', *SP,* lxxi (1974), 291–313.

111 Trans. McWilliam, p. 831.

112 *Alberti opera,* ed. Borgnet, xviii, 358, 360.

113 *Biblia glossata,* iii, 432–3.

114 *Polychronicon Ranulphi,* i, 18.

115 *Ovide moralisé,* vol.i, ed. C. de Boer, Verhandelingen der Koninkijke Akademie van Wetenschappen te Amsterdam, Afdeeling Letterkunde, deel xv (Amsterdam, 1915), 61.

116 *The Metamorphoses, translated by W. Caxton, 1480* (New York, 1968), i, unfol.

117 *Malory: Works,* ed. E. Vinaver, 2 ed. (Oxford, 1971), p. xv. Cf. the similar use of Romans xv.4 in the prologue to Caxton's second edition of *The Game and Playe of the Chesse,* ed. W. J. B. Crotch, *The Prologues and Epilogues of William Caxton,* EETS (OS) clxxvi (Oxford, 1928), pp. 10–11.

118 For discussion, see A. J. Minnis, 'A Note on Chaucer and the *Ovide moralisé', Medium Aevum,* xlviii (1979), 254–7.

119 *Works,* ed. Robinson, p. 265. Cf. *The Ellesmere Chaucer reproduced in Facsimile* (Manchester, 1911), ii, unpaginated. The Hengwrt Chaucer is imperfect at the end, so we do not know if it contained the 'retracciouns' or not. On these two MSS, the work of a single scribe, see, now, A. I. Doyle and M. B. Parkes, 'The Production of Manuscripts of the *Canterbury Tales* and the *Confessio amantis* in the early fifteenth century', *Medieval Scribes, Manuscripts and Libraries: Essays presented to N. R. Ker,* ed. M. B. Parkes and A. G. Watson (London, 1978), pp. 163–210.

120 *The Ellesmere Chaucer,* ii, unpag.

121 Cf. G. L. Kittredge, 'Chaucer's Lollius', *HSCP,* xxviii (1917), 47–133, esp. pp. 49–55. On Chaucer's antiquarianism in *Troilus,* see M. W. Bloomfield, 'Chaucer's Sense of History', *JEGP,* li (1952), 301–13, esp. p. 308, n.17. R. A. Pratt suggested that Chaucer gained 'a sense of chronology, a sense of the past, and a sense of history' from Nicholas Trevet's Cronicles: see 'Chaucer and *Les Cronicles* of Nicholas Trevet', *Studies in Language, Literature and Culture of the Middle Ages and Later,* ed. E. B. Atwood and A. A. Hill (Austin, 1969), pp. 308–9. However, Chaucer could have acquired these senses from Vincent's 'Estoryal Myrour', Higden's *Polychronicon* or, indeed, from many another medieval compilation.

122 See esp. Apologia totius operis, capi i, iii–vi, viii (ed. v. den Brincken, pp. 465–6, 467–74, 475–7); *Polychronicon Ranulphi,* i, 2–6, 16–20. The parallels with Higden are particularly close.

123 In *De vulgari eloquentia,* ii.6, Dante gives examples of word-formation from 'modern' writers like Guido Guinicelli and Guido Cavalcanti, whom he labels as *auctores:* he seems deliberately to be awarding the accolade because, immediately afterwards, he lists 'ancient' *auctores* who also provide examples of word-formation (*Le Opere latine di Dante Allighieri,* ed. G. Giuliani (Florence, 1878–1882), i, 62–4). Cf. the *Epistle to Can Grande,* where Dante's *Divine Comedy* is described in terms of authorial modes cit. above, pp. 144–5. The first commentators on Dante and on other great Italian writers transferred the medieval critical vocabulary—developed in the exposition of 'ancient' *auctores*—to their 'modern' *auctores:* see Sandkühler, *Die frühen Dantekommentare.*

124 Boccaccio's 'self-commentary' is pr. in *Giovanni Boccaccio: Teseida,* ed. S. Battaglia (Florence, 1938).

EPILOGUE

1   *Francisci Petrarcae epistolae de rebus familiaribus,* ed. I. Fracassetti (Florence, 1859–63), iii, 258; trans. M. E. Cosenza, *Petrarch's Letters to Classical Authors* (Chicago, 1910), p. 14.

2   This 'affectionate veneration' of Petrarch's is discussed by P. de Nolhac, *Pétrarque et l'humanisme* (Paris, 1907), i, 216–20; cf. R. Weiss, *The Spread of Italian Humanism* (London, 1964), p. 26.

3   See R. Pfeiffer, *History of Classical Scholarship 1300–1850* (Oxford, 1976), pp. 9–10, who emphasises that the evidence for Petrarch's knowledge of Cicero's *Epistolae ad familiares* is inconclusive.

4   *In libros de reb. fam.,* praefatio (ed. Fracassetti, i, 25; trans. Cosenza, pp. x–xi).

5   *De reb. fam.,* xxi.10 (ed. Fracassetti, iii, 85–6).

6   Cf. Petrarch's statement to this effect in *De reb. fam.,* xxiv.2 (ed. Fracassetti, iii, 259; trans. Cosenza, p. 10).

7   *De reb. fam.,* xxiv.3; xxiv.4 (ed. Fracassetti, iii, 262, 266).

8   *De reb. fam.,* xxiv.3 (ibid., iii, 263).

9   *De reb. fam.,* xxiv.4 (ibid., iii, 264).

10   *De reb. fam.,* xxiv.2 (ibid., iii, 258–61).

11   *Speculum historiale,* vi, capi vi–xxxii (*Speculi maioris* (Venice, 1591), i, fols 59ᵛ ff.).

12   *Gualteri Burlaei liber de vita et moribus philosophorum mit einer altspanischen Übersetzung der Eskurialbibliothek,* ed. H. Knust, Bibliothek des Litterarischen Vereins in Stuttgart, clxxvii (Tübingen, 1886), 2.

13   *Lib. de vita et mor. phil.,* cap. xcv (ibid., p. 318).

14   Pars iv, cap.xvi (*Compendiloquium.* ed. L. Wadding (Rome, 1655), pp. 283–6).

15   For Aquinas's attitude to Cicero see E. K. Rand, *Cicero in the Courtroom of St Thomas Aquinas,* The Aquinas Lecture 1945 (Marquette, 1946).

16   *Vita di Dante,* xxv (ed. D. Guerri, *Il Comento alla Divina Commedia e gli altri scritti intorno a Dante,* i (Bari, 1918), p. 46; trans. J. R. Smith, *The Earliest Lives of Dante,* Yale Studies in English, x (New York, 1901; repr. 1968), p. 51).

17   Trans. Smith, pp. 58–9.

18   Ibid., p. 60.

19 See the 'Aristotelian prologues' to the Dante-commentaries cit. by Sand-
    kühler, *Die frühen Dantekommentare*.

20 Lib.i, lect.3, 55 (trans. Rowan, i, 24).

21 *De reb. fam.*. x. 4 (ed. Fracassetti, ii, 82–4; trans. J. H. Robinson and
    H. W. Rolfe, *Petrarch* (New York, 1968), pp. 261–5).

22 *Vita di Dante*. xxii (ed. Guerri, p. 42). Cf. his *Geneal. deor. gent.*. xiv.8, xv.8
    (ed. Romano, pp. 705, 769); also the *Comento alla Divina Commedia*. iii
    (ed. Guerri, p. 142).

23 *Vita di Dante*. xxii (ed. Guerri, p. 40; trans. Smith, p. 51).

24 *Geneal. deor. gent.*. xiv.9 (ed. Romano, p. 707).

25 Ibid., xiv.14 (p. 725).

26 Ibid., xiv.17 (p. 731); cf. *Vita di Dante*. xxii (ed. Guerri, pp. 39–40),
    and esp. the *Redazioni compendiose della vita di Dante*. xix[bis] (ibid., p. 92).
    For a (perhaps unduly high) estimate of Boccaccio's 'emancipation' of the
    modus poeticus from the other modes, see F. Tateo, 'Poesia e favola nella
    poetica del Boccaccio', in his *Retorica e poetica fra medioevo e rinascimento*.
    Biblioteca di filologia romanza, v (Bari, 1960), 67–202.

Bibliography

SOURCES: MANUSCRIPT

ALEXANDER OF HALES. Commentary on St John's Gospel. Paris, Bibliothèque Nationale, MS Lat. 14438.

ANONYMOUS. Commentary on Juvenal's Satires. Oxford, Bodleian Library, MS Auct. F.6.9.

—. Distinctions on the Psalter. Cambridge, Corpus Christi College, MS 217.

—. *Liber judiciorum*. Oxford, Bodleian Library, MS Bodley 581.

—. *The Poor Caitiff*. Oxford, Bodleian Library, MS Rawlinson C.69.

COMESTOR, PETER. Commentary on St John's Gospel. Oxford, Bodleian Library, MS Bodley 494.

—. Commentary on St Matthew. Oxford, Bodleian Library, MS Laud. Misc. 291.

COSSEY, HENRY. Commentary on the Psalter. Cambridge, Christ's College, MS 11.

DOCKING, THOMAS. Commentary on St Paul's epistle to Galatians. Oxford, Magdalen College, MS 154.

GILBERT OF POITIERS. Commentary on the Pauline Epistles. Oxford, Magdalen College, MS 118.

—. Commentary on the Psalter. Oxford, Balliol College, MS 36. Also, Oxford, Bodleian Library, MS Auct. D.2.1.

GORRAN, NICHOLAS. Commentary on the Psalter. Oxford, Bodleian Library, MS Bodley 246.

HIGDEN, RALPH. *Ars componendi sermones*. Oxford, Bodleian Library, MS Bodley 5.

HUGUTIO OF PISA. *Magnae derivationes*. Oxford, Bodleian Library, MS Bodley 376.

JOHN OF WALES. *De quattuor predicabilibus.* Oxford, Bodleian Library, MS Bodley 571.

LANGTON, STEPHEN. Commentary on Exodus. Oxford, Trinity College, MS 65.

—. Commentary on Machabees. Oxford, Bodleian Library, MS Laud. Misc., 149.

—. Commentary on Numbers. Oxford, Trinity College, MS 65.

—. Commentary on the Song of Songs *(reportatio).* Oxford, Bodleian Library, MS Bodley 528.

—. Commentary on the Song of Songs (another *reportatio*). Oxford, Bodleian Library, MS Bodley 87.

—. Commentary on the Twelve Minor Prophets. Oxford, Bodleian Library, MS Rawlinson G. 427.

NECKAM, ALEXANDER. *Distinctiones verborum.* Oxford, Bodleian Library, MS Hatton 101.

PETER OF POITIERS. Distinctions on the Psalter. Oxford, Corpus Christi College, MS 48.

PETER THE CHANTER. Commentary on Genesis. London, British Library, MS Royal 2. C. VIII.

—. Commentary on the Four Evangelists. London, British Library, MS Royal 10.C.V.

—. Commentary on the Psalter. Oxford, Corpus Christi College, MS 49.

—. *Verbum abbreviatum.* Paris, Bibliothèque Nationale, MS Lat. 15565.

PRAEPOSITINUS. *Summa super Psalterium.* Paris, Bibliothèque Nationale, MS Lat. 454.

RUSSEL, JOHN. Commentary on the Apocalypse. Oxford, Merton College, MS 172.

TREVET, NICHOLAS. Commentary on Boethius, *De consolatione philosophiae.* Typescript of unfinished ed. by the late E. T. Silk.

—. Commentary on Seneca's *Declamationes.* Oxford, Bodleian Library, MS Rawl. G. 186.

—. Literal commentary on the Psalter. Oxford, Bodleian Library, MS Bodley 738.

WHETELEY, WILLIAM. Commentary on Boethius's *De consolatione philosophiae.* Oxford, New College, MS C.264.

WILLIAM OF ARAGON. Commentary on Boethius's *De consolatione philosophiae.* Cambridge, University Library, MS Ii.3.21 (part 2).

WILLIAM OF CONCHES. Commentary on Boethius's *De consolatione philosophiae*. London, British Library, MS Royal 15.B.III.

WILLIAM OF LIDLINGTON. Commentary on the Evangelists. Oxford, New College, MS 47.

WILLIAM OF MIDDLETON. Commentary on the Twelve Minor Prophets. Oxford, Bodleian Library, MS Laud. Misc. 160.

SOURCES: PRINTED

ABELARD, PETER. *Historia calamitatum*, ed. J. Monfrin, 2 ed. (Paris, 1962).

—. *Opera theologica*, ed. E. M. Buytaert, CCCM, xi–xii (1969).

—. *Peter Abelard's Ethics*, ed. D. E. Luscombe (Oxford, 1971).

—. *Sic et non*, pr. *PL*, clxxviii, 1337–1610.

ALAN OF LILLE. *Contra haereticos*, pr. *PL*, ccx, 305–430.

ALBERIC OF MONTE CASSINO. *Flores rhetoricii*, ed. D. M. Inguanez and H. M. Willard, Miscellanea Cassinese, xiv (Montecassino, 1938).

ALBERT THE GREAT, ST. *Opera omnia* (Aschendorff, 1951–   ).

ALCUIN. *The Rhetoric of Alcuin and Charlemagne*, ed. W. S. Howell (Princeton, 1941).

ALEXANDER OF HALES. *Glossa in quattuor libros sententiarum Petri Lombardi*, Bibliotheca Franciscana scholastica medii aevi, xii–xv (Quaracchi, 1951–7).

—. *Summa theologica* (Quaracchi, 1924–48).

ALEXANDER OF VILLA DEI. *Ecclesiale*, ed. L. R. Lind (Lawrence, Kansas, 1958).

AMBROSE, ST. *De apologia prophetae David*, ed. C. Schenkl, CSEL, xxxii (1897), 299–355.

—. *Apologia David altera*, ed. C. Schenkl, CSEL, xxxii (1897), 359–408.

—. *Enarrationes in XII psalmos Davidicos*, pr. *PL*, xiv, 963–1238.

AMMONIUS. See WILLIAM OF MOERBEKE.

ANONYMOUS. *An English Fourteenth-Century Apocalypse Version with a Prose Commentary*, ed. E. Fridner, Lund Studies in English, xxix (Lund and Copenhagen, 1961).

—. *Everyman*, ed. A. C. Cawley (Manchester, 1961).

—. *Incerti auctoris impugnationes contra Aegidium Romanum contradicentem Thomae super primum sententiarum*, ed. G. Bruni, Bibliotheca Augustiana medii aevi, ser. 1, Textus theol. et phil., i (Rome, 1942).

—. *Ovide moralisé,* vol. i, ed. C. de Boer, Verhandelingen der Koninkijke Akademie van Wetenschappen te Amsterdam, Afdeeling Letterkunde, deel xv (Amsterdam, 1915).

?ANSELM OF LAON. *Enarrationes in cantica canticorum,* pr. *PL,* clxii, 1187–1592.

AQUINAS, ST THOMAS. *Commentary on Aristotle's Physics,* trans. R. J. Blackwell, R. J. Spath and W. E. Thirlkel (London, 1963).

—. *Commentary on the Metaphysics of Aristotle,* trans. J. P. Rowan (Chicago, 1961).

—. *Commentary on the Nicomachean Ethics,* trans. C. I. Litzinger (Chicago, 1964).

—. *In metaphysicam Aristotelis commentaria,* ed. M.-R. Cathala (Turin, 1935).

—. *Opera omnia,* ed. S. E. Frette, apud L. Vivès (Paris, 1871–80).

—. *Opuscula omnia,* vi, ed. P. Mandonnet (Paris, 1927).

—. *Quaestiones quodlibetales,* 8 ed., ed. R. Spiazzi (Marietti, 1949).

—. *Scriptum super libros sententiarum* (Paris, 1927–47).

—. *Summa theologiae,* Blackfriars ed. (London and New York, 1964–81).

—. *Summa theologiae,* Iterata editio (Madrid, 1955–8).

—. *Super epistolas S. Pauli lectura,* ed. P. R. Cai (Marietti, 1953).

—. *The Division and Methods of the Sciences,* trans. A. Maurer, 3 ed. (Toronto, 1963).

ARISTOTLE. *The Politics,* trans. T. A. Sinclair (Harmondsworth, 1962).

—. *The Works of Aristotle translated into English,* ed. W. D. Ross (Oxford, 1928–52).

ARNULF OF ORLÉANS. *Glosule super Lucanum,* ed. B. M. Marti, Papers and Monographs of the American Academy in Rome, xviii (Rome, 1958).

AUGUSTINE, ST. *Contra Cresconium,* ed. M. Petschenig, *CSEL,* lii (1909), 325–582.

—. *Contra mendacium,* ed. I. Zycha, *CSEL,* xli (1900), 469–528.

—. *De civitate Dei,* ed. E. Hoffmann, *CSEL,* xl (1899–1900).

—. *De consensu Evangelistarum,* ed. F. Weihrich, *CSEL,* xliii (1904).

—. *De doctrina christiana,* ed. G. M. Green, *CSEL,* lxxx (1963).

—. *De Genesi ad litteram,* ed. I. Zycha, *CSEL,* xxviii (1894), 3–435.

—. *Enarrationes in psalmos,* ed. E. Dekkers and J. Fraipont, *CCSL,* xxxviii–xl (1956).

—. Epistola xciii, pr. *PL*, xxxiii, 321–47.

—. *Soliloquia*, pr. *PL*, xxxii, 869–904.

(Pseudo-) AUGUSTINE, ST. *De spiritu et anima*, pr. *PL*, xl, 779–832.

AURIOL, PETER. *Compendium Biblie totius* (unloc., 1514).

AVERROES. *Commentarium medium in Aristoteles poetriam*, ed. W. F. Boggess (unpub. Ph.D. thesis, University of N. Carolina, 1965).

—. *Middle Commentary on Aristotle's 'Poetics'*, trans. C. E. Butterworth (Princeton, 1986).

AVICENNA. *Commentary on the 'Poetics' of Aristotle*, ed. I. M. Dahiyat (Leiden, 1974).

BARTHOLOMEW THE ENGLISHMAN. *De proprietatibus rerum* (Lyon, 1481).

BEDE. *De arte metrica*, ed. H. Keil, *Grammatici Latini, vii* (Leipzig, 1880).

—. *Explanatio Apocalypsis*, pr. *PL*, xciii, 129–206.

(Pseudo-) BEDE. *In psalmorum librum exegesis*, pr. *PL*, xciii, 477–1098.

BERNARD OF CLAIRVAUX, ST. *S. Bernardi opera*, ed. J. Leclercq *et al*. (Rome, 1957–   ).

BERNARD SILVESTER. *Commentum quod dicitur Bernardi Silvestris super VI libros Eneidos*, ed. J. W. Jones and E. F. Jones (Lincoln, Nebraska, and London, 1977).

BERSUIRE, PIERRE. *Reductorium morale* (Venice, 1583).

—. *Reductorium morale, liber xv: Ovidius moralizatus, cap.i: De formis figurisque deorum*, ed. J. Engels (Utrecht, 1966).

BOCCACCIO, GIOVANNI. *Decameron*, trans. C. H. McWilliam (Harmondsworth, 1972).

—. *De genealogie deorum gentilium libri*, ed. V. Romano (Bari, 1951).

—. *Il Comento alla Divina Commedia e gli altri scritti intorno a Dante*, i, ed. D. Guerri (Bari, 1918).

—. *Opere*, ed. C. Segre, 4 ed. (Milan, 1967).

—. *Teseida*, ed. S. Battaglia (Florence, 1938).

BOETHIUS. *In Isagogen Porphyrii commenta*, ed. S. Brandt, *CSEL*, xlviii (1906).

—. *In Topica Ciceronis commentaria*, pr. *PL*, lxiv, 1039–1174.

(Pseudo-) BOETHIUS. *De disciplina scolarium*, ed. O. Weijers (Leiden, 1976).

BOKENHAM, OSBERN. *Legendys of Hooly Wummen*, ed. M. S. Serjeantson, EETS (OS), ccvi (Oxford, 1938).

—. *Mappula angliae*, ed. C. Horstmann, *Englische Studien*, x (1887), 1–34.

BRADWARDINE, THOMAS. *Sermo epinicius*, ed. H. A. Oberman and J. A. Weisheipl, *AHDLMA*, xxv (1958), 295–329.

BRITO, WILLIAM. *Summa Britonis sive Guillelmi Britonis expositiones vocabulorum Biblie,* ed. L. W. Daly and B. A. Daly, Thesaurus mundi, xv (Padua, 1975).

BRUNETTO LATINI. *Li Livres dou Tresor,* ed. F. J. Carmody (Berkeley, 1948).

?BRUNO THE CARTHUSIAN, ST. *Expositio in psalmos,* pr. *PL,* clii, 637–1420.

BURLEY, WALTER. *Liber de vita et moribus philosophorum mit einer altspanischen Übersetzung der Eskurialbibliothek,* ed. H. Knust, Bibliothek des Litterarischen Vereins in Stuttgart, clxxvii (Tübingen, 1886).

BURY, RICHARD OF. *Philobiblon,* trans. E. C. Thomas and ed. M. MacLagan (Oxford, 1960).

'CAMBRIDGE COMMENTATOR', *Commentarius Cantabrigiensis in epistolas Pauli,* ed. A. Landgraf, Notre-Dame University publications in Medieval Studies, ii (Notre Dame, Indiana, 1937–45).

CASSIAN, ST JOHN. *Conlationes,* ed. M. Petschenig, *CSEL,* xiii (1886).

CASSIODORUS, *Expositio psalmorum,* ed. M. Adriaen, *CCSL,* xcvii–xcviii (1958).

—. *Institutiones,* ed. R. A. B. Mynors (Oxford, 1937).

—. *Institutiones,* trans. L. W. Jones, *An Introduction to Divine and Human Readings by Cassiodorus* (New York, 1946).

CAXTON, WILLIAM. *The Metamorphoses, translated by W. Caxton, 1480* (New York, 1968).

—. *The Prologues and Epilogues of William Caxton,* ed. W. J. B. Crotch, EETS (OS) clxxvi (Oxford, 1928).

CHAUCER, GEOFFREY. *The Ellesmere Chaucer reproduced in Facsimile* (Manchester, 1911).

—. *The Works of Geoffrey Chaucer,* ed. F. N. Robinson, 2 ed. (Oxford, 1957).

CHRISTIAN OF STAVELOT. *Expositio in Matthaeum,* pr. *PL,* cvi, 1261–1504.

CICERO. *Brutus, Orator,* ed. H. H. Hubbell (London and Cambridge, Mass., 1939).

—. *De oratore,* ed. H. Rackham (London and Cambridge, Mass., 1942).

DANTE ALIGHIERI. *Epistolae,* ed. P. Toynbee, 2 ed. by C. G. Hardie (Oxford, 1966).

—. *Le Opere latine,* ed. G. Giuliani (Florence, 1878–1882).

DIONYSIUS THE CARTHUSIAN. *Opera omnia* (Tournai, 1906).

DONATUS, TIBERIUS CLAUDIUS. *Interpretationes Vergilianae,* ed. H. Georgii (repr. Stuttgart, 1969).

DURAND OF ST POURÇAIN. *In sententias theologicas Petri Lombardi* (Venice, 1571).

FISHACRE, RICHARD. Commentary on the Sentences, prologue, ed. R. J. Long, 'The Science of Theology according to Richard Fishacre', *Med. Stud.*, xxxiv (1972), 71–98.

FITZRALPH, RICHARD. *Summa in quaestionibus Armenorum* (Paris, 1512).

GEOFFREY OF AUXERRE. *Expositio in cantica canticorum*, ed. F. Gastaldelli (Rome, 1974).

GEOFFREY OF VITRY. *The commentary of Geoffrey of Vitry on Claudian de raptu Proserpinae*, ed. A. K. Clarke and P. M. Giles (Leiden, 1973).

GERHOH OF REICHERSBERG. *Commentarium in psalmos*, pr. *PL*, cxci, 619–1814.

—. *Letter to Pope Hadrian about the Novelties of the Day*, ed. N. M. Häring (Toronto, 1974).

GILES OF ROME. *De erroribus philosophorum*, ed. J. Koch (Milwaukee, 1944).

GIOVANNI DE'BALBI. *Catholicon* (Venice, 1495).

Glossa Ordinaria, pr. *PL*, cxiii–cxiv.

GODFREY OF ST VICTOR. *Fons philosophiae*, ed. P. Michaud-Quentin, Analecta Mediaevalia Namurcensia, viii (Namur, 1956).

GORRAN, NICHOLAS. *In acta apostolorum et singulas apostolorum* (Antwerp, 1620).

(Pseudo-) GORRAN, NICHOLAS. See PETER OF TARANTASIA.

GOWER, JOHN. *The English Works*, ed. G. C. Macaulay, EETS (ES) lxxxi–lxxxii (Oxford, 1900–1).

—. *The Major Latin Works*, trans. E. W. Stockton (Seattle, 1962).

—. *Works*, ed. G. C. Macaulay (London, 1899–1902).

GREGORY THE GREAT, ST. *Dialogorum libri quatuor*, in *PL*, lxxvii, 149–430.

—. *Homilia in Ezechielem prophetam*, *PL*, lxxvi, 785–1072.

—. *Moralia in Job*, pr. *PL*, lxxv, 509–1162.

GUIBERT OF NOGENT. *Liber quo ordine sermo fieri debeat*, pr. *PL*, clvi, 19–32.

GUIDO DA PISA. *Expositiones et glose super Comediam Dantis*, ed. V. Cioffari (Albany, New York, 1974).

GUNDISSALINUS. *De divisione philosophiae*, ed. L. Baur (Munster, 1903).

(Pseudo-) HAIMO OF HALBERSTADT. *Explanatio in psalmos*, pr. *PL*, cxvi, 191–696.

HARVEY OF NEDELLEC. *In quatuor libris sententiarum commentaria* (Paris, 1647).

HENRY OF GHENT. *Summa quaestionum ordinariarum* (Paris, 1520).

HENRYSON, ROBERT. *The Poems and Fables,* ed. H. H. Wood, 2 ed. (Edinburgh, 1958).

HERMAGORAS. *Fragmenta,* ed. D. Matthes (Leipzig, 1962).

HERMANN THE GERMAN. *Averrois Corubensis commentarium medium in Aristoteles poetriam,* trans. by Hermannus Alemannus, ed. W. F. Boggess (Ph.D. thesis, University of N. Carolina, 1965). Pub. by University Microfilms, Ann Arbor.

HIGDEN, RALPH. *Polychronicon Ranulphi Higden; together with the English translations of John Trevisa and of an unknown writer of the fifteenth century,* ed. C. Babington and J. R. Lumby (London, 1865–86).

HOCCLEVE, THOMAS. *The Minor Poems,* ed. F. J. Furnivall and I. Gollancz, EETS (ES) lxi and lxxiii (Oxford, repr. 1970).

HOLCOT, ROBERT. *Sapientiae regis Salomonis praelectiones* (Basel, 1586).

—. *Super librum Ecclesiastici* (Venice, 1509).

HONORIUS 'OF AUTUN', *Expositio in cantica canticorum,* pr. *PL,* clxxii, 347–496.

—. *Expositio psalmorum,* pr. *PL,* clxxii, 269–312.

HUGH OF ST CHER. *Opera omnia in universum Vetus et Novum Testamentum* (Venice, 1754).

HUGH OF ST VICTOR. *De sacramentis christianae fidei, PL,* clxxvi, 173–618.

—. *De tribus maximis circumstantiis gestorum,* ed. W. M. Green in *Speculum,* xviii (1943), 484–93.

—. *Didascalicon,* ed. C. H. Buttimer, Catholic University of America, Studies in Medieval and Renaissance Latin, x (Washington, 1939).

—. *Didascalicon,* trans. J. Taylor (New York and London, 1961).

—. *Expositio in hierarchiam coelestem,* pr. *PL,* clxxv, 923–1154.

—. *Opera exegetica,* pr. *PL,* clxxv.

HUMBERT OF ROMANS. *Opera de vita regulari,* ed. J. J. Berthier (Rome, 1888–9).

(Pseudo-) IRNERIUS. See ROGERIUS.

ISIDORE OF SEVILLE. *Etymologiae,* ed. W. M. Lindsay (Oxford, 1911).

JACQUES OF VITRY. *The Exempla or illustrative stories from the Sermones vulgares of Jacques de Vitry,* Folk-Lore Society (London, 1890).

JEAN DE MEUN. *Roman de la Rose,* ed. E. Langlois, Société des anciens textes français (Paris, 1914–24).

—. *The Romance of the Rose,* trans. R. W. Robbins and ed. C. W. Dunn (New York, 1962).

JEROME, ST. *Commentaria in Isaiam prophetam,* pr. *PL,* xxiv, 18–900.

—. *Commentarius in Ecclesiasten,* ed. M. Adriaen, *CCSL,* lxxii (1959), 248–361.

—. Epistola xxx, pr. *PL,* xxii, 441–5.

—. Epistola cxl, pr. *PL,* xxii, 1166–1179.

—. *Liber Hebraicarum quaestionum in Genesim,* pr. *PL,* xxiii, 983–1062.

–. *Praefatio in librum psalmorum iuxta Hebraicam veritatem,* pr. *PL,* xxviii, 1123–8.

JOHN OF GARLAND. *Parisiana Poetria,* ed. T. Lawlor (New Haven and London, 1974).

JOHN OF ROCHELLE. Inception Lectures, ed. M. Delorme, 'Deux leçons d'ouverture de cours biblique données par Jean de la Rochelle', *La France franciscaine,* xvi (1933), 345–60.

JOHN OF SALISBURY. *Metalogicon,* ed. C. C. J. Webb (Oxford, 1929).

—. *Policraticus,* ed. C. C. J. Webb (Oxford, 1909).

JOHN OF WALES. *Communiloquium* (Lyon, 1511).

—. *Compendiloquium,* ed. L. Wadding (Rome, 1655).

KILWARDBY, ROBERT. *De natura theologiae,* ed. F. Stegmüller, Opuscula et textus historiam ecclesiae illustrantia, xvii (Aschendorff, 1935).

—. *De ortu scientiarum,* ed. A. G. Judy, Auctores Britannici Medii Aevi, iv (Oxford, 1976).

LATHBURY, JOHN. *In threnos Ieremiae* (Oxford, 1482).

LETBERT OF LILLE. *In Psalmos LXXV commentarius,* pr. *PL,* xxi, 641–960. Falsely attributed to Rufinus.

LOMBARD, PETER. *Collectanea in Epist. d. Pauli,* pr. *PL,* cxci, 1297–1696; *PL,* cxcii, 9–520.

—. *Commentarius in psalmos Davidicos,* pr. *PL,* cxci, 61–1296.

—. *Sententiae in IV libros distinctae,* i, pars 1, ed. I. Brady, Spicilegium Bonaventurianum, IV (Grottaferrata, 1971).

MALORY, SIR THOMAS. *Works,* ed. E. Vinaver, 2 ed. (Oxford, 1971).

MAP, WALTER. *De nugis curialium,* ed. M. R. James, Anecdota Oxoniensia, xiv (Oxford, 1914).

—. *Dissuasio Valerii ad Rufinum,* pr. *PL,* xxx, 254–61.

—. *Walter Map: Of Courtiers' Trifles,* trans. F. Tupper and M. B. Ogle (London, 1924).

NECKAM, ALEXANDER. *Sacerdos ad altare*, ed. C. H. Haskins in *Studies in the History of Medieval Science* (Cambridge, Mass., 1924), pp. 372–6.

ORIGEN. *Commentarium in cantica canticorum*, in *Origenes Werke*, viii, ed. W. A. Baehrens, Die griechischen christlichen Schriftsteller der ersten drei Jahrhunderte, xxx (Leipzig, 1925), 61–241.

—. *Origen: The Song of Songs, Commentary and Homilies*, trans. R. P. Lawson, Ancient Christian Writers, xxvi (Westminster, Maryland, and London, 1957).

PAPIAS. *De linguae latinae vocabulis* (unloc., 1476).

PECOCK, REGINALD. *Donet*, ed. E. V. Hitchcock, EETS (OS) clvi (Oxford, 1918).

—. *Folewer to the Donet*, ed. E. V. Hitchcock, EETS (OS) clxiv (Oxford, 1923).

—. *Reule of Cristen Religioun*, ed. W. C. Greet, EETS (OS), clxxi (Oxford, 1926).

PETER OF POITIERS. *Allegoriae super tabernaculum Moysi*, ed. P. S. Moore and J. A. Corbett (Notre Dame, Indiana, 1938).

PETER OF TARANTASIA. *Innocentius V sententiarum commentaria* (Toulouse, 1652).

—. *In omnes d. Pauli epistolas elucidatio authore Nicolao Gorrano* (Antwerp, 1617). Falsely attributed to Nicholas Gorran.

PETER THE VENERABLE. *The Letters of Peter the Venerable*, ed. G. Constable (Cambridge, Mass., 1967).

PETRARCH, FRANCIS. *Epistolae de rebus familiaribus*, ed. I. Fracassetti (Florence, 1859–63).

—. *Petrarch's Letters to Classical Authors*, trans. M. E. Cosenza (Chicago, 1910).

PHILIP OF HARVENGT. *Commentaria in cantica canticorum*, pr. *PL*, cciii, 181–490.

QUINTILIAN. *Institutio oratoria*, ed. H. E. Butler (London and New York, 1921–2).

REMIGIO DEI GIROLAMI OF FLORENCE. *Per lo studio di Fra Remigio dei Girolami (†1319): Contra falsos ecclesie professores cc.5–37*, ed. E. Panella, Memorie Domenicane, n.s., ix (Pistoia, 1979).

REMIGIUS OF AUXERRE. *Commentarium in cantica canticorum*. pr. *PL*. cxvii, 295–358.

—. *Commentum in Martianum Capellam*, ed. C. Lutz (Leiden, 1962).

—. *Enarratio in duodecim prophetas minores*, pr. *PL*, cxvii, 9–294.

—. *Expositio in apocalypsin*, pr. *PL*, cxvii, 937–1220.

—. *In Artem Donati minorem commentum*, ed. W. Fox (Leipzig, 1892).

—. *In d. Pauli epistolas expositio*, pr. *PL*, cxvii, 361–938.

(Pseudo-) REMIGIUS OF AUXERRE. *Enarrationes in psalmos*, pr. *PL*, cxxxi, 133–844.

RICHARD OF ST VICTOR. *In cantica canticorum explicatio*, pr. *PL*, cxcvi, 405–524.

RIDEVALL, JOHN. *Fulgentius metaforalis*, ed. H. Liebeschütz (Leipzig, 1926).

RINGSTEAD, THOMAS. *In proverbia Salomonis* (Paris, 1515). Falsely attributed to 'Robert Holcot or Thomas Waleys'.

ROGERIUS. *Summa codicis des Irnerius*, ed. H. Fitting (Berlin, 1894). Falsely ascribed to Irnerius.

ROLLE, RICHARD. *English Writings*, ed. H. E. Allen (Oxford, 1931).

RUFINUS. *Summa decretorum des Magister Rufinus*, ed. H. Singer (Paderborn, 1902).

RUPERT OF DEUTZ. *De trinitate et operibus eius*, pr. *PL*, clxvii, 199–1828.

—. *De victoria verbi Dei*, pr. *PL*, clxix, 1215–1502.

SCOTUS, SEDULIUS. *In Donati artem minorem, etc.*, ed. B. Löfstedt, *CCCM*, xl^c (1977).

—. *In Maiorem Donatum grammaticum*, ed. D. Brearley, Pontifical Institute of Mediaeval Studies, Studies and Texts, xxvii (Toronto, 1975).

SERVIUS. *In Vergilii carmina commentarii*, ed. G. Thilo and H. Hagen (Leipzig, 1881).

—. *In Vergilii carmina commentariorum*, Harvard Edition (1946).

SIMPLICIUS. See WILLIAM OF MOERBEKE.

STEPHEN OF BOURBON. *Anecdotes historiques, légendes et apologues tirés du recueil inédit d'Étienne de Bourbon*, ed. A. Lecoy de la Marche, Société de l'histoire de France (Paris, 1877).

THIERRY OF CHARTRES. *Commentaries on Boethius by Thierry of Chartres and his School*, ed. N. M. Häring, Pontifical Institute of Mediaeval Studies, Studies and Texts, xx (Toronto, 1971).

THOMAS OF CITEAUX. *Commentarii in cantica canticorum*, *PL*, ccvi, 17–862.

THOMAS OF IRELAND. *Flores omnium pene doctorum collecti per Thomam Hibernicum* (Lyon, 1555).

THOMAS OF STRASSBURG. *Thomae ab Argentina commentaria in IV libros sententiarum* (Venice, 1564).

TREVET, NICHOLAS. *Commentarius literalis in Psalterium iuxta Hebreos S. Hieronymi,* selections, ed. B. P. Shields (Ph.D. thesis, Rutgers, 1970). Pub. by University Microfilms, Ann Arbor, Michigan.

—. *Il Commento di Nicola Trevet al Tieste di Seneca,* ed. E. Franceschini, Pubb. dell' Università Cattolica del Sacro Cuore, Orbis Romanus (Milan, 1938).

—. *Nicolai Treveti expositio Herculis furentis,* ed. V. Ussani, Biblioteca degli Scrittori Greci e Latini (Rome, 1959).

—. *Nicolai Treveti expositio Senecae Agamemnonis,* ed. P. Meloni, Università di Cagliari, Facoltà di Lettere e di Magistero, iii (Sassari, 1961).

—. *Nicholai Treveti expositio Senecae Herculis oetaei,* ed. P. Meloni, Univ. di Cagliari, Fac. di Lett., vii (Rome, 1962).

TREVET, NICHOLAS and WALEYS, THOMAS. *In libros B. Augustini de civitate Dei commentaria* (Toulouse, 1488).

TREVISA, JOHN. *On the Properties of Things: John Trevisa's Translation of Bartholomaeus Anglicus de proprietatibus rerum,* ed. M. C. Seymour *et al.* (Oxford, 1975).

—. See also HIGDEN, RALPH.

ULRICH OF STRASSBURG. *Summa de bono, lib.i,* ed. J. Daguillon, Bibliothèque Thomiste, xii (Paris, 1930).

USK, THOMAS. *Testament of Love,* in *The Works of Geoffrey Chaucer, vol.vii: Chaucerian and other pieces,* ed. W. W. Skeat (Oxford, 1897), pp. 1–145.

VINCENT OF BEAUVAIS. *Speculum maius* (Venice, 1591).

—. *Speculum maius,* apologia totius operis, ed. A.-D. v. den Bricken, 'Geschitsbetrachtung bei Vincenz von Beauvais', *Deutsches Archiv für Erforschung des Mittelalters,* xxxiv (1978), 410–99.

WALEYS, THOMAS. *Postilla super primos xxxviii psalmos* (London, 1481).

—. See also TREVET, NICHOLAS.

WALSINGHAM, THOMAS. *De archana deorum,* ed. R. A. van Kluyve (Durham, N.C., 1968).

WILLIAM OF AUVERGNE. *De bono et malo,* ed. J. R. O'Donnell, *Med. Stud.,* viii (1946), 245–99.

—. *Opera omnia* (Venice, 1591).

WILLIAM OF CONCHES. *Glosae super Platonem,* ed. E. Jeauneau, Textes philosophiques du moyen âge, xiii (Paris, 1965).

WILLIAM OF MOERBEKE. *Ammonius: Commentaire sur le Peri hermemeias d'Aristote, traduction de Guillaume de Moerbeke,* ed. G. Verbeke, Corpus latinum commentariorum in Aristotelem graecorum, ii (Louvain and Paris, 1961).

——. *Simplicius, Commentaire sur les Categories d'Aristote; traduction de Guillaume de Moerbeke,* ed. A. Pattin, Corpus latinum commentariorum in Aristotelem graecorum, v.1 (Louvain and Paris, 1971).

WILLIAM OF OCKHAM. *De sacramento altaris,* ed. and trans. T. B. Birch, Lutheran Literary Board (Iowa, 1930).

WILLIAM OF ST THIERRY. *De natura et dignitate amoris,* pr. *PL,* clxxxiv, 379–408.

——. *Exposé sur le cantique des cantiques,* ed. M. M. Davy, Bibliothèque des textes philosophiques (Paris, 1958).

——. *Exposé sur le cantique des cantiques,* ed. J.-M. Dechanet and M. Dumontier, Sources chrétiennes, lxxxii (Paris, 1962).

——. *The Works of William of St Thierry,* ii, trans. C. Hart, Cistercian Fathers Srs, vi (Shannon, 1970).

WYCLIFFE, JOHN. *The Holy Bible made from the Latin Vulgate by John Wycliffe and his Followers,* ed. J. Forshall and F. Madden (Oxford, 1850).

SECONDARY MATERIAL

AIKEN, P. 'Vincent of Beauvais and Dame Pertelote's Knowledge of Medicine', *Speculum,* x (1935), 281–7.

——. 'The Summoner's Malady', *SP,* xxxiii (1936), 10–14.

——. 'Chaucer's Legend of Cleopatra and the *Speculum historiale*', *Speculum,* xiii (1938), 232–36.

——. 'Vincent of Beauvais and the Green Yeoman's Lecture on Demonology', *SP,* xxxv (1938), 1–9.

——. 'Vincent of Beauvais and Chaucer's *Monk's Tale*', *Speculum,* xvii (1942), 56–68.

——. 'Vincent of Beauvais and Chaucer's Knowledge of Alchemy', *SP,* xli (1944), 371–89.

ALLEN, H. E. 'The *Manuel des pechiez* and the Scholastic Prologue', *The Romanic Review,* viii (1917), 434–62.

ALLEN, J. B. *The Friar as Critic* (Nashville, 1971).

——. 'Commentary as Criticism: Formal Cause, Discursive Form, and the Late Medieval *accessus*', in *Acta Conventus Neo-Latini Lovaniensis,* ed. J. Ijsewijn and E. Kessler (Munich, 1973), pp. 29–48.

—. 'Hermann the German's Averroistic Aristotle and Medieval Literary Theory', *Mosaic,* ix (1976), 67–81.

—. 'Commentary as Criticism: The Text, Influence and Literary Theory of the "Fulgentius Metaphored" of John Ridewall', in *Acta Conventus Neo-Latini Amstelodamensis,* ed. P. Tuynman, G. C. Kuiper and E. Kessler (Munich, 1979), pp. 25–47.

AUERBACH, E. *'Figura',* in *Scenes from the Drama of European Literature,* trans. R. Manheim and C. Garvin (New York, 1959), pp. 11–76.

BALDWIN, J. W. *Masters, Princes, and Merchants: The Social Views of Peter the Chanter and his Circle* (Princeton, 1970).

BASWELL, CHRISTOPHER. 'The Medieval Allegorization of the "Aeneid": MS Cambridge, Peterhouse 158', *Traditio,* xli (1985), 181–237.

BATAILLON, L. J. See DONDAINE, A.

BAUDOUX, B., 'Philosophia "Ancilla theologiae" ', *Antonianum,* xii (1937), 293–326.

BERGER, S. *La Bible française au moyen âge* (Paris, 1884; repr. Geneva, 1976).

—. *Les Préfaces jointes aux livres de la Bible dans les manuscrits de la Vulgate,* Mémoires présentés par divers savants à l'Académie des Inscriptions et Belles-Lettres, première série, xi (1902).

BERTOLA, E. 'Le critiche di Abelardo ad Anselmo di Laon ed a Guglielmo di Champeaux', *RFN,* lii (1960), 459–522.

—. 'I precedenti storici del metodo del *Sic et non* di Abelardo', *RFN,* liii (1961), 255–80.

BILLANOVICH, G. *Petrarca litterato, i: Lo scrittoio del Petrarca,* Storia e letteratura, xvi (Rome, 1947).

BISCHOFF, B. 'Living with the Satirists', in *Classical Influences on European Culture a.d. 500–1500,* ed. R. R. Bolgar (Cambridge, 1971), pp. 83–94.

BLANCHE, F. A. 'Le Sens littéral des écritures d'après S. Thomas d'Aquin', *Rev. thom.,* xiv (1906), 192–212.

BLUMENKRANZ, B. *'Siliquae porcorum:* l'exégèse médiévale et les sciences profanes', in *Mélanges d'histoire du moyen âge dédiés à la mémoire de L. Halphen* (Paris, 1951).

BOGGESS, W. F. 'Aristotle's *Poetics* in the Fourteenth Century', *SP,* lxvii (1970), 278–94.

BOLTON, D. K. *Manuscripts and Commentaries on Boethius, De consolatione philosophiae in England in the Middle Ages* (unpub. B. Litt. thesis, Oxford, 1965).

BORN, L. K. 'Ovid and Allegory', *Speculum,* ix (1934), 362–79.

BORNECQUE, H. *Les Déclamations et les déclamateurs d'après Sénèque le Père* (Lille, 1902).

BOUGEROL, J. G. *Introduction to the Works of Bonaventure*, trans. J. de Vinck (Paterson, New Jersey, 1963).

BRADY, I. 'The Rubrics of Peter Lombard's *Sentences*', *Pier Lombardo*, vi (1962), 5–25.

—. 'The "Distinctions" of Lombard's *Book of Sentences* and Alexander of Hales', *Fran. Stud.*, xxv (1965), 90–116.

BRUMMER, J. (ed.). *Vitae Vergilianae* (Leipzig, 1912).

—. 'Zum Ueberlieferungsgeschichte der sogenannten Donat-Vita des Vergil', *Philologus*, lxxii (1913), 278–97.

BRUNI, G. 'The "De differentiae rhetoricae, ethicae et politicae" of Aegidius Romanus', *New Schol.*, vi (1932), 1–18.

BRUYNE, E. DE. *Études d'esthétique médiévale* (Brugge, 1946).

BUCK, A. 'Aus der Vorgeschichte der "Querelle des Anciens et des Modernes" in Mittelalter und Renaissance', *Bibliothèque d'humanisme et renaissance, travaux et documents*, xx (1958), 527–41.

BURROW, JOHN. *Ricardian Poetry* (London, 1971).

CALLUS, D. A. 'The "Tabula super originalia patrum" of Robert Kilwardby O.P.', *Studia medievalia in honorem R. J. Martin* (Bruges, 1948), 243–70.

—. 'New Manuscripts of Kilwardby's "Tabula super originalia patrum" ', *Dom. Stud.*, ii (1949), 38–45.

—. 'The Contribution to the Study of the Fathers made by the Thirteenth-Century Oxford Schools', *JEH*, v (1954), 139–48.

—. *Robert Grosseteste, Scholar and Bishop: Essays in Commemoration of the Seventh Centenary of his Death* (Oxford, 1955).

—. 'The Function of the Philosopher in Thirteenth-Century Oxford', *Miscellanea mediaevalia*, iii (Berlin, 1964), 153–62.

CAPPUYNS, M. *Jean Scot Erigène* (Paris, 1933).

CHADWICK, O. *John Cassian: A Study in Primitive Monasticism*, 2 ed. (Cambridge, 1968).

CHAMBERS, R. W. 'Long Will, Dante, and the Righteous Heathen', *Essays and Studies*, ix (1923), 50–69.

CHATILLON, F. 'Vocabulaire et prosodie du distique attribué à Augustin de Dacie sur les quatre sens de l'écriture', in *L'Homme devant Dieu: Mélanges offerts au père Henri de Lubac* (Lyon, Fourvière, 1963–4), ii, 17–28.

CHENU, M.-D. 'Auctor, actor, autor', *Bull. du Cange*, iii (1927), 81–6.

—. 'Notes de lexicographie philosophie médiévale: *collectio, collatio*', *RSPT*, xvi (1927), 435–46.

—. 'Antiqui, Moderni', *RSPT*, xvii (1928), 82–94.

—. 'Les "philosophes" dans la philosophie chrétienne médiévale', *RSPT*, xxvi (1937), 27–40.

—. *La Théologie au douzième siècle*, 2 ed., Études de philosophie médiévale, xlv (Paris, 1966).

—. 'The Masters of the Theological "Science" ', in *Nature, Man and Society in the Twelfth Century*, trans. J. Taylor and L. K. Little (Chicago and London, 1968), pp. 270–309.

—. *La Théologie comme science au XIIIe siècle*, 3 ed., Bibliothèque Thomiste, xxxiii (Paris, 1969).

COMPARETTI, D. *Vergil in the Middle Ages*, trans. E. F. M. Benecke (London, 1895).

COPLESTON, F. C. *Aquinas* (Harmondsworth, 1955).

COTTIAUX, J. 'La Conception de la théologie d'Abélard', *RHE*, xxviii (1932), 247–95.

COURCELLE, P. *Late Latin Writers and their Greek Sources*, trans. H. E. Wedeck (Cambridge, Mass., 1969).

COURTES, J. M. 'Figures et tropes dans le psautier de Cassiodore', *Revue des études latines*, xiii (1964), 361–75.

CROSS, F. L. and LIVINGSTONE, E. A. (eds.). *The Oxford Dictionary of the Christian Church*, 2 ed. (Oxford, 1974).

CUERVO, M. 'La Teologia como ciencia y la sistematización teologica según S. Alberto Magno', *Ciencia tomista*, xlvi (1932), 173–99.

D'AVRAY, DAVID. *The Transformation of the Medieval Sermon* (unpub. D. Phil. thesis, Oxford, 1976).

—. *The Preaching of the Friars: Sermons diffused from Paris before 1300* (Oxford, 1985).

DAVY, M. M. *Théologie et mystique de Guillaume de St Thierry, i, La Connaissance de Dieu*, Études de théologie et d'histoire de la spiritualité, xiv (Paris, 1954).

DEAN, R. J. 'The Earliest Medieval Commentary on Livy', *Med. et hum.*, iii (1945), 86–98; iv (1946), 110.

—. *The Life and Works of Nicholas Trevet* (unpub. D.Phil. thesis, Oxford, 1948).

—. 'Unnoticed commentaries on the *Dissuasio Valerii* of Walter Map', *MARS*, ii (1950), 128–50.

DECHANET, J. M. 'L'Amitié d'Abélard et de Guillaume de St Thierry', *RHE*, xxxv (1939), 761–73.

—. *Guillaume de St Thierry, L'Homme et son oeuvre,* Bibliothèque médiévale, spirituels préscolastiques, i (Bruges and Paris, 1942).

DELHAYE, P. 'La Place de l'éthique parmi les disciplines scientifiques au XIIe siècle', in *Miscellanea moralia in honorem A. Janssen* (Gembloux, 1948), 29–44.

—. 'L'Enseignement de la philosophie morale au XIIe siècle', *Med. Stud.,* xi (1949), 77–99.

—. ' "Grammatica" et "Ethica" au XIIe siècle', *RTAM,* xxv (1958), 59–110.

DELISLE, L. 'Les Écoles d'Orléans au XIIe et au XIIIe siècles', *Annuaire: Bulletin de la société de l'histoire de France,* vii (1869), 139–54.

DEMATS, P. *Fabula: Trois études de mythographie antique et médiévale,* Publications Romanes et Françaises, cxxii (Geneva, 1973).

DENIFLE, H. *Die Entstehung der Universitaten des Mittelalters* (Berlin, 1885).

—. 'Das Exemplar Parisiense', *Archiv für Literatur und Kirkengeschichte des Mittelalters,* iv (1888), 277–92.

DICKEY, M. 'Some Commentaries on the *De inventione* and *Ad Herennium* of the Eleventh and Early Twelfth Centuries', *MARS,* vi (1968), 1–41.

DONDAINE, A., and BATAILLON, L. J. 'Le Commentaire de S. Thomas sur les Météores', *AFP,* xxxvi (1966), 81–152.

DONDAINE, H. F. *Le Corpus Dionysien de l'Université de Paris au XIIIe siècle* (Rome, 1953).

DOUCET, V. 'Quelques commentaires sur les "Sentences" de Pierre le Lombard', in *Miscellanea Lombardiana* (Novara, 1957), pp. 275–94.

DOUIE, D. L. *Archbishop Pecham* (Oxford, 1952).

DOYLE, A. I., and PARKES, M. B. 'The Production of Manuscripts of the *Canterbury Tales* and the *Confessio amantis* in the early fifteenth century', *Medieval Scribes, Manuscripts and Libraries: Essays presented to N. R. Ker,* ed. M. B. Parkes and A. G. Watson (London, 1978), pp. 164–210.

DRONKE, P. *Fabula: Explorations into the uses of Myth in Medieval Platonism,* Mittellateinische Studien und Texte, ix (Leiden, 1974).

—. *Dante and Medieval Latin Traditions* (Cambridge, 1986).

DUNPHY, W. B. 'St Albert and the Five Causes', *AHDLMA,* xxxiii (1967), 7–21.

EDER, C. E. *Die Schule des Klosters Tegernsee im frühen Mittelalter im Spiegel der Tegernseer Handschriften,* Münchener Beiträge zur Mediävistik und Renaissance-Forschung, lxxxiii (Munich, 1972).

EDWARDS, M. C. *A Study of Six Characters in Chaucer's Legend of Good Women with reference to medieval scholia on Ovid's Heroides* (unpub. B. Litt. thesis, Oxford, 1970).

ELDER, E. R. 'William of St Thierry: Rational and Affective Spirituality', in *The Spirituality of Western Christendom*, ed. E. R. Elder (Kalamazoo, Michigan, 1976), pp. 85–105.

ELSWIJK, H. C. VON. *Gilbert Porreta, sa vie, son oeuvre, sa pensée*, Spicilegium sacrum Lovaniense, études et documents, xxxiii (Louvain, 1966).

EVANS, G. R. *Old Arts and New Theology: The Beginnings of Theology as an Academic Discipline* (Oxford, 1980).

—. *The Language and Logic of the Bible: The Road to Reformation* (Cambridge, 1985).

FLINT, V. I. J. 'Some Notes on the Early Twelfth Century Commentaries on the Psalms', *RTAM*, xxxvii (1971), 80–5.

—. 'The "School of Laon": A Reconsideration', *RTAM*, xliii (1976), 89–110.

FONTAINE, J. *Isidore de Seville et la culture classique dans l'Espagne wisigothique* (Paris, 1959).

—. 'Les Symbolismes de la cithare dans la poésie de Paulin de Nole', in *Romanitas et christianitas: Studia I. H. Waszink oblata*, ed. W. Den Boer, *et al.* (Amsterdam and London, 1973), pp. 123–43.

FREDBORG, K. M. 'The Commentary of Thierry of Chartres on Cicero's *De inventione*', *CIMAGL*, vii (1971), 1–37.

—. 'The Dependence of Petrus Helias' *Summa super Priscianum* on William of Conches' *Glose super Priscianum*', *CIMAGL*, xi (1973), 1–57.

—. 'Petrus Helias on Rhetoric', *CIMAGL*, xiii (1974), 31–41.

—. 'The Commentaries on Cicero's *De inventione* and *Rhetorica ad Herennium* by William of Champeaux', *CIMAGL*, xvii (1976), 1–39.

GASTALDELLI, F. 'L'esegesi biblica secondo Goffredo di Auxerre', *Salesianum*, xxxvii (1975), 219–50.

GAUTHIER, R. A. 'Notes sur les débuts (1225–1240) du premier "averroïsme" ', *RSPT*, lxvi (1982), 321–74.

GEENEN, G. 'S. Thomas et ses sources pseudépigraphiques', *Ephemerides theologicae Lovanienses*, xx (1943), 71–80.

GENET, J.-P. (ed.). *Four English Political Tracts of the Later Middle Ages*, Camden Fourth Srs (London, 1968).

GHELLINCK, J. DE. 'La Carrière de Pierre Lombard: Nouvelle précision chronologique', *RHE*, xxx (1934), 95–100.

—. 'Patristique et argument de tradition au bas moyen âge', *Beiträge zur Geschichte der Philosophie und Theologie des Mittelalters*, suppl. III.i (1935), 403–26.

—. ' "Originale" et "originalia" ', *Bull. du Cange,* xiv (1939), 95–105.

—. 'Nagi et gigantes', *Bull. du Cange,* xviii (1945), 25–9.

—. *Le Mouvement théologique du XIIe siècle,* 2 ed. (Bruges, 1948).

GHISALBERTI, F. 'Arnolfo d'Orléans, un cultore di Ovidio nel s. XII', *Memorie del Reale Istituto Lombardo di Scienze e Lettere,* xxiv (1932), 157–234.

—. 'Medieval Biographies of Ovid', *JWCI,* ix (1946), 10–59.

GILLESPIE, V. '*Doctrina* and *predicacio:* The Design and Function of Some Pastoral Manuals', *Leeds Studies in English,* n.s. xi (1980), 36–50.

GILSON, E. *The Mystical Theology of St Bernard,* trans. A. H. C. Downes (London, 1940).

—. *History of Christian Philosophy in the Middle Ages* (London, 1955).

—. *The Elements of Christian Philosophy* (New York, 1963).

GLORIEUX, P. 'L'enseignement au moyen âge: techniques et méthodes en usage à la faculté de théologie de Paris au XIIIe siècle', *AHDLMA,* xxxv (1968), 65–186.

GLUNCZ, H. H. *History of the Vulgate in England from Alcuin to Bacon* (Cambridge, 1933).

GNEUSS, H. *Hymnar und Hymnen in Englischen Mittelalter* (Tübingen, 1968).

GOSSELIN, E. A. *The King's Progress to Jerusalem: Some Interpretations of David during the Reformation Period and their Patristic and Medieval Background,* Humana Civilitas, ii (Malibu, 1976).

GOUGAUD, L. 'La Théorie dans la spiritualité médiévale', *RAM,* (1922), 381–94.

GRABMANN, M. *Die Geschichte der scholastichen Methode* (Freiburg, 1909–11).

—. *Mittelalterliches Geistesleben* (Munich, 1926–56).

—. 'I divieti ecclesiastici di Aristotele sotto Innocenzo III e Gregorio IX', in *Miscellanea historiae pontificae,* v.7 (Rome, 1941).

GREER, R. A. *Theodore of Mopsuestia, Exegete and Theologian* (London, 1961).

GRÜNDEL, J. *Die Lehre von den Umständen der menschlichen Handlung im Mittelalter,* Beiträge zur Geschichte der Philosophie und Theologie des Mittelalters, xxxix.5 (1963).

HAHN, T. G. *God's Friends: Virtuous Heathen in Later Medieval Thought and English Literature* (Ph.D. thesis, University of California, Los Angeles, 1974). Pub. by University Microfilms, Ann Arbor.

HAILPERIN, H. *Rashi and the Christian Scholars* (Pittsburg, 1963).

HALM, C. (ed.). *Rhetores Latini Minores* (Leipzig, 1863).

HAMILTON, G. L. 'Theodulus, a Medieval Textbook', *MP,* vii (1909), 1–17.

HARDISON, O. B. 'The Place of Averroes' Commentary on the *Poetics* in the History of Medieval Criticism', *Medieval and Renaissance Studies 4*, ed. J. L. Lievsay (Duke Univ. Press, 1970), pp. 57–81.

HÄRING, N. M. 'The Lectures of Thierry of Chartres on Boethius *De trinitate*', *AHDLMA*, xxv (1959), 113–226.

—. 'Two Commentaries on Boethius by Thierry of Chartres', *AHDLMA*, xxvii (1960), 65–136.

—. 'Thierry of Chartres and Dominicus Gundissalinus', *Med. Stud.*, xxvi (1964), 271–86.

—. 'Chartres and Paris Revisited', in *Essays in Honour of A. C. Pegis*, ed. J. R. O'Donnell (Toronto, 1974), pp. 268–329.

HARTMANN, W. 'Psalmenkommentare aus der Zeit der Reform und der Frühscholastik', *Studi Gregoriani*, ix (1972), 346–54.

HAZELTON, R. 'The Christianization of Cato', *Med. Stud.*, xix (1957), 157–73.

HINNESBUSCH, W. A. *The History of the Dominican Order* (New York, 1966–73).

HUNT, R. W. 'Chapter Headings of Augustine *De trinitate* ascribed to Adam Marsh', *BLR*, v (1954), 63–8.

—. 'Manuscripts containing the Indexing Symbols of Robert Grosseteste', *BLR*, iv (1955), 241–55.

—. 'The Library of Robert Grosseteste', in *Robert Grosseteste. Scholar and Bishop: Essays in Commemoration of the Seventh Centenary of his Death*. ed. D. A. Callus (Oxford, 1955), pp. 121–45.

—. 'English Learning in the Late Twelfth Century', in *Essays in Medieval History*, ed. R. W. Southern (London, 1968), pp. 106–28.

HUYGENS, R. B. C. 'Notes sur le *Dialogus super auctores* de Conrad de Hirsau et le commentaire sur Théodule de Bernard d'Utrecht', *Latomus*, xiii (1954), 420–8.

JAUSS, H. R. *Alterität und Modernität der mittelalterlichen Literatur* (Munich, 1977).

—. 'The Alterity and Modernity of Medieval Literature', *New Literary History*, x (1979), 385–90.

JEAUNEAU, E. 'L'Usage de la notion d'*integumentum* à travers les gloses de Guillaume de Conches', *AHDLMA*, xxiv (1957), 35–100.

—. 'Deux rédactions des gloses de Guillaume de Conches sur Priscien', *RTAM*, xxvii (1960), 212–47.

—. ' "Nagi gigantum humeris insidentes": Essai d'interprétation de Bernard de Chartres', *Vivarium*, v (1967), 79–99.

—. 'La Lecture des auteurs classiques à l'école de Chartres durant la première moitié du XIIe siècle', in *Classical Influences on European Culture a.d. 500–1500,* ed. R. R. Bolgar (Cambridge, 1971) pp. 95–102.

—. 'Les Écoles de Laon et d'Auxerre au IXe siècle', in *Settimane di studio del Centro Italiano di Studi sull'alto Medioevo,* xix (Spoleto, 1972), ii, 794–839. 794–839.

JEFFERSON, B. L. *Chaucer and the Consolation of Philosophy of Boethius* (Princeton, 1917).

JENARO-MACLENNAN, L. *The Trecento Commentaries on the Divina commedia and the Epistle to Cangrande* (Oxford, 1974).

JOLIVET, J. 'Sur quelques critiques de la théologie d'Abélard', *AHDLMA,* xxxviii (1963), 7–51.

JOURDAIN, C. 'Des Commentaires inédits de Guillaume de Conches et Nicolas Traveth sur la Consolation de Boèce', *Notices et extraits de manuscrits de la Bibliothèque Impériale,* xx.2 (1862), pp. 40–82.

KANTOROWICZ, H. *Studies in the Glossators of the Roman Law* (Cambridge, 1938).

KENNEDY, G. *The Art of Rhetoric in the Roman World* (Princeton, 1972).

KER, N. R. *Medieval Manuscripts in British Libraries* (Oxford, 1969–).

KNOWLES, D. *The English Mystical Tradition* (London, 1961).

KÖPF, U. *Die Anfänge der theologischen Wissenschaftstheorie im 13. Jahrhundert,* Beiträge zur historischen Theologie, xlix (Tübingen, 1974).

KURZ, E. (ed.). *Die Persius-Scholien nach den Berner Handschriften* (Burgdorf, 1875).

LACOMBE, G. *La Vie et les oeuvres de Prévostin,* Bibliothèque Thomiste, ix (Le Saulchoir, 1927).

LACOMBE, G., and SMALLEY, B. 'Studies on the Commentaries of Cardinal Stephen Langton', *AHDLMA,* v (1931), 5–220.

—. 'The Lombard's Commentary on Isaias and other fragments', *New Schol.,* v (1931), 123–62.

LAMBOT, C. 'Lettre inédite de S. Augustin relative au *De civitate Dei, Rev. bén.,* li (1939), 109–21.

LANDGRAF, A. 'Recherches sur les écrits de Pierre le Mangeur', *RTAM,* iii (1931), 341–72.

—. 'Die Zuweisung eines Psalmenkommentars an Anselm von Laon', *Biblica,* xxiii (1942), 170–4.

LECLERCQ, J. 'Le Commentaire du Cantique des Cantiques attribué à Anselme de Laon', *RTAM*, xvi (1949), 23–39.

—. 'Les Deux rédactions du prologue de Pierre Lombard sur les épitres de S. Paul', in *Miscellanea Lombardiana* (Novara, 1957), pp. 109–112.

—. *Études sur le vocabulaire monastique du moyen âge*, Studia Anselmiana, xlviii (Rome, 1961).

—. *The Love of Learning and the Desire for God*, trans. C. Misrahi (Fordham, 1961).

—. *Monks and Love in Twelfth Century France* (Oxford, 1979).

LEFF, G. *Bradwardine and the Pelagians* (Cambridge, 1957).

—. *Paris and Oxford Universities in the Thirteenth and Fourteenth Centuries* (New York and London, 1968).

—. *William of Ockham* (Manchester, 1975).

LEWIS, C. S. *The Allegory of Love* (Oxford, 1936).

LEWRY, O. *Robert Kilwardby's Writings on the Logica vetus studied with regard to their teaching and method* (unpub. D. Phil. thesis, Oxford, 1978).

LIVINGSTONE, E. A. See CROSS, F. L.

LUSCOMBE, D. E. *The School of Peter Abelard* (Cambridge, 1969).

LUTZ, C. E. 'Remigius' Ideas on the Origin of the Seven Liberal Arts', *Med. et Hum.*, x (1956), 32–49.

—. 'The Commentary of Remigius of Auxerre on Martianus Capella', *Med. Stud.*, xix (1957), 137–56.

—. 'One formula of *accessus* in Remigius's Works', *Latomus*, xix (1960), 774–80.

MAINZER, H. C. *A Study of the Sources of the Confessio amantis of John Gower* (unpub. D. Phil. thesis, Oxford, 1967).

MANCINI, A. 'Un commento ignoto di Remy d'Auxerre ai *Disticha Catonis*', *Rendiconti della Reale Accademia dei Lincei*, ser. v, xi (1902), 175–98, 369–82.

MANDONNET, P. *Siger de Brabant*, Les philosophes Belges, vi–vii (Louvain, 1908–11).

MANITIUS, M. *Geschichte der lateinischer Literatur des Mittelalters* (Munich, 1911).

—. 'Remigius von Auxerre und Mico von St Riquier', *Neues Archiv*, xxxvi (1911), 43–57.

MANZALAOUI, M. A. *The Secreta secretorum in English Thought and Literature from the Fourteenth Century to the Seventeenth Century* (unpub. D. Phil. thesis, Oxford, 1954).

MARROU, H. S. Augustin et la fin de la culture antique (Paris, 1938).

—. Histoire de l'éducation dans l'antiquité, 6 ed. (Paris, 1965).

MARSHALL, M. H. 'Theatre in the Middle Ages: Evidence from Dictionaries and Glosses', Symposium, iv (1950), 1–39.

MARTIN, R. M. 'Notes sur l'oeuvre littéraire de Pierre le Mangeur', RTAM, iii (1931), 63–4.

MATHEW, G. The Court of Richard II (London, 1968).

MCEVOY, J. Man and Cosmos in the Philosophy of Robert Grosseteste (unpub. D. Phil. thesis, Louvain, 1974).

MCKEON, R. 'Rhetoric in the Middle Ages', in Critics and Criticism, Ancient and Modern, ed. R. S. Crane (Chicago, 1952), pp. 260–96.

MENHARDT, H. 'Der Nachlass des Honorius Augustodunensis', Zeitschrift für deutsches Alterum und deutsche Literatur, lxxxix (1958), 23–69.

MEYER, P. 'Les manuscrits français de Cambridge', Romania, viii (1879), 305–42.

MEYVAERT, P. 'John Erghome and the Vaticinium Roberti Bridlington', Speculum, xli (1966), 656–64.

MICHALSKI, C. 'Le Problème de la volonté à Oxford et à Paris au XIVe siècle', Studia philosophica, ii (Lemberg, 1936), 233–65.

MILLER, J. M. et al. (eds.), Readings in Medieval Rhetoric, ed. and trans. J. M. Miller, M. H. Prosser and T. W. Benson (Bloomington and London, 1973).

MINNIS, A. J. ' "Authorial Intention" and "Literal Sense" in the Exegetical Theories of Richard FitzRalph and John Wyclif', Proceedings of the Royal Irish Academy, lxxv, section C, i (Dublin, 1975).

—. 'Discussions of "Authorial Role" and "Literary Form" in Late-Medieval Scriptural Exegesis', PBB, xcix (1977), 37–65.

—. 'Late-Medieval Discussions of Compilatio and the Role of the Compilator', PBB, ci (1979), 385–421.

—. 'A Note on Chaucer and the Ovide moralisé', Medium Aevum, xlviii.2 (1979), 254–7.

—. 'Literary Theory in Discussions of Formae Tractandi by Medieval Theologians', New Literary History, xi (1979), 133–45.

—. 'John Gower, sapiens in ethics and politics', Medium Aevum, xlix.2 (1980), 207–229.

—. 'Langland's Ymaginatif and Late-Medieval Theories of Imagination', Comparative Criticism, iii (1981), 71–103.

—. 'The Influence of Academic Prologues on the Prologues and Literary

Attitudes of Late-Medieval English Writers', *Med. Stud.*, xliii (1981), 342–83.

—. 'Aspects of the Medieval French and English Traditions of the *De consolatione philosophiae*', in *Boethius: His Life, Thought and Influence*, ed. M. T. Gibson (Oxford, 1981), 312–61.

—. 'Chaucer and Comparative Literary Theory', in *New Perspectives in Chaucer Criticism (Papers of the Second International Conference of the New Chaucer Society, at New Orleans, April 10–12, 1980)*, ed. D. M. Rose (Norman, Oklahoma, 1981), pp. 53–69.

—. (ed.) *Gower's Confessio amantis: Responses and Reassessments* (Cambridge, 1983).

MOORE, P. S. *The Works of Peter of Poitiers* (Washington, 1936).

MURPHY, J. J. 'Cicero's Rhetoric in the Middle Ages', *Quarterly Journal of Speech*, liii (1967), 334–41.

—. *Rhetoric in the Middle Ages* (Berkeley, 1974).

MURRAY, A. V. *Abelard and St Bernard* (Manchester, 1967).

MYNORS, R. A. B. *Catalogue of the Manuscripts of Balliol College, Oxford* (Oxford, 1963).

NARDI, B. 'Osservazioni sul medievale "accessus ad auctores" in rapporto all' "Epistola a Cangrande" ', in *Saggi e note di critica Dantesca* (Milan and Naples, 1966), pp. 269–89.

NASH, P. W. 'Giles of Rome and the Subject of Theology', *Med. Stud.*, xviii (1956), 61–92.

NOLHAC, PIERRE DE. *Pétrarque et l'humanisme* (Paris, 1907).

OBERMAN, H. A. *Archbishop Thomas Bradwardine: A Fourteenth-Century Augustinian* (Utrecht, 1958).

—. ' "Facientibus quod in se est Deus non denegat gratiam": Robert Holcot and the Beginnings of Luther's Theology', *Harvard Theological Review*, iv (1962), 317–42.

—. *The Harvest of Medieval Theology* (Michigan, 1967).

OLSON, G. 'The Medieval Theory of Literature for Refreshment and its Use in the *Fabliau* Tradition', *SP*, lxxi (1974), 291–313.

—. *Literature as Recreation in the Later Middle Ages* (Ithaca and London, 1982).

ORME, N. *English Schools in the Middle Ages* (London, 1973).

OWST, G. R. *Preaching in Medieval England* (Cambridge, 1926).

—. *Literature and Pulpit in Medieval England,* 2 ed. (Oxford, 1961).

PAETOW, L. M. *The Arts Course at Medieval Universities with special reference to grammar and rhetoric* (Champaign, Illinois, 1910).

PANTIN, W. A. 'John of Wales and Medieval Humanism', in *Medieval Studies presented to Aubrey Gwynn* (Dublin, 1961), pp. 279–319.

PARENT, J. M. *La Doctrine de la création dans l'école de Chartres,* Publications de l'Institut d'Études Médiévales d'Ottawa, viii (Paris and Ottawa, 1938).

PARKES, M. B. 'The Influence of the Concepts of *Ordinatio* and *Compilatio* on the Development of the Book', in *Medieval Learning and Literature: Essays presented to R. W. Hunt,* ed. J. J. G. Alexander and M. T. Gibson (Oxford, 1975), pp. 115–41.

—. See also DOYLE, A. I.

PEPPERMÜLLER, R. *Abelards Auslegung des Römerbriefes,* Beiträge zur Geschichte der Philosophie und Theologie des Mittelalters, Neue Folge, Bd. x (Aschendorff, 1972).

PERGAMO, B. 'De quaestionibus ineditis Fr Odonis Rigaldi, Fr Gulielmi de Melitonia et codicis Vat. Lat. 782 circa naturam theologiae deque earum relatione ad Summam theologicam Fr Alexandri Halensis', *AFH,* xxix (1937), 3–54.

PETERSEN, K. O. *Sources of the Nonnes Preestes Tale,* Radcliffe College Monographs, x (Boston, 1898).

—. 'Chaucer and Trevet', *PMLA,* xviii (1903), 173–93.

PFEIFFER, R. *History of Classical Scholarship 1300–1850* (Oxford, 1976).

PINBORG, J. *Die Entwicklung der Sprachtheorie im Mittelalters,* Beiträge zur Geschichte der Philosophie und Theologie des Mittelalters, xlii (1967).

PONTET, M. *L'Exégèse de S. Augustin prédicateur* (Paris, 1946).

PORCHER, J. 'Le *De disciplina scholarium,* traité du XIIIe siècle faussement attribué à Boèce', *Positions des thèses soutenues par les élèves de la promotion de 1921 de l'École des Chartes* (Paris, 1921), pp. 91–3.

POWICKE, F. M., and EMDEN, A. B. (eds.). Rashdall's *Universities of Europe in the Middle Ages* (Oxford, 1963).

PRATT, R. A. 'Chaucer and the Hand that Fed Him', *Speculum,* xli (1966), 619–42.

—. 'Chaucer and *Les Cronicles* of Nicholas Trevet', *Studies in Language, Literature and Culture of the Middle Ages and Later,* ed. E. B. Atwood and A. A. Hill (Austin, 1969), pp. 303–11.

—. 'Some Latin Sources of the Nonnes Preest on Dreams', *Speculum,* lii (1977), 538–70.

PRZYCHOCKI, G. 'Accessus Ovidiani', *Rozprawy Akademii Umiejetnosci,* wydzial filologiczny, serya III, tom. iv (1911), 65–126.

QUADLBAUER, F. *Die antike Theorie der genera dicendi im lateinischen Mittelalter,* Sitzungsberichte der österreichischen Akademie der Wissenschaften, phil.–hist. klasse, Bd. cclxi, 2 Abh. (Wien, 1962).

QUAIN, E. A. 'The Medieval *Accessus ad auctores*', *Traditio,* iii (1945), 228–42.

RAND, E. K. *Cicero in the Courtroom of St Thomas Aquinas,* The Aquinas Lecture 1945 (Marquette, 1946).

REEVES, M. *The Influence of Prophecy in the Later Middle Ages: A Study in Joachimism* (Oxford, 1969).

RICHÉ, P. *Education and Culture in the Barbarian West,* trans. J. J. Contreni (Columbia, S. Carolina, 1976).

RICKERT, E. 'Chaucer at School', *MP,* xxix (1931/2), 257–74.

RIQUET, M. 'St Thomas et les *auctoritates* en philosophie', *Archives de philosophie,* iii.2 (1925), 117–55.

ROBERT, BROTHER S. 'Rhetoric and Dialectic: According to the First Latin Commentary on the Rhetoric of Aristotle', *New Schol.,* xxxi (1957), 484–98.

ROBERT, G. *La Renaissance du XII siècle: les écoles et l'enseignement,* Publications de l'Institut d'Études Médiévales d'Ottawa, iii (Paris and Ottawa, 1933).

ROBINSON, J. H., and ROLFE, H. W. *Petrarch* (New York, 1968).

ROLFE, H. W. see ROBINSON, J. H.

ROUSE, R. H. 'La Diffusion en occident au XIIIe siècle des outils de travail facilitant l'accès aux textes autoritatifs', *Revue des études islamiques,* xliv (1976), 115–47.

——. 'Florilegia and Latin Classical Authors in Twelfth- and Thirteenth-Century Orléans', *Viator,* x (1979), 131–60.

ROUSE, R. H., and ROUSE, M. A. 'The Texts called *Lumen anime*', *AFP,* xli (1971), 5–113.

——. 'Biblical Distinctions in the Thirteenth Century', *AHDLMA,* xli (1974), 27–37.

——. 'The Verbal Concordance to the Scriptures', *AFP,* xliv (1974), 5–30.

——. *Preachers, Florilegia and Sermons: Studies on the Manipulus florum of Thomas of Ireland* (Toronto, 1979).

——. '*Statim invenire:* Schools, Preachers and New Attitudes to the Page', forthcoming in *The Renaissance of the Twelfth Century,* ed. R. Benson and G. Constable.

RUSSELL, D. A., and WINTERBOTTOM, M. (eds.), *Ancient Literary Criticism, The Principal Texts in New Translations* (Oxford, 1972).

SALTER, E. *Nicholas Love's 'Myrrour of the Blessed Lyf of Jesu Christ'*, Analecta Cartusiana, ix (1974).

SANFORD, E. M. 'The Manuscripts of Lucan: Accessus and Marginalia', *Speculum,* ix (1934), 278–95.

SAVAGE, J. J. 'The Scholia in the Virgil of Tours, Bernensis 165', *HSCP,* xxxvi (1925), 163–4.

SEBASTIAN, H. F. *William Wheteley's commentary on the Pseudo-Boethius' tractate De disciplina scolarium and medieval grammar school education* (Ph.D. thesis, Columbia University, 1970). Pub. by University Microfilms, Ann Arbor, Michigan.

SEDLMAYER, H. S. (ed.). *Prolegomena critica ad Heroides Ovidianas* (Vienna, 1878).

SHARP, D. E. *Franciscan Philosophy at Oxford in the Thirteenth Century,* British Society of Franciscan Studies, xvi (Oxford, 1930).

—. 'The *De ortu scientiarum* of Robert Kilwardby', *New Schol.,* viii (1934), 1–30.

SILK, E. T. *Cambridge Ii.3.21 and the relation of Chaucer's Boethius to Trevet and Jean de Meung* (Ph.D. thesis, Yale, 1930). Pub. by University Microfilms, Ann Arbor, Michigan.

SILVESTRE, M. 'Le Schema "moderne" des *accessus*', *Latomus,* xvi (1957), 684–9.

SMALLEY, B. 'Gilbertus Universalis, Bishop of London (1128–34), and the Problem of the *Glossa ordinaria*', *RTAM,* vii (1935), 235–62.

—. 'Gilbertus Universalis, contd.', *RTAM,* viii (1936), 24–60.

—. 'La *Glossa ordinaria*', *RTAM,* ix (1937), 365–400.

—. 'A Collection of Paris Lectures of the Later Twelfth Century in the MS Pembroke College, Cambridge 7', *Camb. Hist. Jour.,* vi (1938), 103–113.

—. 'A Commentary on Isaias by Guerric of St Quentin O.P.', *Studi e testi,* cxxii (1946), 383–97.

—. 'Robert Bacon and the Early Dominican School', *TRHS,* 4 ser., xxx (1948), 1–19.

—. 'John Russel O.F.M.', *RTAM,* xxiii (1956), 277–320.

—. 'John Baconthorpe's Postill on St Matthew', *MARS,* iv (1958), 91–145.

—. 'Wyclif's *Postilla* on the Old Testament and his *Principium*', in *Oxford Studies presented to D. Callus*, Oxford Historical Society, New Srs, xvi (Oxford, 1964), 253–96.

—. 'The Bible in the Medieval Schools', in *The Cambridge History of the Bible, vol. ii: The West from the Fathers to the Reformation*, ed. G. W. H. Lampe (Cambridge, 1969), pp. 197–220.

—. 'William of Auvergne, John of la Rochelle and St Thomas Aquinas on the Old Law', in *St Thomas Aquinas 1274–1974, Commemorative Studies*, ed. A. Maurer *et al.*, Pontifical Institute of Mediaeval Studies (Toronto, 1974), ii, 11–71.

—. Review of Gosselin, *The King's Progress to Jerusalem*, in *Speculum*, liii (1978), 368–9.

—. 'Peter Comestor on the Gospels and his Sources', *RTAM*, xlvi (1979), 84–129.

—. 'An Early Paris Lecture Course on St Luke', in *Sapientiae Doctrina: Mélanges offerts à Dom H. Bascour*, Réch. de théol. anc. et méd., numéro spécial, i (Leuven, 1980), 299–311.

SMITH, J. R. (trans.). *The Earliest Lives of Dante*, Yale Studies in English, x (New York, 1901).

SOMMER-SECKENDORFF, E. M. F. *Studies in the Life of Robert Kilwardby, O.P.*, Institutum historicum FF. Praedicatorum, Dissertationes historicae, viii (1937).

SOUTHERN, R. W. 'Humanism and the School of Chartres', in *Medieval Humanism and other Studies* (Oxford, 1970), pp. 61–85.

—. 'History as Prophecy', *TRHS*, 5 ser., xxii (1972), 159–80.

—. *Platonism, Scholastic Method, and the School of Chartres*, The 1979 Stenton Lecture, University of Reading.

SPITZ, H.-J. *Die Metaphorik des geistigen Schriftsinns*, Munstersche Mittelalter-Schriften, xii (Munich, 1972).

STACY, R. H. *Defamiliarization in Language and Literature* (Syracuse, 1977).

STOELEN, A. 'Les Commentaires scripturaires attribués à Bruno le Chartreux', *RTAM*, xxv (1958), 177–247.

—. 'Bruno le Chartreux, Jean Gratiadei et la "Lettre de S. Anselme" sur l'euchariste', *RTAM*, xxxiv (1967), 18–83.

SUCHOMSKI, JOACHIM. *'Delectatio' und 'Utilitas': Ein Beitrag zum Verständnis mittelalterlicher komischer Literatur* (Bern, 1975).

SYNAVE, P. 'La Question disputée *De sensibus Scripturae*: La Doctrine de S. Thomas d'Aquin sur le sens littéral des écritures', *Rév. bib.*, xxxv (1926), 40–65.

SYPHERD, W. O. *Studies in Chaucer's House of Fame,* Chaucer Society Publications, 2 ser., xxxix (London, 1907).

TATEO, F. 'Poesia e favola nella poetica del Boccaccio', *Retorica e poetica fra medioevo e rinascimento,* Biblioteca di filologia Romanza, v (Bari, 1960), 67–202.

TAYLOR, RUPERT. *The Political Prophecy in England* (New York, 1911; repr. New York, 1967).

THOMSON, S. HARRISON. 'Grosseteste's Topical Concordance of the Bible and the Fathers', *Speculum,* ix (1934), 139–44.

—. 'Robert Kilwardby's Commentaries *In Priscianum* and *In Barbarismum Donati', New Schol.,* xii (1958), 52–65.

THUROT, C. 'Documents relatifs à l'histoire de la grammaire au moyen âge', *Academie des Inscriptions et Belles Lettres, Comptes Rendus,* n.s., vi (1870), 242–51.

—. 'Extraits de divers manuscrits latins pour servir à l'histoire des doctrines grammaticales au moyen âge', *Notices et extraits des manuscrits de la Bibliothèque Nationale et autres bibliothèques,* xxii, pt.2 (1868).

TORRELL, J.-P. *Théorie de la prophétie et philosophie de la conaissance aux environs 1230: La Contribution d'Hughes de Saint-Cher,* Spicilegium Sacrum Lovaniense, Études et documents, xl (Louvain, 1977).

TRAPP, D. 'Augustinian Theology of the Fourteenth Century', *Augustiniana,* vi (1956), 146–274.

UPSON, H. R. 'Mediaeval Lives of Virgil', *CP,* xxxviii (1943), 103–111.

VACCARI, P. A. 'Il genuino commento ai salmi di Remigio di Auxerre', in *Scritti di erudizione e di filologia,* i (Rome, 1952), 283–329.

VAN DEN EYNDE, D. 'Literary Note on the Earliest Scholastic *Commentarii in psalmos', Franciscan Studies,* xiv (1954), 121–54.

VIARRE, S. *La Survie d'Ovide dans la littérature scientifique de XIIe et XIIIe siècles* (Poitiers, 1966).

WARD, J. O. 'The Date of the Commentary on Cicero's *De inventione* by Thierry of Chartres', *Viator,* iii (1972), 219–73.

—. 'Glosses and Commentaries on Cicero's *Rhetorica',* in *Medieval Eloquence: Studies in the Theory and Practice of Medieval Rhetoric,* ed. J. J. Murphy (Berkeley, 1978), pp. 25–67.

WEDEL, T. O. *The Medieval Attitude to Astrology, particularly in England,* Yale Studies in English, lx (New Haven, 1920).

WEINBERG, B. *A History of Literary Criticism in the Italian Renaissance* (Chicago, 1961).

WEISHEIPL, J. A. 'The Curriculum of the Faculty of Arts at Oxford in the Early Fourteenth Century', *Med. Stud.*, xxvi (1964), 143–85.

—. 'Classification of the Sciences in Medieval Thought', *Med. Stud.*, xxvii (1965), 54–90.

—. *Friar Thomas d'Aquino* (Oxford, 1975).

WEISS, R. *The Spread of Italian Humanism* (London, 1964).

WELTER, J. T. *L'Exemplum dans la littérature religieuse et didactique du moyen âge* (Paris and Toulouse, 1927).

WESTERINK, L. G. (ed.). *Anonymous Prolegomena to Platonic Philosophy* (Amsterdam, 1962).

WETHERBEE, W. *Platonism and Poetry in the Twelfth Century* (Princeton, 1972).

WICKERT, MARIA. *Studien zu John Gower* (Cologne, 1963).

WIERUSZOWSKI, H. 'Rhetoric and the Classics in Italian Education of the Thirteenth Century', *Studia Gratiana*, xi (1967), 169–208.

WILMART, A. 'Le Commentaire sur les psaumes imprimé sous le nom de Rufin', *Rev. bén.*, xxxi (1914/19), 258–76.

—. 'Un Commentaire des psaumes restitué à Anselme de Laon', *RTAM*, viii (1936), 325–44.

WRIGHT, T. (ed.). *Political Poems and Songs*, Rolls Srs (London, 1859–61).

ZECHMEISTER, J. (ed.). *Scholia Vindobonensia ad Horatii artem poeticam* (Wien, 1877).

ZIMMERMAN, H. *Antiqui und Moderni: Traditionbewusstein und Fortschrittskewusstein im späten Mittelalter* (Berlin, 1973).

ZUMTHOR, PAUL. 'Comments on H. R. Jauss's Article', *New Literary History*, x (1979), 385–90.

Index of Latin Terms

accessus introduction, prologue: 15,
21, 35, 41, 47, 50, 62, 126, 140,
203, 206, 224n, 225n, 228n,
231n, 241n, 276n

actor writer, in contrast with *auctor*:
26, 157

affectus affections, disposition: 49–52,
61, 90, 119–22, 126, 127, 129–
30, 134, 137, 139, 144, 239n,
252n, 264n

affirmare to affirm: 194

affirmator one who affirms: 100–101

allegoria allegory. *See* General Index
s.v. allegory

ante opus before the work (series of
headings): 15

ars dictaminis art of letter-writing: 62,
191, 242–43n

artes praedicandi arts of preaching:
136–38 passim, 161–62, 174–76,
263–64n

artifex master, practitioner, craftsman: 31, 81

aspectus gaze of the intellect: 120–22,
137; *finis aspectus* objective of looking: 120

assertio assertion: 193, 194

assertor one who asserts: 100–102

auctor and *auctoritas* author and authority, major definitions: 1–2,
10–12; *auctoritas* in sense of extract
from an *auctor*: 10, 59, 95, 116–
17, 146, 155–56, 157, 158, 166,
182, 183, 184, 192, 197, 201,
202

cantus song: 134

capitula chapter-divisions: 227n,
274n

capitulum chapter-summary: 171,
274n, 275n

carmen song, poem: 135; *carminis species* species of poetry: 135

causa, causae cause, causes: 32, 162–
63, 174; *causa scribendi* cause of the
writing: 41, 244n; *causae libri*
causes of the book: 172; *causae operis*
causes of the work: 31

causa distinctionis case of the divisions:
64–65, 66, 87

causa frequentationis case of frequent
use: 64–65, 66

causa inscriptionis cause of the title:
240n

causa nominis case of the name: 64–65,
66

causa propinqua immediate or near
cause: 77; cf. 102, 255n

causa quantitatis case of the quantity:
64–65, 66

causa remota remote or far cause: 77;
cf. 102, 255n

causae introductoriae introductory causes, being the Aristotelian four causes: 79, 249–50n

causa efficiens efficient cause: 5, 9, 28, 39, 74–84, 90–102 passim, 113, 117, 162, 163, 173, 175, 176, 230n, 249n, 251n

  causa effectiva librorum effective cause of the books: 80

  causa efficiens extra external efficient cause: 76, 77

  causa efficiens intra internal efficient cause: 76, 77

  causa efficiens principalis principal efficient cause: 93

  duplex causa efficiens twofold efficient cause: 79–80, 102, 118, 164–65, 173–75 passim

  quadruplex causa efficiens fourfold efficient cause: 81, 170

  triplex causa efficiens threefold efficient cause: 80–81, 175

causa finalis final cause: 5, 28, 29, 56, 77, 78, 79, 93, 129–30, 162, 163–64 passim, 187, 188, 204–209 passim, 230n, 249n, 253n

causa formalis formal cause: 5, 28, 29, 39, 76, 77–78, 79, 117–59 passim, 161–62, 230n, 249n, 253n

causa materialis material cause: 5, 28–29, 78, 79, 161, 230n, 249n, 253n, 271n

causae moventes ad scribendum causes moving one to write: 80; *causae moventes ab intrinseco/ab extrinseco* causes moving from within/from outside: 249n

characteres scripturae styles of writing (exegematic, dramatic, and mixed): 22, 57–58

circa artem, *circa librum* concerning the art, concerning the book (two series of headings): 30–32

circumstantia litterae circumstances of the letter: 270n

circumstantiae circumstances, summaries: 16–17, 19, 223n, 224n

collectio literary collection: 97, 153, 205

collectio ratiocinative 'gathering together': 123, 146

collector collector: 92, 112

commentator commentator: 94–95, 98, 113

compilatio compilation: 96–97, 98, 113, 155, 191–210 passim, 254n

compilator compiler: 94, 98, 100, 101, 102, 112, 113, 192, 196, 198, 204, 208, 210

conquestio complaint: 133, 238–39n

continuatio syntactical structure: 222n

cui parti philosophiae supponitur which branch of learning the text pertains to: 18, 19, 23–27, 32, 71

definitio definition: 122–23, 146

delectare to delight: 241n

delectatio delight: 241n

distinctio distinction: 32, 63–64, 66, 68, 148, 153, 243n

divisio division of a subject into parts: 123, 146

divisio libri division of the book: 148, 180

divisio textus division of the text: 118, 145, 149, 151, 154, 158, 162, 171, 268n, 269n

dramatica dramatic poems: 57, 135

editor editor: 100, 112

elegia elegies: 135

ethice supponitur it pertains to ethics: 25, 56, 182–83, 188

exempla examples. *See* General Index *s.v.* exemplification

explanatio explanation: 15, 16

expositio litterae exposition of the letter: 222n

extrinsecus and *intrinsecus* extrinsic and intrinsic, being two kinds of introduction: 30–32, 63–71, 77, 86–87, 231n, 244n, 246n, 247n, 249n

fabula fable, myth: 11, 48, 57, 139, 140–41, 142–43, 144, 166, 183, 198, 205, 206–207, 216, 236n, 265n, 266n

figura figure. *See* General Index *s.v.* prefiguration

finis end, objective: 20, 29, 31, 32, 41, 52, 92, 93, 120, 126–27, 129–30, 132, 147–48, 174, 179, 217, 240n

forma form: 29, 118, 148–49; *duplex forma* twofold form: 29, 118, 148–49; *forma tractandi* form of treatment: 4, 29, 76, 118–45, 147, 148, 166, 167, 168, 192, 204; *forma tractatus* form of the treatise: 29, 76, 118, 145–59

forma prophetialis literary form of prophecy. See *modus prophetialis* s.v. *modus agendi*

genera dicendi kinds of speaking (the high, middle, and low styles): 15, 49, 223n

grammaticus grammarian: 13, 33–34

historia history: 104–108, 152; *nuda historia* plain/bare history: 143. *See also* General Index *s.v.* history and historical context

in ipso opere in the work itself (a series of headings): 15

indignatio indignation: 133, 238–39n

ingressus introduction, prologue: 15, 65–66, 68, 223n

inscriptio operis title of the work: 18, 51

inspirator inspirer: 38

integumentum fictional garment: 21, 140, 142–43

intellectus intellect: 119–20, 121, 129, 137, 264n

intentio intention, purpose: 15, 16, 19, 20–21, 27, 31, 32, 41, 45, 50, 52, 54, 55–56, 60–62, 64, 66, 70, 73, 93, 109–110, 111, 127, 154, 170, 171, 178, 180, 181, 182, 189, 190, 191, 196, 199, 225n, 226n, 227n, 236n, 240n, 244n, 245n, 272n, 274n; *communis intentio* common intention: 54, 241n; *generalis intentio* general intention: 55–56, 62; *intentio extrinseca* extrinsic intention: 69–71; *intentio intrinseca* intrinsic intention: 69–71; *prima intentio* primary intention: 85, 251n; *specialis intentio* special intention: 55–56

intentiones chapter-summaries: 154, 275n

inter lineas ipsas within the lines themselves (*re* positioning of authors' names): 157

introitus introduction, prologue, lecture: 15, 134, 222–23n

lectoris arbitrium freedom of the reader: 201

locus place (of composition): 17, 225n, 236n

materia material: 19, 21, 27, 28, 32, 41, 45, 46, 50, 51, 52, 54–55, 62, 64, 66, 70, 93, 108, 126, 153, 155, 162, 163, 170, 171–74 passim, 180, 181, 183, 189, 191, 197, 199, 201–202, 209, 226n, 227n, 236n, 240n, 249n, 272n, 274n; *communis materia* common material: 54, 241n; *materia extrinseca* extrinsic material: 69–70; *materia intrinseca* intrinsic material: 69–70; *principalis materia* principal material: 183, 184, 185, 188 *materia* material, in sense of introduction, prologue: 15, 227n, 241n, 244n

mens auctoris mind/purpose of the author: 100, 154, 172

mens prophetiae mind/purpose of the prophet: 91

modus agendi/procedendi/scribendi/ tractandi mode of literary treatment/procedure: 17, 21–22, 23, 29, 31, 41, 45, 49, 51, 52, 54, 56, 57, 62, 66, 70, 84, 90, 93, 111, 118, 119, 124–45 passim, 148, 151, 162, 168, 170, 171, 172–73, 177, 178, 182, 191, 216–17, 225n, 226n, 236n, 239n, 240n, 244n, 281n; *modus abbreviationis* mode of abbreviation: 79; *modus affectivus, desiderativus et contemplativus* affective, desiderative, and contemplative mode: 129–30; *modus argumentativus* argumentative mode: 263n; *modus definitivus, divisivus et collectivus* definitive, divisive, and collective mode: 76, 122–23, 144–46, 147; *modus disputativus* disputative mode: 87, 128; *modus dramatis* dramatic mode: 57; *modus excerptoris* mode of the excerptor: 192, 204; *modus exemplorum suppositivus* mode of applying examples: 123–24, 125, 182, 261n; *modus exhortativus* exhortative mode: 124; *modus historicus et exemplificativus* historical and exemplifying mode: 124; *modus lamentativus* lamentative mode: 130, 133; *modus laudis et orationis* mode of praise and prayer: 87, 90, 93, 152, 205, 261n; *modus narrativus* narrative mode: 87, 125, 136, 261n, 263n; *modus orativus* orative, praying mode: 124, 125; *modus parabolicus* mode of parable: 131, 132; *modus poeticus* poetic mode: 139, 140, 217; *modus poeticus, fictivus, descripti-*
vus, etc. poetic, fictive, descriptive . . . mode: 144–45; *modus praeceptivus* perceptive mode: 124; *modus praeceptivus, exemplificativus, exhortativus, etc.* preceptive, exemplificative, exhortative . . . mode: 87, 122, 124–25; *modus probativus et improbativus* mode of proving and disproving: 123; *modus prophetialis* mode of prophecy: 132–33, 136, 168–77 passim; *modus revelativus* revelatory mode: 124; *modus sacrae poetriae* mode of sacred poetry: 135; *multiplex modus* multiple mode: 126–29 passim; *uniformis modus* uniform mode: 126

modus docendi mode of teaching: 156
modus exponendi mode of exposition: 87
modus legendi mode of reading: 252n
modus praedicandi mode of preaching: 136, 138

nomen auctoris name of the author: 20, 28, 32
nomen interpretatoris name of the interpreter: 252n
nomen libri name of the book: 41, 179; *nomen libelli* name of the little book: 180, 181, 189
nomen scribentis name of the writer: 170, 274n
numerus librorum number of books: 15, 16

officium office: 5, 31, 39; *officium praedicatoris* office of preacher: 174–77 passim
ordinatio partium organisation/arrangement of parts: 118, 145, 147–48, 152–55 passim, 191, 192, 197, 200, 201, 208, 254n
ordo literary order: 15, 16, 18, 22–23, 31, 32, 43, 64, 76, 225n, 236n; *ordo tractandi* order of treatment: 148, 150; *ordo tractatus* order of the treatise: 148

ordo artificialis artificial order: 22–23, 152

ordo naturalis natural order: 22–23, 227n

originalia originals (authoritative texts in their entirety): 153–59 passim, 202, 270n

pars philosophiae part/branch of learning: 26, 27, 41, 46, 240n

pars/genus prophetiae type of prophecy: 27, 46, 47, 50, 91, 240n

persona person, character: 22, 57–58, 90, 111, 189–90, 253n

persona person responsible for a work: 17

philomites lover of myth: 140, 216

philosophi the philosophers: 114

prelectio lecture, explanatory reading: 13–14, 34

principia inaugural lectures: 134–35

prodesse to profit: 241n

prolusio introductory lecture: 275n

qualitas carminis quality of the poem: 15, 16

recitare to report, repeat: 194

recitatio reporting, repeating: 101–102, 158, 193–200 passim

reportatio reporting: 101–102

salutatio salutation: 243n

satira satire: 22

scriptor scribe: 94, 98, 101, 102

scriptus intus et foris written within and without: 68–69, 70, 71, 246–47n

secundum proprietatem sermonis according to the proper meaning of speech: 74

sensus sense, meaning: 14, 33, 176, 232n

sensus auctoris sense of the author: 157

sensus litteralis literal sense. *See* General Index *s.v.* literal sense

sententia deep meaning, profound saying: 10, 14, 95, 111, 129, 131, 196, 202, 213, 222n

sermones ad status sermons for different states: 137–38

tempus time (of composition): 17, 225n, 236n

theologia theology, science of: 114, 119–20, 121, 233n

tituli chapter-headings: 153, 155, 201

tituli psalmorum titles of the psalms: 44, 47–48, 90–92, 238n

titulus operis/libri title of the work/book: 15, 16, 19–20, 31, 32, 41, 44, 52, 64, 66, 98, 162, 163, 226n, 272n

translatio transference: 74

utilitas usefulness, utility: 18, 19, 23–24, 29, 31, 32, 46, 56, 93, 162, 180, 182, 187, 188, 204, 225n, 226n, 236n

vita auctoris life of the author: 15, 16, 19, 112–13, 211–17 passim, 272n

General Index

Abelard, Peter: 3, 41, 58–63, 72, 102, 125, 158, 235n, 242n, 270n
acrostics: 170, 175, 193
Acts of the Apostles: 70, 72, 78–79, 124, 249n
Aesop: 11, 161
Aiken, P.: 191
Alan of Lille: 161, 231n, 265n
Alberic of Monte Cassino: 243n
Albert the Great: 5, 32, 73, 76, 80, 82, 99, 106, 114, 139, 140, 141, 156, 166, 204–205, 216, 217, 236n, 247n, 251n, 264n; Pseudo-Albert: 79, 132, 133, 266n
Alexander of Hales: 5, 78, 99, 119–22, 124, 125, 126–27, 128, 130, 131, 132, 137–38, 144, 153, 157, 249n, 259n, 264–65n
Alexander of Villa Dei: 3
Alexander the Great, King: 179, 183, 184
Al-Farabi: 265n
allegory: 5, 34, 39, 44, 45, 46–48, 63, 64, 66, 69–72, 73–74, 85–88, 90, 103, 104, 105, 109, 129, 131, 143, 151, 216, 238n, 246n, 247n, 248n, 252n
Ambrose, St: 43, 104, 157, 237n
Ammonius of Alexandria: 18, 225n
'ancients' and 'moderns': 12, 19, 86, 112, 136, 175–76, 190, 209–10,

211–12, 214, 216, 217, 221–22n, 226n, 279n
Anselm of Laon: 26, 40, 41, 44, 45, 49, 50, 54, 58, 60, 157, 235n, 236n, 239n, 240n, 241n
Apocalypse: 17, 22, 27, 41, 61, 67, 69, 79, 81, 124, 125, 126, 132–33, 169–71, 177, 187, 188
Aquinas, St Thomas: 5, 28, 32, 73–74, 80, 83–84, 86–90, 102, 107–108, 109, 114, 124, 128, 130, 131, 132, 135, 139, 141, 146–48 passim, 156, 194, 214, 216, 217, 221n, 247n, 248n, 251n, 253n, 261n, 262n, 264n, 268n, 270n; Pseudo-Aquinas: 136, 143, 150–51, 226n
Arab scholarship: 76, 114, 141, 265n
Aristotle and Aristotelianism: 5, 6, 13, 18, 28–29, 32, 58, 75–77 passim, 80, 82–84 passim, 92–93, 114, 115, 118, 123, 125, 140, 141, 143, 146–47, 149, 163, 167, 174, 177–78, 179, 182, 183, 184, 197, 202, 216, 231n, 232n, 251n, 257n; Pseudo-Aristotle: 184
Arnulf of Orléans: 19, 23, 227n
Ars concionandi: 264n
Arundel, Thomas: 168, 275n
Asaph: 43, 44, 47, 90, 91
Ashenden, John: 196, 197, 199

astrology: 194–97
Auerbach, E.: 88–89
Augustine, St: 33, 34–35, 43, 44–
    45, 49, 59, 73, 80, 90, 96, 102,
    104, 105, 112, 119, 120, 134,
    140, 143, 153, 154, 157, 158,
    161, 233n, 237n, 247n, 251n, 264n,
    273n; Pseudo-Augustine: 120
Augustine of Dacia: 232n
Augustinus: 224n
Auriol, Peter: 135, 141–42, 166
authenticity: 10–12
Averroes: 141, 265n
Avianus: 23, 161
Avicenna: 76, 265n

Bacon, Roger: 141
Baconthorpe, John: 144
Bartholomew the Englishman: 97,
    155, 192
Baruch: 82, 99, 101, 204–205, 225n
Bathsheba: 89, 103, 104, 105, 106,
    108, 215
Bede: 17, 57, 64; Pseudo-Bede: 105
Bernard of Chartres: 13, 25–26,
    222n, 231n
Bernard of Clairvaux, St: 51, 58,
    129, 236n, 238n
Bernard of Utrecht: 16, 19, 23–24,
    50, 57, 135, 227n
'Bernard Silvester': 11, 18, 22, 23,
    225n
Bersuire, Pierre: 142–43, 155, 162–
    63
Bible. See under titles of its various
    parts and books
Boccaccio, Giovanni: 2, 6, 7, 195,
    203–204, 209, 210, 214–17,
    264n, 265n, 272n, 273n, 281n
Boethius: 9, 13, 18, 20, 22, 23, 29,
    31, 77, 133–34, 143, 165, 179,
    208, 224n, 225n, 231n; Pseudo-
    Boethius: 9, 11
Boethius of Dacia: 257n
Bokenham, Osbern: 164–65, 193,
    271n

Bonaventure, St: 5, 32, 80–81, 94–
    95, 98–99, 110–11, 126–27,
    132, 146, 148, 157, 165, 189,
    249n, 258n, 259n, 264n
Bradwardine, Thomas: 277n
Brito, William: 220n
Bruno the Carthusian, St: 26, 27, 41,
    237n
Bulgarus: 226n, 227n
Burley, Walter: 213

Callus, D. A.: 121
'Cambridge Commentator' on St
    Paul: 242n, 243n
Cassian, John: 34
Cassiodorus: 33, 35, 43, 44, 45, 47,
    54, 105, 233n, 237n
Cato: 17, 19, 161
Cavalcanti, Guido: 279n
Caxton, William: 206, 208, 279n
Chaucer, Geoffrey: 6, 7, 9, 160, 165–
    66, 167, 190–210 passim, 272n,
    273n, 279n
Chenu, M.-D.: 2, 102, 125
Christian of Stavelot: 17
Cicero: 13, 20, 29, 30–31, 49, 62,
    125, 133, 179, 211–14, 231n,
    243n, 264n
Claudian: 227n
Clement of Lanthony: 273n
comedy: 23, 57, 241n, 273n
Conrad of Hirsau: 11, 19, 35, 227n
Constantine the African: 13
Core and his sons: 43, 44, 47, 90–91
Cossey, Henry: 87, 252n
Curtius, E. R.: 144

Daniel: 129, 136, 137, 138, 169,
    177, 183, 184
Dante Alighieri: 144–45, 161, 165,
    214–16, 256n, 272n, 279n
David, King and Psalmist: 6, 43–49
    passim, 67, 79, 88–92 passim, 97,
    103–112, 129, 134, 152, 163,
    167, 214–16 passim
De contemptu mundi: 161

despoliation. *See* spoliation
D'Eyncourt, William: 142
Diogenes: 194
Dionysius, Pseudo-: 141, 151, 264–65n
Dionysius the Carthusian: 269n
Docking, Thomas: 124, 132, 262n
Donatus, Aelius: 13, 15, 17, 33, 123, 147
Donatus, Tiberius Claudius: 223n
drama: 22, 48, 57–58, 135–36, 241n
Dunn, C. W.: 197
Durand of St Pourçain: 149

Elias, disciple of Ammonius: 18
Elias Brunetti: 77, 267n
Elyas, Paris Master of Arts: 77
Erigena, John Scotus: 16, 223n
Esdras: 92, 97, 152–53
Eusebius: 60
Evangelists, Four. *See* Gospels
Everard of Béthune: 220n
Everyman: 272n
Excerpta rhetorica: 224n
exemplification: 55–56, 61, 104, 109, 110, 111–12, 123–24, 125, 127, 135, 144, 147, 182, 185, 264n
Ezechiel: 17, 69

Fishacre, Richard: 78, 98, 99, 120, 121–22, 259n
FitzRalph, Richard: 100–102, 194, 247n
Floretus Sancti Bernardi: 161
Foliot, Gilbert: 243n
Fortunatianus: 224n
Fulgentius, St: 130
Fulgentius, the mythographer: 142

Galen: 13, 251n
Gellius, Aulus: 213
Geoffrey of Auxerre: 38
Geoffrey of Vinsauf: 218n

Geoffrey of Vitry: 227n
Gerhoh of Reichersberg: 22, 157, 237n, 239n
Ghisalberti, F.: 113
Gilbert of Poitiers: 4, 41, 50, 52, 130, 139, 157, 169–71, 190, 239n, 243n
Gilbert the Universal: 238–39n, 262n
Gilby, T.: 83
Giles of Rome: 5, 38, 82, 125–26, 129–30, 134, 148, 257n, 261–62n
Giovanni de'Balbi of Genoa: 10, 220n, 222n
Glorieux, P.: 2
Glossa Ordinaria: 26, 40–49 passim, 60, 87, 89, 96, 108, 156, 229n, 235n, 236n, 239n, 242n, 243n
Godfrey of St Victor: 229n
'good pagans': 37, 114, 257n, 258n, 272n
Gorran, Nicholas: 80, 81, 107, 249n, 253n, 255n, 256n, 262n
Gospels: 26, 27, 61–62, 99–100, 124, 149, 241n, 259n, 267n; St Matthew: 17, 144, 167, 273n; St Mark: 70, 72, 78–79; St Luke: 80–81, 148, 244n; St John: 78, 82, 133, 148, 249n
Gower, John: 6, 160, 165, 167–90, 200, 201, 209–210, 274–75n
Gratian: 13, 21, 157, 158, 226n, 270n
Gregory the Great, St: 17, 33–34, 36–38, 136–37, 157, 213, 232n, 256n
Grosseteste, Robert: 83, 85, 120–21, 251n, 259n
Guerric of St Quentin: 79
Guibert of Nogent: 34
Guido da Pisa: 165
Guinicelli, Guido: 279n
Gundissalinus, Dominicus: 20, 23, 31–32, 226n, 231n

Haimo of Halberstadt: 41, 54–55, 237n
Harvey of Nedellec: 262n

Henry of Ghent: 5, 81–82, 106–
107, 128–29, 148, 247n, 261n
Henryson, Robert: 166
Herbert of Bosham: 156–57, 240n
Hermagoras: 224n
Hermann the German: 141, 265n
Higden, Ralph: 113, 174, 193–94,
196, 200, 205, 210, 256n, 258n,
279n
Hilary, St: 91
Hilduin: 245n
history and historical context: 22–23,
34, 46–47, 48, 59, 89, 104–106,
109, 124, 125, 131, 135, 136,
143, 152, 210
Hoccleve, Thomas: 166
Holcot, Robert: 5, 95–96, 142, 158,
165, 166, 178–80, 181, 182,
241n, 257n, 258n, 259n, 262n,
272n, 274n
Homer: 15, 21, 191, 209, 210
Honorius 'of Autun': 26, 41, 105,
118, 236n, 237n, 238n
Hopeman, Thomas: 142
Horace: 21, 113, 241n
Hraban Maur: 95
Hugh of St Cher: 5, 11, 17, 35, 66–
67, 68, 70–72, 78–79, 97, 107,
116, 134, 148, 150, 153, 182,
223, 245n, 246–7n, 249n, 253n, 255n,
256n, 273n
Hugh of St Victor: 14, 17, 18, 25,
27, 46, 72, 134, 225n, 228n,
233n, 247n
Hugutio of Pisa: 10, 113, 219–20n,
222n
Humbert of Romans: 156, 174n
Hunt, R. W.: 15, 16, 18, 32, 231n
Huygens, R. B. C.: 224n
Hyginus: 13

Idithun: 43, 44, 47, 90, 91–92
imagination: 141, 217, 265n
Isaiah: 67, 79, 131, 135, 150–51
Isidore of Seville: 26, 58, 113, 157,
205, 228n

Jauss, H. R.: 219
Jean de Meun: 197–98, 201, 202,
203, 204, 273n
Jeremiah: 6, 61, 99, 101, 135, 216,
238n
Jerome, St: 33, 35, 43, 44, 54, 60,
85, 86, 87, 88, 90, 91, 92, 95,
96, 106, 110, 134, 135, 152,
156, 157, 236n, 237n, 245n, 256n
Jesus, son of Sirach: 96
Jews: 43, 60, 62, 67, 70, 84, 95–96,
106, 110, 116; Jewish exegesis:
44, 75, 85–87, 91–92, 150,
252n, 255n
Johannes Bassianus: 227n
'John of Bridlington': 161, 168
John of Bristol: 85
John of Garland: 218n, 271n
John of Rochelle: 116, 121, 134,
249n, 259n
John of Salisbury: 13, 14, 222n,
257n
John of Wales: 157–58, 175, 191,
213–14, 257n
Jonah: 101
Jordan, Paris Master of Arts: 76, 147,
248n, 267n
Jordan of Saxony: 248n, 267n
Justinian, Emperor: 20, 21
Juvenal: 23, 25, 226n, 228n, 230n

Kantorowicz, H.: 25
Kilwardby, Robert: 32, 76, 78, 98,
99, 120, 121, 122–23, 147, 149,
154, 158, 248n, 249n, 259n,
267n, 269n, 274n
Kings, Second Book of: 103, 106,
107

Lamentations: 6, 130, 135, 165, 238
Langton, Stephen: 27, 68–71, 96,
153, 156, 241n
Lathbury, John: 6, 130, 142, 165,
180
Latini, Brunetto: 155, 184, 192,
200, 278n

Letbert of Lille: 104, 237n, 238n, 240n, 268n
Lewis, C. S.: 188
Liber cartulae. See De contemptu mundi
Liber judiciorum: 196
Liber sex principiorum: 76
literal sense: 5, 34, 39, 43, 46, 47, 69–72 passim, 73–159 passim, 214, 238n, 246n, 247–48n, 251n, 255n, 270n
Livy: 161
Lollards: 144, 247n
Lombard, Peter. *See* Peter Lombard
Lucan: 10, 19, 21, 23, 25, 40, 50, 191, 209, 227n
Lumiere as lais: 163

Machabees, Books of: 96–97, 134
Macrobius: 222n
Malory, Thomas: 206, 208
Map, Walter: 11–12, 161
Marrou, H.-I.: 33
Martianus Capella: 13, 16–17, 22, 223n
Matthew of Vendôme: 161
Moses: 37, 64, 70, 78, 91, 100–101, 102, 129, 216, 245n

Neckam, Alexander: 220n, 222n
Nicholas of Lyre: 5, 80, 84, 86, 91–92, 93, 96, 97, 100, 107, 108–109, 132, 148–49, 152–53, 167, 177–78, 205, 208, 247n, 252n, 259n, 273n
Nicholas of Paris: 147

Odo Rigaldi: 124–25
Origen: 26, 58, 136
Ovid: 3, 4, 11, 16, 21, 25, 43, 47, 51, 55–57, 113, 142–43, 161, 165, 182, 183, 185, 188, 191, 203, 205–208 passim, 209, 229n, 242n, 275–76n
Ovide moralisé: 205–207, 208

Papias: 131
parable: 48, 74, 97, 136, 137, 140–41, 144, 252n, 273n
Parkes, M. B.: 154–55
Paul, St, and the Pauline Epistles: 32, 40, 41, 47, 58–63, 73, 104, 105, 110, 124, 128, 132, 156, 157, 235n, 241n, 242–43n, 244n, 250n
Pecham, John: 130
Pecock, Reginald: 271–72n
Pentateuch: 22, 61, 100, 134, 135, 246n; Exodus: 64, 69–70, 246n; Genesis: 34, 100, 245n, 246n; Numbers: 68–69
Persius: 21–22, 23, 225n, 230n
Peter Comestor: 11, 63, 64, 65, 68, 96, 236n
Peter Helias: 231n
Peter Lombard: 13, 29, 32, 47–48, 54, 60, 63, 64, 68, 78, 80, 90, 94–95, 98–99, 104–105, 146, 151, 153, 156–57, 190, 229n, 237n, 240n, 242n, 243n, 249n
Peter of Aldgate: 243n
Peter of Capua: 148
Peter of Corbeil: 244n
Peter of Poitiers: 63–66, 69, 223, 243n, 245n, 254n
Peter of Spain: 123
Peter of Tarantasia: 132, 249n, 250n, 262n
Peter the Chanter: 67–68, 236n, 241n, 243n, 245n
Petrarch, Francis: 2, 6, 7, 209, 211–17 passim, 264n, 280n
Philip of Harvengt: 236n, 238n, 239n, 241n
Philo the Jew: 95–96, 179
Philoponus: 18
Plato: 10, 14, 18, 76, 102, 179, 183, 225–26n
Plautus: 15
Poor Caitiff, The: 192
Porphyry: 13, 18

Praepositinus: 63–68 passim, 223n, 244n, 245n
Pratt, R. A.: 191, 279n
preaching: 49, 136–38, 156, 174–77, 187, 248n, 263n, 264n
prefiguration: 45, 88–90, 104, 105, 109
Priscian: 11, 13, 17, 31, 76, 147, 222n, 231n
prologue, academic, main types of: Type A: 16–17, 18, 226n; Type B (Servian): 15–16, 17–18, 226n, 230n; Type C: 18–25, 27, 29, 31, 32, 38, 40–72 passim, 171, 190–91, 225n, 226n; Type D: 31; Aristotelian prologue: 5, 28–29, 32, 38, 39, 70, 72, 74–84, 91–95, 129–30, 148, 160–65, 168, 172, 190, 249n, 281n; extrinsic and intrinsic prologues: 30–33, 64–71, 86–87, 177–82, 188, 275n; sermon type: 64
Przychocki, G.: 225n
Psalter: 4, 22, 26–27, 35, 40, 41, 42–50, 52–56, 63, 65–68, 75, 79, 84, 85–93, 104–109, 124, 133, 134, 135, 151–53, 205, 216, 223n, 229n, 235n, 236n, 244n, 246n, 248n, 251n, 252n, 253n, 267n, 268n
Pseudo-Dionysius. See Dionysius, Pseudo-
Ptolemy: 13

Quain, E. A.: 18, 225n
Quintilian: 13

Ralph Niger: 156
Raoul Ardent: 110
Reginald of Piperno: 156
Remigio dei Girolami: 248n
Remigius of Auxerre: 16–17, 19, 26–27, 40, 41, 44, 47, 104, 223n, 224n, 226n; Pseudo-Remigius: 237n, 238n
Revelation. See Apocalypse

reverent interpretation: 43, 56
rhetoric: 1, 6, 14, 25, 30–32, 35, 49–50, 59, 61, 64, 90, 125–26, 130, 133, 136, 138, 144, 173, 186–87, 212, 241n, 261n, 264n, 274n
Rhetorica ad Herennium: 49, 125, 223n, 231n
Richard de Bury: 12, 156
Richard of St Victor: 26, 236n
Riché, P.: 2, 54
Ridevall, John: 142
Ringstead, Thomas: 131, 142, 165, 180
Robert of Basevorn: 136–37, 138, 161–62, 175, 176, 264n, 274n
Robert of Paris: 249n
Rogerius: 20
Roland of Cremona: 114, 268n
Rolle, Richard: 190–91
Rufinus: 26, 58, 226n
Rupert of Deutz: 35, 151, 246n
Russel, John: 81, 170
Ruth, Book of: 113, 246n

Sapiential Books: 95, 96, 115–17, 124, 178, 182, 258n, 267n; Ecclesiastes: 26, 110–11, 132, 134, 165, 189, 246n; Ecclesiasticus: 71, 96, 134, 135, 179, 182, 246n; Job, Book of: 36–38, 128, 131, 134, 136, 213, 216, 247n; Proverbs: 26, 97, 131, 132, 135, 148, 150, 165; Wisdom: 95–96, 97, 134, 135, 165, 178, 182, 259n, 274n
satire: 21, 22, 23, 227n, 228n, 241n
Sedulius: 16
Sedulius Scotus: 224n
Seneca the elder: 154, 161
Seneca the younger: 161, 179, 213, 214, 276n
Servius: 15–16, 17–18, 22, 58, 224n, 227n, 230n
Sicardus of Cremona: 226n
Siger of Brabant: 257n

Simplicius: 18, 225n
Sinclair, T. A.: 183
Smalley, B.: 39, 115, 142, 149, 235n
Socrates: 179
Solomon, King: 26, 38, 41, 42–43, 47, 48, 51, 58, 65, 84, 88, 91, 95–96, 97, 103–104, 110, 111–12, 125, 130, 132, 150, 179, 182, 184–85, 189, 214, 215, 216
Song of Songs: 4, 22, 26, 27, 38, 41, 42–43, 45, 47, 48, 50, 51–52, 57–58, 63, 129–30, 132, 134, 135, 148, 150, 236n, 239n, 241n, 246n
Southern, Sir Richard: 3
spoliation: 113, 115, 258n
Statius: 40, 191, 209
Stephen of Bourbon: 155
subordination of the sciences: 146–48

Tempier, Stephen: 257n
Terence: 23
Theodore of Mopsuestia: 87–88, 107, 252n
Theodulus: 16, 50, 161
Thierry of Chartres: 20, 30–31, 223n, 230n, 231n
Thomas of Citeaux: 236n
Thomas of Ireland: 143, 256n
Thomas of Strassburg: 149, 262n
tragedy: 57, 191, 276n
Trevet, Nicholas: 5, 84–86, 87, 90–91, 107, 131, 133, 143, 151–52, 154, 160–61, 166, 251n, 252n, 255n, 262n, 269n, 272n, 276n, 279n
Trevisa, John: 192, 193–94, 196, 200

Twelve Minor Prophets: 41, 43–44, 69, 70, 132, 135

Ulrich of Strassburg: 140–41, 162, 166
Usk, Thomas: 163–64, 167

Valerius Maximus: 12
Victorinus: 30, 224n
Vincent of Beauvais: 97, 154–55, 157, 158–59, 162, 191, 192, 194, 197, 199, 200, 201, 210, 213, 254n, 258n, 279n
Virgil: 10, 15–16, 22, 23, 40, 47, 113, 114, 133, 152, 191, 209, 214, 223n, 224n, 229n

Waleys, Thomas: 80, 106, 137, 154, 158, 160, 262n, 263–64n, 269n
Walsingham, Thomas: 230n
Westerink, G. L.: 18, 225–26n
Wheteley, William: 9, 219n
Wickert, Maria: 274n
William of Aragon: 143
William of Auvergne: 106, 121, 258n
William of Auxerre: 121
William of Conches: 11, 13–14, 22, 23, 25–26, 143, 221n, 222n, 226n, 228n, 230n, 231n
William of Middleton: 132, 259n
William of Moerbeke: 125, 225n
William of Ockham: 74, 258n
William of St Thierry: 48, 51–52, 57–58, 129, 139, 236n
Wilmart, A.: 41
Wyclif, John: 143–44, 277n

Zumthor, Paul: 219n